Beginning Windows 8

Mike Halsey
Microsoft MVP for Windows

apress·

Beginning Windows 8

ISBN-13 (pbk): 978-1-4302-4431-8

ISBN-13 (electronic): 978-1-4302-4432-5

President and Publisher: Paul Manning
Lead Editor: Jonathan Hassell
Developmental Editors: Chris Nelson and Tom Welsh
Technical Reviewers: Todd Meister and Jeff James
Editorial Board: Steve Anglin, Ewan Buckingham, Gary Cornell, Louise Corrigan, Morgan Ertel,
    Jonathan Gennick, Jonathan Hassell, Robert Hutchinson, Michelle Lowman, James Markham,
    Matthew Moodie, Jeff Olson, Jeffrey Pepper, Douglas Pundick, Ben Renow-Clarke, Dominic Shakeshaft,
    Gwenan Spearing, Matt Wade, Tom Welsh
Coordinating Editor: Mark Powers
Copy Editor: Kimberly Burton-Weisman
Compositor: SPi Global
Indexer: SPi Global
Artist: SPi Global
Cover Designer: Anna Ishchenko

This book is dedicated to everyone who has ever dreamed of writing a Windows or other technical book, but didn't know where to start. Never give up the dream because the sky's the limit.

Contents at a Glance

Contents

xviii

About the Author

Mike Halsey is the author of several books on Microsoft's operating system, including *Troubleshoot and Optimize Windows 8 Inside Out* (Microsoft Press, 2012) *and Windows 8: Out of the Box* (O'Reilly Media, 2012).

An English and math teacher by trade, he puts his experience with explaining often complex subjects in non-intimidating language, and sincerely hopes you find this book an example of this.

He is a Microsoft MVP (Most Valuable Professional) awardee and a recognized Windows expert. He regularly makes help and how-to videos and holds live regular webcasts.

Mike has an open mailbag and always welcomes questions and comments from readers. He lives in an ecohome in Sheffield (Yorkshire, UK) with his rescue border collie, Jed.

2011-2012 MVP

About the Technical Reviewers

Todd Meister has been working in the IT industry for more than 15 years. He's been a technical editor for over 75 titles, ranging from SQL Server to the .NET Framework. Besides technical editing, he is the senior IT architect at Ball State University in Muncie, Indiana. He lives in central Indiana with his wife, Kimberly, and their five excellent children.

Jeff James has been the editor-in-chief of both *Windows IT Pro* and *Microsoft Technet Magazine,* and has served as an editorial director at the LEGO Company. Jeff has nearly 20 years of experience as a technology writer and journalist. He started his career writing technology articles for AmigaWorld, Computer Gaming World, and other tech publications and web sites in the early 1990s.

Acknowledgments

Since I first self-published my first Windows guides, there have been so many people offering help, support, and encouragement that it would be impossible to name them all here. Thanking them is simpler however. Thank you.

Two people do stand out though as having seen the full potential of those original books in 2006 and 2009. Those people are my parents. I consider myself very fortunate to have parents as grounded and provident as they, and I wish to thank them for the encouragement that has brought me such good fortune. . .

. . .but this doesn't mean they can have all the money!

—Mike Halsey

Introduction

Windows 8 is something new for Microsoft. Since the very first version of Windows was released in 1985, the main "desktop" user interface is taking a back seat to something new and, dare I say, radical.

This can present challenges for some users and there is certainly a learning curve. This book is here to help with that.

Why would you want to stop there though? All that was in Windows 7 still exists along with a lot more new features. This book will help guide you from computer novice to the stage where you can feel comfortable maintaining, safeguarding, and even customizing your own copy of Windows 8, giving clear instructions and easy-to-follow step-by-step guides.

Beginning Windows 8 will show you how to be productive, protect your family, and how to unlock the hidden features and power that exist within this operating system—helping you to become comfortable, feel confident, and take your first steps toward becoming a Windows power user.

Who This Book Is For

This book is for people—be they a computer novice or an enthusiastic amateur—who have already mastered the basics of using their computer for web browsing and e-mail, but who are either new to Windows 8 or want to delve deeper into the OS to do more with it and to get more benefit from having it.

How This Book Is Structured

This book is arranged in a chapter structure that will help you build your confidence and skills as you read.

- **Chapter 1** introduces the new interface in Windows 8 and shows you how to get the most from it.

- **Chapter 2** shows you how to get around Windows 8, including the desktop and certain software and utilities.

- **Chapter 3** helps you connect your computer to the Internet, to other computers in your home or work network, and to other hardware devices.

- **Chapter 4** shows you how to share your life, files, pictures, and more with friends, colleagues, and family via the Internet and on home and work networks.

- **Chapter 5** helps you make sense of the myriad collections of folders, files, and documents that can accumulate on your computer with clever searching, sorting, and filtering techniques.

- **Chapter 6** answers all your printing questions, from attaching a Wi-Fi printer to setting different printers for work and home.

- **Chapter 7** shows you all the ways the operating system can help you to have fun with your Windows 8 computer.

- **Chapter 8** covers Windows 8 features that can help you use your computer productively and efficiently for work.

- **Chapter 9** helps you make your copy of Windows 8 your own, from personalizing the interface to changing settings in order to make better use of your computer.

- **Chapter 10** introduces you to the vast array of accessibility features the operating system has to offer everyone, including those with vision or motor impairments.

- **Chapter 11** shows you how to make sure your computer and files are safe and secure.

- **Chapter 12** shows you how to keep your copy of Windows and your files safe, updated, and backed up.

- **Chapter 13** is a master class in the myriad ways that Windows 8 can be customized, from simple changes through more advanced customization using the registry.

- **Chapter 14** is your introduction to the sometimes complex world of virtualization, showing you how to get the best out of Windows 8 Pro's new virtualization tools.

- **Chapter 15** guides you through installing Windows 8 on an existing computer.

Contacting the Author

Mike Halsey has an open mailbag. He can be contacted via his web site at www.thelongclimb.com. You can also keep up with him regularly with news, reviews, and tutorials at the same web site and at his author page on Amazon.com (www.amazon.com/author/mikehalsey).

Video and Webcasts

You can find help and video tutorials at www.youtube.com/TheLongClimb. Mike also holds tutorial webcasts on the first Thursday of each month (see www.oreilly.com/webcasts for archived webcasts and to register for upcoming ones).

Social Networking News, Help and Support

You can follow Mike on Facebook and Twitter:

www.facebook.com/HalseyMike

www.twitter.com/HalseyMike

CHAPTER 1

Introducing Windows 8

When Microsoft first began talking about "the next version of Windows" in January 2011, they used words like "bold" and "risky" to describe both it and the venture that the company was undertaking. Microsoft was already some years behind the competition in the ever-expanding consumer tablet market, and they needed desperately to catch up.

At the Windows BUILD developers' conference that September, it was actually no surprise to discover Microsoft's entirely new tablet-centric interface based on their highly praised Windows Phone user interface. What did come as a surprise, however, was the beginning of a move toward a new user interface paradigm for Windows, the relegation of the desktop to an app.

The truth isn't actually anywhere near simplistic. Windows 8 is a far more detailed and complete operating system than it was before. The new interface doesn't replace the desktop, but it does offer new ways for both power and casual users get the very best out of the OS. Moreover, many of the administrative resources are now easier to access than ever before.

In this chapter, I'll talk you through this version's most significant changes to Windows, and help you decide where this operating system fits within your digital world. We'll cover

- How Windows 8 differs from its predecessors

- The differences between the various SKUs (editions) and processor versions

- The new features in Windows 8

- How to use, customize, and configure the new Windows 8 lock screen

What Is Windows 8?

Windows 8 is the 2012 release of Microsoft's popular Windows operating system. It is based around a small kernel called MinWin, which provides all the core operating system functions. MinWin is also the basis for the Windows Server operating system and possibly others in the future, including Windows Phone.

Having a single kernel powering Microsoft's operating systems helps maintain compatibility across devices and platforms, reduces development time, and helps increase security. It is also what Apple does; its OS X desktop operating system and the iOS operating system on the iPhone and iPad are based on the same kernel.

Windows 8, like Vista and Windows 7 before it, is a *modular operating system*. This means that features can be switched on or off, and some features can be removed completely without affecting the resiliency of the whole system. It is what happens with the desktop and server versions of Windows: the features and modules differ while the kernel remains the same.

This modular approach helps Windows 8 maintain compatibility with older "legacy" software and hardware, while still being as customizable as previous versions of the operating system.

How Windows 8 Differs from Windows 7 and Windows Vista

When you first start Windows 8, the changes from Windows 7 are significant and very obvious. The biggest change is the use of the new UI (see Figure 1-1) as the default method for interacting with software programs and apps. The desktop has effectively been downgraded to an app itself, but it retains all the power and functionality of Windows 7.

Figure 1-1. *The Start screen*

Windows 8 is also the very first version of Windows to feature a built-in antivirus as standard. The new Windows Defender software is not like the version in Windows XP, Vista, and Windows 7, where it was a basic malware protection tool. In Windows 8, it is a fully rebadged copy of Microsoft's free Security Essentials software.

The final major change is the addition of Microsoft's Ribbon interface throughout the desktop, File Explorer, and other aspects of the OS. Other than some new features (as you would expect with any new version of an operating system), the underlying base for Windows 8 is exactly the same as its predecessor. Microsoft hasn't changed or tinkered with anything other than the Task Manager, which has had a major overhaul. What they have done is add a whole raft of new features over the top. This means that if you are familiar with using Windows 7, you won't get lost because almost everything is where you would expect to find it—certainly when you drill down into the advanced features on the desktop. Some of the new features may come as a pleasant surprise, however, as they expand the core power and flexibility of Windows in new and exciting ways.

How Window 8 Differs from Windows XP

If you're moving from the "comfortable old shoe" of Windows XP to Windows 8, then you're probably in for a very pleasant surprise. That may surprise you, given the move away from the desktop as the default UI and the fact that software and hardware compatibility is no better in Windows 8 than in Windows 7.

This compatibility issue, however, is one that I will come back to several times in this book. It's very common for us to have older software and possibly hardware that we're either very comfortable using, or that we have to use for work or to perform another specific task. I have an aging graphics package from Microsoft that was released over ten years ago, and consequently, not all the features work properly now in Windows 8. That said, the virtualization technologies built into Windows 8 Pro and Windows 8 Enterprise, as well as the application compatibility wizard, address some of the issues. Overall, the way Windows has advanced to this version makes upgrading extremely worthwhile.

The simple fact remains that all support for Windows XP is ending in April 2014. After that, there will be no further security and stability patches for the operating system, so it will become a big target for malware writers and criminals. Windows XP Mode in Windows 7, while good, is based on older Virtual PC technology and it, too, will no longer be supported after April 2014 (although Windows 7 itself will be supported until 2020). Conversely, the Hyper-V virtualization technology built into Windows 8 will continue to be supported for many years.

Windows 8 is the most secure operating system that Microsoft has ever produced, especially with its first-ever built-in antivirus protection. Security was difficult to maintain in Windows XP, but doesn't really need to be considered in Windows 8—so long as you are aware that criminals and malware writers will try to trick you into bypassing the operating system's built-in security. I cover this later in the book.

I will talk more about security and virtualization in Chapters 11 and 14, respectively.

32-bit (x86) and 64-bit (x64) Explained

Windows 8 is reportedly the last version of the desktop operating system to come in both 32- and 64-bit variants. The reason for this is to maintain compatibility with older hardware that may still be in use in some environments.

What do the terms "32-bit" and "64-bit" mean? Well, a *bit* is a binary digit. Binary is the mathematical number base that uses only the digits 0 and 1. The number zero is represented as 0, and the number one is represented as 1; but as there is no digit 2 in binary, representing the number two requires an additional digit, just as the number ten does in decimal. In binary, the number two is represented as 10, three as 11, four as 100, and so on.

A 32-bit number is represented by 32 digits, and thus cannot be larger than 65,535. There are ways of getting around this limit using software, which involves using two or more 32-bit numbers together to achieve greater numbers, but this adds significant overhead and can slow down performance. With a 64-bit system, the largest number that can be processed is 18,446,744,073,709,551,616. This is significantly higher than any maximum value that can be processed by a 32-bit system. As a result, computers running 64-bit operating systems can directly address vastly more memory (the limit with a 32-bit operating system is 4GB, including any graphics memory in the machine) and processing larger numbers means the computer can do more things simultaneously.

The main benefits of a 64-bit system being able to process larger numbers come not just in being able to address more memory, but also in being able to perform operations in a single step. For example, if you were working with very large numbers in a 32-bit operating system, let's say the number 100 billion, performing a calculation on this would require multiple memory registers to be used simultaneously. With a 64-bit operating system, memory is used more effectively because fewer memory registers are required to perform calculations on numbers. All new computing hardware from the last few years is able to run 64-bit operating systems, but the Windows 8 installer will tell you if there is a problem. Conversely, not all older hardware has 64-bit driver support; and if you have older hardware in or attached to your computer, you should check for 64-bit driver availability before changing to 64-bit.

If 64-bit compatible drivers for all the hardware in and attached to your computer exist, and you either already have or plan to upgrade to more than 4GB of memory, including the memory on your graphics card, you should use the 64-bit version of Windows 8.

What's New in Windows 8

As I have already mentioned, Windows 8 presents the biggest change to the user interface since Windows 95 was launched. Underneath this new interface, however, are hundreds of additions and changes, small and large, which I will talk about in Chapter 2.

The Start Screen

First of all, what is this new user interface? Why does it exist and how do you use it? The Start screen came about in Windows 8 because of Microsoft's need to get into the tablet computing market. It is based on a design created for the company's Windows Phone operating system and can be traced back in various forms to the Zune media player and even Windows Media Center before that.

The Start screen is based around a series of "live tiles," each of which gives you real-time information from a particular app. For example, they may display the number of e-mails you have waiting, or the sender and subject of those e-mails. They may show you calendar appointments, currency exchange rates, stock market values, or the latest photographs in your collection.

I will talk a lot more about how to use and navigate Windows 8 in Chapter 2; for now, suffice it to say, the system is much more powerful, useful, and flexible than it might appear at first sight.

Refresh and Reset

Windows Vista first introduced "system image" backup, where you could create an image of your entire Windows installation—including all your settings and installed software—and restore from this backup in the event of a catastrophe. With Windows 7, this feature was included in every edition of the OS.

Windows 8 still contains this feature, but it also adds two more. Refresh is a system that allows you to reinstall Windows if you encounter a problem—while maintaining all your settings, data, and apps (see Figure 1-2).

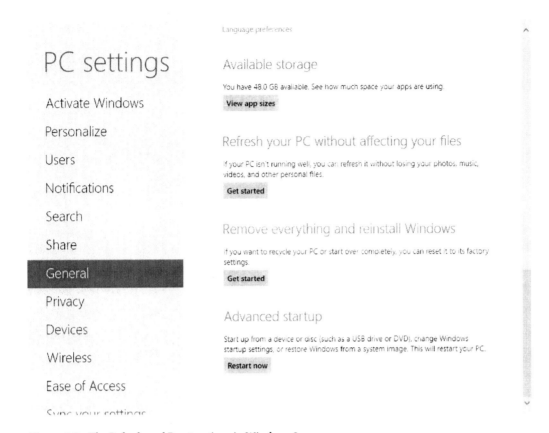

Figure 1-2. *The Refresh and Reset options in Windows 8*

■ **Tip**   Using Refresh to fix your computer retains all your apps, but it wipes out all the desktop software you have installed on your computer. You can create a custom refresh image, however. I cover how to do this in Chapter 12, where I also discuss how it differs from a system image backup and why this is important.

When you use the Reset feature, all your files, settings, and apps are deleted, and your computer is returned to its factory default state. This can be useful if you want to give away or sell your computer.

Windows To Go

The Windows To Go system allows you to create a bootable USB flash drive containing your copy of Windows 8 with its software and settings. It is compatible with both USB 2.0 and USB 3.0 drives, and on BIOS and UEFI motherboards.

Windows To Go sounds like a takeaway for a very good reason. No longer will people have to worry about finding mobile versions of apps, or using cloud services. With Windows To Go, you really can carry around your entire Windows installation, safely and securely.

Windows To Go is an Enterprise-only feature in Windows 8, however, and so it isn't included in the standard and Pro editions of the operating system.

Hyper-V

Probably the most talked-about feature in Windows 8, after the new UI, is the inclusion of Microsoft's Hyper-V virtualization software (see Figure 1-3). First released in 2008 as part of the Windows Server 2008 operating system, this is a virtualization tool that allows other operating systems—including earlier versions of Windows and GNU/Linux—to be run inside the main installed *host* operating system, this being Windows 8.

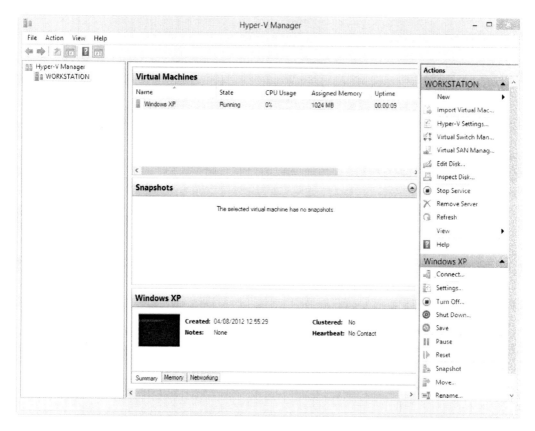

Figure 1-3. *Hyper-V in Windows 8*

Each virtualized OS runs effectively in a self-contained ISO disk image file. You can run multiple operating systems side by side on a single Windows desktop.

Hyper-V is a Type-1 hypervisor, which means it can communicate directly with your computer's hardware and take full advantage of it. One advantage of hypervisors such as this is that they can be programmed to take full control of a specific processor core in a multicore chip. This maximizes processing efficiency and ensures there is no latency while each running operating system waits for processing resources to become available.

By contrast, older Type-2 hypervisors used the host operating system to *simulate* the hardware of a computer, not allowing access to the actual PC's hardware. This type included the now-aging Microsoft Virtual PC.

Storage Spaces

Storage Spaces is a feature that allows you to aggregate multiple hard disks into a single large storage location. For example, if you have a 750GB HDD and a 2TB HDD, you can pool these into a single 2.75TB drive. You can also use USB-attached disks with the feature.

Windows 8 manages the data distribution and can also create built-in resiliency with mirroring or striping of data across the various physical hard disks to prevent data loss.

Secure Boot

One of the more controversial features of Windows 8 is Secure Boot, a feature that prevents any UEFI-equipped motherboard from booting an operating system that is not signed with a security certificate. This feature, sometimes called Trusted Boot, will most commonly be found on the computers you buy from manufacturers such as Samsung, HP, Dell, and so forth, where it will be enabled by default.

The reason behind Secure Boot is to stop unauthorized firmware, operating systems, or UEFI drivers from loading at boot time. This is to prevent the spread of malware and viruses that can attack the computer at boot time.

░ **Note**   Secure Boot can be disabled, but UEFI systems vary across manufacturers. To disable it, you need to refer to the documentation for the system used on your computer.

What Else Is New?

There are many other new features in Windows 8, including new multimonitor support; drivers for new hardware types such as USB 3.0; an improved Task Manager, Windows Live ID, and SkyDrive integration; improved boot times that make use of hibernation; and a new security system for product activation.

Configuring the Windows 8 Lock Screen

The new lock screen in Windows 8 is much more useful than those of previous Windows versions in that it can display additional information about Internet connectivity, battery status (very useful), e-mail, appointments, and more.

You can also plug third-party apps into the Logon screen as they become available. But how do you do this?

░ **Tip**   On a desktop PC or laptop, you can quickly open the Logon screen without having to swipe upward with your mouse. Just press any key on your keyboard—and the Logon screen opens.

You access the Logon screen settings using the new PC Settings in the interface. This is a multistep action. If you are using touch, swipe your finger in from the far right of the screen to bring up the charms (see Figure 1-4). I talk about charms in detail in Chapter 2 and discuss touch in Windows 8 later in this chapter.

Figure 1-4. *The charms, located on the right side of the Start screen or desktop in Windows 8*

1. Press **WinKey + C** on your keyboard or move your mouse to the bottom right of the Start screen.

2. Click the **Settings** icon.

3. Click **Change PC Settings** near the bottom right of the screen.

You are automatically taken to the Lock Screen settings in the Personalize section (see Figure 1-5), where you can change the wallpaper for the lock screen, and add and remove apps from it.

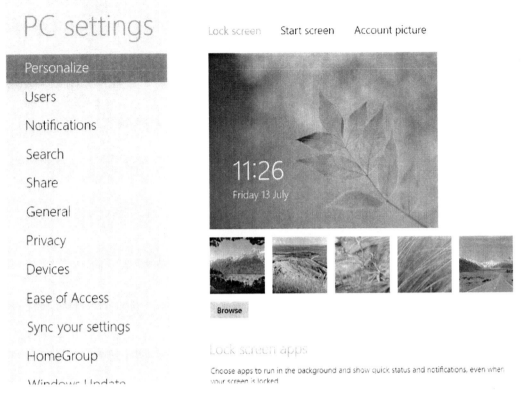

Figure 1-5. *The lock screen settings*

To add an app, click one of the available + icons; you can have a maximum of seven apps on the lock screen. To remove an app, click or tap it, and from the context menu that appears, select **Don't display a badge here**.

Note You cannot change the order of apps on the lock screen by dragging and dropping. You need to unpin and repin apps in the order you want them displayed.

You can choose one app to display a detailed status at the bottom of the lock screen options. By default, this is set to the calendar; but you can remove it by clicking it and selecting **Don't show detailed status on the lock screen** from the context menu that appears.

Not every app is capable of displaying detailed information, and only those that are will appear in this section, in the same way that only apps capable of displaying lock screen information will show in the main Lock Screen Apps options.

Using a Pin or Picture Password on the Lock Screen

It is always advisable to have a strong password, but if you log into your copy of Windows 8 using a Live ID, you won't always want to type a long string of 12 or more uppercase and lowercase letters, numbers, and symbols.

Windows 8 offers two alternatives, though it is up to each individual user to decide how secure these are. One is to unlock your computer with a four-digit PIN number (it is advisable to never use the same code you use for your credit card or alarm system) and the other is to use a picture password or to create a password if you do not currently have one assigned to your account (see Figure 1-6).

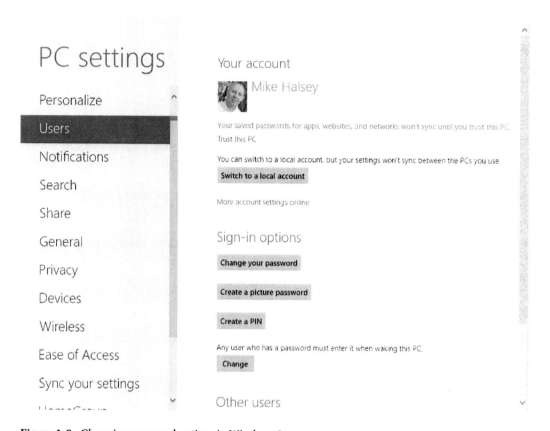

Figure 1-6. Changing password options in Windows 8

To access these options, go to PC Settings, as detailed earlier, and click or tap the Users section. You will see the options to create (or remove) a picture password and a PIN.

When creating a picture password, you are asked to select a photograph or picture from your Pictures library and to perform three actions on it. These can be taps, swipes, or a combination of both. Picture passwords are best used on touchscreens because the movement involved can be quite laborious with a mouse.

Changing Your Login Method

Creating a picture password or a PIN doesn't automatically change the way you sign in to Windows 8. You are still required to use your password the next time you log in. Just underneath the sign-in password box, click the new link, Sign-in options. This displays icons allowing you to switch to a picture password or a PIN.

Your selection is remembered and used in the future. This is where security considerations come into play; you can switch back to a full password for extra security if, for example, you are taking your computer on the road.

Mastering Touch in Windows 8

Touch has assumed a central role in Windows 8. Not all Windows machines currently support touch, but the technology is moving more and more in that direction. In this section, I want to briefly talk about how to use touch in Windows 8.

The touch interface is remarkably intuitive and operates in a way that you might expect it to work on any other tablet or touch operating system. The following are the main gestures:

- **Tap** the screen to select an item or to open it in the new user interface.

- **Double-tap** to open an item on the desktop.

- **Swipe** either up, down, left, or right from the edges of the screen to bring up menus or options, or swipe on the screen to perform an action in an app or program.

- **Drag** an item on screen by tapping and holding it, and then dragging it to move it.

- **Tap and pull downward** to highlight an item on the screen.

- **Pinch inward** to zoom out of a view.

- **Pinch outward** to zoom into a view.

When you are swiping in from the edges of the screen, try to start on the actual screen bezel because this will produce better results. For some screens, however, the bezel and screen may not be completely flat against each other. In this case, practice may be required to get the best results. See Appendix A for more information on using touch with Windows 8.

■ **Note** Microsoft's Kinect for PC sensor can also be used to swipe using gesture controls; but please note that this form of control in Windows 8 is both limited and imprecise.

Using the Onscreen Keyboard in Windows 8

Windows 8 is very good at detecting when you have selected something with a mouse or with a keyboard. It pops up the onscreen keyboard if it detects a finger tap on an input field such as the password box.

There are several different keyboards you can choose from in Windows 8. I would like to describe each one for you, as follows:

- The **default keyboard** is a standard affair; you can see the QWERTY keyboard in Figure 1-7. There is the &123 key to bring up numbers and symbols, and an Emoticon button to bring up happy and sad faces for e-mail, social networking, and instant messaging. On the bottom right of the keyboard is a key that allows you to change your input method to one of the next four options.

Figure 1-7. *The onscreen keyboard in Windows 8*

- **Split keyboard** splits the keys to the far left and right of the screen, making it much simpler to hold a tablet in both hands and type with your thumbs.

- **Written input** allows those with a tablet stylus to input text, numbers, and symbols using Windows 8's excellent handwriting recognition. This is useful for writing notes while carrying a tablet.

- **Full keyboard**'s full keyboard option gives you all the keys you expect to find on a PC keyboard, including a number row across the top of the keyboard.

- **Hide keyboard** is the final option; it allows you to hide the onscreen keyboard.

The Maximize and Close buttons are located at the top right of the keyboard window when you are viewing it on the desktop. The Maximize button expands the keyboard to fill the width of the computer's screen. It does not make the keys larger, but it does effectively put the keyboard in its own locked dock. Pressing the Maximize button again returns the keyboard to its normal mode.

■ **Tip** Tap and briefly hold a letter on the onscreen keyboard to display international variations for that letter, including accented letters.

In normal mode, the keyboard floats on the desktop, and can be dragged around and placed where you want it. This is very useful if the keyboard is obscuring something that you need to see or read.

■ **Tip** The default onscreen keyboard doesn't show the full PC keyboard layout with number row and page control keys. You can activate a full onscreen keyboard by searching for *keyboard* at the Start screen (see Figure 1-8).

Figure 1-8. *The full onscreen keyboard*

Privacy and Security for Personal and Business Data

Throughout this book, I highlight where privacy and personal or business data security are relevant.

On the lock screen, an app showing detailed information can be displayed to anyone viewing your computer when it is locked and you are away from it. You should not leave an app showing detailed sensitive, private, or personal information on your Windows 8 lock screen. It is for this reason that the e-mail app only displays the current number of unread e-mails.

Summary

Windows 8 is very different from Windows 7, though it is built on the same code and everything that is in Windows 7 sits underneath the new UI. In the chapters that follow, I discuss all the features in the desktop and Start screen interfaces, and how you can maximize the best benefits in both. I also help you learn how to use Windows 8 to get maximum enjoyment, maximum performance, and maximum productivity.

CHAPTER 2

▨ ▨ ▨

Finding Your Way Around Windows 8

The first thing that you notice when you use Windows 8 for the first time is the new interface. It is very much unlike anything that we've ever seen on the desktop, and on initial inspection, it seems very focused on tablet devices.

The new Start screen dates back to early versions of Windows Media Center, but perhaps in a more pronounced way, to Microsoft's Zune HD media player, which was released in 2009.

The main purpose of the Start screen is to use the types of iconography that are commonly found in our daily lives to help us get information quickly and easily; the familiar signs and symbols that navigate us around roads, public transport systems, and in public spaces. Primarily, it involves transportation signage, which is designed specifically to give us relevant information quickly and simply.

The new user interface and the new Start screen in Windows 8 are aiming to do just that for operating systems. The use of different shapes, sizes, colors, and iconography can help you quickly locate the information you need, and the live tiles on the Start screen can then provide better and more in-depth detail about a particular subject.

While the "traditional" desktop is still beneath this new interface, the Start screen is now the default way to interact with Windows and it's more usable and powerful than you might first presume.

In this chapter, I show you how to get the very best out of the Start screen and all its new features by using either touch or a keyboard and mouse.

Using the Start Screen

The main elements of the Start screen are

- Square and rectangular tiles for apps

- Square tiles for desktop software

- Live tiles for apps that show up-to-date information from within the app itself

- A pop-up menu at the bottom of the screen with main options called the *App bar*

- A pop-down menu at the top of the screen with additional options

- Thumbnails of running apps that pop-in from the left of the screen

- The charms, which pop from the right of the screen

Each app that runs in Windows 8 will, by default, run fullscreen, though it is possible to have two apps running side by side, one in a narrow pane on the left or right of the screen and one filling the rest of the screen space. This allows you to use a main app—let's say a game or even the Windows desktop—with another small pane alongside containing perhaps e-mail, stock-market figures, or a chat program, see Figure 2-1.

Figure 2-1. *The side-by-side app view*

■ **Note**   Your screen needs to be at a minimum resolution of 1366×768 pixels to view apps side by side.

It is not possible to run more than two apps on a screen at one time, though apps such as Internet Explorer support multiple tabs. If you want to run more than two apps simultaneously, you will need to use software on the traditional desktop.

The Start screen is the hub of everything in Windows 8. It is where you launch, not only apps and programs, but also the desktop itself. In Windows 8, to reduce memory usage, the desktop doesn't load unless you call it. Some say this is reducing it to another app, but it contributes to a memory-efficient operating system nonetheless.

When you first launch Windows 8, the Start screen already has apps and programs split into different groups. You can define and name these groups as you want. I will show you how to do this later in the chapter.

■ **Tip**   On some higher-resolution displays, Windows 8 can display more tiles vertically on the screen. To activate this feature, open the Charms menu and click Settings, and then at the top right of your screen, click Tiles. If your screen can support this feature, you will see the Show More Tiles option.

In a change to the way many of us are used to interacting with our computers, the tiles on the Start screen scroll left and right instead of the more customary up and down. When you install new apps or programs into Windows 8, their tiles appear on the far right of the Start screen, although they can be rearranged, as I will detail shortly.

Locking the Computer and Signing Out

The word "Start" appears in the top left of the screen (see Figure 2-2), but it doesn't do anything if you click or right-click it.

Figure 2-2. *The Start screen*

Your user name and photo appear in the top right of the screen. You can click it to perform the following actions:

- **Change the Account Picture** takes you to the Personalization options in PC Settings, where you can upload a new profile picture; take a picture using a webcam, if you have one attached to your computer; or use an installed app, if one is compatible, to take or create a picture.

- **Lock** is the option you choose to lock the computer without turning it off. It is useful if you are leaving your computer for a short break. You can also lock the computer the more traditional way by pressing Ctrl + Alt + Del on your keyboard and selecting Lock from the options; or you can press WinKey + L to lock the computer instantly.

Tip   Use WinKey + L to lock your computer quickly.

- **Sign Out** is the option to use if you are finished with your computing session and want to let somebody else use the computer with his own user account. This option will not shut down the computer.

Note   There is no option to restart, shut down, hibernate, or sleep the computer directly from a menu on the Start screen. To do this, you need to access the charms (more on this shortly) and select Settings.

Controlling the Windows 8 Start Screen

The new interface is designed with touch in mind. You can control it with a keyboard and mouse, but this can create complexity due to several ways to operate and control various aspects of the screen, and in trying to find ways to mimic touch controls with a keyboard and mouse.

You control the Start screen by swiping left and right with your finger on a touchscreen or by moving your mouse left or right on the screen to scroll sideways. When you use a mouse, you also see a scrollbar appear at the bottom of the screen. You can grab this scrollbar and use it just like a scrollbar in a desktop program.

When the scrollbar is visible, you see a small button in the bottom-right corner of the screen, as shown in Figure 2-3. Clicking it will show the Start screen zoomed out so that you can quickly find and locate a specific group of programs, apps, or links, and so that you can perform additional actions on groups, such as naming them. If you are using a touch interface, you can zoom out with a pinch gesture.

Figure 2-3. *The Zoom control next to the Start screen scrollbar*

■ **Tip** Hold down the Ctrl key and use your mouse's scroll wheel to zoom in and out of the Start screen.

When you are looking at the zoomed-out Start screen, you are able to see buttons for individual apps, programs, and links. This helps you locate things that you may have difficulty finding.

You cannot run any app or program directly from the zoomed-out view; however, clicking or tapping anywhere on that view will zoom back into that place on the Start screen (see Figure 2-4). This is very useful when you have a great many tiles on the screen.

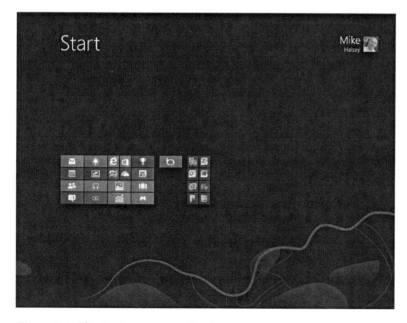

Figure 2-4. *The Start screen zoomed out*

Context menus, known as the *App bar*, appear on the Start screen from the top and bottom of the screen, depending on the app or feature you are using. You can swipe downward from the top of the screen, or upward from the bottom to bring up a context menu. If you are using a mouse, right-click in any unused space to bring up the context menus, as shown in Figure 2-5. When opening this menu from the keyboard, the combination WinKey + Z opens the context menus for you.

■ **Tip**   Use WinKey + Z to open the App bar.

Figure 2-5. *The new App bar in Windows 8*

Controlling Apps and Live Tiles

You open (launch) an app or program (software that runs on the desktop) from the Start screen with a single click or tap. This launches an app fullscreen or switches to the desktop to run a program. You want to be able to organize and perform additional actions on apps and programs, which includes running them as an administrator, resizing the live tiles, and so on. More importantly, you will want to arrange these tiles into groups that make it easy to find your most-used apps and programs, and hide the ones you don't use as often.

■ **Tip**   You can get back to the Start screen at any time by pressing the Windows key on your keyboard.

Performing Functions on Apps and Live Tiles

The equivalent of a right-click in a tile in Windows 8 is *still* a right-click; but if you are using touch, then you need to touch a tile and drag it slightly downward in the same movement to perform the same task. You cannot touch and hold a tile to perform actions on it.

■ **Tip** You can deselect a tile or select multiple tiles by swiping down or right-clicking. There is no need to hold the Ctrl or Shift keys when selecting or deselecting multiple tiles.

The actions you can perform on a tile will vary depending on what it is you have selected.

- **Unpin from Start** allows you to remove a tile from the Start screen. It is still available in the All Apps view (more on this shortly) and it can be launched from there. It is useful for programs and apps that you only use occasionally.

- **Pin to/Unpin from Taskbar** is useful if you want quick access to desktop programs from the Windows desktop taskbar. This option adds or removes a button on the desktop taskbar for a particular program. Apps cannot be pinned to the desktop taskbar.

- **Uninstall** is the option you use to uninstall *both* an app and a program from your computer. You can still manage and uninstall programs from Programs and Features, as with Windows 7, but this new quick method makes it easier to remove software from your PC.

- **Smaller** and **Larger** allows you to resize compatible app tiles from a square to a rectangle and back. You may have, for instance, a live tile for e-mail that gives you previews of your current e-mail in rectangle view, but as a square, it gives you only the number of unread e-mails (see Figure 2-6). You may decide that you want to make some tiles smaller so that your organized groups on the Start screen take up less space or look more organized.

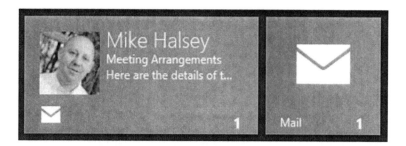

Figure 2-6. *The large and small live tile views*

- **Turn Live Tile Off** deactivates the live component of a compatible tile. You may want a larger rectangular tile for e-mail to make it easier to find and open, but not have the tile display the subjects and senders of your most recent e-mails.

- **Open New Window** allows you to open multiple instances of a program. Let's say, for example, you have Internet Explorer open from the Start screen and you want to open a web site, but not in a new tab because you want to view two web pages side by side. This option on compatible apps and programs allows you to open a new instance of the app or program.

- **Open File Location** works only on installed desktop programs and Windows desktop components. It opens a File Explorer window and navigates directly to the folder on your hard disk where the program or link you have selected is located. I discuss File Explorer in in Chapter 5.

- **Run as Administrator** allows you to run the program or feature with full admin privileges.

- **Clear Selection** cancels the current selection apps and/or programs.

Arranging Live Tiles into Groups

As I have already mentioned, you can arrange your tiles on the Start screen into customizable groups, and rearrange them within those groups. This is something that can be used to bring your most commonly used programs to the beginning (left) of the Start screen, and to group together related tiles such as Internet links or development software.

You can rearrange tiles within a group or move one to a different group by dragging and dropping it using touch or the mouse. You can only do this with one tile at a time because the Start screen doesn't permit the selection and moving of multiple tiles simultaneously.

When you move a tile between groups, a highlighted vertical bar appears between groups as you move from one to another. If you drop a tile onto this highlighted bar, then a new group is created.

By default, the Windows 8's Start screen does not give names to groups, but it is possible to do this. To name a group or groups, you first need to zoom out of the Start screen by clicking the Zoom control on the far right of the mouse scrollbar, or by holding the Ctrl key while using your mouse's scroll wheel, or by performing a pinch gesture (see Figure 2-7).

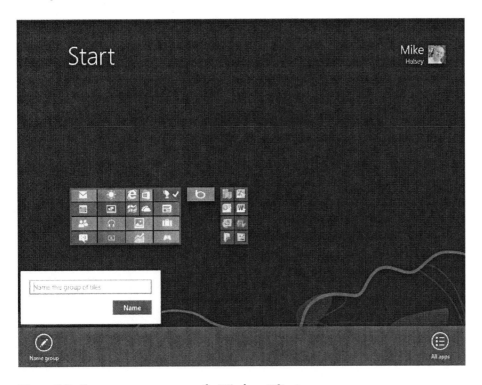

Figure 2-7. You can name groups on the Windows 8 Start screen

With the full Start screen zoomed out, you can name a group by selecting it with a right-click or a touch-and-drag downward movement. This will open the App bar with a Name Group option. Selecting this enables you to name an individual group. Click anywhere on the screen to return to the normal view.

Tip In this zoomed-out view, you can also rearrange entire groups in the same way that you would move tiles on the Start screen: simply by dragging and dropping.

Hiding and Adding Apps and Tiles

When you are customizing and arranging your Start screen, you will want to hide tiles, which can be done by selecting one or several, bringing up the App bar, and selecting Unpin from Start. When you install software onto Windows 8, every program and installed app has a tile on the Start screen. This can create a very messy environment that includes sub-utilities and uninstallers that you don't need, or at least won't want to use very often. You certainly want to remove these tiles from the Start screen.

But what if you want to restore some of these afterward? What if you want to restore all the Start screen programs that you weren't previously using, but now want easier access to?

Tip You can pin an app or program back to the Start screen by selecting it and clicking Pin to Start in the App bar.

By default on the Start screen, the App bar displays All Apps. This brings up a screen showing all the apps and programs that are installed on Windows 8, including those tiles that are hidden from the Start screen or the desktop taskbar.

On the left of this screen, which also scrolls left and right, you are first shown all the apps that are installed. Further to the right, you find Windows features and all the software you have installed in Windows 8 sorted into groups as they would appear in the Start menu.

You cannot edit this screen as you do in the Start menu, which allows you to drag and drop programs and Windows features between folders. The way that programs and apps are organized in the All Apps view is static. You also cannot rearrange the groups; they are always presented in alphabetical order, see Figure 2-8.

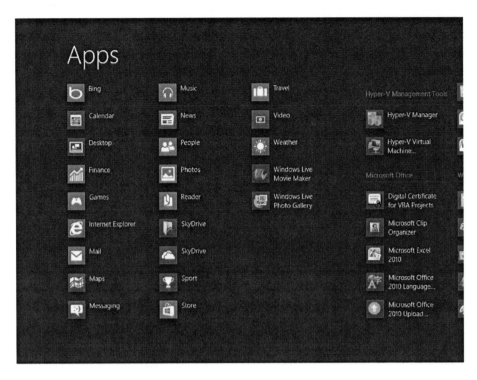

Figure 2-8. *The All Apps view*

To help with this issue, you can zoom out of view in the same way as you zoom out of the main Start screen, either by a pinch gesture, by clicking the zoom control on the far right of the scrollbar, or by holding down the Ctrl key and using the scroll wheel on your mouse.

This additional zoomed-out view (see Figure 2-9) shows apps arranged alphabetically. Software packages and Windows features are arranged by folder.

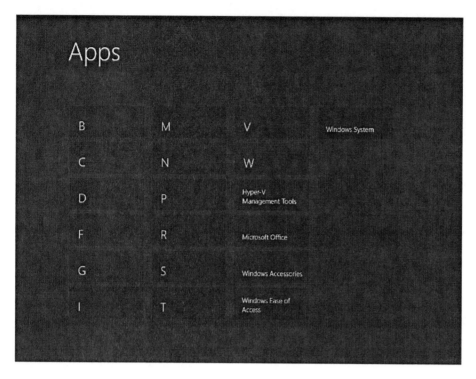

Figure 2-9. *You can zoom out of the All Apps view to see programs and apps arranged into groups*

With this view, you can quickly navigate to Microsoft Office, Camtasia Studio, Windows System, or other folders and groups that appear in the All Apps view by simply clicking or tapping.

Using the Charms

The charms include the Start button, also known as the Windows orb, along with several new features in Windows 8.

You open the charms (see Figure 2-10) in several ways: by swiping your finger in from the *bezel* (the area around your touchscreen) on the right of your screen, by moving your mouse to the top left or bottom right of the screen, or by pressing Win + C on the keyboard. The charms open in both the Start screen and the desktop.

Figure 2-10. *The charms*

There are five charms:

- **Search** allows you to search apps, settings, and files.

- **Share** is a new feature in Windows 8 that allows you to share text, images, and other items between apps, including sharing a photo with a social networking app to publish it there.

- **Start** is now where the Start button (which replaces the desktop Windows orb) appears. In Windows 8 it has been redesigned with a new look. Pressing it, just as with pressing the Windows key on your keyboard, cycles between the Start screen and the most recently running app or program.

- **Devices** is a quick way to access devices such as USB peripherals and secondary displays.

- **Settings** is the new home for the slimmed-down version of the Control Panel. There are now several different Control Panels in Windows, which offer different ways to access the settings of the operating system.

The charms are not configurable; you cannot manually add apps or hardware to the Share and Devices charms. You also cannot customize the Settings options or add extra charms. When Windows 8 detects apps and hardware that are compatible with the Share and Devices features, they are added automatically.

Share is a new feature that allows apps to share items, similar to the way that we copy and paste things between programs. This share functionality works with apps *only* and not with programs on the desktop.

Note   Third-party customization software for Windows 8 already exists, and by the time you read this, there may be software that allows you to customize the charms. Check my web site, `www.theLongClimb.com`, for details.

Configuration Options in PC Settings

When Microsoft introduced Windows 8, they needed to provide a way, from within the standard interface, for people to be able to change the basic settings that would most commonly apply to them. This has become the new PC Settings window (see Figure 2-11). You access it by clicking the Settings charm. Because we will use PC Settings often in the book, I want provide an initial overview.

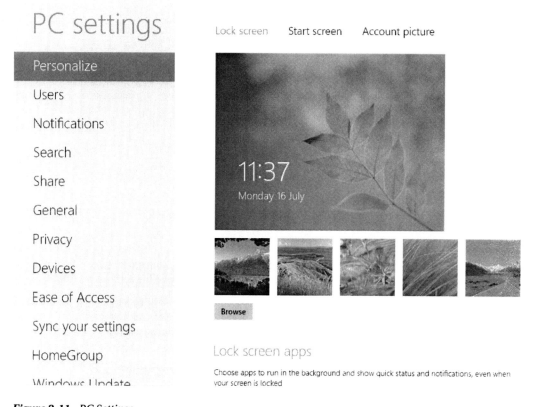

Figure 2-11. *PC Settings*

PC Settings is not a replacement for the full Windows Control Panel, which has been expanded with this Windows release (see Chapter 13 for detailed coverage of the Control Panel). For access to many of the basic settings that a user needs, however, PC Settings is an excellent place to start and is very well laid-out. I would like to describe how some of the PC Settings controls are an excellent alternative to the full Control Panel.

Some Control Panel options have become harder to find in recent releases. With Windows 8, we have the Control Panel, PC Settings, and the Devices and Printers panel. Some controls are duplicated. PC Settings controls perform one task in the Start screen but the equivalent Control Panel option only controls the desktop. There is also Administrative Tools, the Computer Management Console, and more. If you look at the number of controls, you discover that these settings pages and controls can nest up to a dozen others. Frankly, it's a big mess.

PC Settings gets around this problem by rationalizing all of the basic controls that a person using Windows 8 will need in a single location. Here you will find controls for personalization, user control, windows notifications (normally very hard to find), search, privacy (again, hard to find), networks, Windows Update, and more. It's really quite well laid-out.

I will talk through each category and describe the controls.

- **Personalize** is where you will find all the options for changing the look and feel of the Start screen and for controlling the information that is displayed on the lock screen.

- **Users** is where new user accounts can be easily created. It is much better than the full Control Panel version, in my opinion, because *only* Standard user accounts can be created. This page makes it very simple to create a Microsoft Account.

- **Notifications** in Windows have always been a pain and I have never seen a simpler or more rational approach taken to managing them than here.

- **Search** is where you can choose the type of in-app searching you want to perform. For example, you might want to exclude searching financial or e-mail apps because you only tend to search documents. This page makes that easy.

- **Share** is where you can control a new Windows 8 feature that allows apps to share data. If you don't want to share your text, photos, and so forth with social networking or Internet apps, you can turn this feature on or off.

- **General** is where you will find time zone controls, which is particularly useful if you travel a lot because it's very easy to change. It also features controls your touch keyboard, language, and spelling, as well as restore options if your computer begins to misbehave.

- **Privacy** is new to Windows. It is now common for new computers to have features with GPS. Here you can control the type of information your apps are allowed to have.

- **Devices** is where you can manage and add new hardware without having to deal with the Device Manager. You can also prevent drivers from being downloaded and updated over mobile broadband connections to save bandwidth. I will talk more about managing devices using this page later.

- **Wireless** is where you can quickly and simply turn your wireless devices on and off, including mobile broadband. It is useful if your computer doesn't come with a physical on/off switch or if you want to turn off mobile broadband while leaving Wi-Fi active. You can also activate Airplane Mode. If you need information about your mobile broadband, perhaps your IMEI number, which is a special code that your mobile operator uses to identify your SIM card or mobile phone, it is easy to find by clicking the name of the mobile broadband provider (see Figure 2-12).

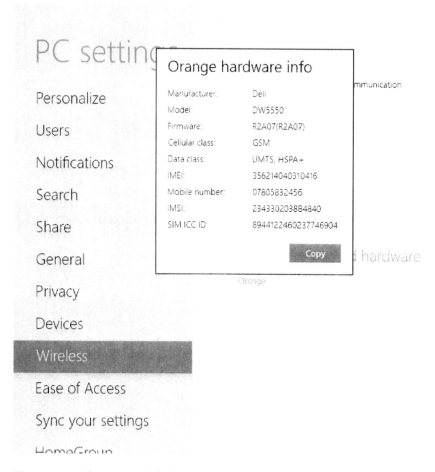

Figure 2-12. *Obtaining mobile broadband details*

- **Ease of Access** contains the most popular and common settings. It is no substitute for the full controls, but if a user has difficulty reading or finding controls due to vision or other problems, the Ease of Access controls can make it easier.

- **Sync Your Settings** is where you can sync your Internet Explorer favorites, user account details, and app preferences across all of the Windows 8 computers you use. You can also confirm the computer that you want information synched with and from.

- **HomeGroup** is where you can set up and manage a simple sharing group for a set of Windows 7 and/or Windows 8 computers in your home. You can share documents, videos, music, pictures, and printers.

- **Windows Update** is a much simpler version of the automatic update controls that you find in the Control Panel. This page simply tells you if anything is available for update and the number of updates available. It also allows you to download and install updates.

■ **Tip** To save your bandwidth, by default, Windows 8 turns off all downloads and syncing in PC Settings for Mobile Broadband connections. If you have unlimited data, PC Settings allows you turn this option on.

Using the Desktop in Windows 8

Using the desktop in Windows 8 is the same as with any previous version of the operating system, except that the Start button (Windows orb) is now gone from the taskbar. You can pin programs to the taskbar by right-clicking them on the Start screen and selecting Pin to Taskbar from the App bar options. You can only pin one program at a time from the Start screen; however, this can make the process a little slow.

■ **Note** Until you get used to the missing Start button on the taskbar, you should make sure that your first taskbar button is something small and quick to load, such as File Explorer, as you will probably click it quite often!

All the usual desktop clicks, such as right-clicking with the mouse to bring up a context menu, still work. On a touchscreen, you can tap and hold to simulate a right-click. In some ways, this is inconsistent with the tap-and-pull downward gesture to select an item. It is, however, more consistent with the right-click touch gesture in Windows XP, Windows Vista, and Windows 7 when used with a touchscreen.

The Windows Administration Menu

Although the Start menu has been removed from the desktop in Windows 8, it isn't gone completely. On both the desktop and the Start screen, right-clicking with your mouse in the very bottom left of the screen (also accessible by pressing Win+X) brings up a menu of options typically found in the Start menu, such as the Run and Command prompt. This menu is also customizable through the use of third-party software. I will talk more about this in Chapter 13.

Using the Desktop Taskbar

The Windows 8 taskbar is the same as in Windows 7. You can pin programs that can be launched with a single click, or that on a click up-and-drag-upward motion (also on a right-click) opens a Jump List with additional options (see Figure 2-13). I will talk more about Jump Lists shortly.

Figure 2-13. *The Windows 8 desktop and taskbar Jump Lists*

On the right side of the taskbar sits the system tray (see Figure 2-14), the area where you commonly see the time and date. The following list describes the other icons in the system tray.

Figure 2-14. *The system tray icons on the desktop taskbar*

- The **Keyboard icon** brings up the onscreen keyboard. It appears by default when Windows 8 detects a touchscreen interface attached to your computer, but it can also be switched on in the Tablet PC Settings in the Control Panel.

- The **system tray** is represented by a small white Up arrow. This is the bucket container for all the system tray icons that are hidden. I show you how to customize the system tray in Chapter 9.

- The **Action Center** is the central location for Windows messages, including those about antivirus, backup, problems, and errors. The irony that the icon for the Action Center is a white flag has never been lost on me!

- The **Battery icon** only shows when you are running Windows 8 on a computer containing a battery. This icon gives you a visual representation of the battery's charge level, and overlays a Plug icon if your computer is currently connected to mains electricity.

- The **Network icon** changes depending on whether you are connected to your network and the Internet by a physical Ethernet cable, Wi-Fi, or a mobile internet connection such as 3G or 4G via a SIM card in your computer or via a dongle. This icon changes to an airplane if you have airplane mode switched on.

- The **Volume icon** offers a quick way to turn the computer's volume up or down, or mute it. If you click this icon, a volume control appears. I talk more about the additional functionality of this icon in Chapter 9.

- The **Date and Time** format can be changed. I talk about how to customize and configure the Date and Time settings in Chapter 9. If you click the time and date in the system tray, a dialog box shows the current month's calendar, the currently displayed clock(s), and any messages relating to daylight saving time. I talk more about using this window shortly.

- The **Show Desktop button** was a visible button on the Windows 7 taskbar, but it is hidden in Windows 8. Hovering over this button temporarily hides all open windows on the desktop. Clicking the far right of the taskbar, however, minimizes all the windows currently open on your desktop, showing just the desktop and any gadgets you may have on it. Clicking the button again restores all previously minimized windows (see Figure 2-14).

Using the Date and Time Dialog Box

The Date and Time dialog box, which is viewable by clicking the date and time on the taskbar, is very powerful. I explain how to configure the settings in Chapter 9, but one of the best features is the calendar. At the top of the calendar are left and right arrows that navigate to either side of the current month (see Figure 2-15).

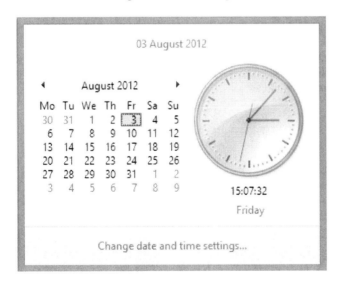

Figure 2-15. *The date and time accessible from the taskbar*

Clicking the month changes the display to show all the months in the current year. Clicking it again displays all the years in the current decade, and clicking it a third time displays all the decades in the current century. This makes it an excellent tool for quickly locating dates.

When you hover your mouse over a button on the taskbar, a pop-up showing a live thumbnail image of the running program appears (see Figure 2-16). If that program is minimized, then mousing over the thumbnail image temporarily brings that application to the foreground without having to restore it to the desktop. This is an excellent way to get a quick peek at what is going on in an app. Because the thumbnails are completely live, you can see any progress bars or motion in the thumbnail that is occurring in the window at that time. This is useful for keeping an eye on programs that you only want running in the background while they complete tasks.

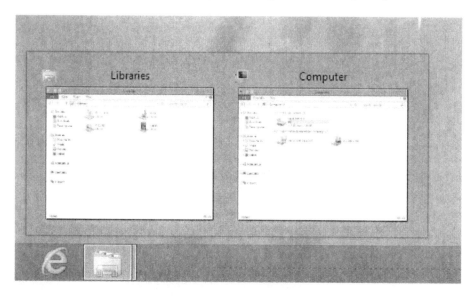

Figure 2-16. *Using live thumbnail previews on the taskbar*

Using Taskbar Jump Lists

I find Jump Lists to be one of the most useful features of Windows (see Figure 2-17). I use them all the time. They are pop-up menus that appear above program buttons on the taskbar. You display a Jump List by right-clicking a taskbar button or by clicking it and dragging upward with your mouse or finger.

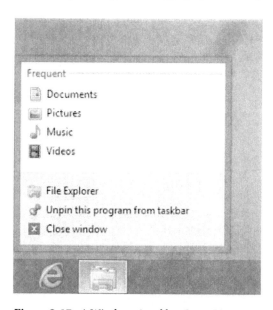

Figure 2-17. *A Windows 8 taskbar Jump List*

Jump Lists can contain any of the following elements:

- **Recently opened files** in a program for quick access
- **Pinned files** that will always display in the Jump Lists for quick file access
- **Tasks** that can be performed with a program
- The **Program Launch**, which can be very useful if you want to start multiple instances of a program
- The **Unpin button** for unpinning the program from the taskbar
- The **Close Window button** for closing the program

Jump Lists are programmable, not only by software packages, but also by web sites. You can drag the button for a web site from the desktop version of Internet Explorer and pin it to the taskbar by dropping it there. Many web sites, such as Facebook, are programmed to provide quick links to specific parts of the site or specific features.

Managing Windows on the Desktop

When you have a lot of windows open on your desktop, things can get very muddled. You can use the taskbar thumbnails to give you previews or quick views of windows. But what if you want to clean away all but the current working window or work on two windows together?

Both of these tasks are easy in Windows 8's Shake and Snap features. Shake allows you to grab and shake a window. This has the effect of automatically minimizing every window except the one you're shaking. If you want to return the desktop to the way it was, just shake the window again and all the minimized windows are restored.

Sometimes you will want to work on two documents side by side, perhaps to move data from one to another, or to compare two web pages or documents. You can do this by dragging windows to the far left or right of the desktop. When you do this, an outline appears, indicating that that window will fill exactly half the screen. You can snap windows to both sides of the desktop screen.

The Preinstalled Windows 8 Apps

There are a great many apps provided with Windows 8. Many are either the standard apps that you now expect to find bundled with an operating system, or are there to showcase the abilities of the system. I will detail the apps with features that can genuinely aid productivity.

░ **Note**   One of the biggest advantages of the default apps in Windows 8 is that they are more regularly updated than we previously experienced.

Calendar

When you log into Windows 8 using a Microsoft Account linked to a Hotmail, Live or Outlook.com account, Windows Calendar automatically syncs your appointments and shows any upcoming appointments on the lock screen. This is especially useful if you use a Windows Phone and manage your calendar there, or if you log in using an ID linked to an exchange server.

Camera

The Camera app lets you take pictures and record video from your tablet, laptop webcam, or the webcam built into or attached to your desktop PC. This app is probably more useful on mobile devices, but eliminates the need for third-party software to do the same job.

Mail

When you sign into Windows 8 using a Microsoft Account linked to an e-mail account or an exchange server, your e-mail is automatically synced to Windows 8. There is no need to configure the account separately. The Mail app is basic e-mail software, however, with features that allow you to arrange mail by folder. It is a good package for very light usage and as a way to separate your home and work e-mail (work e-mail may be best read with Windows Live Mail or Outlook).

You can add email accounts from the app by opening the Settings charm and you will see an Add Accounts link appear in the top right of the screen.

■ **Note**   If the e-mail account you use in Mail has a calendar and contacts, those features appear in the Calendar and People apps.

Maps

Maps is one of the most useful and powerful apps in Windows 8. It does everything you expect a standard mapping app to do, such as support both road and aerial views, but it also contains a quick and effective route planner with the ability to use an Internet connection to show traffic congestion and its built-in GPS to pinpoint your location.

Messaging

Messaging is the app version of Windows Live Messenger, which you probably want to use in a side pane on the screen. It may be updated at a later stage to include chat services such as Facebook, but it is unlikely to include integration with Microsoft's Lync services.

Music

Music is a fairly basic music player. Windows now has three types: Music, Windows Media Player, and Windows Media Center. If you include the excellent Zune desktop software, you will be spoiled with choices.

People

On the face of it, the People app doesn't look very useful—maybe a bit like a stripped-down social network aggregator. It is actually more powerful than you might imagine. But before you can use it to its full effect, you need a Windows Live ID to which you can connect third-party services.

To connect other services to your Live ID, go on the web to profile.live.com. In the Connected To section (see Figure 2-18), there are links to connect you to additional services and manage (i.e., remove) existing services.

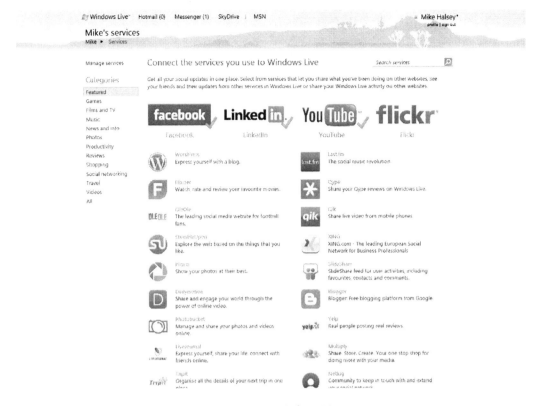

Figure 2-18. *Connecting services to your account in Windows Live*

There are dozens of services that can be integrated into Windows Live, including Facebook, LinkedIn, YouTube, Flickr, and more. Linked services appear in your People app, making it much more useful and interesting.

Photos

The Photos app is a fairly basic picture and photo viewer; however, like the People app, it integrates with services you have linked in your Microsoft account. This means that it automatically allows you to view your photos on Facebook, Flickr, and other services without any configuration.

Video

Video is a basic video playing app that connects to other services through a Microsoft account.

Windows Reader

For the first time, Windows comes bundled with software that opens Adobe PDF and Microsoft XPS files natively. There is no longer the need to download Adobe Reader software separately. This app only allows opening PDF files in Windows 8. If you want to read PDF files on the desktop, you need third-party software.

The Preinstalled Desktop Programs

As you might expect to find with Windows, the bundled desktop programs are much more powerful than their app equivalents. Not much has changed in recent years, but improvements have been made and some of the apps are indeed very powerful and flexible.

Calculator

If you are used to the basic Windows calculator from XP, then you're in for a surprise and a treat. The calculator in Windows 8 is extremely flexible. In addition to the default standard mode, there are scientific, programmer, and statistics modes available in the View menu (see Figure 2-19).

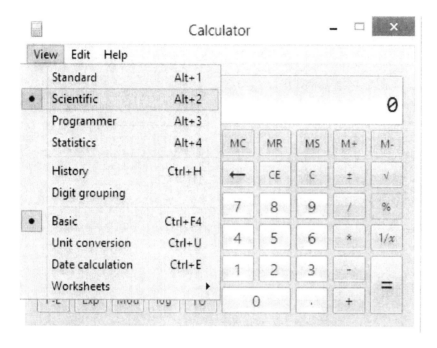

Figure 2-19. *The calculator in Windows 8*

You can also use the Windows calculator for unit conversions and date calculations, and there are additional worksheets integrated to help you figure out common calculations, including fuel economy.

Character Map

The Character Map allows you to view all available text characters from the installed fonts on your computer. You can copy these characters, many of which are not available via a keyboard combination, and paste them into your documents.

Math Input

If you have stylus for your computer or tablet, Math Input is useful for turning scribbled equations and formulas into text that can be inserted into your documents. It is extremely good at recognizing handwriting, as you can see in Figure 2-20 (it's not easy writing on my laptop's screen, honest).

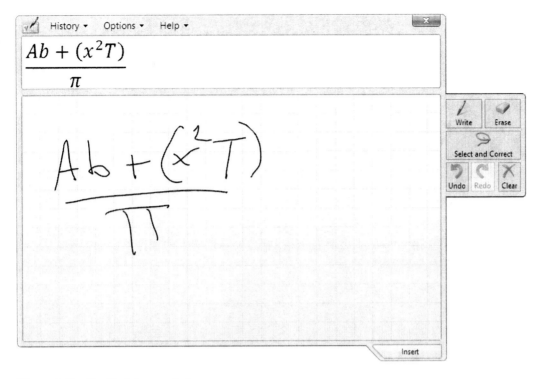

Figure 2-20. The Math Input window

Notepad

Notepad is still here. The old favorite hasn't changed at all. Why would you want it to?. This basic text editor and note taker has always been a popular inclusion in Windows, especially with programmers.

Paint

If you have used Paint in Windows 7, you are familiar with the Ribbon interface. For basic graphics work, such as cropping images and light touchup work, it's fine too. I have used it extensively in creating the images for this book.

Snipping Tool

While Windows 8's new feature for automatically saving screen grabs using the Win + PrntScrn key combination is welcome, sometimes you just want to capture a specific window or a part of the screen. This is where the Snipping Tool is useful. It can grab any part of your screen, in any shape, and save it as file (see Figure 2-21).

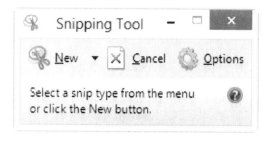

Figure 2-21. The Snipping Tool

Sound Recorder

As a basic sound recording tool, the Windows Sound Recorder has always worked well. As a basic alternative to third-party apps, it is very good at what it does and has also been carried over from previous versions of Windows.

Sticky Notes

Sticky Notes were formerly gadgets on the Windows Vista sidebar, but in Windows 7, they made their way into the Start menu as a full program. Sticky Notes exist in Windows 8 as a useful way to put notes on your desktop without getting glue all over it.

Windows Fax and Scan

Despite the fact that every scanner and multifunction printer in the world comes with its own custom scanning package, the scanning software in Windows is extremely accomplished in its own right—with excellent configuration and management options as standard. The app has full faxing capabilities, including fax history, header pages, and more.

Windows Journal

The Windows Journal is a note-taking app designed primarily for touchscreens. It is the "little brother" of the incredibly powerful and flexible Microsoft OneNote. The little brother hasn't had a makeover in Windows 8, but for tablets and touchscreen laptops, he still exists as a free alternative to OneNote (see Figure 2-22).

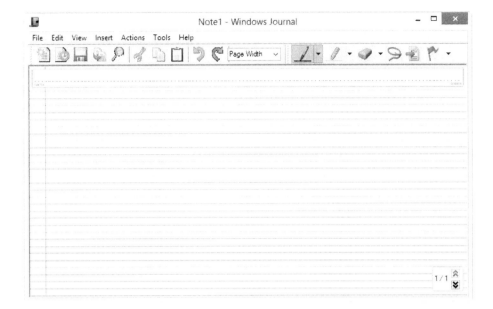

Figure 2-22. *Windows journal*

Windows Media Center/Windows Media Player

I'll talk in-depth about Windows Media Center and Windows Media Player in Chapter 7, but they exist to allow you to view pictures and video, to listen to music, and to watch and record live TV.

WordPad

If you bought your computer from the manufacturer (e.g., Dell, Samsung, or HP), then you probably have Microsoft Office Starter installed on it. If you don't have Office Starter installed on your computer, WordPad is an effective basic word processor that comes with every version of Windows 8 including retail copies. It also supports the latest Microsoft Word file formats (see Figure 2-23).

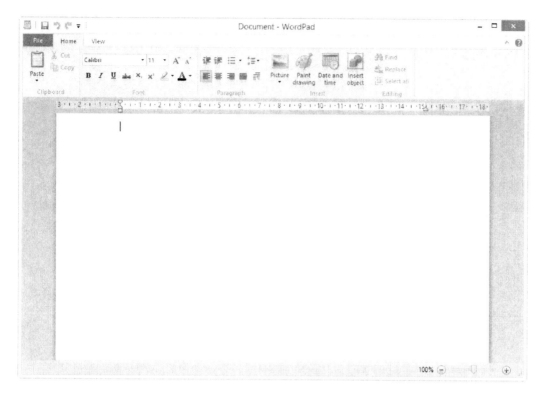

Figure 2-23. *WordPad in Windows 8*

XPS Viewer

XPS has long been Microsoft's alternative to Adobe's PDF file format, and although it's not as popular, it's not going anywhere. Whereas Windows Reader is set as the default app for opening XPS views, the desktop XPS Viewer exists to open XPS files when you don't want to use the app.

Installing and Uninstalling Apps and Programs

When you install an app onto Windows 8, there is only one way to do it and one place to do it: the Windows Store. This makes it very simple to find, install, and update your apps. If updates are available, a counter appears on the Windows Store Live Tile. You can click the Store app update indicator, which appears in the top right of your screen, to install updates (see Figure 2-24).

⊖ App updates 1 update available

Figure 2-24. *Updating apps in the Windows Store*

■ **Note**   If you manage your computers through Windows Server, you can deploy, manage, and remove apps and desktop programs in Windows 8 using AppLocker. This also works with Windows ARM tablets.

You can install Windows desktop software the same as always: by inserting a CD or DVD with the software installer or by running it from a USB flash drive or other external storage through File Explorer.

■ **Tip**   Always choose advanced options when installing software because many software packages also want to install third-party toolbars and utilities that you won't need and may not want.

To uninstall software in Windows 8, you can access Programs and Features from the Control Panel. Here you find all the desktop software installed on your computer. You can click the column headers (Name, Publisher, Installed On, etc.) to sort and arrange the software to make it easier to organize (see Figure 2-25). You may want to arrange it by date, for example, to see the most recently installed software first.

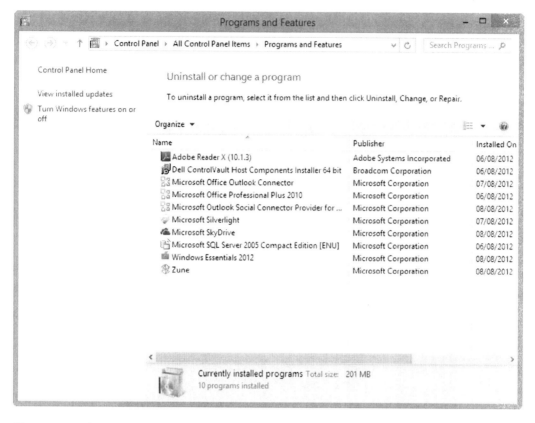

Figure 2-25. *The Programs and Features page in Windows 8*

To uninstall apps (and desktop software) from the Start screen, right-click (or touch and drag down) an app and select Uninstall from the App bar (see Figure 2-26). If you uninstall an app this way, it is uninstalled. If you uninstall a desktop program this way, you are redirected to the Programs and Features page—from where you will need to select and uninstall it.

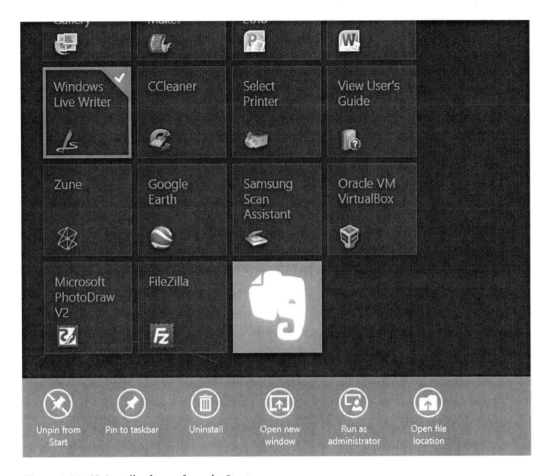

Figure 2-26. *Uninstall software from the Start screen*

This might seem a bit of a cheat but it does at least provide a more accessible and far easier way to uninstall all types of software from your Windows 8 computer.

Summary

The Start screen is a completely new way of working with Windows. It offers its own challenges and its own learning curve. Some people will love and enjoy it, other people will prefer to use the desktop. In Windows 8, it is much easier to stay on the desktop than you might think, and with the exception of the Start menu, all the functionality from previous versions of Windows remains.

In the next chapter, we will look at how we can get Windows 8 connected to our home and work networks, devices, peripherals, and the wider world via wired, wireless, and mobile broadband connections.

CHAPTER 3

Connecting

Windows 8 is the best-connected version of the Windows operating system yet. It includes support for new wireless standards like 4G mobile broadband. With this added flexibility, however, comes some pitfalls. Getting online and connecting to networks is now far more than turning on a connection and entering a password.

In this chapter, I want to take a holistic look at safely and securely connecting to networks and the Internet. You don't want to have to worry about securely checking your e-mail. Worse still, you don't want to have to worry about your business or personal data being open and available to hackers and drive-by Wi-Fi thieves.

In this chapter, I want to give you the knowledge you need to use network and Internet connections safely and securely, whether you are at home, at work, or on the move. This is especially important as we keep more of our personal and business lives in digital files and in online cloud services. With all of our precious photographs, music, documents, and business projects now stored digitally, we need to be certain that we're protected on any device, because everything is now interconnected in ways we've not previously experienced.

Getting Online with Windows 8

One of the very first things you're going to do with a computer is get it connected to the Internet. So much of what we do these days is online, with e-mail and social networking now part of the fabric of society. Long gone are the days when we might use an MSN or IRC chat client for a couple of hours on a weekend. Now it's constant access to chat via PCs and smartphones, social updates across multiple platforms, and access to e-mail, even work e-mail, 24 hours a day.

There really is no getting away from the Internet wherever we go. If you are a web enthusiast, a gamer, an IT pro, at work or running a business, or even just on your daily commute looking for something to occupy yourself with, odds are you'll be on a computer and that you'll be online. Tablets recently out from major manufacturers offer features not seen in other tablet operating systems, including multiuser setups. Use of Windows 8 will be more widespread than in the previous Windows editions that were only used on desktop PCs and laptops. We really do need to make sure that all of our data is safe and secure.

Understanding Public and Private Networks

Before I show you how to connect to networks in Windows 8, I want to talk a bit more about the main network types. Windows splits networks into three different categories: Home, Work, and Public. When you connect to a network for the first time, Windows 8 asks you which of these three networks applies to your usage. On the face of it, these might seem quite straightforward, and indeed they are intended to be this way, but I want to talk a little about each network type and why they are or are not suitable for certain purposes.

Home Networks

Home networks are the types where you simply trust everything. You are, after all, in complete control of the network and all the hardware attached to it, including other computers, smartphones, tablets, game consoles, and maybe even storage attached to your home Wi-Fi router. What could possibly go wrong with all of this?

Well, for starters, many people are confused by or simply don't understand home network security. Why should they? As consumers, we're used to home electronics being like a television, a microwave, or a DVD player. It's not true that all consumer electronics are simple to use. Take the new Internet-connected televisions, for example. Some of these TVs can take three-quarters of an hour to set up the first time you use them. They have myriads of menus controlling different tuners, movie and TV downloads, plug-in services, and 3D and surround sound. A friend of mine bought a new TV in 2011 that he couldn't tune into at all. He simply couldn't get a signal on it, so he called me to look at it. I figured out that both the digital and the old analog tuners had completely different onscreen menus, and they were accessed by pressing different buttons on the remote control. The reason he'd been unable to get a signal was because he'd been using the wrong tuner in a place where the old analog signal had been switched off.

With home computer equipment, it can be even more complicated. The most common piece of hardware at fault is the router that connects your home to the Internet. While Internet Service Providers (ISPs) are much better than they used to be at programming individual Wi-Fi passcodes into devices, they still usually leave the administration password as the default.

When coupled with the fact that the name of your Wi-Fi network commonly includes the make and model of the router itself, it's simple for a neighbor or a drive-by hacker to casually access the router and gain access to your network and the devices on it.

While this type of drive-by hack is rare, it is commonly blamed in file-sharing cases where unsuspecting people are accused by the authorities and big movie studios of downloading the latest Johnny Depp movie.

The first thing to do with your own Home network is make sure that you have unique passwords on both your Wi-Fi access and your router's administration interface. How you do this depends on the make and model you have, but your ISP will be able to talk you through it, and the router should come with a manual or help files.

You won't only connect to Home networks in your own house. You may also connect to Home networks at friends' and family members' houses. You have no control over their network or hardware, nor have any idea if they have adequate anti-malware protection on their network-connected computers and devices.

When you connect to their Wi-Fi, however, you know if they have a strong password or even no password at all (be very careful when connecting to networks where you don't know if any of the computers are infected with malware).

Home networks are really only for use in your own safe and secure environment, where you absolutely know the state of your security, and where you can implicitly trust the person who put it all together.

Work Networks

Workplace networks are inherently more trustworthy than home networks because they are managed by qualified personnel. In a work network, the other computers attached to the network won't be able to see the documents, pictures, music, or video you have shared in a HomeGroup (more on these in Chapter 4), but well-written malware can still infect network-connected computers.

Work networks are really only useful in managed server environments where a company is running its own Windows Server and you have to access to shared storage. If you are connecting to a work network that's run from a Windows Server system, for example, then telling Windows you are connected to a Work network is essential to ensuring that all the relevant network systems in Windows 8 have permission to talk to the server and receive data back from it.

If you are in a workplace, however, where you are only using the network for Internet access, and your computer is stand-alone or not connected to a server (for example, when you're visiting a client), then I wouldn't recommend telling Windows you are connected to a Work network. The reason for this is that in your own company, you have to take it on trust that the IT department has set security appropriately on the network. You may even manage that network yourself. If it's somewhere else though, and especially if it's a small business, you won't have any reliable knowledge about how security is set on the network and the router.

Public Networks

For everywhere else, and for your peace of mind, there are Public networks. It is what you should *always* use if you are in a public place such as a coffee shop, library, or even connected via a mobile dongle or SIM card.

When a network is set in Windows to Public, the operating system throws up its full defenses against other computers and network devices, not allowing file sharing or other sharing unless you explicitly permit it.

If you are ever uncertain about the network you are connected to, or perhaps don't need access to a server or shared storage on that network, then I recommend you tell Windows 8 that it is Public. It is the best way to avoid problems and security concerns.

Connecting to Networks in Windows 8

Connecting to networks in Windows 8 is slightly different from previous versions of the operating system. If you are on the desktop, you can still click the network connection icon in the system tray area of the taskbar, but from the Start screen, you first need to open the charms, and then click Settings. (You can open the charms with a touch swipe in from the right of your screen, or by moving your mouse to the bottom right of the screen, or by pressing Win + C on your keyboard.)

In Settings, your network connection button is in the group of six small buttons that pop out from the right of the screen. It is the first of the six, in the top left of the group.

When you click it, you are shown various options (see Figure 3-1). I want to talk about each of these in turn.

Figure 3-1. The network connection window in Windows 8

Airplane Mode was first introduced on mobile phones because radio signals given off by the phones can cause interference with airplane computer systems during take off and landing; they can also interfere with other equipment, such as sensitive medical equipment. The Airplane Mode feature is present in Windows 8 because people now commonly use laptops and tablets with mobile broadband while traveling. Switching on Airplane Mode in Windows 8 deactivates all communication signals, effectively cutting off all radio communication from being sent and received by the computer. You are reminded by signage onboard the aircraft or by the cabin crew when you need to activate Airplane Mode on your computer.

Mobile broadband networks are those you access through a SIM card in your laptop or tablet, or through a USB mobile broadband dongle. There are data usage concerns with mobile broadband in Windows because of networks commonly capping data usage. I will talk more about this shortly.

Wi-Fi networks are standard home, workplace, or public networks. They have limited range and do not work when you move away from the router or base station.

When you choose a network to connect to, you are asked for the network password (if there is one— and remember to be extremely wary about networks that don't). There is a box that allows you to see the full characters of the normally hidden password. This is useful to make sure you are typing a complex password correctly. But don't select this option if someone might be looking over your shoulder!

You are also asked if you want to always connect automatically to this network; this box is checked (selected) by default, but unless you want to connect to this network regularly, you should uncheck it. Just because you are fairly sure that a given network is safe, don't assume that it will always stay secure. All it takes is a single setting to be changed.

Managing Mobile Broadband

As I mentioned earlier, one of the problems with network connections in Windows is that they can be set (deliberately or accidentally) to connect automatically whenever you are in range. I will show you how to manage your network connections shortly, but with 3G or 4G mobile broadband, this can be a problem, especially if your laptop or tablet has a built-in SIM card.

Mobile data packages regularly cap usage, so it's bad if your computer connects to such a network when you don't specifically want it to. This can result in hefty data usage bills if you go over your allotted limit (or you may find you can't get a connection when you need to because you used up your allotment).

While you can set your mobile broadband connection to *not* connect automatically, the only way to be completely safe and secure is to switch it off when you don't need it. Why do I recommend this? It's simply because while we're all used to uncapped Wi-Fi usage at home and at work, mobile broadband is still very expensive. Personally, I am not prepared to risk running up huge bills on my laptop and Windows tablet (both of which have a SIM card slot), so I always have mobile broadband switched off in Windows when I'm not using it.

To access the mobile broadband on/off switch, you need to go into PC Settings, which is the new, simplified Control Panel in Windows 8. Open the charms and select Settings. In PC Settings, click Change PC Settings at the bottom of the menu to display the full PC Settings page (see Figure 3-2).

Figure 3-2. *The wireless controls in PC Settings*

PC Settings gives you the basic controls you need to use Windows 8 on a day-to-day basis, though the full Control Panel also exists (more on this in Chapter 13). The mobile broadband on/off switch is located in the Wireless section (see Figure 3-2), which you can select on the left of the screen by touching or clicking it.

If you have a SIM card, USB mobile broadband dongle, or a modem attached to your computer, you see Mobile Broadband in the right pane of the Wireless Devices section. You can toggle this on and off by touching or clicking the switch.

Connecting to Hidden Networks and VPNs in Windows 8

By default, Windows 8 only shows you networks that are not hidden; it's designed to make things as easy as possible for you. The new Windows 8 interface doesn't show any of the advanced features of Windows. To connect to a hidden Wi-Fi network or a workplace Virtual Private Network (VPN), perform the following steps: Note that if you are connecting to a VPN that has been set up for your company, you will need settings that can be provided by your network administrator.

1. Open the Windows desktop.

2. Right-click the Network button to the right of the taskbar.

3. Select Open Network and Sharing Center.

■ **Note** You can also search for the Network and Sharing Center from the Start screen.

---

4. Click **Set up a new connection or network to open the new connection page** (see Figure 3-3).

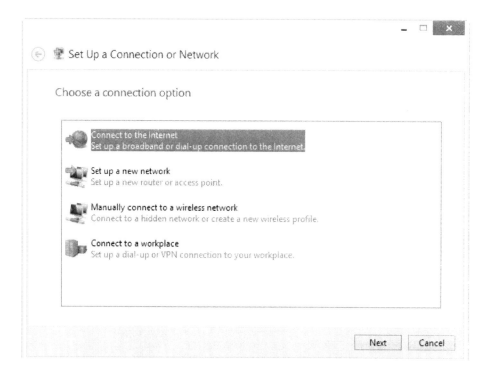

Figure 3-3. The Network and Sharing Center in Windows 8

5. To connect to a hidden Wi-Fi network, click **Manually connect to a wireless network**. Press Next.

6. To connect to a company VPN, click **Connect to a workplace**. Press Next.

The wizards to connect to hidden Wi-Fi networks and VPNs are very straightforward and easy to use, but you will need specific information for them, such as the hidden network's SSID name and security passphrase type, or the IP address of the VPN.

Managing Network Connections

You also use the Network and Sharing Center for managing your broadband and other networks. You can access the Network and Sharing Center by either searching for it or navigating to the desktop and right-clicking the Network button, where there is an option to open it.

To access the networks you have stored on your computer, click Change Adapter Settings in the left-hand pane. The window that opens contains all the saved network connections that you have in Windows (see Figure 3-4).

Figure 3-4. *Managing network connections in Windows 8*

You can right-click these connections to perform various actions, but the following actions are also available on the toolbar at the top of the window:

- **Disable** the connection so that you keep it in your network settings, but the network cannot be accessed.

- **Connect** or **Disconnect** from the network.

- Check the **Status** of the network, which is useful if you are having connection difficulties.

- **Diagnose** a problem or a fault with the connection. This runs an automated troubleshooter that resets the connection to its default state.

- Check the **Properties** of the connection. This is where you can change specific settings with the network adaptor. Use your computer to share this connection with other computers by turning your PC into a mobile hotspot, or turn on/off specific features that may be causing problems, such as IPv6.

- There is no direct option to delete a connection or change its autoconnect or stored password settings. To delete a connection, highlight it and press the **Delete (Del) key** on your keyboard.

- To change the autoconnect or stored password status of a Wi-Fi or mobile broadband connection, select its Status. In the dialog box, click the **Wireless Properties button**. This brings up another dialog box showing an autoconnect check box that you can toggle on and off. There is also a Security tab in this dialog box containing the stored password (called the network security key), which can be removed if you wish (see Figure 3-5).

51

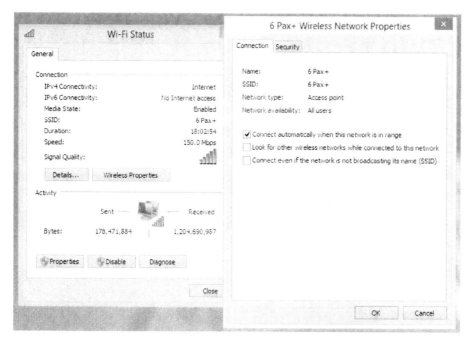

Figure 3-5. *Changing the security properties of a wireless connection*

■ **Note** Windows 8 only allows you to select the status of a connected network or Internet connection. Sometimes it is simpler to simply delete the connection.

Network Management Best Practice

If you manage a network at home or at work, you should take a holistic view of security and network management, including consideration for who will be using the network.

It is worth the money, especially in a small business environment, to buy a router that allows you to set up multiple main and guest SSIDs. The advantage of doing this is that you do not have to worry about visitors to your work environment having accidental access to your computers, the files stored on them, or any shared storage you have in the workplace.

Many high-end routers offer this functionality, and in the workplace, I couldn't recommend it more. It can also be useful in the home, especially if you have shared network storage, such as a NAS drive or USB hard disk attached to your router, on which you keep backups and private files.

You should always make sure that the router has two passwords on it, one for the administration interface and another for the Wi-Fi. These should *always* be different. If you have a router that supports multiple SSIDs, then each one should have its own unique password. This is the best way to guarantee, as much as is humanly possible anyway, that you have excellent security on your network.

■ **Tip** To create a secure password, make sure it is at least 12 characters in length and includes a mixture of uppercase and lowercase letters, numbers, and symbols. You can also use some numbers and symbols to represent letters, such as 5 instead of S, 1 instead of i or L, and & instead of A.

Securing Wi-Fi Networks

When you set up your Wi-Fi network, it can be difficult to decide which type of security to use on the password; after all, there are so many. Do you choose WEP, WPA-Personal, WPA2-Personal, WPA-Enterprise, or WPA2-Enterprise encryption? As these are all combinations of letters and numbers, what does each one mean? There is a temptation to choose a basic encryption type such as WEP because it allows for the use of short passwords that are easy to remember. This makes it very insecure, however. The higher the level of encryption you add, the longer and more complex the default password requirement.

Suffice it to say, however, that WEP, WPA, and WPA2 have all been compromised, especially in the business space, by a drive-by hacker (a person sitting outside the building in a car or on a bench who hacks into a network from a laptop). So unless your router offers additional security options that can be used in conjunction with the key—such as AES encryption or a RADIUS authentication server—you are never completely protected.

Each type of secure encryption and authentication you add to a Wi-Fi network makes the password longer with requirements that are more stringent. On the upside, it only has to be entered on each computer once; but on the downside, it still has to be entered.

I bring this up because, especially for business, it's a legitimate security concern. On the other hand, you need to think about the likelihood of a drive-by hacker trying to crack your security.

What do you have on your network? How sensitive are your files and documents? Are you really a hacking target? Most enthusiasts and IT pros reading this have the same types of files on their networks as any consumer, but also have business files. Only if you store particularly sensitive data on your network—you work in the biochemical industry or for a government agency, for example—are you likely to be the target of drive-by hackers.

This isn't to say hacking will never happen to you, but I want to present a balanced argument. For home users, I recommend WPA2 encryption. The minimum password length might be a bit long to remember, but it is always recommended by security professionals to have long passwords. You should keep the password written in a safe location—a desk drawer in your home or workplace, for example, is good because it is unlikely that someone will physically break in to the building to access your Wi-Fi network. WEP and WPA simply don't offer enough security, so I recommend you avoid them.

Managing Mobile Broadband Data Usage

If you use your computer on a mobile broadband connection (3G/4G), you probably want to make sure that you don't go over your usage limits.

With Live Tiles on the Start screen, Windows 8 quietly helps you both monitor your usage and limit the amount of data used.

When you connect to a mobile broadband network, Windows tells you the amount data you have used so far. If you are on a monthly contract in which you have a fixed amount of data, you can reset the data counter every month by clicking Reset (see Figure 3-6).

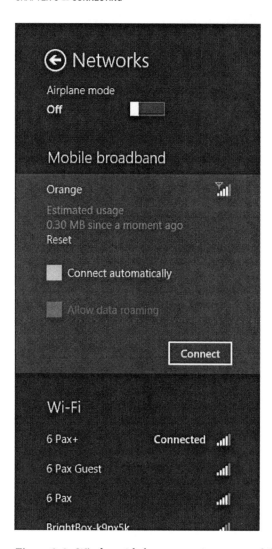

Figure 3-6. *Windows 8 helps you monitor your mobile broadband usage*

From this page, you can also turn Airplane Mode on and off. You can also specify whether your mobile broadband connection can be used for data roaming abroad, because it can be very expensive.

The Live Tiles on the Windows 8 Start screen consumes data every time they automatically update. You can limit the amount of data they consume, however.

1. From the Start screen, open the charms and click **Settings**.

2. At the top right of the screen, click **Tiles**.

The Tiles window (see Figure 3-7) allows you to specify the maximum amount of data Live Tiles are allowed to use each month. Once this limit is reached, the Live Tiles will no longer update over your mobile broadband connection.

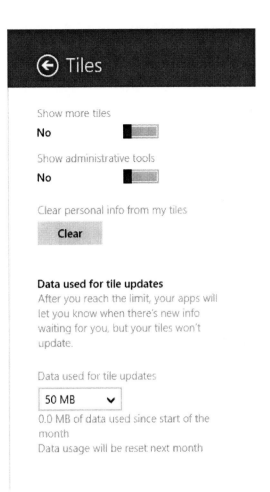

Figure 3-7. *Control the amount of mobile data Live Tiles uses*

■ **Note** Sometimes a Wi-Fi network that you connect to misbehaves or suddenly won't connect any more. This often occurs because the settings for that network have become corrupt. To fix this, instead of clicking on a network's name to connect to it, right-click on its name and select **Forget this network** from the options that appear. This deletes the settings for that network, and the next time you connect, it will be like the first time (so you will probably need the password). This normally rectifies connection problems.

Using Internet Explorer 10

Windows 8 comes with two different versions of the Internet Explorer web browser. One of these is an app, run from the Start screen, and the other is the more traditional desktop program. Although these two browsers might appear completely separate, they do share favorites and stored information, such as website usernames and passwords.

As you might imagine, though, they operate in different ways. The IE10 app is a slimmed-down version containing just the controls most people need for everyday web browsing. The desktop version, on the other hand, is a full-featured browser with support for plug-ins, toolbars, and the more advanced features that many computer users like to have. In this section I will talk you through the differences and show you how to get the best out of each browser.

Using the Internet Explorer 10 App

Life is usually complicated enough, but Windows 8 includes two completely different versions of the Internet Explorer web browser. There are two fundamental differences between them.

IE10 in Windows 8 does not support *any* plug-ins, so web content written in languages such as Flash and Java simply do not display or work.

IE10 also cannot share your Internet Favorites with its desktop counterpart. Any favorites you have in Internet Explorer in Windows Vista or Windows 7 will appear only in the desktop version of the browser in Windows 8.

That said, it isn't all bad news. For starters, the lack of plug-ins and a focus on the new HTML5 web standard makes the browser much more secure. This isn't just a decision Microsoft has made. It was Apple that first blocked browser plug-ins on the iPad and iPhone. The reasoning behind the move, which was deeply unpopular at the time, was that it made the browser more secure and prevented third-party plug-ins from slowing down the browser (something that Flash did rather well on Apple devices). Plus, with HTML5 web sites beginning to appear, there was a shrinking need for plug-ins.

If you want to use plug-ins and toolbars in Internet Explorer in Windows 8, the desktop version of the browser and some third-party web browsers continue to support them.

As with all apps, Internet Explorer runs fullscreen. A swipe upward from the bottom of the screen, or down from the top brings up the App bar (see Figure 3-8).

Figure 3-8. *Internet Explorer 10 in Windows 8*

The controls in this version of Internet Explorer are limited. It is not as full-featured as its desktop counterpart is. On the bottom of the screen, the App bar shows the following features:

- The **Back button** takes you back to the previous web page.

- The **Address bar** allows you to tap and enter a web address or a search term.

- The **Refresh button** reloads the current page.

- The **Pin to Start button** pins a quick link to the current web site to the Start screen.

- The **Settings button**. The only available settings for IE10 are

  - **Find on Page**, where you can search for text on the currently displayed web page.

  - **View on Desktop** opens the current page in the desktop version of IE10.

  - The **Forward button** takes you forward a page if you have already moved back.

On the top App bar, you find the following:

- **Thumbnail images of the open browser tabs**; you can click one to display it fullscreen.

- A **Plus (+) button** to open a fresh tab.

- A button with three dots with two more options:

  - An **Open in Private tab** opens a tab in private browsing mode. In this mode, no history is stored of the web pages you visit, and no cookies or downloadable files from the web site are stored on the computer (this is useful when shopping for gifts).

  - **Clean Up Tabs** closes all but the currently displayed tab.

All the usual touch and swipe gestures in Windows 8 work in Internet Explorer, including on the desktop, including pinch gestures to zoom in and out of a page.

Using Favorites in Internet Explorer

You can display your favorite links in IE10 by clicking in the Address bar. The screen changes to show your favorites, including all your frequently used ones and those that are pinned to the Start screen.

You can select a favorite to load by tapping or clicking it. If you want to open a favorite in a new tab or delete it from a tab, you can right-click it with your mouse (you can only select one at a time this way) or tap and hold to bring up the context menu with touch.

▓ **Note**   This right-click touch gesture is different from the ones used elsewhere in Windows 8, where you tap and pull downward. A tap-and-pull down motion in IE10 doesn't do anything.

In the Favorites view, you can return to the current web page at any time by clicking or tapping the Left arrow button in the top left of the screen.

Unless you choose to turn off the Windows 8 synching feature in the Sync Your Settings page of PC Settings, all of your Internet Explorer favorites are automatically synched between computers that you log onto using a Microsoft Account. This is a tremendous time-saver because you can go to any Windows 8 computer, log in with your Microsoft Account, and all of your favorites in both versions of Internet Explorer—standard Windows 8 and desktop—are there.

This is not without its concerns, however, especially if you temporarily use another person's computer and do not use it again. I discuss this security subject in more detail later in the book.

Using Internet Explorer 10 on the Desktop

Unlike its slimmed-down cousin, Internet Explorer on the desktop is the fully featured version with all the trimmings. It is the same cosmetically as Internet Explorer 9, and if you are familiar with that browser in Windows 7, then you will feel at home straightaway.

It is a very powerful browser (see Figure 3-9) and highly configurable too, so I want to spend some time in this chapter showing you how to get the very best from it.

Figure 3-9. *Internet Explorer on the Windows 8 desktop*

One of the most useful features of the browser is in its toolbars and extras, which can be switched on by right-clicking anywhere in the blank space at the top of the window (see Figure 3-10).

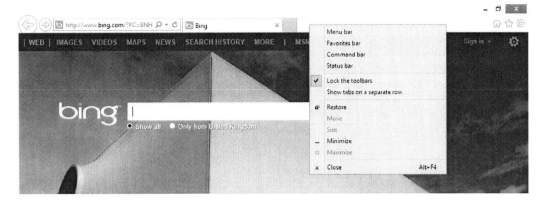

Figure 3-10. *Right-click the top of the IE10 desktop browser to display additional options*

IE10 toolbars and extras include the following features:

- The **Menu bar** is the traditional drop-down menu with the typical Internet Explorer options displayed. There is really no need for this now because the options are all easy to get at, and as almost nothing else in Windows 8 has

- drop-down menus. This is only a legacy feature.

- The **Favorites bar** is a quick way to launch commonly-used links to web sites. It is a far quicker way to launch web sites than the Favorites menu.

- The **Command bar** contains tools now found in the Settings menu, including Print, Home, RSS, and Safety.

- The **Status bar** sits at the bottom of the browser and gives feedback on loading and other aspects of the page.

- The **Address bar** offers extra display options. If you want a full-width Address bar or if you want to place a toolbar next to the Address bar, you can choose to **Show tabs on a separate row**, which moves the browser tabs below the Address bar.

■ **Tip**   Do not unpin Internet Explorer from the Windows taskbar because it does not appear in any searches or in the All Apps view!

- To the left of the Address bar are **Back** and **Forward buttons**. Inside the Address bar are buttons for Search, Compatibility (for a web site that doesn't display properly in the browser, but worked in earlier versions of Internet Explorer) and Refresh (reloads the current page). To the far right of the tabs are buttons for Home, Favorites, and Settings.

■ **Tip**   You can pin a web site to the Windows taskbar by dragging its button (found to the left of the Address bar) onto the taskbar.

Managing Browser Tabs in IE10 on the Desktop

Web browser tabs in Internet Explorer 10 work in the same way they have in previous versions of the browser and in other web browsers. Each tab, when you mouse over it, displays a Close button (represented by an ×) on its right. You can also drag and drop browser tabs to rearrange them in any order you wish.

■ **Tip** You can drag a tab out of Internet Explorer to open it in its own Window.

Internet Explorer 10 Safety Features

Some features in the Settings menu may be familiar, but there are some that deserve special attention. The Safety options are chief among these because Internet safety is very important to us all (see Figure 3-11).

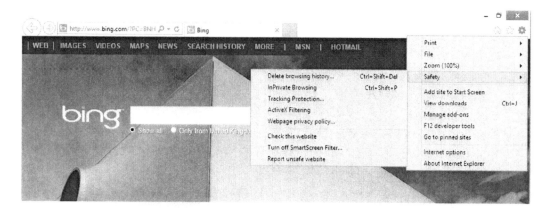

Figure 3-11. *The Safety options in Internet Explorer*

IE10 includes the following Safety features:

- **Delete Browsing History** deletes all record of the web sites that you have visited in Internet Explorer. You may not want anyone else seeing the web sites you have visited because these appear automatically in the Address bar when a user clicks in it or searches in it.

- **InPrivate Browsing** is a special mode within Internet Explorer that doesn't keep any record of the web sites you visit and that doesn't allow those web sites to leave cookies or other tracking files on your computer. This is useful for gift shopping.

- **Tracking Protection** is a feature that was introduced in IE9. Sometimes you visit web sites where cookies are placed on your computer by third-party web sites, often through advertisements. Turning this feature on can block cookies from being stored on your computer.

- **ActiveX Filtering** is a feature that blocks small programs, sometimes used to play video, from running in your web browser. ActiveX controls can be programmed to run malicious code on your computer when activated.

- **Webpage Privacy Policy** displays the privacy policy, if available, of the web site that is currently displayed.

Using the SmartScreen Filter to Block Malicious Web Sites

The Windows 8 SmartScreen Filter runs in IE10 to help prevent malicious code from running on web sites that can infect your computer. Unless you turn it off in the Safety options, it automatically checks every web page you visit against a list of known malicious sites compiled in collaboration with other browser makers and security companies.

In the Safety menu, you can manually check a web site against the SmartScreen database. If you suspect a web site to be malicious, then you can use this menu to manually report the web site as potentially unsafe to Microsoft.

Managing Add-ons and Toolbars in IE10

Toolbars and add-ons are incredibly useful in Internet Explorer, including the Flash Player and Java. Occasionally, however, they can get in the way, slow down your browser, or be malicious and hijack your search submissions.

You can manage and remove toolbars from Internet Explorer 10 in the Settings menu by selecting Manage Add-ons. In the window that appears (see Figure 3-12), you can highlight an add-on or a toolbar; an Enable or Disable button appears.

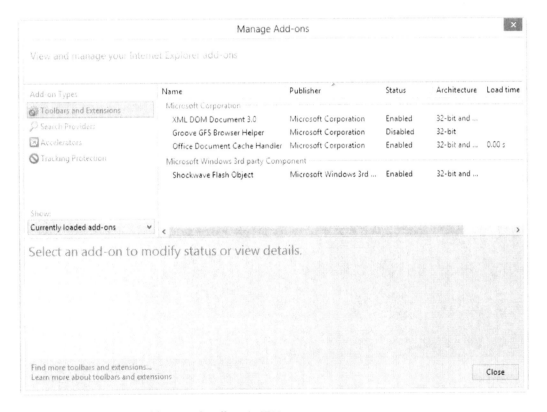

Figure 3-12. *Managing add-ons and toolbars in IE10*

■ **Note**   Disabling an IE add-on or toolbar is not the same as uninstalling it from your computer. You can uninstall add-ons and toolbars in Programs and Features in the Control Panel.

Internet Explorer 10 Options and Configuration

The extensive Internet options in IE10 (see Figure 3-13) also deserve a mention. I want to talk you through some of these. You access Internet Options from the Settings button to the far right of the browser tabs.

Figure 3-13. *The General tab in Internet Options*

The first tab to appear in Internet Options is the General tab. Under this tab, you can set a single or multiple home pages for your web browser. You can also set IE to automatically reload all the pages from your last browsing session when you start it.

The Tabs options are interesting. When you open a tab from another browser tab, IE color-codes them automatically. It also opens all new tabs next to the existing one. These are features that many power users find irritating. They can be switched off.

You can also turn off tabbed browsing completely if you wish, forcing each new web site to open in its own window.

Managing Safety and Privacy in Internet Explorer 10

Two things that concern people greatly these days, especially parents whose children use the Internet, are safety and privacy. Internet Explorer 10 comes with built-in options to help with this. Click the Settings button near the top right of the window and select Internet Options from the menu.

The Safety options, also selected from the Settings button, block potentially unsafe web sites or allow web sites that IE10 blocks by default. These settings can be further customized, but unless you have real reasons for changing this control, you will probably find that it proves more of a hindrance than a help because all manner of useful and perfectly legitimate web sites will be blocked if you turn the settings up.

The Security tab (see Figure 3-14) allows you to set general rules for your Internet security, such as whether to allow or block certain types of cookies, which are small tracking files placed by web sites on your computer to permit actions such as remembering login passwords.

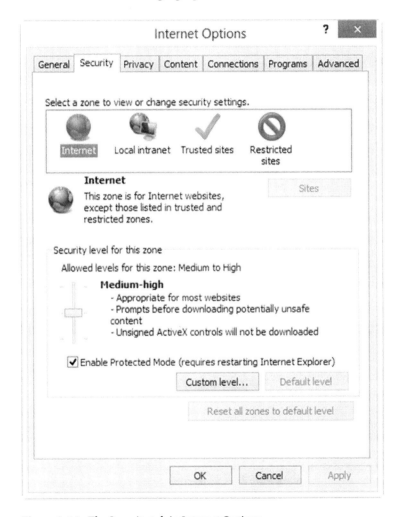

Figure 3-14. *The Security tab in Internet Options*

Of more interest are the Privacy options (see Figure 3-15), which allow you to block tracking and other cookies from web sites, depending on your own criteria. The feature also allows you to import whitelists and blacklists from third parties (perhaps parental or privacy groups).

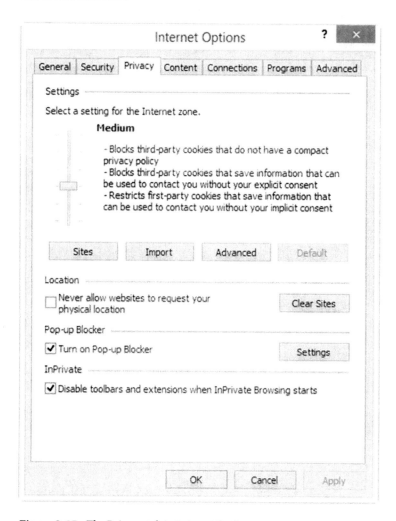

Figure 3-15. *The Privacy tab in Internet Options*

In the Location Services section of this tab, you can block web sites from being sent to your physical location. This is useful because computers now come fitted with GPS systems.

It is also on this tab that you can turn Internet Explorer's built-in pop-up blocker on and off. It is turned on by default.

The Content tab (see Figure 3-16) is commonly of interest to parents. Windows 8's Family Safety can be accessed from here. The Content Advisor is a feature that, with lists specified by the user, automatically blocks specific web sites or groups of web sites. You might wish to block Facebook, for example, if you have young children who should not be using it or you can block web sites based on content such as violence or nudity.

Figure 3-16. *The Content tab in Internet Options*

■ **Note** The IE10 Content Filter is no substitute for a full family safety suite or an office web-filtering appliance specifically installed to control the types of web sites that users can visit, and where the blacklists and whitelists of web sites are maintained by the company that provided the appliance. It may miss web sites that would ordinarily fall into banned categories.

Staying Safe Online

Staying safe online is a challenge these days. Criminals are everywhere, ready to infect our computers with malware or steal our credit card information or identities. So when we increasingly spend our time on online social networks and Internet shopping sites, how can we know that we are safe and secure?

I want to discuss online threats; how you can spot them; and how you can protect yourself, your friends, and your family against them.

Internet Threats Explained

There are several major types of Internet threats.

- **Malware** is malicious software that infects a computer to steal information, steal or encrypt files, or simply corrupt a machine and delete things. It can come from various different sources, including *macros* (small programs than run inside files, usually word processor or spreadsheet files); *keyloggers* that record everything you type, including credit card information and bank logins; and browser plug-ins that pretend to be something that you need, such as a codec required to view a video online.

- **Phishing** e-mails try to trick you into revealing sensitive information, such as passwords, by pretending to be from a reputable bank or business institution.

- **Compromised web sites** may look perfectly legitimate, but they ask for sensitive information that can be used to hijack your account or that are programmed to download and run infected files to your computer.

■ **Tip**   No legitimate web site will *ever* e-mail you asking you to confirm your security details. If you notice the web site that you regularly use has changed and is asking for additional login information, e-mail abuse@companyname.com (where "companyname.com" is the web address of the company) to report it.

Identifying Safe and Unsafe Web Sites in IE10

Internet Explorer is great at telling you whether a web site is safe or not. It displays a padlock in the Address bar that indicates the site is a known, secure web site. Also, the Address bar is green when the URL is a safe web site, and it is red when it is known to be used by criminals (see Figure 3-17).

Figure 3-17. IE10 desktop version highlights a safe web site

Sadly, these features are best highlighted in the desktop version of IE10 because the Address bar is hidden from normal view in Windows 8. If you are doing financial transactions or shopping on a laptop or desktop PC, I strongly recommend you use the desktop version of IE because it gives you more and better feedback about web sites.

The web site safety reporting in Internet Explorer, or any web browser for that matter, is not infallible and is only as good as its last update.

Identifying Unsafe Downloads in IE10

Again, with malicious downloads, Internet Explorer is only as good as the most recent update from Microsoft; but its SmartScreen Filter is generally quite good at warning you that a download should be avoided.

SmartScreen is a system that shares information between Microsoft, other browser makers, and security companies to identify malware. Windows warns you with a fullscreen alert when the SmartScreen Filter detects software that it considers malicious, and gives you the choice of whether or not you wish to download and run it.

Summary

Windows 8 offers new ways to connect to the Internet. These new ways also bring challenges. The worry that comes from being accidentally connected to your 3G or 4G network and using expensive data, for example.

There are also challenges with staying safe on the Internet. Internet Explorer does an excellent job of keeping you safe, but the weak link will always be the user. Malware writers and criminals will prey on you, trying to trick you into entering sensitive information on the pretense that it's perfectly safe to do so.

On my web site (`www.TheLongClimb.com`), I write regularly about the security and privacy concerns facing Internet users. You can always find more information there.

CHAPTER 4

■ ■ ■

Sharing with Family and Friends

Windows 7 introduced the concept of HomeGroup, enabling us to share our files, music, photos, and video easily within small networks. Windows 8 is taking sharing to the next logical level with built-in sharing for apps of all description.

With Windows 8, apps that send or receive information, such as pictures, don't need to be programmed to import and export files to and from other programs. Windows 8 now handles it all. This opens new opportunities for sharing, but some of the traditional methods of sharing files, folders, and network hardware still exist. In this chapter, I'll show you how to share a wide variety of hardware, file types, and data libraries in Windows 8.

Working with User Accounts

One of Windows' traditional strengths has been its support of multiple users. On the face of things, this may seem relatively minor, but when you work from home, do school work, or just want some privacy, the usefulness of this feature steps up to another level.

Windows 8 practically begs users to log on with a Microsoft Account—the same ID you use to log on to a Live, Hotmail, or MSN e-mail account. When you do this, much of the system is automatically set up for you, including the Windows Store and the e-mail and calendar apps. This presents issues for multiple user systems, however, because you might not want other people in your household or workplace reading your e-mail.

There is also the matter of file security. We trust the people we live with, but accidents happen. If somebody doesn't know the importance of a particular file or Internet favorite, it can be deleted accidentally.

The ability to set up Windows 8 so that each user has his or her own account is a benefit. It is also a task that's simpler than ever to perform.

Setting Up Users

In Windows 8, Microsoft has removed the need to navigate through the full Control Panel to add users. This task was often seen as complicated and off-putting. Now you simply add users through the PC Settings panel, with the whole process clearly detailed.

To create a local user account, follow these instructions:

1. Open the charms and select Settings.

2. At the bottom right of the screen, click More PC Settings.

3. In PC Settings, click Users (see Figure 4-1).

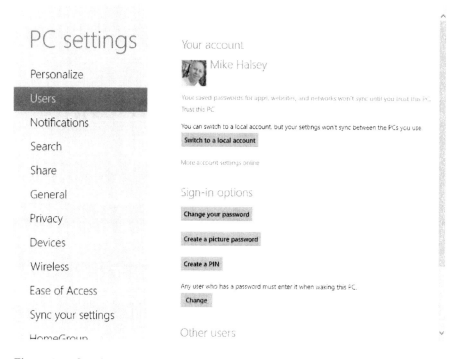

Figure 4-1. Creating a new user account in PC Settings

4.   In the Other Users section, click **Add a user**, which opens the screen shown in Figure 4-2.

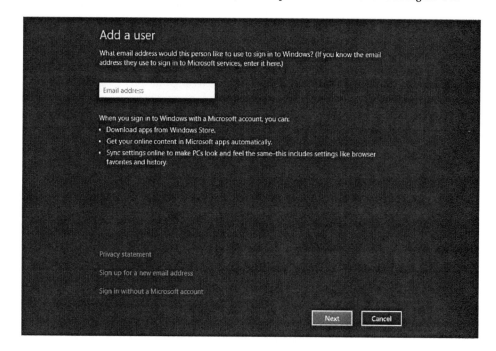

Figure 4-2. Adding a new user

5. To create a local account, click **Don't want this user to sign in with a Microsoft account?** to open the screen shown in Figure 4-3.

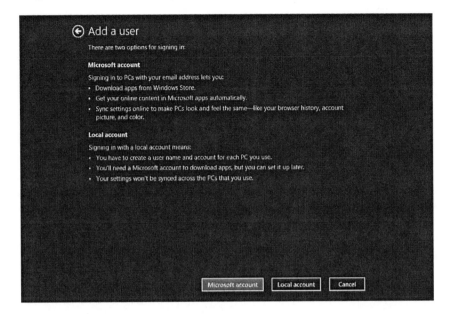

Figure 4-3. Windows 8 tells you the difference between a Microsoft account and a Local account

6. Click the Local Account button. You will be asked for a username and (optionally) a password for the new user (see Figure 4-4).

Figure 4-4. It is not necessary for local accounts to have a password, which is especially helpful for young children

7. Enter the name of the user and, optionally, a password and password hint. When you are finished, you are asked if you want to turn on Family Safety to get reports of what a child does online (see Figure 4-5).

Figure 4-5. *The account is created*

■ **Note** The "Using Family Safety" section, which appears later in this chapter, covers this topic.

---

8. The local account is created. Click Finish to complete the process.

Managing User Accounts

There are two types of users in Windows 8: *administrators*, who have authority to make any changes to the operating system and computer's files that they want to, and *standard users*, who can only make changes that affect their own user account.

The first user account created when you start using Windows 8 will always be an administrator, but any accounts you create for the computer after that will be standard users unless you specify otherwise. As we just saw in the preceding section, you create a new user account in the Users panel of PC Settings.

To manage user accounts, you need to open the full Windows 8 Control Panel, which you can do by searching for **control** at the Start screen. Managing user accounts is done from the User Accounts section of the Control Panel. When you load this panel, you are first shown your own user account (see Figure 4-6). Here you can perform various actions, as follows.

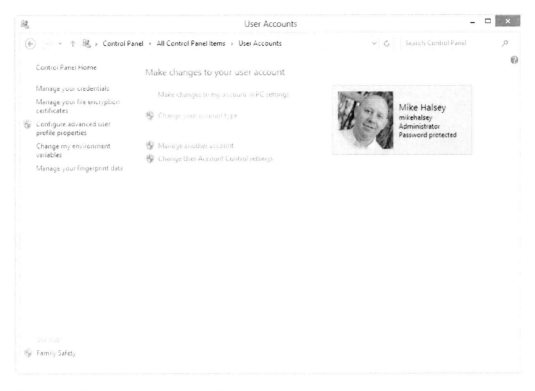

Figure 4-6. *Managing user accounts in Windows 8*

- **Change your account type** from standard user to administrator (or vice versa). This might be useful to upgrade a user to an administrator.

- **Manage your credentials** allows you to view, edit, and delete the stored password for Windows, Windows software, and web sites that are associated with your account. This can be useful if something has become corrupt and Windows or Internet Explorer gets confused when you change your password.

- **Manage your file encryption certificates** allows you to back up and restore any EFS encryption keys associated with this account. For more on this, see Chapter 12.

- **Change advanced user profile properties** is used if your user account has been created as part of a Windows Server domain.

- **Change my environment variables** allows you to change certain aspects of your profile, such as where your user and temporary files are stored by default.

- **Manage your fingerprint data** appears if your computer has a biometric fingerprint reader.

Tip   If you have friends or family members using your computer occasionally but you don't want to configure specific user accounts for them or have them use your account, you can turn on the Guest Account by clicking Manage Another Account in the User Accounts panel. The Guest Account gives you a quick and secure way to allow other people to use your computer.

If you click Manage Another Account, you are shown a list of the other user accounts on your computer. Clicking an account allows you to change the settings for that user (see Figure 4-7).

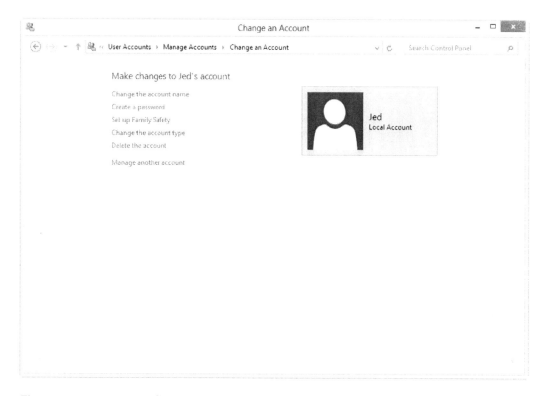

Figure 4-7. *Managing another user account*

The options found here include the following:

- **Change the account name**.

- **Create a password** for the account if it doesn't have one. If it does, you will see options to change or remove the password.

- **Set up Family Safety** allows you to place the Family Safety feature on the account.

- **Change the account type** from standard user to administrator (or vice versa). All secondary users are standard users by default.

- **Delete the account** alerts that the user has files on the computer and gives the opportunity to save these files to a desktop folder before the account is deleted.

■ **Tip** If you log on to someone else's computer with your Microsoft account but you aren't going to use that computer very often, be aware that Windows 8 might have downloaded your Internet Favorites or other personal files to the computer. Obviously you won't want these to remain on someone else's computer, so you can remove them by performing a few steps. When logged on as another user, open User Account in the Control Panel; otherwise, open Manage Another Account. Click the name of the account you want to delete. Next, click Delete the Account, and when prompted, click Delete Files. This will remove the files, but you should make certain by checking the C:\Users folder. If a folder still exists for that user account, delete it manually.

Using Family Safety

When you create a new user account in Windows 8, you are asked if the user you are adding is a child (see Figure 4-8). Checking this option activates Family Safety Activity Reports, which is accessed through the Family Safety page. You can specify that an account is for a child by checking the **Is this a child's account?** box after you input the name and other details about the new user.

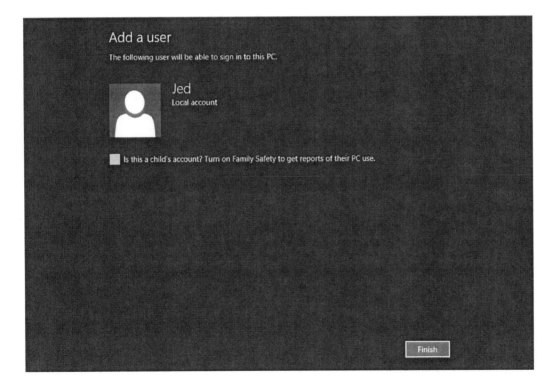

Figure 4-8. You can specify if a new user is a child

Family Safety is very powerful and flexible in Windows 8 and includes web filtering for the first time. The Activity Report is a very helpful addition to these controls because they show you the types of activities your child is participating in online and which web sites they visit.

You access the Activity Report from the main Family Safety page. To open it, search for **parent** on the Start screen. On the right side of the window, you can View Activity Reports of your child's time on the computer (see Figure 4-9). Your child cannot see these reports; they are only visible to administrators on the computer.

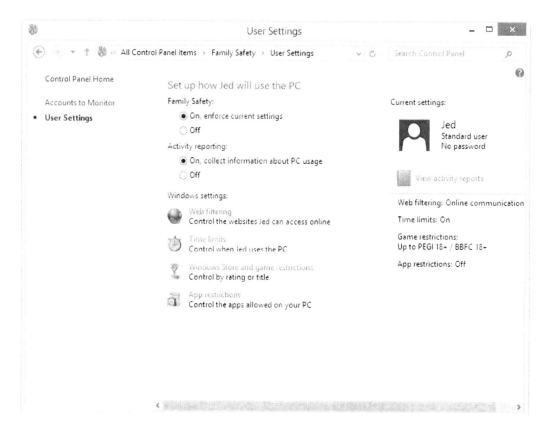

Figure 4-9. *The Family Safety page*

While the content filtering in Internet Explorer is useful, it is much easier to use Windows 8's Family Safety (see Figure 4-10). You find these by searching for the word **family** on the Start screen: simply type the word and Family Safety appears in the Settings search results. There is more about searching in Chapter 5.

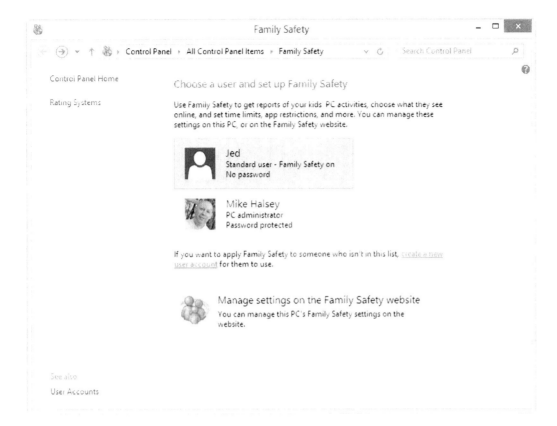

Figure 4-10. *Windows 8 asks you which user you wish to have Family Safety controls*

At the main Family Safety screen, select the user you want to set controls for. You can only set Family Safety for Standard Users. This is because administrators have permission to perform whatever actions they want, including deactivating Family Safety Controls.

■ **Note** You will need to have a password on your main user account to use Family Safety in Windows 8.

After you have selected which user you wish to set Family Safety for, you are taken to the main Family Safety page (see Figure 4-11).

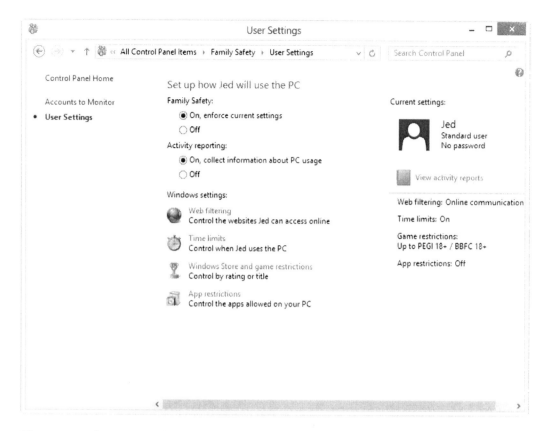

Figure 4-11. *The main Family Safety options*

On the Family Safety page, you have several options:

- Turn the controls on or off for a particular user.
- Set **Web Filter** parameters to decide which web sites are suitable for your children.
- Set **Time Limits** on when children are allowed to use the computer.
- Choose what types of **Games** are suitable for your children.
- Choose which **Programs** your children are allowed to use.

I want to spend a little time discussing each of these settings in detail. Web filtering in Family Safety (see Figure 4-12) is much simpler than it is in the IE10 Content Advisor page. In Family Safety, you can choose from five web category types:

- Allow list only (where you can manually specify which web sites to allow)
- Child-friendly
- General interest
- Online communication
- Warn an adult

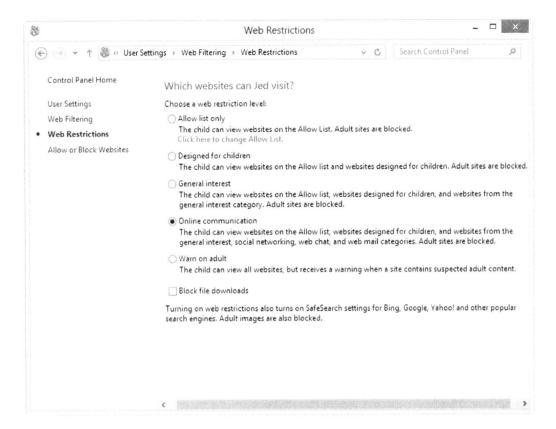

Figure 4-12. *Choose the web sites that are suitable for your child*

Each category has a clear description of what it is, so you can feel certain that your children are only seeing appropriate web sites. You can also block Internet downloads, which helps protect your computer from malware.

Additionally, if you click Edit the Allow and Block List, you can choose specific web sites to permit or completely block. You might want to allow your child to view web sites in the Online Communication category, but you want to block Facebook and Twitter until she is slightly older.

The Time Restrictions page is extremely useful (see Figure 4-13). Here you can set the times your child is allowed to use the computer. You can say, for example, that they're not allowed to use the computer after 8 p.m. Monday through Friday, but on weekends they can stay on the computer until 9 p.m.

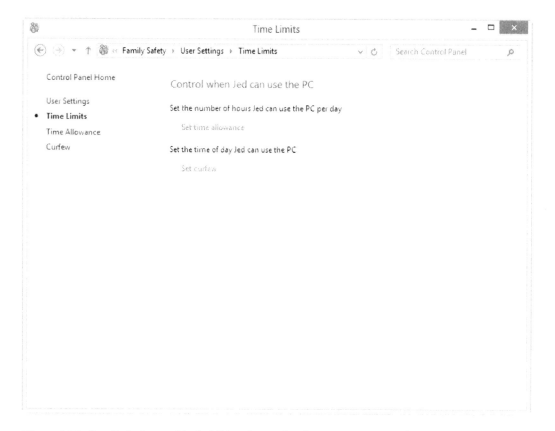

Figure 4-13. *Family Safety can block children from using the computer at specified times*

You set time restrictions in the curfew options by coloring in time blocks on a chart; it's simple and intuitive.

Not all games come with ratings and there is no guarantee that inappropriate games won't slip through. Parents may find, however, that the age ratings system on games is a great indicator for which games are suitable for their children (see Figure 4-14).

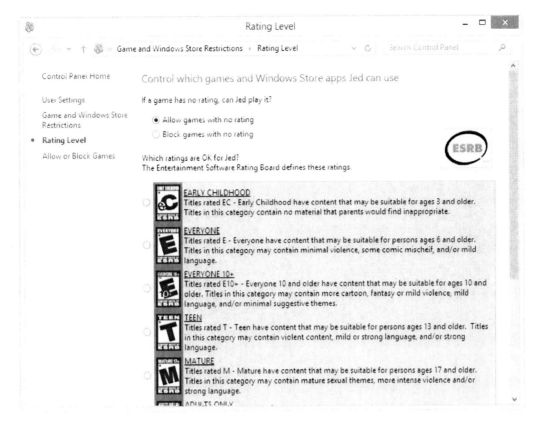

Figure 4-14. Parents can choose the games suitable for their children

Select a maximum game rating and all ratings below that are automatically included in your selection. This means that you can block games rated as more mature from running on your computer.

The last section of options, Application Restrictions, is complex; most parents will want to leave it alone (see Figure 4-15). On this page, you can choose the software that your child is allowed to use. The list of software in a computer can be extremely long, however, with new packages and apps being added all the time.

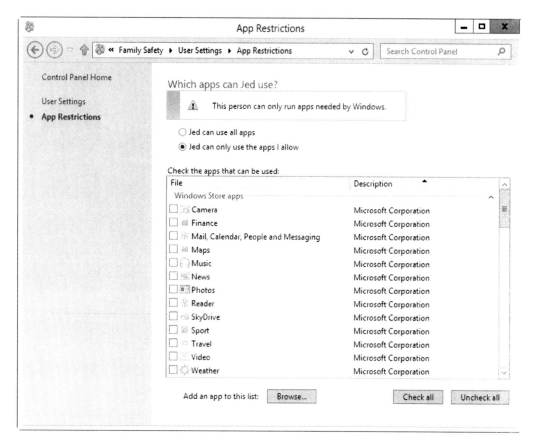

Figure 4-15. *Parents can select the programs and software their children are allowed to use*

If you find a third-party solution that allows you to block specific programs, you might find it more useful.

The Application Restrictions feature is only really useful when you use a computer for both home and work, and want to stop children from accessing your work programs.

Sharing Files and Folders with HomeGroup

HomeGroup was introduced in Windows 7 as a means of sharing documents, pictures, music, video, and printers across small, protected home networks. Think of a HomeGroup as a quick way to share files between your home computers. This is because Windows knows which environment you're sharing things in, and as a result, automatically sets all the correct permissions and parameters on the files, folders, and networking settings for you, minimizing your configuration.

HomeGroup still exists in Windows 8. It's easy and straightforward to set up and configure. HomeGroup is in PC Settings (see Figure 4-16), which is available by opening the charms on the right side of the screen and selecting Settings.

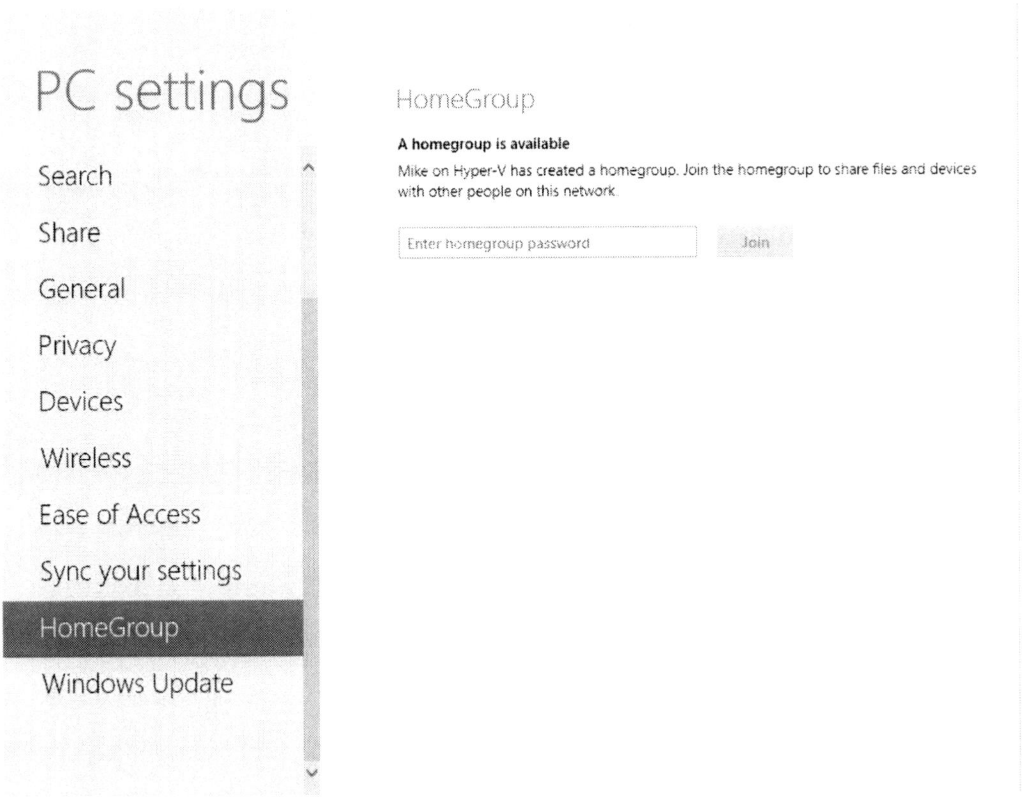

PC settings

Search

Share

General

Privacy

Devices

Wireless

Ease of Access

Sync your settings

HomeGroup

Windows Update

HomeGroup

A homegroup is available

Mike on Hyper-V has created a homegroup. Join the homegroup to share files and devices with other people on this network.

Enter homegroup password   Join

Figure 4-16. *The HomeGroup page in PC Settings*

If a HomeGroup has already been set up on another computer, you are asked to enter the password. You may have a Windows 7 computer on which you have previously set up and configured a HomeGroup, for example.

If a HomeGroup does not exist, or if Windows 8 cannot detect one on the network, then you are asked if you wish to set up one.

■ **Note** HomeGroup only works over Wi-Fi for networks that you have identified as Home. It is automatically disabled and blocked on Work and Public networks to help maintain your file and computer security.

Once you are connected to a HomeGroup, the HomeGroup page in PC Settings gives you controls for sharing files and devices, including documents, pictures, music, videos, printers, and devices like USB attached storage and external hard disks (see Figure 4-17).

Figure 4-17. *The HomeGroup settings in Windows 8*

Next, however, is a very interesting option. Do you want to allow your TVs and other devices, such as game consoles, to share the media on your home network? HomeGroup allows you to use your computers as UPnP (Universal Plug and Play) devices.

UPnP devices can share media, commonly pictures, music, and video over a network. They are used by media streamers to play music from your PC on your Hi-Fi or video from your laptop on your television. You can use this, for example, to share your media with your Xbox 360 or Playstation 3 to view on a big screen, or to listen to an Internet radio station in the garden.

There are security concerns to take into account, however. With a HomeGroup, you have a secure password, which is also shown in the HomeGroup page in PC Settings; but when you share media via this setting, all that is required is access to your network. You need not worry about having a very secure password on your Wi-Fi router because media connectors and modern routers have a pairing button on them, usually called WPS, which connect secure devices without the need to enter complex passwords using awkward interfaces.

If you do not have a password on your Internet router, then you should create one straightaway. Unsecured routers provide outsiders with access to both your home Internet connection and the shared files on your computers and devices.

Media shared on a HomeGroup cannot be deleted from your computer, and it does not include your documents. It is always wise to know who has access to what before you share it, however.

■ **Tip** You can still manage a HomeGroup from the full Control Panel, but the management options in PC Settings are so much better that I wouldn't bother.

Sharing Files and Folders on a Network

There are several ways to share files and folders across a network in Windows 8. First, I want to discuss why you might want to share files and folders, and in what environments you do it.

In the home environment, by far the simplest way to share files and folders is in a HomeGroup, as I have detailed already. HomeGroup gives you easy and simple ways to share devices such as printers, which means you save money from not having to buy expensive new Wi-Fi printers.

You may have set up a HomeGroup and decided to share your pictures, music, and video, but not your documents. You may decide to keep your documents private, but want to share a folder or two's worth of documents with another person in the family.

HomeGroup can have connection difficulties, however, and you may only want to share a particular folder with another person or persons. Let's say, for example, you are collaborating with another individual in a home office or at work, and you want to be able to share the resources and workflow documents.

In a Windows Server environment, you have all this managed by SharePoint or by a similar or alternative service like Office 365; but many small businesses can't afford their own server system and don't have an Office 365 cloud-services subscription. This is where the built-in sharing in Windows 8 is very useful.

Again, in an office environment, you may want to set up a computer as a file store. I've done this myself, placing project documents and resources—in my case, teaching resources, lesson plans, schemes of work, and contractual paperwork—on a single machine (with a backup kept on another). I provided network access to the main PC with a desktop shortcut to the shared files to make it easy for everyone to access them.

Sharing with Individuals

Let's say several people use the same computer in your home, and you want to be able to share files such as household documents, bills, legal documents, and perhaps homework assignments. File Explorer and Microsoft have made this type of sharing simpler than ever.

In File Explorer, navigate to and highlight the folder you wish to share. Then, in the Ribbon, click the Share tab; you see a section called Share With. Here, you highlight to share file(s) and/or folder(s) and click the name of the person(s) with whom you wish to share. Windows 8 automatically and silently sets the sharing permissions.

If you want to choose a specific user, perhaps because he doesn't appear on the list, or if you want to choose the privileges for users, select Specific People to display a full list of the users on your computer (see Figure 4-18).

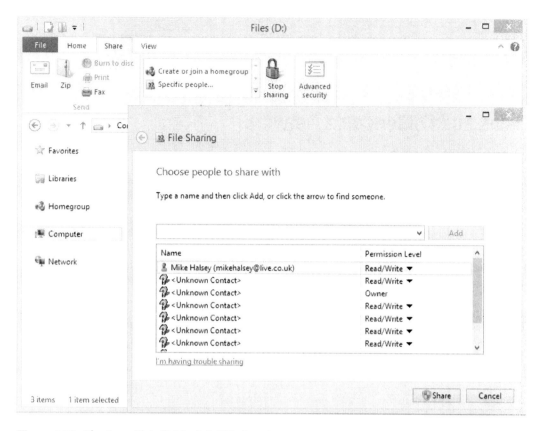

Figure 4-18. *Sharing with individuals in Windows 8*

This dialog comes in handy when you want to choose specific privileges for a user, such a Read Only, so that files can be accessed but not modified—and, crucially, not deleted!

■ **Caution**   Be careful giving others access to files and folders that you do not want changed or deleted.

For most sharing scenarios within a home with one PC, this is all you need; but many homes now have multiple computers to share across. In a business environment, it is rare for several people to use the same PC, except in instances of small businesses where people only need occasional access to a computer.

Sharing with Groups of People

If you have a multicomputer setup and don't want the risk that comes with sharing absolutely everything in your Documents folder, you will want finer control over sharing. Windows 8 offers finer control in an easy-to-manage way.

This is managed by right-clicking a folder and selecting its properties. A Sharing tab contains all the controls (see Figure 4-19). There are only three, the first of which takes you to the settings dialog that I talked about in the last section.

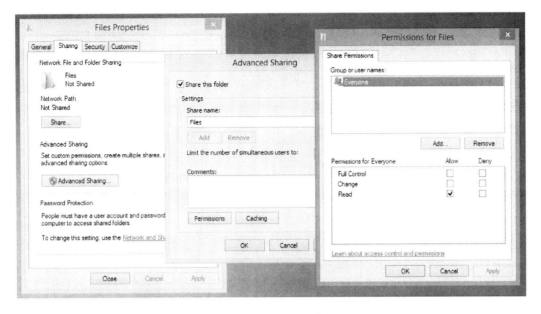

Figure 4-19. *Setting advanced file and folder sharing in Windows 8*

Click the Advanced Sharing button to get access to the settings for sharing a folder across a network. There is a simple check box to turn sharing on and off, making it simple to rescind sharing at a later stage, perhaps when a project has completed and you want to archive the folder. You can also give the shared folder a custom name. By default, sharing gives others permission to read files within the folder, but nothing else. This means that while others can access the files in a folder and read them, if they modify a file, they aren't able to save it back to that folder. They also aren't able to create or copy new files into the folder.

To change these settings, click the Permissions button. You are offered, for separate user lists, a variety of permissions options.

- **Full Control** grants the ability to create new files, and copy files to and delete files from a folder. This is something you should be aware of when setting full control on any shared folder.

- **Change** allows people to make changes to files that already exist in the document; for example, opening, working on, and saving the updated copy of the file in the folder.

- **Read Only** grants permission to only open and read the contents of a folder.

■ **Note**   If you want to share folders from a computer running Windows 7 or Windows Vista with a Windows 8 computer, the sharing setup works the same way as described here.

Sharing with Non-Windows Computers

Setting the advanced sharing properties for folders is also useful if you want to share with non-Windows computers, such as Apple computers or PCs running GNU/Linux. These network shares are accessible, although additional configuration may be required on the other computer to deal with minor incompatibilities that can arise from time to time.

> ■ **Caution**   Be cautious about sharing files with a computer running Windows XP unless you are certain that the security on that computer is properly maintained. Any files hosted on an XP machine are generally far more vulnerable to malware than those in Windows Vista, Windows 7, and Windows 8.

Sharing Files with Windows 8 Tablets, Ultrabooks, and Laptops

There are several issues associated with sharing files with tablets, laptops, and ultrabooks running Windows 8. First, there is the amount of available storage on these devices. Even Windows 8 tablets with Intel/AMD processors commonly come with solid-state storage, as do ultrabooks. These severely limit the amount of storage space available; and when we commonly have hundreds of gigabytes worth of documents, pictures, music, and video, you couldn't possibly hope to hold it all on a mobile device.

This brings me to security. You can never consider any mobile computer as being completely secure. While some laptops (and perhaps even a few tablets and ultrabooks) come with Trusted Platform Module (TPM) security chips onboard to support full-disk encryption, the vast majority do not; this includes laptops. These chips store encryption and keys for your hard disks in their firmware, and as such are very secure. I talk more about TPM chips and encrypting your files and computer in Chapter 12.

If you are carrying volumes of data around, it probably includes personal and sensitive information, and the simple fact remains that tablets, ultrabooks, and laptops are highly desirable items for thieves.

The next consideration is what you will actually be able to *do* with those files on these portable devices. Do you want Word, Excel, and PowerPoint documents, which are far more difficult to edit with touch than they are with a keyboard and mouse? Do you want your entire photo or music library when you'll likely only ever access a small portion of it when you're on the move?

I believe it is folly to assume that any portable device is completely secure unless it is encrypted properly with a TPM chip and a technology like BitLocker. There are just too many risks associated with carrying round your entire libraries of documents, photos, and more to justify carrying it around when out and about.

The final consideration is whether the computer is properly password protected. You may have a local account on your tablet (or other device) that doesn't require a password. This means that anyone picking up your device will have complete access to all your files.

Alternatively, you may have a Windows Live ID that you use to log onto your device. This could be a long, super-secure password containing a mixture of uppercase and lowercase letters, numbers, and symbols at least 10 characters long. But there's a temptation to create a PIN or picture password for Windows 8 access because you won't want to have to enter such a long password every time you start your device.

A PIN code instantly reduces a secure multicharacter password to a simple, four-digit numeric code, which isn't anywhere near as secure; and while a picture password might be more secure if presented with a photo of three or more people, the temptation would be to poke the first three people on the nose. Is this what you would do? Is this what you might consider for a picture password? While web enthusiasts and IT pros are generally more security-aware than consumers are, a great many people think that a "plonk, plonk, plonk" approach to picture passwords in a pattern that's a bit fun would also be secure. Believe me, it isn't any more secure than having a password that's the name of your dog.

Using Microsoft SkyDrive to Share

One of the best ways to back up and synchronize files between different computers is via a cloud service. Microsoft's Live Mesh has been a popular choice with Windows users for some time. The company has responded to user requests and released a dedicated SkyDrive app, which is available through the Windows Marketplace.

Using SkyDrive with Windows 8, you can easily access your cloud-stored files from within Windows 8; but you are also able to access SkyDrive and its services directly from File Explorer on the desktop (see Figure 4-20).

Mike's SkyDrive ∨ 5 items

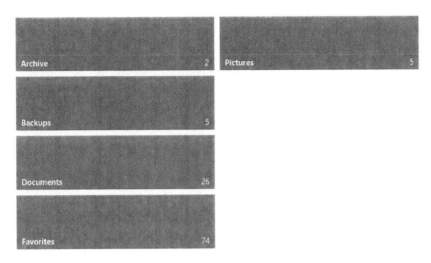

Figure 4-20. *The SkyDrive app for Windows 8*

The introduction of desktop support makes it much simpler to synchronize and back up files and folders to SkyDrive than it is to Windows Live Mesh, which has always been a catch-all type of backup solution that lacks the refinement and flexibility of packages like Dropbox.

The File Explorer integration of SkyDrive (see Figure 4-21) allows you to specify the files to back up and synchronize directly from within File Explorer. This helps in two ways.

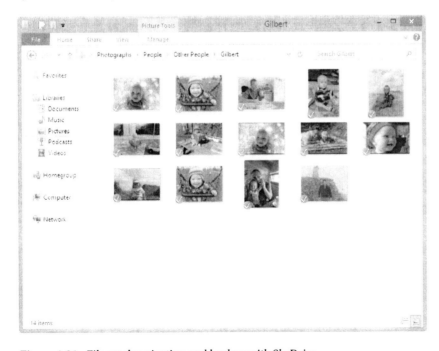

Figure 4-21. *File synchronization and backup with SkyDrive*

First, you are able to see the files that are synchronized and backed up, but you can also see the current backup status on a file-by-file basis.

Synchronization and cloud backup are excellent ways to get files and documents onto mobile devices like tablets, especially ones running on the ARM architecture—most of which won't connect to devices like USB hard disks and flash drives in the way that a laptop or a desktop computer will.

One of the main advantages of using the SkyDrive app to read files from the cloud, rather than synchronizing the files so that they download directly to the drive, is that there is nothing actually stored on the tablet. Even physically removing the storage from the drive or reformatting and trying to recover deleted files won't display them. This makes it a more secure approach.

On the downside, in order to do this, you need an active data connection. Unless you have a SIM card slot in your tablet with a live mobile broadband package, then you are unable to view this content when you are away from a Wi-Fi connection.

■ **Caution**   Viewing any file from a cloud service requires the file to be temporarily downloaded. Depending on the software or service you use, these files may not be automatically deleted afterward; they may also be recoverable.

Sharing Files and Documents

One of the best new features in Windows 8 is the ability to share content directly from one app to another. This is done without the apps having to know how it is done and without the developers having to add any code into the app other than support for the sharing service.

How this will actually be used over time remains to be seen as industrious app developers will no doubt constantly find new and innovative ways to use the feature. At its most basic, however, it is a way to share photos vie e-mail or with photo-sharing services such as Flickr, Facebook, and PhotoBucket.

You can also highlight text, perhaps on a web page, and share it between apps; you can share any type of content really. This is where it will be fascinating to see how app developers use this feature. There's not really been anything quite like it in an operating system before, so anticipating how it will be used over time is impossible to guess right now.

You can share in Windows 8 by highlighting the item or items you wish to share, opening the charms, and clicking Share. All compatible apps for that type of content appear (see Figure 4-22). Just click the app you wish to share the content with and the content is transferred to the other app for sharing.

Figure 4-22. *Sharing via Windows 8*

Of course, this sharing feature comes with risks. The easier it is to share content with apps, web sites, and the like, the easier it becomes to accidentally put content where you didn't intend for it to go, or for it to go on web sites where your privacy settings mean that it is generally accessible to the whole world. I always recommend, strongly in fact, that you make sure your privacy settings on web sites are set to automatically block all content from those you have not *deliberately* invited to view it.

Sharing Optical Drives

One of the biggest challenges facing users of Windows tablets and ultrabooks is the lack of an optical drive. Sure, you can install software (and even Windows 8) from a USB flash drive or the Internet, and Windows 8 will allow you to mount ISO files; but there will be occasions when you'll need an optical drive.

One solution is to buy a USB optical drive, but this isn't always a practical solution. Indeed, I bought one last year for my Windows tablet and then promptly left it at a Microsoft Research event in Cambridge, where it isn't doing me much good.

A better solution is to share the optical drive on another computer. To do this in both Windows 8 and Windows 7 (because the instructions are the same), do the following:

1. On the host computer (the one with the optical drive), open File Explorer (Windows Explorer in Windows 7) and click Computer in the left pane.

2. Right-click the optical drive you want to share. From the options, click Share With ➤ Advanced Sharing (see Figure 4-23).

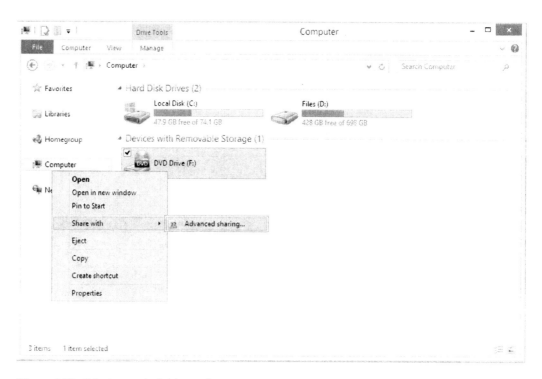

Figure 4-23. *Select an optical drive to share*

3. In the dialog box, click the Advanced Sharing button (see Figure 4-24).

Figure 4-24. *Select the Advanced Sharing settings*

4. Check the Share This Folder box and then give the share an appropriate name, such as
    DVD-Share (see Figure 4-25).

Figure 4-25. *Share the drive and give it a name*

5.   Click OK. You are then shown the full network name of the share, in this case
     \\WORKSTATION\\DVD-Share. WORKSTATION is the name of the host PC (seeFigure 4-26).

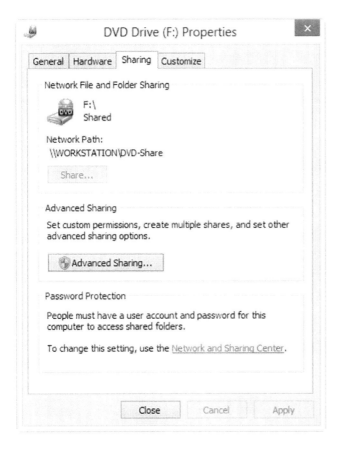

Figure 4-26. *The full share name of the drive*

■ **Note** For the drive to be visible on other computers, you need to have File and Printer Sharing turned on in the Advanced Sharing Settings of the Network and Sharing Center. Users of other computers may also need the username and password of the host computer to gain access to the shared drive.

This optical drive is now accessible to people on other computers when they are attached to the same network and the computer containing the optical drive is switched on; this includes those using ultrabooks and tablets.

Streaming Music and Video to Devices and Computers

At the beginning of the chapter, I showed you how to set up a HomeGroup to share your documents, music, pictures, and videos with other Windows 8 and Windows 7 computers. Among the HomeGroup settings was one to "Allow devices such as TVs and games consoles to play my shared content."

Activating this feature turns your computer, when it is switched on anyway, into a UPnP server. Many devices support this feature, including Internet radios, MP3-playing Hi-Fi systems, external network-attached storage (NAS) and USB hard disks, game consoles, and even devices you wouldn't normally expect to work happily with Windows, like Apple TV.

Not only can Windows 8 (and previous versions of Windows) share content in this way, it can also stream content from other UPnP devices that are connected to your home network. UPnP devices are found in the Network section of File Explorer (see Figure 4-27).

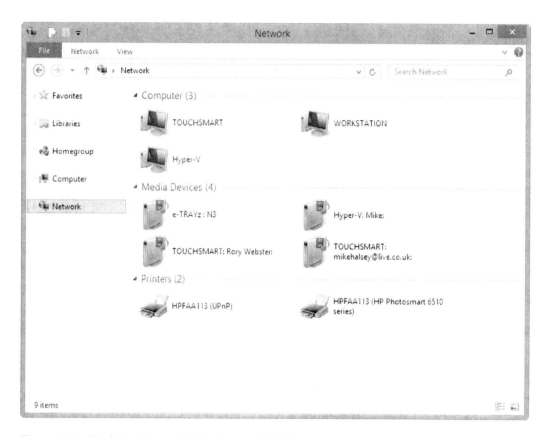

Figure 4-27. *Displaying Network Media Devices in Windows 8*

■ **Note**   Microsoft does not include DVD and Blu-Ray playback support as standard in Windows 8. Instead, they have made it a chargeable extra. You can Add Features to Windows in the Control Panel to purchase and upgrade to Windows 8 Pro with Media Center. This adds these features, but only within Windows Media Center itself, not through the Video app or Windows Media Player.

Here you can check if Windows 8 is sharing your content properly and also, I think somewhat crucially, check that nothing is being shared by accident.

Windows 8 shares only media files such as pictures, music, and video; you can be sure your documents will not be shared with media devices. This comes in particularly handy if you have downloaded movies or TV shows onto your computer and you want to watch them on your TV, perhaps through your Xbox 360.

Changing Advanced Sharing Settings in Windows 8

Sometimes you may have trouble with network sharing in Windows. This could be caused by something switched off in the Advanced Sharing Settings page. Alternatively, you may wish to deliberately switch something off if you no longer want a certain type of sharing to take place from a specific computer.

You can access the Advanced Sharing Settings page from the Network and Sharing Center, itself accessible from either the Ribbon in the Network view of File Explorer, or by right-clicking the Network icon on the desktop taskbar.

Once in the Network and Sharing Center, there is a link to Change Advanced Sharing Settings in the left-hand pane.

There are a great many options in the Advanced Sharing Settings page (see Figure 4-28), and some are very important and significant.

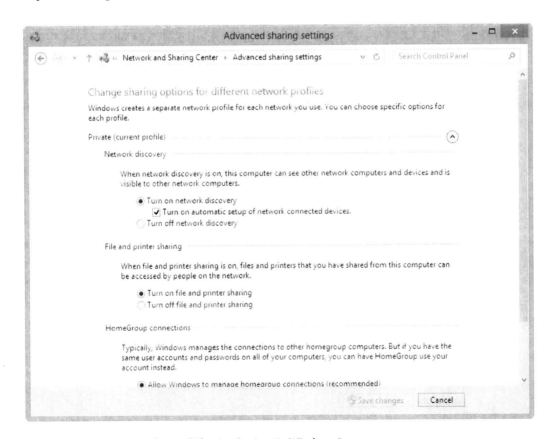

Figure 4-28. *Changing Advanced Sharing Settings in Windows 8*

The network settings are separated into three groups: Private, Guest or Public, and All Networks. The sharing settings for Public networks are understandably different from those for Private networks. The following describes the main settings:

- **Network Discovery** is the setting to go to when your computer can't be found on a network or you can't see any other computers and devices. There is a switch here to automatically turn on Setup for Network Connected Devices. You may not want this on, however, if you are commonly in environments where networked devices such as storage might be prone to malware infection and distribution.

- **File and Printer Sharing** is the main switch for sharing all your files, documents, pictures, music, and videos on networks. Printer sharing only affects printers physically attached to the computer.

- **HomeGroup Connections** is a useful setting if you want to choose between Windows automatically managing user access from computers in HomeGroup, or if you want finer control with specific user accounts and passwords required.

- **Public Folder Sharing** isn't what you might first believe. It's not about sharing your files and folders with the public. Instead, it is about the public folders Windows has always set up in user accounts to aid the sharing of files. These folders are not commonly used, however.

- **Media Streaming** controls the options for live broadcasting of pictures, audio, and video over a network to UPnP devices.

- **File Sharing Connections** is the setting for controlling the amount of encryption used on the network when sharing files. This should not ever be changed from the default.

- **Password Protected File Sharing** is something that you shouldn't normally change; however, if you do not have a password on the computer from which you use to share files, you will find that you are not able to access those files from another computer unless you turn this setting off.

Connecting to Network Shared Storage

These days, most networked shared storage automatically appears in the Network section of File Explorer. This is the case whether you're on a home or a work network, and can include NAS boxes, file servers (though you may need to log in to access these), and USB hard disks plugged into compatible routers.

In Windows 7, you can view a full network map through the Network and Sharing Center to locate devices. You can no longer do this in Windows 8, but the operating system is much better at connecting to network resources than its predecessors.

Unfortunately, with the removal of the network map, the option to automatically log into the network storage administration interface is also gone. In Windows 8, if you want to change a configuration option, you have to know the IP address of the device, which you can get through your router or through the Devices and Printers page.

▒ **Note** The default IP address of a router is normally 192.168.0.1 or 192.168.1.1. You can type this into your web browser address bar to gain access.

Why You Might Not See Network Storage on Your Computer

Sometimes network resources fail to appear. This is usually a problem caused by your router. A typical home router provided by your ISP can be unreliable at simultaneously managing multiple devices on the network.

In my own home, for example, I regularly have a desktop PC, a laptop (perhaps even a second laptop), an Xbox 360, a Windows phone, and an NAS drive on at the same time; so six devices plus the router. I regularly find that

Windows starts with a message that it has detected an IP address conflict. This is where the router has incorrectly assigned the IP addresses of the computers and devices on the network, and one device thinks it has a different IP address than the one the router has assigned it.

In practice, however, Windows is very good at sorting out these types of problems on its own. It is very rare that you are completely unable to see a networked device.

You can manually set the IP addresses for computers and devices on your router, but the facility to manually set IP addresses in Windows has been removed from previous versions. If a device still fails to appear, then restarting that device (and the router) normally rectifies the problem.

Another thing that can prevent your computer from seeing network storage is a firewall that has settings that are too aggressive. I have found some security suites have this problem with the default configuration. The solution depends on your security suite and the way its configuration options work. It is always worth checking if you experience problems. You can best check by temporarily switching the firewall off.

Viewing the Status of Network Drives

When you use the Network page in File Explorer, it's simple to view and access other hard disks and attached storage on your network. The ability to see the amount of remaining storage is more difficult. There's no point in performing a backup to a network drive, for example, if you don't know that you first need to clear some space.

You can do this by connecting your computer to a folder on the drive; any folder will do, but it's usually a good idea to create a root folder on the disk into which you put everything else. This way, when you open the shared drive, you will be able to see and work with all of its contents.

To do this, follow these instructions:

1. Open File Explorer and click Network in the left pane.

2. Double-click the network drive you wish to attach to your computer.

3. Right-click a folder within that drive. From the options, click **Map network drive** (see Figure 4-29).

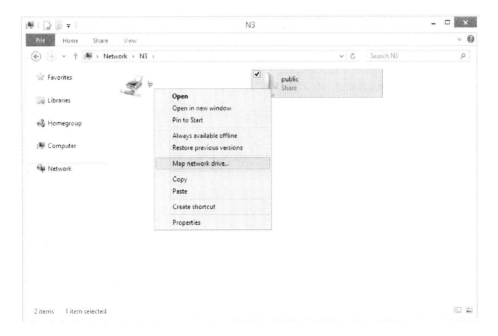

Figure 4-29. *Connecting a network drive*

4. In the dialog box, choose any free drive. If you want Windows to automatically connect to this drive every time you start your computer, make sure Reconnect at Logon is checked. If the mapped drive is on another computer, you may need to log into it with different credentials; these will be the username and password for the host PC (see Figure 4-30).

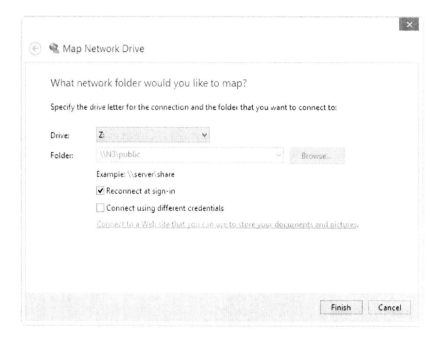

Figure 4-30. *Map Network Drive options*

5. Click Finish when you are done.

The network drive now appears in File Explorer in the Network Location section of the Computer window. It displays the total size of the drive along with the amount of available free space (see Figure 4-31). As you can see from this screenshot, it's good that I checked.

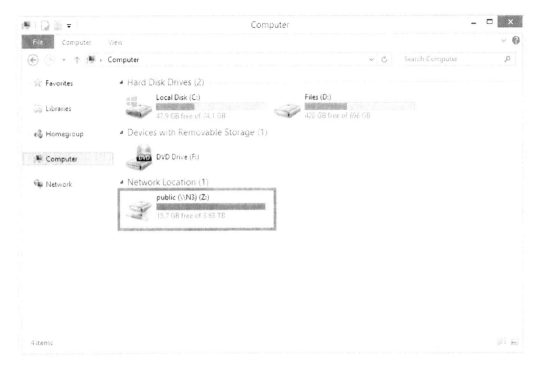

Figure 4-31. *Viewing a mapped drive in File Explorer*

■ **Tip** Sometimes your network drives won't show up in File Explorer, perhaps because they're on a subnetwork such as a powerline system in your home or office. You can manually connect to them in the Address bar by typing \\ followed by the name of the network drive; for example, \\N3 to connect to the drive called N3.

Summary

There are more ways to share documents, media, and network resources in Windows 8 than ever before offered in a Windows operating system. The new sharing integration with apps is something that I am personally excited to see developers use to push sharing in new directions.

Of course, there are security considerations. You should always make sure that you have up-to-date antivirus protection.

The Devices and Printers page is far more powerful than it first appears to be. The networking settings for sharing are also very powerful. When it comes to sharing media files and printer access, Windows 8 is a great operating system to use, especially with its helpful wizards—something Microsoft has always been good at—walking you through each step.

Despite the removal of a couple of Windows 7 features that I personally found very useful, it is still very possible to robustly work with network resources.

CHAPTER 5

▨ ▨ ▨

Organizing and Searching Your Computer

Our computing devices, be they desktop PCs, laptops, tablets, smartphones, or new ultrabooks are all about content. We either make it or consume it, but we all have ever-growing quantities of it. You may store it on a network share, in the cloud, on an external hard disk, or on the computer's hard disk or SSD (solid-state drive)—but there will probably be a lot of it wherever it is stored.

Of this content, you'll likely have an ever-ballooning collection of digital photographs, a big music Library, and possibly a growing video collection. These files take a lot of space to store and can make finding exactly what you're looking for problematic, especially with photos.

At the other end of the file-size scale are all your Word, Excel, PDF, and other file types, which you have for personal, household, work, and school purposes. Although they may not take up large amounts of space, these files can be equally difficult to find and organize.

Traditionally, the way to organize files and documents was to use a folder structure. I remember using software such as XTree on the first IBM PCs to perform this task (see Figure 5-1).

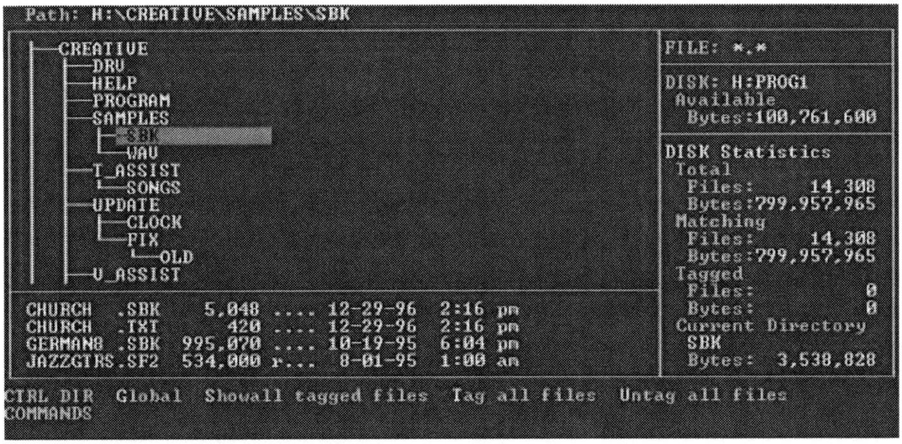

Figure 5-1. *XTree on the original IBM PC*

Folders aren't always a suitable way to organize our files and documents because some have crossovers between categories; and as the volume of files, music, pictures, and videos we collect expands, even the most organized folder structure can become unwieldy and difficult to navigate.

103

For many years now, Windows has tried to help us organize our files through user folders, My Documents, and so forth. These still exist but there are much more powerful ways to help you organize. In this chapter, I'll show you how to optimize file organization and access.

Using File Explorer

Before moving into newer features, the place to start a discussion about organizing your files is File Explorer. Actually, File Explorer is new in a way, as it was previously called Windows Explorer. In Windows 8, it has been significantly overhauled with the inclusion of the Ribbon interface, which was first introduced in Microsoft Office 2007).

■ **Note**   The Ribbon interface is minimized by default in Windows 8, appearing only when you click a tab header. You can show or hide the Ribbon at all times in File Explorer by clicking the small arrow on the right of the Ribbon headers (see Figure 5-2).

Figure 5-2. *File Explorer in Windows 8*

File Explorer in Windows 8 is split into several different sections, and some can be used with great effect to aid productivity or save time when searching for and working with files. At the very top left of the File Explorer, there is a File Explorer button that can be clicked to perform various actions on the program, including minimizing it and closing it.

■ **Tip**   Double-clicking a program button in the top left of its window will close the program.

The Quick Access Toolbar

The Quick Access Toolbar remains next to the program button at the top of the window (see Figure 5-3). This area allows you single-click access to commonly used commands. It is customizable too, with the Down arrow to its right bringing up a list of additional buttons that you can add to the toolbar, including Undo, Delete, and Rename.

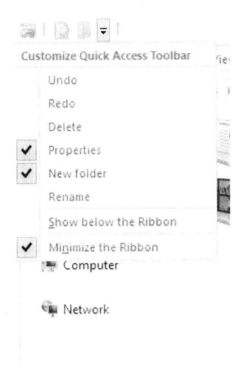

Figure 5-3. *The Quick Access Toolbar in File Explorer*

You can add and remove items from the Quick Access Toolbar by selecting and deselecting them in the toolbar options menu.

The Address Bar

Just below the Ribbon, which I shall talk about in depth shortly, is the Address bar, sometimes known as the Address bar. On the left of this are buttons to move backward and forward in the current view. These buttons remember where you have been and allow you to return to locations, even if they are out of the current folder tree (see Figure 5-4).

Figure 5-4. *The Address bar in File Explorer*

Next to these buttons is an Up arrow that takes you one level up in the current folder hierarchy. To the right of the Address bar is a search box that allows you to search for any type of file or text within a file. By default, the search prioritizes the contents of the current folder. For example, if you are looking at pictures, then pictures are prioritized in your search results over other types of document.

The Address bar is so called because it offers you ways back in the current folder tree that provide easy access to other parts of that tree. Figure 5-5 shows Computer ➤ Local Disk (C:) ➤ Windows ➤ Web ➤ Wallpapers. Each of the two folder names has a small black arrow separating them.

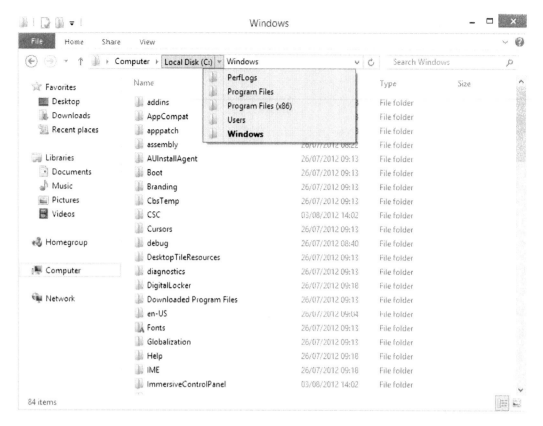

Figure 5-5. *Using the Address bar in File Explorer*

If you click one of the arrows between folders, you are given quick links to jump to any other folder in that part of the tree. This can make it extremely quick and easy to navigate to different parts of your hard disk(s) and find what it is you are looking for.

■ **Tip**   To find out the exact current folder location or to manually type a folder address into the Address bar, click the button located on the far left of the Address bar. The exact current folder address will appear, highlighted, so you can immediately start typing a new folder address if you wish.

The Navigation Pane

To the left of the window is the Favorite Links pane, which is split into different categories. In the first, Favorites, you can drag and drop folders (not files) that you want quick one-click access to, perhaps because you use them often.

Beneath Favorite Links is access to your Libraries, which I discuss in detail in Chapter 5. If you do not want a specific library to display in this pane, then you can right-click it and select **Don't show in navigation pane**.

■ **Tip** You can pin Libraries and Favorite Links to the Start screen by right-clicking them in the navigation pane and selecting Pin to Start.

Beneath the Libraries in the navigation pane are quick, expandable groups for

- **HomeGroup**, which I discuss in detail in Chapter 4
- **Computer**, which displays all the hard disks and attached storage on your computer
- **Network**, which displays all available attached network locations, networked computers, and network storage

The Status Bar

Running along the bottom of File Explorer is the Status bar. It gives basic information about the current folder of the currently selected items, such as the number of files. Unlike Windows 7, this Status bar doesn't contain details about files; these have been moved to a Details pane, which I will talk about shortly.

■ **Tip** At the far right of the Status bar are buttons to quickly access two of the most common views in File Explorer: the Details view and the Thumbnail view. Clicking these buttons immediately changes the File Explorer view of the current folder.

The Main Explorer View

In the main File Explorer pane, you see all your files and folders. These can be arranged in a great many ways. You can also select files in the main view in several ways, including

- **Right-click**. You can right-click a file or folder with your mouse to bring up a context menu of the actions you can perform on it.
- **Tap and hold**. You can tap and hold a folder or file to bring up the actions context menu.
- **Hover your mouse**. You can hover your mouse over a file or folder to bring up a check box to select the item. You can use this method to select multiple items if you wish.

■ **Tip** To select multiple files and/or folders with your mouse and keyboard, you can use one of these options. To select everything between two items, click the first item, hold down the Shift key, and then click the item at the end of the list. To select multiple, randomly placed items, hold the Ctrl key while clicking the items you want to select.

Hiding Picture File Names

One very useful feature that has not made it into the Ribbon is the ability to hide the file names of pictures in File Explorer. If you are looking at holiday photos or similar, why do you need to look at reams of DSCxxx file names anyway?

You can hide the file names for pictures by right-clicking in any blank space, and then in the View menu, select **Hide file names** (see Figure 5-6).

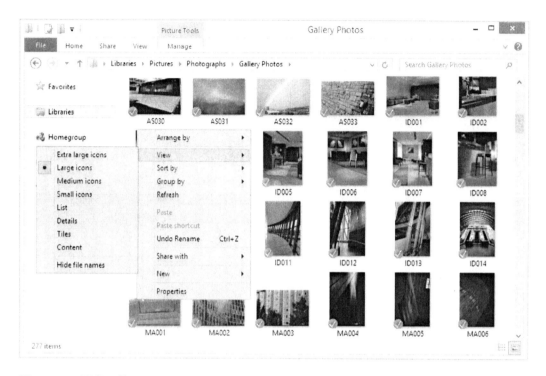

Figure 5-6. *Hiding file names in picture views*

The File Explorer Ribbon

I have left the Ribbon until last because I want to spend a little more time on it and talk about each tab.

By default, the Ribbon in File Explorer is hidden, and you display it but clicking one of the tabs at the top of the window. These are: File, Home, Share, and View. Other tabs can appear, however, such as Computer, Library, or Picture. These extra tabs contain functions specific to those file types. When the Ribbon is open a *pin* icon will appear on the right of the window. You can click this to lock the Ribbon so that it is always displayed.

I'm not going to discuss every Ribbon function in depth because, frankly, I don't think you'd want me to, but I want to concentrate on the Ribbon functions that I think are most useful, most interesting, or most likely to give you a valuable productivity boost.

You may find that the Ribbon is hidden in File Explorer and you can only see the tab names. If you click one of these, the Ribbon will appear temporarily, but you can show and hide the Ribbon by clicking the small Up/Down arrow (this changes depending on whether the Ribbon is currently displayed or hidden) that appears next to the Help button on the far right of the tab name, on the right of the window.

The File Tab

The main file tab, which is blue—a different color from the other tabs, is where you find options like Open or Open in a New Window. One of the most interesting and useful features in the File tab is the Delete History option, which can either delete your recent places, your Address bar, or both, should you wish. This is very useful for clearing out the temporary files associated with your Explorer history, as well as hiding what you have been viewing (especially if you are working on a custom birthday card for someone!).

The Computer Tab

The Computer tab is accessible from the computer or network main drive (see Figure 5-7). The Computer tab provides context-sensitive options to perform actions such as adding a network location to File Explorer. You also get easy access to the Windows 8 Control Panel.

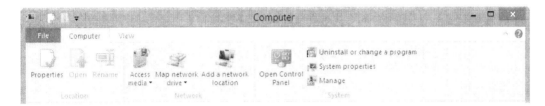

Figure 5-7. *The Computer tab*

The Home Tab

The Home tab (see Figure 5-8) is where you find all the common options associated with files and folders in Windows. These include Cut, Copy, Paste, Move, and Delete. You can also create new folders and files in the New section of the Ribbon. Of particular interest are the History button and the Selection buttons.

Figure 5-8. *The Home tab in File Explorer*

■ **Tip** You can perform cut, copy, and paste actions in Windows using the Ctrl + X (Cut), Ctrl + C (Copy), and Ctrl + V (Paste) hotkeys.

Windows 8 includes a better file versioning system than what was included in Windows 7. I discuss how to use the feature in depth in Chapter 12, but if you have a single file selected, the History button brings up the versioning for that file, including any previous versions of the file that Windows 8 has backed up.

Also, the Open section has a Properties button that you can click to quickly bring up the Properties dialog box for any file, folder, or a selection of files and/or folders. In the Properties dialog box for files, you can change or update information about a file, including artist and track information for music, as well as tags and ratings.

In the Selection section, a very handy Invert Selection button has been included. It can be very helpful when you want to work with some files, perhaps to change their properties, and then need to perform another action on all the other files in the same folder.

Note that if you select a location such as a DVD or non-hard-disk location, the options on the Home tab will change to better reflect the actions you can perform with that device.

The Share Tab

The Share tab (see Figure 5-9) contains the tools and utilities you need to share and back up your files and folders. This includes syncing and backing up to Microsoft's SkyDrive service, sending files via e-mail, creating a zipped archive file, burning files to disc (CD/DVD/Blu-ray), and printing or faxing files.

Figure 5-9. *The Share tab in File Explorer*

If you are sharing files on your computer or across a network, or would like to, you can set who you want to share files with by using this tab.

The View Tab and Customizing File Explorer

In the View tab (see Figure 5-10), you can customize File Explorer to look and work the way you like.

Figure 5-10. *The View tab in File Explorer*

There are different panes that can be switched on and off in File Explorer. The Navigation pane has a button to switch it off or to customize it. There is no way to turn on the traditional folder view, not that you were necessarily used to it in earlier versions of Windows anyway, but turning on Show All Folders in the Navigation pane displays the same result in the Computer section.

The Preview and Details panes are slightly different, though they can be confused with one another. Both these panes appear on the right side of the Explorer window and cannot be seem simultaneously. If you turn on the Preview pane, then a live image of the file appears, which you can review. This includes being able to scroll through an entire Word, Excel, or Acrobat document.

■ **Tip** When you group items in File Explorer, each group is separated by a horizontal line. You can click this line to select all items in the group or right-click the line to display an option to hide the group. This makes folders that contain many files easier to navigate.

The Details pane in File Explorer gives you detailed information about a file that you select. The information presented in the Details pane is editable, meaning that you don't have to bring up the separate Properties dialog box to edit information such as Author, Track Number, or Rating.

In the Layout section of the Ribbon are some very useful tools for customizing the current view.

- The **Small**, **Medium**, **Large**, and **Extra Large buttons** change the default button size in the current view.

- **List** displays all items in view as a simple list, like in the very early versions of Windows.

- **Details** is a very common view. It can also be accessed from a button on the Status bar at the bottom of the window. This view displays extra information about files and folders that many people find useful, such as the file size and the date/time the file was created and last modified.

- **Tiles** and **Content** present files and folders in much friendlier ways than the default view, in my opinion. Tiles is an upgraded button view. Content presents more details about files in a way similar to the Details view.

In the Current View section are tools to help you sort and group content in different ways. You may want, for example, to sort items by Date Modified or Created By. Grouping files and folders is an excellent way to keep yourself organized so that you know exactly what you have and where. Grouping files and folders by Type, for example, groups all the folders together, all the Word documents together, all the PNG images together, and so on.

■ **Tip** At the bottom of the Sort By and Group By drop-down menus is a Choose Columns option. If you select it, then many more sort and group options appear, including album artist or rating for music or EXIF data for digital photographs.

In the Show/Hide are two functions previously hidden to many Windows users: the ability to show and hide file extensions. These are hidden by default for all known file types. The second option is to show and hide hidden files. This option is extremely useful if you need to drill down into the Windows system folder or your User folder to find specific information or a specific hidden file.

■ **Tip** In the Ribbon, you can set all folders to display in the same way as the current folder by clicking Options ➤ Folder and Search Options ➤ View ➤ Apply to Folders.

Copying and Moving Files in File Explorer

The feedback you get when copying and moving files in Windows 8 has significantly improved. There is more feedback and more control when duplicate copies of files are found. The copied file dialog box is shown in Figure 5-11.

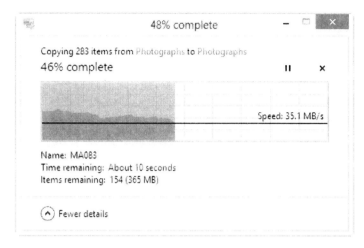

Figure 5-11. *The improved Copy/Move file dialog box in Windows 8*

One of the most significant improvements to copy and move file operations is that all operations now appear in the same window. This means that if you have several copy or move operations running simultaneously, you now only have one window on your screen that contains them all.

The other significant improvement is the addition of a Pause button to the dialog box. You can now pause copy and move operations should you need to do something else or put your computer to sleep at the end of the day. When you return to Windows, you can continue with the operation by unpausing it.

When you click More Details on a Copy or Move File dialog box, you are shown a graph of the copy or move operation. This graph gives you live feedback on the current speed of the copy, the number of megabits per second being copied, and a filled graph showing how the speed of the copy has changed. This is useful for diagnosing problems with copy or move operations when something else is happening in the background.

The Replace dialog boxes have also been upgraded in Windows 8 (see Figure 5-12), as you will notice when you copy or move files into a folder or onto a drive where another copy already exists.

Figure 5-12. *The improved Replace or Skip dialog box*

The Replace or Skip Files dialog box is now much simpler with choices to replace or skip all the files, or to choose which ones you want to keep in the destination folder.

Should you want to choose which files you want to keep or overwrite, this dialog box has improved as well. You still have a tick box to select everything to keep or replace, but each individual file is more easily identifiable.

Tip To keep all the source *and* destination files in a copy or move operation, check the Files From and Files Already In check boxes at the top of both the left and the right columns (see Figure 5-13).

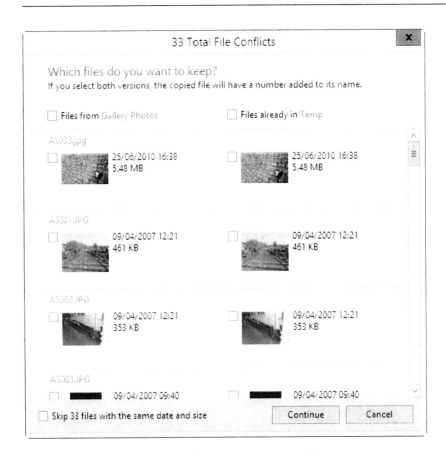

Figure 5-13. *You can easily select files to overwrite in Windows 8*

Pictures have a thumbnail image, but other file types just display the opening program's button. This new dialog box makes it much easier to decide which files to keep and which to replace than withWindows 7, where you were only given text information such as the date and time stamps.

Managing Files and Folders from Apps

Managing files and folders in Windows 8 apps is a much simpler affair, though the new interface can make it difficult to manage large volumes of files or to perform complex actions because the commands available in the App bar are not as extensive as in the desktop File Explorer.

To select any file in an app that you want to perform an action on, tap it and drag downward. You can also right-click it with a mouse. You can select multiple files, but the options available for working with those files in the App bar may change depending on the app you are currently working in.

Using Libraries in Windows 8

The common view of Windows 7 users is that Libraries are the same as the shell user folders—those folders with "My" in front of their names. Libraries actually are aggregated storage for many locations. They are customizable, for specific types of content. They're actually very powerful with the way that content can be displayed.

You access Libraries in File Explorer, where they are linked in the left pane, as seen in Figure 5-14. By default, there are libraries of Documents, Music, Pictures, and Videos; although if you install other software (such as the Microsoft Zune player), others (such as Podcasts) may be added.

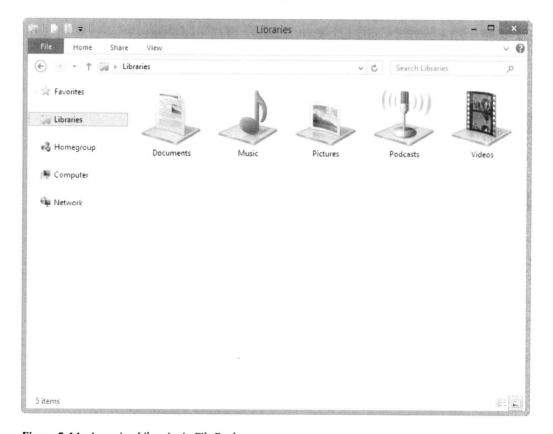

Figure 5-14. *Accessing Libraries in File Explorer*

You can create your own Libraries to view and arrange content in specific ways; for instance, you might want one for your work or school documents, and so on.

Using Tags and Ratings to Organize Files

Tags and Ratings are two of the best ways to organize and categorize files. Tags are labels that help you find relevant documents. For example, you might have documents tagged as "work," "school," "household," or "auto." Thus, tags might help you locate documents related to your car quickly and easily.

If you have a lot of photos, you might label them "vacation," "children," or "Spain" to help you find them quickly for display to friends and family (this is, after all, why you took them in the first place).

You are probably already familiar with tags called *metadata* with your music files, where the artist, album name, track number, track name, and more are all tags. They are labels used to help you identify the contents of a file.

You don't need to be limited to a single tag per file either. You can stack multiple tags together so your recent vacation photos in Orlando might be tagged "vacation," "Orlando," "Disney," "Jessica," and "Matthew."

Ratings are slightly different, but easier to understand. Ratings in Windows 8 use one to five stars that indicate how significant the file is. In your music, you probably already use 4- and 5-star ratings to identify your favorite tracks; you may have been doing this for years. If you use the Like tag for music tracks in the Zune Desktop software, for example, it automatically adds a 5-star rating to each file you like.

You can view the tags and ratings for any file or files in File Explorer by clicking the Details pane button on the Ribbon under the View tab (see Figure 5-15). This opens a pane on the right side of the windows, showing all manner of information, which changes from file type to file type. Tags and Rating are always at the top of the list.

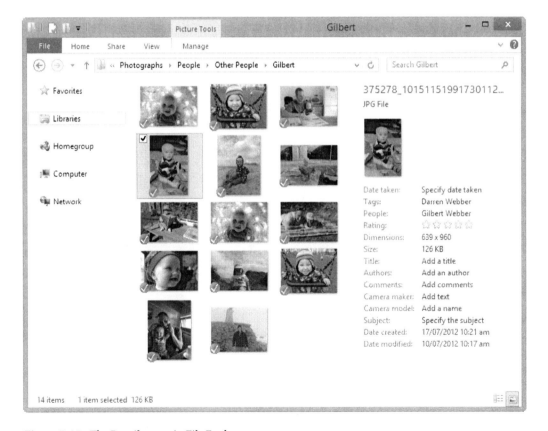

Figure 5-15. *The Details pane in File Explorer*

To add a tag or multiple tags to a file or a selection of files (remember you can press Ctrl+click to select files, and then Shift+click to mark the end of a selected group), click next to Tags in the Details pane and type as many as you like, each one separated by a semicolon (;). When you have finished adding tags, click the Save button to finish.

You can add a rating or change a rating by clicking the appropriate number of stars. Click Save when you are done.

Simplify Adding Tags and Ratings with Windows Live Photo Gallery

It can be a laborious process adding tags and ratings to files, but the important thing to remember is that *you only need to do this once*. There are tools that can make the process much easier for you as well. Windows Live Photo Gallery, part of the Windows Live Essentials suite, can be downloaded for free from download.live.com. In the View tab on the Ribbon, you have the option to view files by tag (seeFigure 5-16).

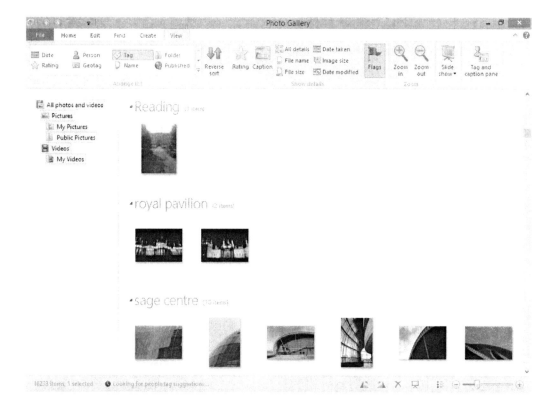

Figure 5-16. *Tagging photos in Windows Live Photo Gallery*

The View tab features a button to open the Tag and Caption Pane. This pane offers a great way to simplify the addition of tags to photos and pictures because it lists all your photos by tag category, and shows all the photos that are *not tagged*. You can select these photos for tagging, making it much easier to know which pictures are already tagged.

When you import new photos to Windows 8 from your digital camera or memory card, you are asked if you want to add tags to them. This is a good time to do it because all the photos are probably related, and having Windows automate the process of adding tags makes things much simpler.

You can also remove and amend tags and ratings later in Windows Live Photo Gallery using simple controls. The options for this appear in the right pane when a photo or photos are selected.

When you see the Import Photos and Videos wizard, click Add Tags and type your tags (see Figure 5-17). This automatically adds the tags you enter to all your imported photos. You may want to use general tags such as "vacation," "family," or "countryside." I talk more about importing photos and videos in Chapter 7.

Figure 5-17. Tagging photos on import from a camera

Tip Most music players help automate adding tags to your music by finding the correct album from an extensive online database.

Creating a Library

You can add new folders to an existing Library (I show you how to do this shortly), but you can also create your own custom Libraries. I have one for Photos where all my pictures are arranged by their tags. You might want one each for your school, work, or household documents. You can have a Library for anything, and it's a great way to organize files.

To create a new Library, perform the following steps:

1. Open File Explorer on the desktop.

2. Click Libraries in the left pane.

3. Right-click (or tap and hold with your finger) any blank space in the main Explorer window (see Figure 5-18).

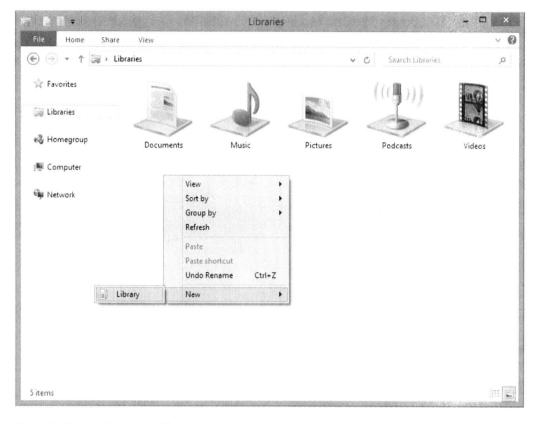

Figure 5-18. *Creating a new Library*

4. From the context menu, select New and then Library. You are presented with a new, empty Library.

5. Click the Include a Folder button and choose a folder to display in the Library (see Figure 5-19).

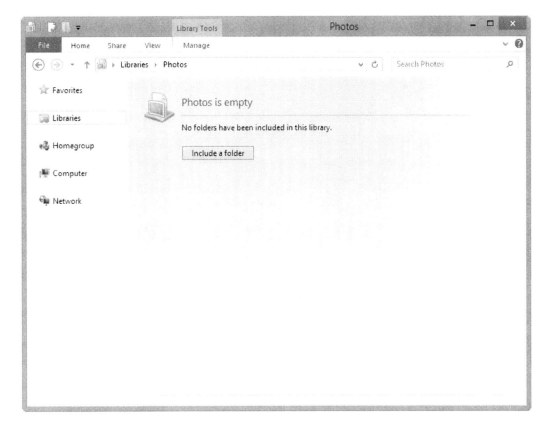

Figure 5-19. *Including a folder in a Library*

Changing the Way a Library Displays Files

You now see your folder listed in the Library, but it just looks like an ordinary explorer Window. It is now that the full flexibility of Libraries can be used because they can display content in ways that the normal Explorer folder view cannot.

1. To change the view, right-click (or tap and hold with your finger) in any blank space in the main window (see Figure 5-20).

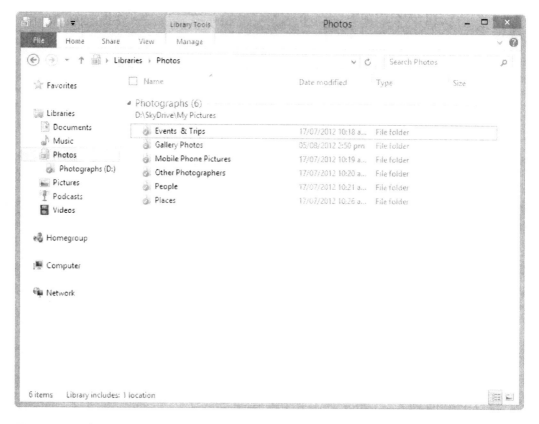

Figure 5-20. *Changing the way a Library is displayed*

2. From the context menu, click Arrange By and then your preferred choice by which to arrange the contents of the Library (see Figure 5-21).

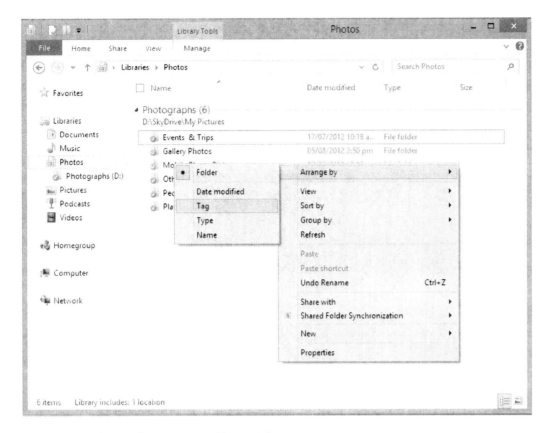

Figure 5-21. *Choosing how to arrange files in a Library*

You see that the Library is now arranged as you want it. In Figure 5-22, I have arranged a Photo Library by tag. Regardless of what folder photographs are stored in, I can view all pictures of Brighton Pier (for example) just by opening the tagged group. A nice benefit.

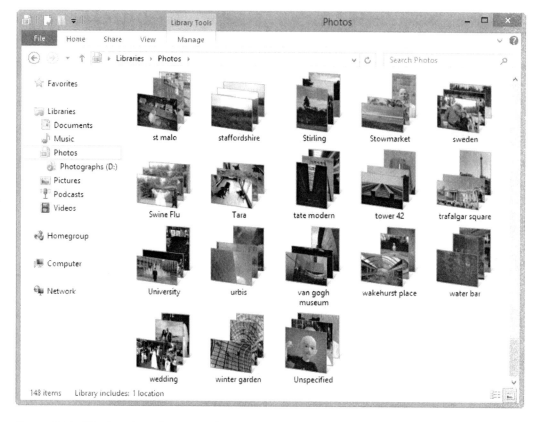

Figure 5-22. *Viewing photos by Tag in Libraries*

These Brighton Pier photos may reside in a dozen or more different folders on my hard disk, but because they all have the same tag, they are all displayed together in the Library when I arrange the files by tag.

Note Within Libraries, you can arrange files by type, where you find stacked groups for Word documents, PDFs, and so on. Sadly, you cannot specify just a single file type to be shown in a Library, only complete folders.

Adding and Removing Folders to Libraries

The folders included by default in the standard Windows 8 Libraries are the default folders found in C:\User\ Username. In addition to the default folders, you can include other folders and remove folders in a Library. When viewing the Library in File Explorer, you see a Library Tools: Manage tab on the Ribbon. Click it to bring up the Library management tools menu, the first of which is Manage Library.

Tip Although Libraries won't allow you to add external hard disks and network locations, it can still be done through a Windows Media Center cheat. See "Adding Network Locations to Libraries" later in this chapter.

Manage Library brings up the Library Locations window with its simple Add and Remove buttons for Library locations. You must have at least one location for a Library, but you can specify as many as you wish (see Figure 5-23).

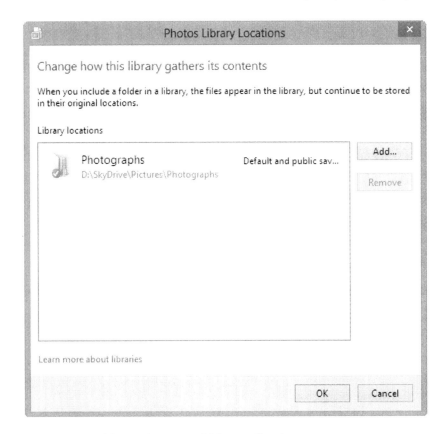

Figure 5-23. *Adding and removing folders to Libraries*

Changing the Default Save Location

A question mark can be raised about where the default save locations for Documents, Music, Pictures, and Video will be when you add new folders to a Library. After all, when you save a file, where does it go? Into your Users folder on the C:\ drive? Into the Library somewhere? Into a specific folder in the Library?

In Chapter 12, I talk about how and why you should move your files away from Windows and onto a separate hard disk or partition to safeguard them, but one way to do it is to change the default save location for a Library. You can do this from the Library Tools tab on the Ribbon in File Explorer when a Library is being viewed.

On the left of the Ribbon, there is a Set Save Location button, which offers a drops-down menu of the folders contained within that Library. To change the default save location, simply click the relevant folder that you want all new files saved to (see Figure 5-24).

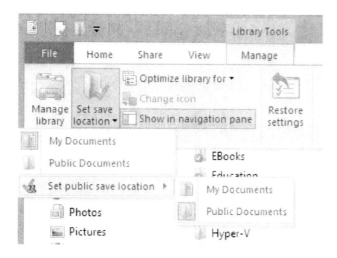

Figure 5-24. *Setting the default save location for Libraries*

Adding Network Locations to Libraries

It's widely known and established that you can't add network locations to Libraries in Windows 8, as was the case with Windows 7 ... or can you? In fact, it's always been possible to add network locations to your Music, Pictures, and Videos Libraries. You do it using Windows Media Center.

Note that in Windows 8, Windows Media Center is no longer a standard feature in the operating system, but is available as a chargeable add-on for Windows 8 Pro and it brings with it DVD and Blu-ray playback. You can purchase an upgrade by clicking Add Features to Windows in the Control Panel.

Open Windows Media Center to add network locations, and from the main menu click Settings ➤ Media Libraries.

You are presented with a wizard that allows you to add or remove folders to/from the Libraries. When asked where the files are located, select On Another Computer (see Figure 5-25). This displays network drives and allows you to add these locations to the Libraries.

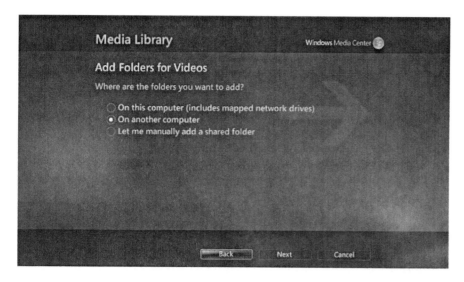

Figure 5-25. *Using Media Center to add network locations to Libraries*

All available network locations, including other computers on your network (that are switched on), appear in a collapsible list (see Figure 5-26). You can check and uncheck media folders to add to the Library. This is a fantastically simple workaround to what is otherwise a missing functionality in Windows Libraries.

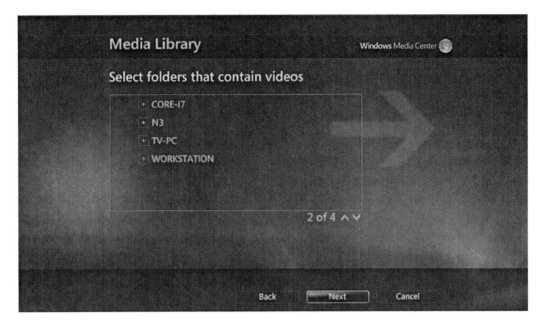

Figure 5-26. *Viewing network drives to add to Libraries in Media Center*

Managing Folder Options

Folder Options offers a huge amount of control over File Explorer and the way files and folders are viewed.

The first tab in this window, General, gives you the option to open files and folders with a single-click instead of a double-click. This is especially useful for people using a professional-grade Windows tablet (see Figure 5-27).

Figure 5-27. Changing the general folder view options

The option to show all folders in File Explorer's navigation pane may be the most popular. If you aren't a fan of the new Favorite Links pane, either you can switch this off completely in favor of the legacy folder view (see Figure 5-28) or you can combine the two. You can also set File Explorer to automatically expand the folder view of the currently viewed folder.

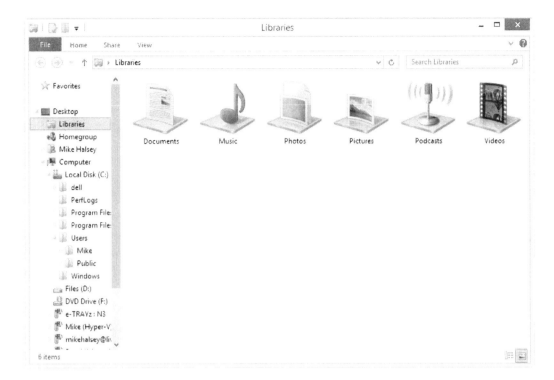

Figure 5-28. *Showing the folder view in File Explorer*

The View tab gives you extra control over the way files and folders are viewed and organized (see Figure 5-29). At the top of this window are buttons to **Apply [the current folder view] to [all] Folders** or to **Reset [all] Folders** to their default view. This enables you to decide the way you want your folders to look. If you would like your folders tiled with items grouped by file type, for example, you could apply this quickly and simply to all the folder views on your computer.

Figure 5-29. Changing advanced folder view options

Brief descriptions of some of the more noteworthy options follow:

- **Hidden files and folders** allows you to show or hide all hidden folders on your computer.

- **Hide empty drives in the Computer folder** is checked by default. It hides empty USB flash drives or memory card drives that you might want to copy files onto.

- **Hide extensions for known file types** is checked by default, but some users want to know the file extensions for all their files.

- **Hide protected operating system files** can be unchecked to display hidden system files that you may need to work with.

- **Show drive letters** shows the legacy drive assignments (C:, D:, etc.) on File Explorer views. Uncheck to remove the ability to see the drive letters.

- **Show encrypted or compressed NTFS files in color** highlights files in blue when BitLocker is turned on. Many people like to uncheck this option.

The last tab, Search, contains options for searching files and folders. For example, by default, Windows 8 doesn't search the content of compressed ZIP, CAB, or RAR files. You might want to turn on this option if you work with compressed files (see Figure 5-30).

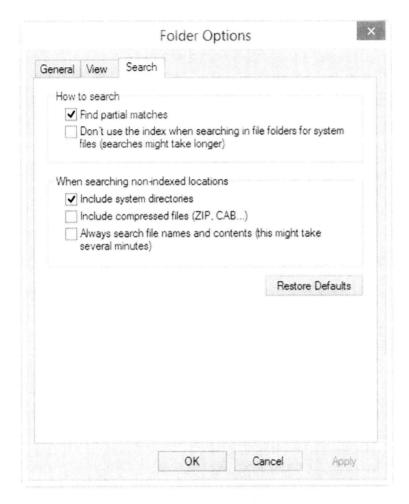

Figure 5-30. *Changing folder search options*

Using Search in Windows 8

It seems that with each new version of Windows, the methods by which we search for programs, settings, and files changes again. Windows 8 is no exception. In its simplest terms, basic search has been greatly improved since Windows 7. In Windows 7, you open the Start menu and simply type a search result; whereas in Windows 8, you start typing at the Start screen.

Windows 7 always contextualizes your searches, and so a search in the Start menu always prioritizes programs and settings. On the other hand, a basic search in Windows 8 isn't quite as good at contextualizing your searches, splitting items into only three categories, Files, Settings, and Apps.

Searching directly in File Explorer, however, still prioritizes the type of content displayed in that window. With the Start menu gone, however, a new way of performing basic searches was introduced.

Searching from the Start Screen

You can now search in Windows 8 directly from the Start screen by simply typing. Whatever it is you are doing, as long as you are looking at the Start screen (even if you have right-clicked on a tile), you can begin typing, and the search results instantly appear. You can also search directly from the Start screen or the Windows desktop by pressing the Win + F key combination.

Search from the Start screen is separated into three categories: Apps, Settings, and Files. Each of these categories has a link in the top right of the screen that can be clicked to switch between them.

By default, searches are in Apps. If you would rather search Settings or Files, you need to click the appropriate link at the top right of the screen (see Figure 5-31).

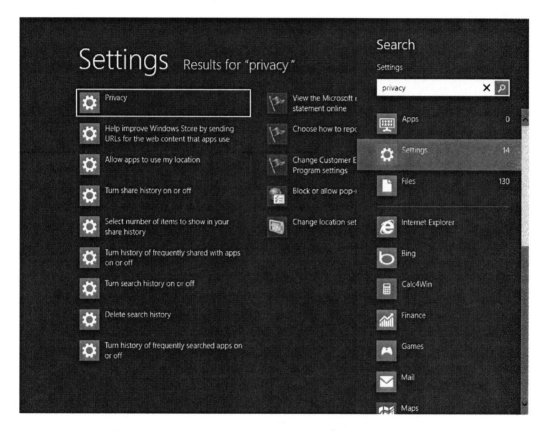

Figure 5-31. *Searching from the Start screen in Windows 8*

Search is intelligent, so it does not search for the words literally as you type them. A search for **Control**, for example, brings up relevant Windows features, including the Device Manager, Remote Assistance, and Accessibility options.

This means that you do not have to know exactly the name of the feature in Windows you are looking for. When you are searching for apps and desktop programs (for which the results appear in the Apps results), the results depend more on how the developer has described and programmed it, but generally the search facility in Windows 8 is excellent.

You can also use additional search syntax on the Start screen, however, and some of it is extremely useful. I detail the full Advanced Query Syntax in Appendix C, but some of the most useful search syntax options include Kind, Datemodified, Type, and Name as shown in Tables 5-1 through 5-4.

Table 5-1. *Kind (to search the properties of a document type)*

Option	Example
Kind:=email	Jake Webster kind:=email
Kind:=task	Meeting kind:=task
Kind:=note	project kind:=note
Kind:=document	Apress kind:=document
Kind:=music	Metallica kind:=music
Kind:=song	Equinoxe kind:=song
Kind:=folder	Book kind:=folder
Kind:=program	paint kind:=program

Table 5-2. *Datemodified (to search by the date a file was modified)*

Option	Example
Datemodified:MM/DD/YYYY	Report datemodified:10/22/2012
Datemodified:MM/DD/YY	Report datemodified:7/4/12
Datemodified:MM/DD/YY..MM/DD/YY	Report datemodified:7/4/12..10/22/12
Datemodified:yesterday	Orders datemodified:yesterday
Datemodified:lastweek	Orders datemodified:lastweek
Datemodified:pastmonth	Orders datemodified:pastmonth

Table 5-3. *Type (to search by file type)*

Option	Example
Type:	Type:image
	Type:image jpeg
	Type:.doc
	Type:.pdf

Table 5-4. *Name (to search by file name or by a property name of a file)*

Option	Example
Name:	Name:vacation
	Name:wedding
	Name:budget

Typing **type:** initially displays a drop-down list of all the file types on your computer; for example, .doc or .pdf, as seen in Table 5-3. If, for example, you continue by typing **type:image** you can filter your search by various image types or search for all image types. You also can use other file types, such as type:document, type:audio, type:video, type:presentation, and so forth.

131

As you begin to type a search filter in File Explorer, a drop-down list (with all the supported filter options) is displayed. Clicking the appropriate one for your search helps you find what you are looking for more quickly. If you are searching for dates, a calendar assists you.

Filtering File Searches in Apps

When you search for files in Apps, there are categories at the top left of the search results screen that allow you to filter the results by document types.

In Figure 5-32, there are a considerable number of documents returned in the search. The results are also filtered by Document, Pictures, and Other, which significantly reduce the search results. In this case, we reduce 10,752 files to just 216 documents, which is more manageable.

Figure 5-32. Filtering file searches in Apps

Note When viewing your search results, pressing the Esc key displays your last three searches. You can click or tap directly to search again.

Searching for Content Inside Apps

The standard Start screen search in Windows 8 also allows you to search your apps and the contents of those apps quickly and simply.

When you type a search, a list of apps appears in the right pane. These are all the searchable apps installed on your computer. You can scroll the list up and down if there are more than fit on screen at one time (see Figure 5-33).

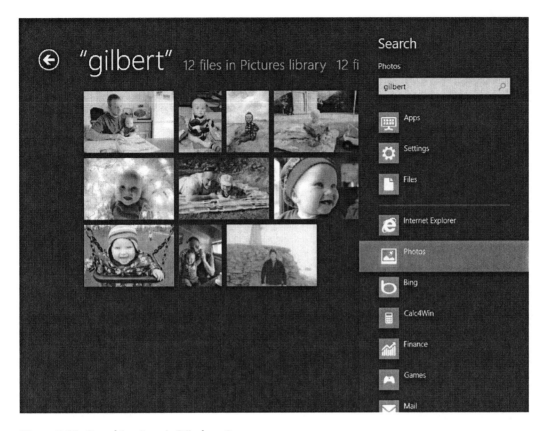

Figure 5-33. *Searching Apps in Windows 8*

When you click an app, the search results are from within that app. The right pane remains in place until you click the app. This allows you to switch between apps to search for the same thing; for example, to see which photos you have in various apps.

While in Search, you can view your previous three searches by pressing the Esc key on your keyboard. The previous three search terms appear underneath the search box (see Figure 5-34). If you wish to search a term again, then simply tap or click it.

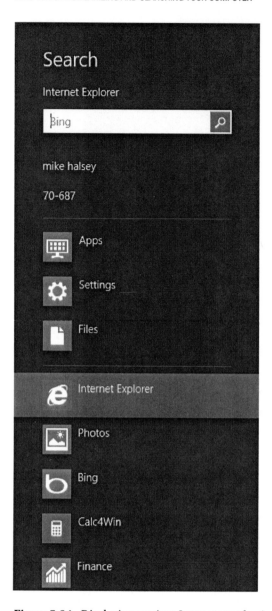

Figure 5-34. *Displaying previous Internet searches in Windows 8*

We can probably expect additional search functionality, both from Microsoft apps and from third parties, to extend the Internet search functionality in Windows 8. You find these in the Books & Reference section of the Windows Marketplace as they are released.

You can also use the search facility to suggest searches for you. If you highlight a search term or terms, the search system suggests related and relevant searches just below the text box (see Figure 5-35). This makes searching more effective in Windows 8.

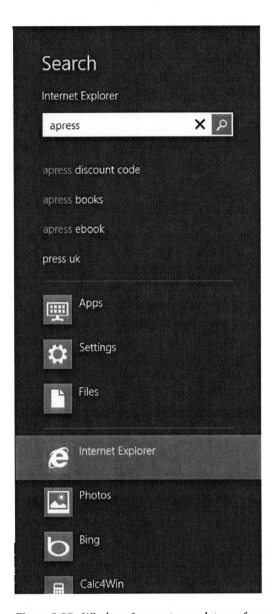

Figure 5-35. *Windows 8 suggests search terms for you*

Searching in File Explorer

File Explorer contains its own context-sensitive search box. In some ways, this is a more efficient way to search for files and documents in Windows 8 than using the Start screen.

The search box prioritizes the content. It might be prioritized by documents, pictures, music, video, a specific disk drive (internal or external), a network location, or something else (see Figure 5-36). In this way, it is flexible and more dynamic than the Start screen search, which looks almost bulky and clumsy by comparison.

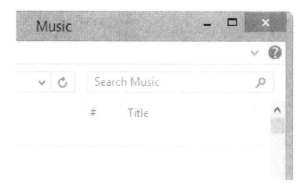

Figure 5-36. *File Explorer has its own Search box*

When searching in File Explorer, a new Search tab appears on the Ribbon. It contains tools and buttons to make search even more powerful and useful, especially for people who are less familiar with search syntax.

The Search tab on the Ribbon (see Figure 5-37), allows you to filter your search by

- the current folder and all subfolders

- Libraries, e-mail, notes, or the Internet

- when the file was last modified (opened)

- the type of file

- the file size

- file names

- specific folders

- file tags

Figure 5-37. *The Search tab on the Ribbon*

These options cover just about any search you would want to undertake in Windows 8. The Search tab on the Ribbon appears automatically the moment you type anything in the search box in File Explorer.

■ **Note**   The Search tab on the File Explorer Ribbon allows you quick access to recent searches you have made, so that you can repeat them.

Expanding Libraries with Saved Searches in Windows 8

One of the criticisms of Libraries is that you can only add folders to them. You cannot specify that a Library should only contain one or two file types, say Word and Excel files. Nor can you specify that Libraries should only contain documents created by "Jed" or tagged as "college".

This is where the true power of search in Windows 8 comes into play. It's such a cool feature that it will probably save you countless hours of lost productivity all on its own!

After you have completed a search, you can save it on the Search tab on the File Explorer Ribbon. Saving a search adds a quick link, named whatever you want, to the Favorite Links pane in File Explorer (see Figure 5-38).

Figure 5-38. *Saving searches in Windows 8*

The upshot of this is that you can create those custom-aggregated folders whenever you want, and each one is automatically and dynamically updated whenever you open it.

Let's say, for example, you search for **type:.pdf** in the search box when looking at your Documents Library. This brings up a list of all your PDF document files in your Documents Library and all subfolders. Saving this search creates something that looks and behaves like a Library consisting entirely of PDF files, which you can use whenever you need. Each time you open this saved search, the search is re-run (it literally takes a fraction of a second if the locations being searched are part of the Windows Index) and the contents are updated automatically.

You can further sort, organize, and group the contents of this search however you want, perhaps by the date they were created or the tags associated with them.

I simply cannot overstate how powerful and useful this feature is, especially when used with properly tagged files. As a way of organizing home or work documents, it is a true time-saver!

Harnessing the Full Power of Saved Searches

Let me give you an example of how powerful I believe saved searches really are. In Figure 5-39, I searched for ***.ppt? authors:mike halsey**, which displays all PowerPoint files created by Mike (and optionally) Halsey.

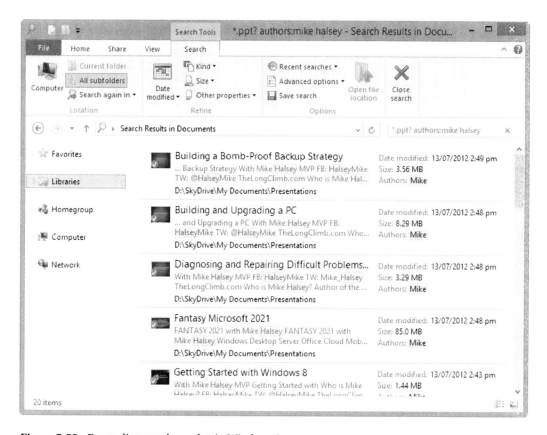

Figure 5-39. *Expanding saved searches in Windows 8*

Saving these search results creates dynamically updated folders where you can quickly and easily find the information you need. Having a saved search for all documents relating to a project name enables you to keep track of all the documents related to the project at a single location.

Saving and Sharing Your Saved Searches

Once you have created a saved search, you can create a copy of it to back it up or perhaps to share with a friend or colleague. You can do this by right-clicking the saved search in the Favorites pane in File Explorer and selecting Open Folder Location from the context menu.

You now see the saved search(es) listed and you can create copies in the same way you would with any other file on your computer. They can be backed up or shared with other computers. Note, however, that if drive assignments are different on the other computers, the search may not function correctly because searches work with drive letters and folders that all have absolute references on your computer.

Tagging Files in Microsoft Office

I've talked about adding tags to documents as you create them to help find them later on, but how do you do this? Obviously, the method by which you can add tags to documents as you save them varies considerably from one software package to another, and it can be expected that many software packages won't support this feature at all.

Microsoft Office has supported tags for some time, however, and if you use Office 2007 or later, it is a simple matter to add tags to documents as you save them.

When you first save a document in Microsoft Office (or select Save As …) you have the option to Add a Tag (see Figure 5-40).

Figure 5-40. *Adding tags to documents in Microsoft Office*

You can add other details here, including authors and title, although the software will probably automatically add some information.

All Microsoft Office programs and many programs from other software vendors support adding tags to your files when you save them. In Microsoft Office, the Save dialog box for Word, Excel, PowerPoint, and so forth, allow you to add tags in the same way. You can also add information like subjects and project managers to make files easier to find.

With other software, you need to check if tags can be added when the file is saved. If not, you can always add tags afterward in the Details pane in File Explorer.

Managing the Search and File Index in Windows 8

The reason search works very quickly in Windows 8, at least for internal storage on the computer, is that details about the files are all stored in an index database. By default, this database stores information on anything in your user folders and default Libraries. You may move, add, or remove folders (or even entire hard disks) to or from the index.

You can find the Indexing Options in the Search tab on the Ribbon in File Explorer, but you need to perform a search for the tab to appear. A simpler approach is to type **Index** at the Start screen and run Indexing Options from the Settings search results.

In the main Indexing Options are all the indexed drive and folder locations and their current indexing status (see Figure 5-41).

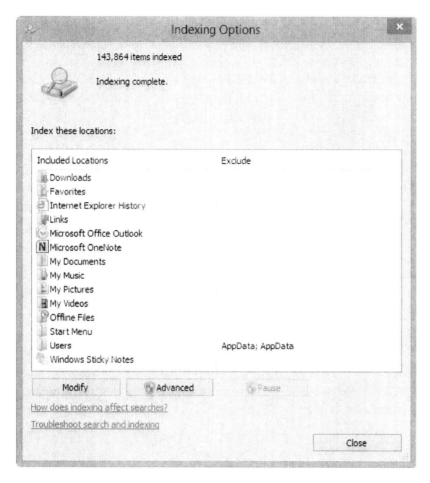

Figure 5-41. *Managing the Search Index in Windows 8*

You may find that not many files are indexed, perhaps because you have a relatively new Windows 8 installation and a great many files. In that case, the results you expect won't appear in the search results. You may see that some critical or important folders don't appear in the index.

Adding Folders to the Index

You can add (or remove) folders to the index by clicking the Modify button on the Indexing Options screen. This displays a folder list of all the drives on your computer. The current folder locations are checked (see Figure 5-42).

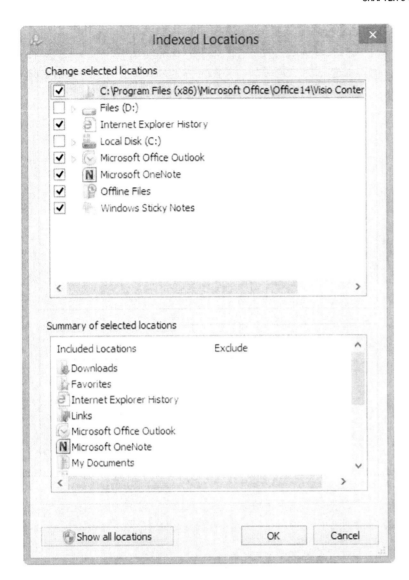

Figure 5-42. *Adding folder locations to the Indexing Options*

To add or remove folders or entire drives to the index, simply check or uncheck their boxes. When you press the OK button, the Index is refreshed to include or exclude the folders you have updated.

■ **Note** It can take some time for Windows 8 to index the contents of your hard drive, and the process slows when you are using the computer. If you need the index built quickly, then leaving the computer switched on overnight can speed up the process significantly.

Changing the Advanced Indexing Options

Clicking the Advanced button at the Indexing Options pane brings up several additional options that you may want to consider (see Figure 5-43). Chief among these, especially if you work in a business environment, is the option to index encrypted files. By default, Windows 8 doesn't index files that you have encrypted with either Microsoft or third-party software. This is because the key searchable contents of the files contained within the index aren't encrypted.

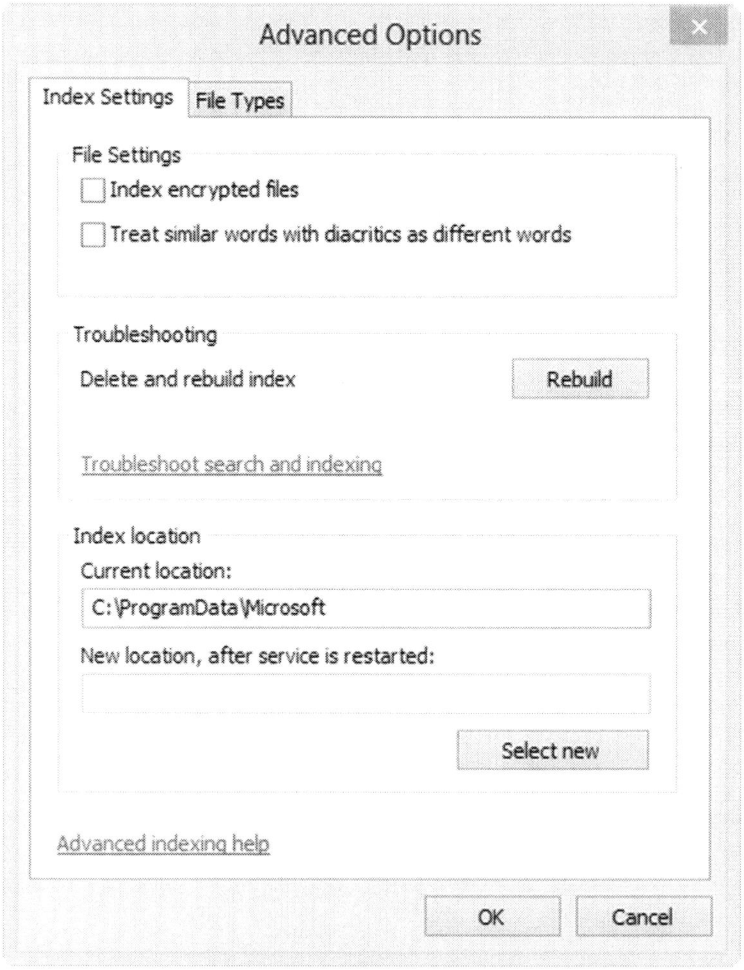

Figure 5-43. *Modifying the Advanced Index options*

For most scenarios, it is perfectly acceptable to tick this box. If you work in a governmental, financial, medical, or research and development organization, you should you seek advice, although the choice will probably be made for you, and Indexing Options will not be available.

■ **Note** Windows 8's indexing of encrypted files includes hard disks in the computer encrypted with BitLocker, if you are a user who has access to those drives.

The next option in the File Settings section enables you to turn off Windows 8's automatic correction feature to accommodate the different (albeit correct) spellings of words and the oddly spelled word.

In the Index location, section is an option to change the default location of the index. I'd like to discuss why you might want to do this and what the benefits are. The most obvious reason to do this is to increase the speed of your hard disk or to improve the resilience of an SSD. If you have a large number of files to index, then this is the only circumstance where it's possibly worthwhile to move the index.

If you have an SSD in your computer (the number of maximum write operations is finite over the life of the disk), then you may want to move the index. On modern SSDs, it shouldn't make a difference because the overall lifespan of the disk should be more than adequate. But you may have an older SSD or perform duties that involve huge amounts of file work and modification every day.

To change the location, type the *new* location of the index into the empty box with its full drive assignment (e.g. D:\Index\) and click the Select New button.

■ **Note** When you move the index, it is rebuilt from scratch when you restart your computer. Also, you cannot reuse an existing index when you reimage your computer; it rebuilds when you restart your computer.

Searching Network Locations in Windows 8

When you add extra folders and drives to the Windows 8 index, the system will not allow you to add network or other locations to the index. If you are a manager in a small office where files are shared on a Network Attached Storage drive, for example, and you want to create a saved search to monitor the progress of a project, you cannot add this location to the index.

However, you can open a network location in File Explorer from Network in the navigation pane. When you are at the correct location, you can then perform a search and save that search.

Searches of network locations can take longer than searches of files on your own computer because the search system has to read each file every time, rather than refer to its information in the index.

If you are logged into a domain on a Windows Server system, the index usually allows you to add mapped server locations to the index.

Searching the Internet from the Start Screen

One of the things we all want to do on our computers is search the Internet. Why should this be any more complex than searching in Apps, Settings, or Files on the computer? The good news is that it isn't. It's a simple job to perform searches online.

To search the Internet from the Start screen, simply start typing what you wish to search for, and when the search results appear, click the Internet Explorer tile in the right pane. This changes the search results to Bing and displays the results instantaneously (see Figure 5-44).

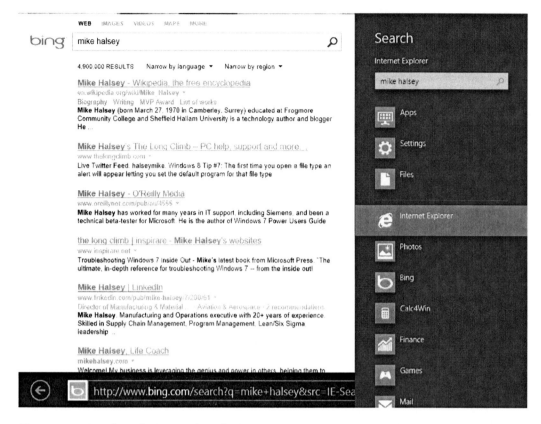

Figure 5-44. *Searching the Internet from the Start screen*

■ **Note**   We can fully expect Chrome, Firefox, and other major browsers to support the search functionality in Windows 8. It may vary from one software vendor to another, however.

Using Advanced Search Syntax in Internet Explorer

In the science-fiction series *The Hitchhiker's Guide to the Galaxy* (Pan Books, 1985), author Douglas Adams wrote, "Space is big. You just won't believe how vastly, hugely, mind-bogglingly big it is. I mean, you may think it's a long way down the road to the shops, but that's just peanuts to space." As a quote, this is an excellent analogy to the Internet.

The question is how do you find what you are looking for online when there are usually millions and sometimes billions of search results? After all, the major search engines, Bing, Google, and so forth, do a reasonable job of filtering the results for you. How do you know though that you're getting the *correct* results for what you type? Surely you're just getting the most popular generalized results.

This is where you can use search syntax options that are commonly supported by all online search engines.

- **"Enclose a few words in double quotes"** to search for those words as a complete sentence. By default, typing the words without quotes returns search results that include one or more of all the words; it does not treat them as a combined whole.

- Use a plus (+) symbol at the front of a word (e.g., **+halsey**) to guarantee that this word *must* appear in the search results. You can also use a plus symbol in front of a string of words (see preceding bullet).

- Use a minus (–) symbol to exclude a particular word or string from the results. You may want to exclude the word **-buy** or **-shopping** if you are looking for technical details of a product and want to exclude shopping and price comparison sites from the results.

- Search only a specific web site for a term by typing **site:*sitename*.com**. You may want to search for **"windows 8" site:thelongclimb.com**, for example.

- Use ***** and **?** wildcard operators. The asterisk represents a selection of letters and the question mark represents only a single letter; for example, you want to search for **"Mike H*"** or **Hals?y** if you are unsure of a spelling.

- Include Boolean operators **OR, AND**, and **NOT** in your search to narrow down the results. **Adobe software 2011 OR 2012**, for example.

There are other search operators that are specific to individual search engines. The ones I have listed here I find to be the most useful and the easiest to remember. I personally only ever use double quotes and the plus and minus signs, for example, and I get search results that I am happy with.

Appendix D features a full list of the Advanced Query Syntax (AQS) options that you can use for Windows 8 searches.

■ **Note** You can use these operators directly from the Start screen when searching for things online.

Summary

Search in Windows 8 is incredibly powerful, but the full features can be hard to remember. I believe that by far the best feature for searching is the saved search, which allows you to search by subject, workflow, author, contributors, file type, location, and more. It also allows you to search for multiple parameters simultaneously. This truly powerful feature can help you get the best out of file management and organization in Windows 8.

Elsewhere, however, the ability to search from the Start screen by simply typing is very welcome. We can expect both Microsoft and third-party providers to plug some extremely useful functionality into this feature in the coming years. It's not quite as powerful and flexible as search in File Explorer, however.

Libraries are also significantly more powerful than you might first believe, with saved search and Windows Media Center able to extend their functionality considerably. I have long argued that Libraries should be more flexible by default, but the ability to create flexibility through simple workarounds greatly increases their usefulness.

CHAPTER 6

Printing and Managing Printers

In these days of external hard drives, flash drives, TV tuners, graphics tablets, HD webcams, cordless headphones, and more, it is always a printer that is commonly the first and most important peripheral that we purchase for our computers.

These days, wireless printers are becoming so common that you no longer need to have the machine physically connected to your computer. It can easily be shared between multiple computers and hidden out of sight where it won't be easily noticeable when you're relaxing.

Network printers in the workplace have already been common for years now, and you'll be pleased to hear that setting up and managing printers in Windows 8 is as straightforward as ever.

Installing Printers in Windows 8

Windows 8 performs a very neat trick that no other version of Windows has ever done before with printers (and other network devices). If these devices exist and Windows 8 sees them on the network, it automatically installs them for you.

This means that the first time you try to print a document you'll probably find that your network printer is already listed. Windows 8 searches Windows Update for a driver and installs these devices quietly in the background. So, ordinarily, you simply plug in your printer, and Windows 8 takes care of the installation.

It is unlikely, however, that Windows 8 will be able to install printers with drivers not included in Windows 8 or not available on Windows Update. If this is the case, you'll need to uninstall and reinstall the printer. You can do this in the Devices and Printers window (see Figure 6-1). Type **devices** at the Start screen and you will find Devices and Printers listed in the Settings search results.

Tip To uninstall a printer or another device (perhaps because the driver is not properly installed), right-click the device, and then select Remove Device from the options.

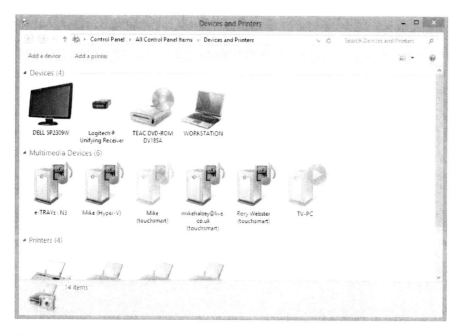

Figure 6-1. *The Devices and Printers window*

There are two main ways to add printers to Windows 8 using Devices and Printers. On the toolbar at the top of the window, you can select the link to **Add devices and printers** or you can choose the **Advanced printer setup**.

Initially, as you will see in Figures 6-2 and 6-3, these options operate in exactly the same way, though they look slightly different. Both options search for network printers and other devices, and display them for you. Where they differ most greatly is in the driver installation for the hardware.

Figure 6-2. *Adding Devices and Printers to Windows 8 in the Add a Device dialog box*

Figure 6-3. *Adding a printer to Windows 8 using Add Printer*

In the Add a Device dialog box (see Figure 6-2), Windows 8 simply installs what it thinks is the best available driver for that piece of hardware. If Windows 8 has previously found your printer on its own and installed it with an incorrect driver, it will reinstall *the same* incorrect driver.

If the printer isn't found automatically, which is common in business environments, the **Not finding what you're looking for?** link simply opens a Help window with a note telling you how the problem may be fixed.

It is the Add Printer dialog box (see Figure 6-3) that you will find helpful for all but the easiest to install printers.

If the printer is not automatically found, you can click **The printer that I want isn't listed** to bring up additional installation options for the device (see Figure 6-4).

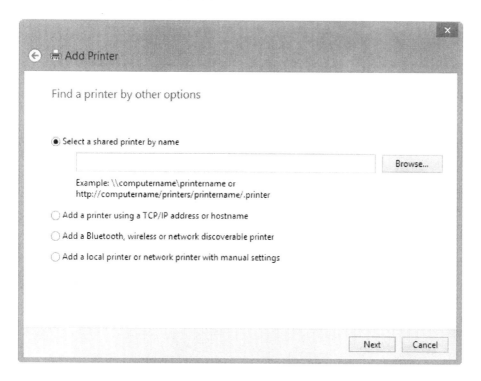

Figure 6-4. *Manually adding a printer*

In the Add Printer window, you have the following options:

- You can add a printer by its name on the network (if you know it; it is usually provided by your IT department).

- You can add it by its IP address (more on finding this in a minute).

- You can add a Bluetooth printer, if you have one.

- You can choose to manually configure the printer depending on which port it is located.

All things being equal, you don't likely know the IP address or the network name of a printer. One quick way around this is to check how the printer is configured on another computer. You can do this in Devices and Printers (in Windows 7 and Windows 8). Right-click the printer and select Printer Properties. Under the Ports tab, you should see the address of the printer (see Figure 6-5).

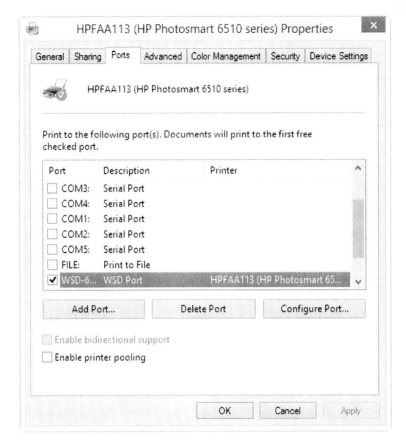

Figure 6-5. *Checking the address of a printer*

▦ **Tip** Let's say you want to add an older parallel device to Windows 8. Choosing the **Add a local printer or network printer with manual settings** allows you to select the LPT port that the printer is plugged into.

On a home or small business network, finding a printer's IP is relatively straightforward, though the actual method varies depending on the make of your router. The following steps provide a general approach, which you should be able to tweak for your own setup.

1. Open Internet Explorer.

2. Access your router login by typing **192.168.0.1** (sometimes 192.168.1.1 or 192.168.2.1) and pressing Enter.

3. Log in to your router with your username and password (if these are still *admin* and *password*, you should change them!).

4. Find the LAN settings.

5. Look for the Ethernet settings.

6. Look for the name of your network printer; its IP address is listed here (see Figure 6-6).

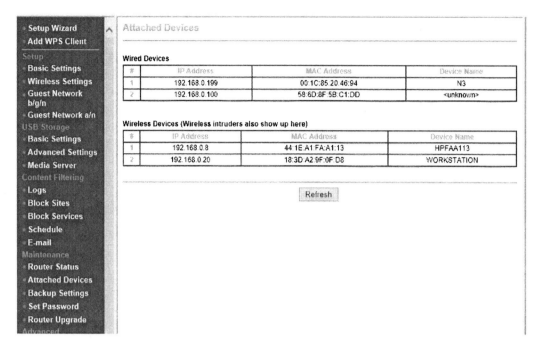

Figure 6-6. *Finding a printer's IP address on the network*

■ **Note** If you have to reset your router, perhaps because your Internet connection has gone down, then the IP address of your printer might have changed. This requires that you uninstall and reinstall the printer on all your computers because Windows locks the driver to a specific IP address. To get around this problem, you can set the printer to a static IP address in your router setup. Consult your manual or contact your ISP for details on how to do this.

Setting Default Printers for Different Places

If you use the same computer in different places, perhaps both at home and at work or in different office locations, you don't want to spend time setting and resetting the default printer whenever you want to print a document.

Windows 8 allows you to set the default printer depending on the network that you are connected to at the time. In Devices and Printers, select a printer and then click the Manage Default Printers on the toolbar at the top of the window.

In the dialog box (see Figure 6-7), you can set a different default printer for each network you connect to. The networks and installed printers are all listed by name and are available from drop-down menus with the defaults showing in the main pane of the dialog box.

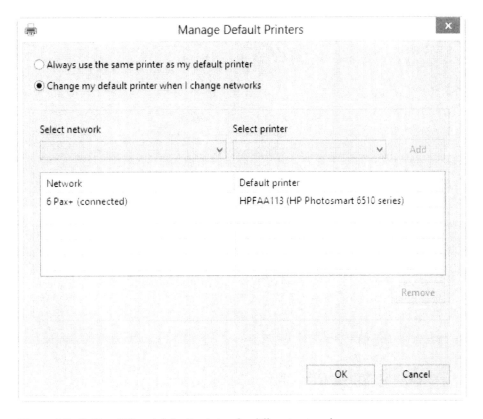

Figure 6-7. *Setting different default printers for different networks*

Using this feature, you are able to set Windows to automatically change the default printer on your computer the moment you connect to a different network. This means that if you have been on this network before and have already installed the printer driver(s), you can be sure that whatever you print is sent to the correct printer.

Managing Printers in Windows 8

Long gone are the days when printers only did a single thing: accept an input and print it onto paper. Now printers come with a huge number of options for controlling every aspect of that output and the hardware itself. This, coupled with new eco-printing features intended to save both ink and paper, can make printers very difficult to manage.

Printers and their driver software differ by make and model, but most of the functionality across devices is the same. Thus, you may find that some of the following screenshots don't match up exactly with what you see on your own computer. Windows 8 does a good job of standardizing the settings for printers, however.

You can manage your printer in Devices and Printers by right-clicking the printer and selecting Printer Properties from the options.

In the main printer properties dialog box under the General tab (see Figure 6-8), you find the name of the printer (which you can change by simply typing a new name). You can also input comments about the machine's physical location, as well as other notes (perhaps about how to insert paper for double-sided printing if there is no duplex unit installed).

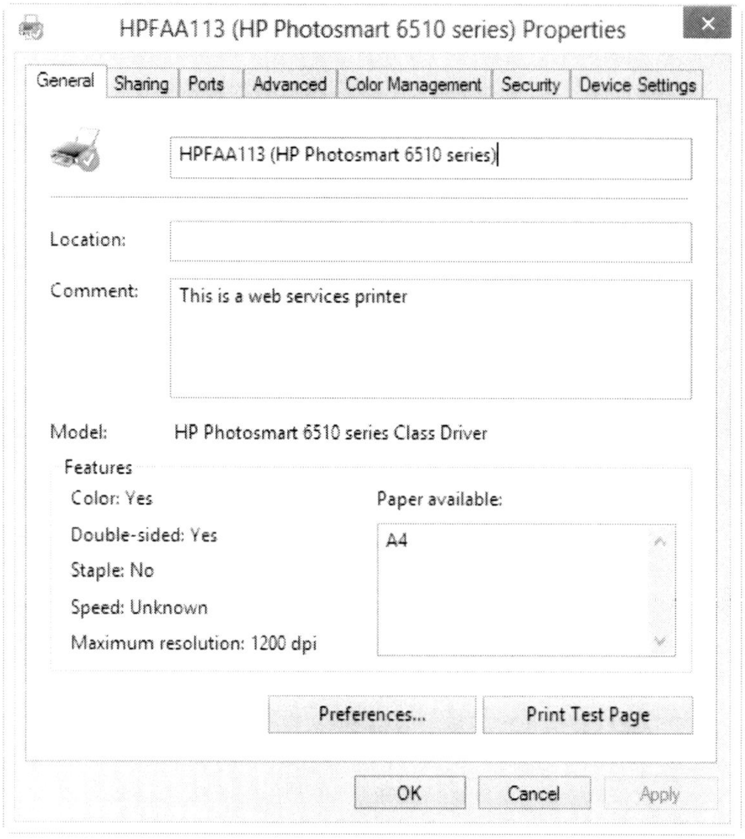

Figure 6-8. *Working with general printer properties*

The Preferences button opens the printing preferences, which I discuss in the "Managing Printing in Windows 8" section later in this chapter. You can also print a test page here to check that the printer is working.

■ **Note**   The configuration and options in the printer dialog boxes vary according to the make and model of the printer.

On the Sharing tab, you can choose whether you want to share the printer over your network (the computer that is sharing the printer needs to be left on for the printer to be accessible) and you can give it a name (see Figure 6-9).

■ **Tip**   Earlier I discussed finding a printer by its name. A printer with a simple name is easier for people to find and remember. Easy names may include a floor number, room number, and/or printer type.

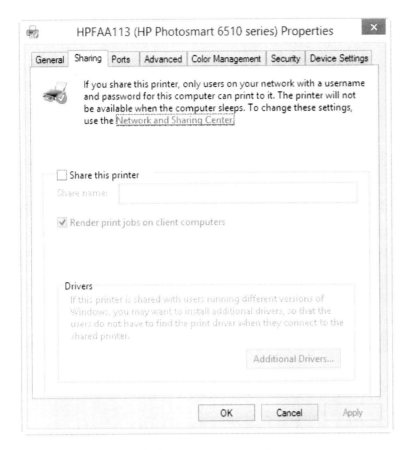

Figure 6-9. *Working with Sharing printer properties*

Shared printers may be accessed by computers running other versions of Windows, such as Windows 7, Windows Vista, or Windows XP. If this is likely, click the Additional Drivers button to choose drivers that automatically load from your computer as needed.

You probably won't want to change anything in the Ports tab (see Figure 6-10), but if you have had to reset your router, the IP address of the printer may have automatically changed. Thus, after resetting a router you may find that you can no longer print to a particular printer—and you will have to reinstall it.

Figure 6-10. *Working with printer ports*

The Ports tab is also useful if you are using older parallel or serial printers, which are very complicated to install and configure correctly, but are still found in use in some business environments.

There are many useful options available in the Advanced tab (see Figure 6-11), including

- The ability to specify that a printer is only accessible between certain hours. This is useful if you are trying to cut down on waste.

- The ability to choose how the printer prioritizes print jobs that are sent to it. You might want to set this option on a shared printer to only spool a job after the previous one has finished (if the printer doesn't have much internal memory). Generally, you should not need to do this because Windows 8 is excellent at managing print jobs.

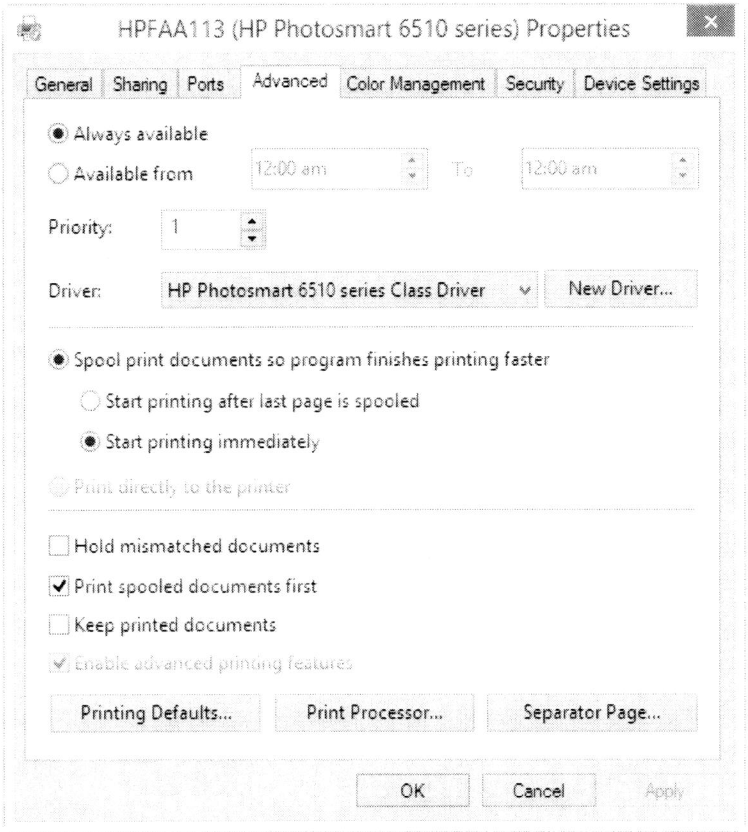

Figure 6-11. *Working with advanced printer properties*

The Color Management options (see Figure 6-12) allow you to set a color profile that matches your monitor. This is especially useful if you have a carefully calibrated screen for color accuracy. (I will talk more about color management shortly.)

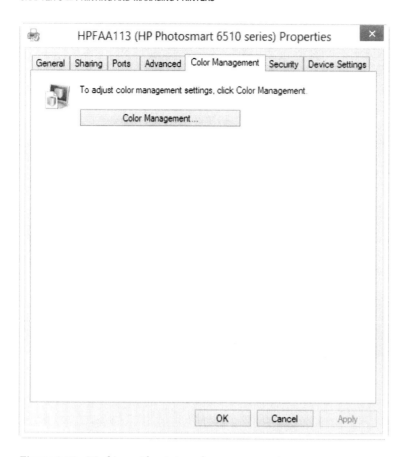

Figure 6-12. Working with printer color management

The options on the Security tab allow you to specify who can control what on the printer (see Figure 6-13). Here you may want to make changes, including giving users computer permissions to manage print jobs (such as deleting stuck jobs).

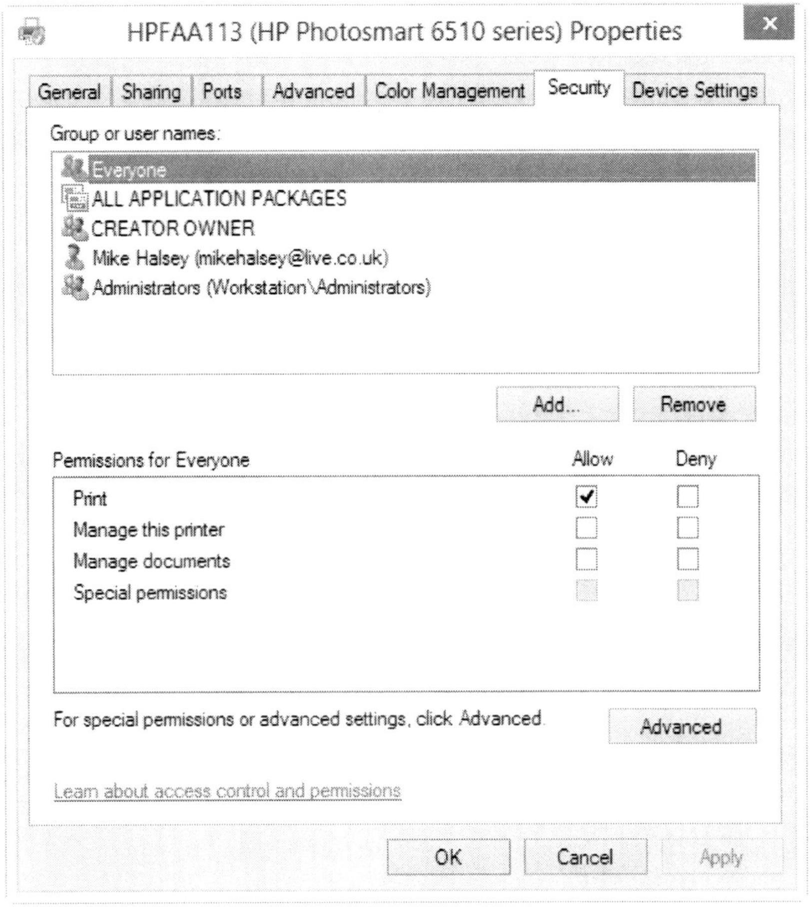

Figure 6-13. *Working with printer security*

To change permissions, select the appropriate users in the top pane. You can then change their options by checking the boxes in the bottom half of the tab. These basic controls are all you need to grant and deny users access to a printer. Should you require more control over access to printers, such as printer availability time and which users can print and how often, click the Advanced button.

It is now common for printer manufacturers to add a custom tab that provides extra information, such as ink and toner status, and links to purchase official consumables and accessories online.

Managing Color Profiles for Printers and Displays

Sometimes you absolutely *must* have color accuracy, perhaps if you are a photographer or graphic artist. To help with this, you can load specific color profiles into Windows 8 for both printers and displays. Open the Color Management window by searching the word **color** at the Start screen and running Color Management from the Settings results.

In Color Management (see Figure 6-14), you can load specific color profiles for both printers and displays if they have the correct manufacturer profile file. The file formats are Color Device Model Profile (*.cdmp), Color Appearance Model Profile (*.camp), Gamut Mapping Model Profile (*.gmmp), and ICC (*.icm).

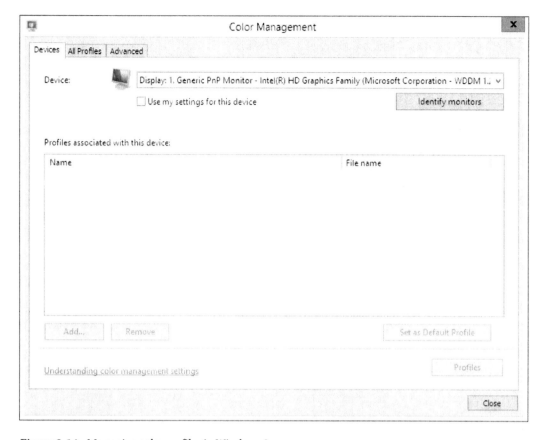

Figure 6-14. *Managing color profiles in Windows 8*

Choose the device you want to view the current color profile in from the drop-down menu at the top of the window. To add a color profile to the currently selected device, check the **Use my settings for this device** box. You can then select an installed color profile.

You can add a profile from the All Profiles tab, where you will find the currently installed color profiles. Click the Add button at the bottom of the window to load a new color profile.

There are controls and options on the Advanced tab that enable you to further specify the way your color profiles are used for different types of images and art. You can also run a tool that helps calibrate the brightness, color, and contrast settings for your monitor so that what you see on screen are faithful representations of true color.

Managing Shared Printers in Windows 8

In the previous section, I talked a little bit about managing the security of a shared printer. This can also be done directly from the Devices and Printers window. When a printer is selected, you can open Print Server Properties from the toolbar.

You can also manage security properties for the printer in the Print Server Properties dialog box (see Figure 6-15), which offers additional security options, such as whether or not users can edit the print queue or change the print settings.

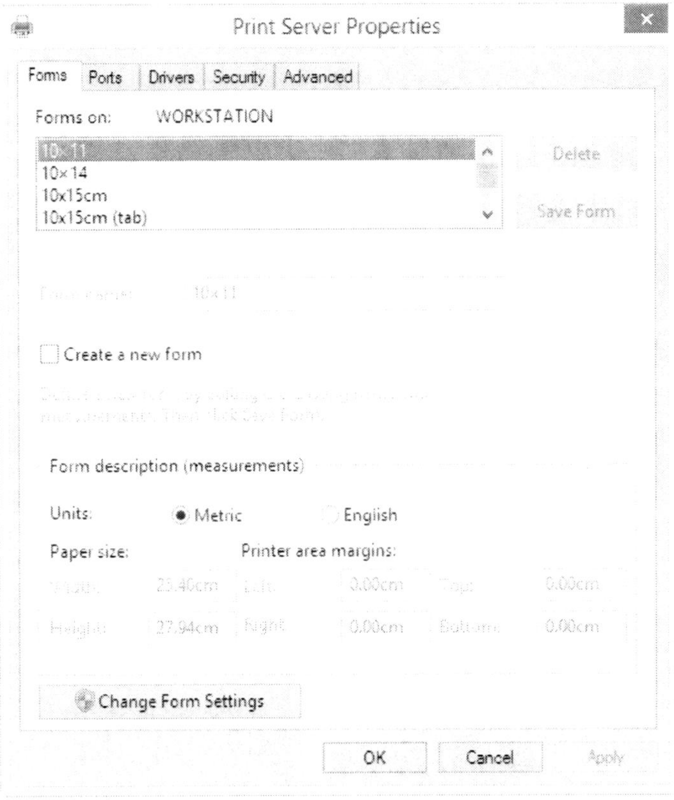

Figure 6-15. *Managing Print Server Properties*

Managing Printing in Windows 8

While there are many options for managing your printer(s), there are usually even more for managing the printing itself. These features differ from one printer to another, but the general printing preferences are the same.

You can most easily access the printing preferences by right-clicking a printer and selecting Printing Preferences from the options.

On the first tab in this dialog box, which may vary in name (see Figure 6-16), are the most common options, including the default page size, page orientation, and whether the printer uses single- or double-sided printing by default (you need an internal duplexing unit to take advantage of this).

Tip Once you know whether your printer's duplex unit flips the paper on the long or short edge of the paper. I recommend writing this information on a label and sticking it to the printer so that it is easy for others to use double-sided printing on their own computers.

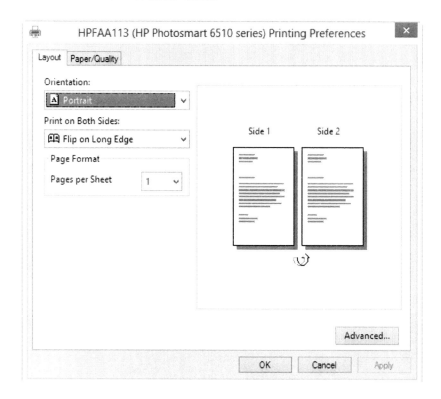

Figure 6-16. *Working with basic printing preferences*

The options on the Paper tab allow you to choose the default paper size, collation of multipage print jobs (a very useful option in an office), and the printer's default source tray.

■ **Tip**   If you want to change the default printing options for the printer, perhaps to set it to print only in black draft mode to save ink or toner, you can do this in the Advanced settings. Every time someone prints from that printer (and on that computer) afterward, these are the default print options (unless changed manually for just one job).

If you want finer control over the printer's settings, click the Advanced button, see Figure 6-17, which displays a list of all the controls.

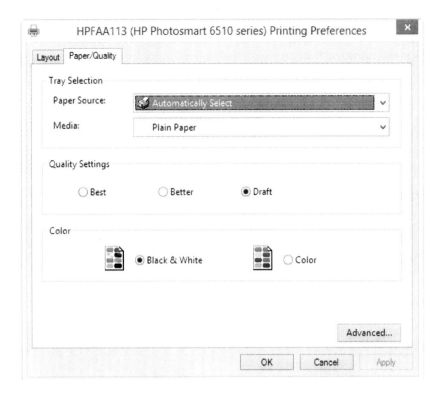

Figure 6-17. *Working with paper preferences*

■ **Tip** If you are printing photographs, you want to make sure that eco and draft features are switched off so that you get the best quality prints.

Working with Wireless Printers in Windows 8

I mentioned earlier in the chapter that resetting your router may also reset the IP address on your network wireless printer.

If this happens, the best option is to uninstall and reinstall the printer. You can set the printer to have a static IP address, however not all routers support this functionality. Check the router's manual or consult your ISP's support department.

Sometimes it is difficult to figure out how to connect a wireless printer to your network. If you have a wired printer, it's easy enough to just plug the printer into the router or switch panel with an RJ45 Ethernet cable.

To connect a wireless printer to your network, you need to find the WPS buttons on both the router and the printer. These buttons allow you to pair the two devices wirelessly without a password.

1. Press the WPS button on your router.

2. As soon as you can (within 30 seconds), press the WPS button on the printer.

These two devices should now pair. Occasionally, however, a router refuses to see a printer, even when the WPS buttons have been pressed. In this event, you should contact your ISP's support department or consult the router manual to find the best way to pair the router with a wireless device.

■ **Tip** You can also pair computers, printers and other devices by pressing the WPS button on your router if the computer—normally tablets or laptops—or device also has a WPS or similarly labeled button. Check the documentation that came with the device to see if this function is supported.

Obtaining the IP Address of a Network Printer

The Devices and Printers page (see Figure 6-18) is a very useful way to manage network resources that your computer can see. You can best access it by searching for "devices" on the Start screen and running it from the search results, which you will find in Settings. All printers and other network devices that Windows 8 can see are displayed here. You can use the information provided to find the IP address of a device.

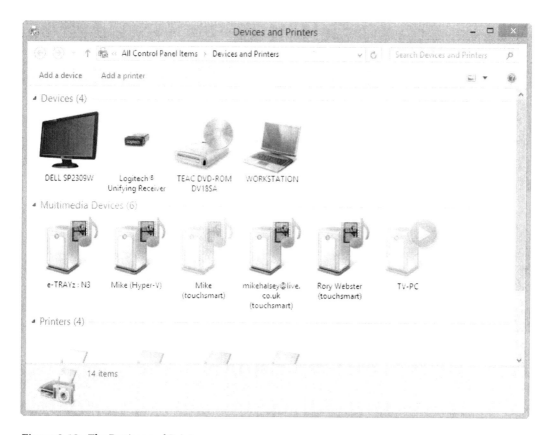

Figure 6-18. *The Devices and Printers page*

Perform the following two steps to find the IP address of a device in the Devices and Printers page:

1. Right-click on the printer you want to find the IP address for.

2. Click the Hardware tab in the window that appears.

The IP address is listed in the location information at the bottom of the window.

░ **Note** Windows may display the IPv6 address for a device. If this happens, you can get the numeric IP address from your router.

Top Printing Tips

There are some great ways to get a little more out of your printer's ink and toner. They begin with purchasing the right printer. When purchasing a printer, follow these tips:

- If you can afford it, buy a printer with in-built duplexing (double-sided printing). This saves paper.

- Check the cost of full-price consumables (ink cartridges and toner) and compare it against prices for similar printers by other manufacturers.

- Do some research online about the printer's TCO (total cost of ownership). This information may be provided in a magazine review or in a product group test.

- Find out if you can use cheaper compatible ink and toner cartridges. Some printers have "chipped" cartridges that require you to use official manufacturer ink.

To get more life out of your ink cartridges and toner, there are a few things you can do to prolong their life.

- If you are not going to use your printer for a while, keep the ink cartridges in a cool, dry place (you can even wrap them in plastic film and put them in the refrigerator). This prevents the ink from drying up. This *does not* apply to toner, which does not dry out.

- When your toner cartridge is low, you can shake the cartridge to loosen up more toner, which results in a longer lifespan. If you do this, you *must* read the following cautionary note!

- Think about if you *really* need to print something. Most of the people I know don't actually use most of the printed material they create.

░ **Caution** When shaking a toner cartridge, you should always make sure your arms are fully covered, that you are wearing disposable gloves, and that you do not breathe in any waste toner. Some laser printer toners are carcinogenic. You should always wash your hands thoroughly after handling cartridges, especially refillable ones.

Summary

Working with and managing printers is always something people ask me about because these peripherals are generally used more than other devices. The one piece of eco advice I give on using printers is to first ask yourself the question, "Do I really need to print this document?" By far the best way to save paper, ink, and money is to not print a document or picture.

The controls for installing and managing printers in Windows 8 are excellent, although some of the most useful ones are hidden. These include the ability to autoset the default printer at different locations and networks, and the color management tools, which are essential to creative professionals and very useful to anybody printing high-quality photographs at home.

■ ■ ■

CHAPTER 7

Having Fun with Games, Photos, Music, and Video

Despite the business origins of the PC, Windows has always been a gaming platform. Despite predictions on the death of PC gaming in favor of consoles, Windows 8 brings some new features to the mix that put gaming front and center of the PC for the first time.

There is new integration between Windows 8 and other Microsoft platforms that will be built upon and expanded in coming years, such as the ability to start a game on one device and then continue it on another.

With gaming on a PC comes some responsibility, especially if you are a parent, because controlling the games your children play is becoming increasingly difficult as the Internet provides access to games, entertainment, and content that may not be suitable for children.

When it comes to nongaming fun, Windows 8 is as good as any version before it—with excellent photo, music, and video playback and editing facilities, and Media Center for watching and recording live TV.

Finally, we have what will probably become the perennial Windows 8 gaming platform: tablets. With their sensors and accelerometers, these devices are perfect gaming platforms.

In this chapter, I'll talk you through how to have fun with your PC: integrating your PC with your Xbox 360; enjoying the latest gaming technologies, including 3D; and viewing your photos and videos.

Managing Games in Windows 8

If you've used the Games Center in Windows Vista or Windows 7 to manage, launch, and update your games, you will find that it's gone in Windows 8. It has been replaced by the new Apps.

The reasons for this include a shift toward apps on the part of Microsoft, but also the rise of game management and delivery platforms—such as Steam—that are central locations for purchasing, updating, and managing your games, your account, and other things. These platforms provide central locations for purchasing, updating, and managing games, player settings, and achievements.

Microsoft has also expanded their own Xbox Live service to cover the Windows Phone platform and Windows 8.

■ **Note**   If you install a Windows game that is not managed by Steam, Xbox Live, or another management service, you need to update the game manually. Updates are posted on the web site of the game's publisher.

One of the biggest issues for gamers is updates. This is primarily why platforms such as Steam and Origin have taken off in such a big way. Through these platforms, users no longer have to manually find, download, and install sometimes complicated updates.

Xbox Games

In some ways, the Xbox branding causes confusion in Windows 8. For example, you can buy games on both the Windows Store and the new Xbox Games app. The difference is purely a matter of branding. Only games whose vendors have bought into Xbox are for sale on the app.

In Chapter 2, I said that Windows Store alerts you when updates are available for your downloaded apps and games. The Xbox Games app also alerts you when updates are available for your games (see Figure 7-1).

Figure 7-1. *Buying games in Xbox Games*

While Microsoft wants the Xbox Games app to be a hub for games that run in Windows 8, these are not the only games that can be bought there. All Xbox Live–branded PC games are available, along with games for your Xbox console if you have one.

You can also use the Xbox Games app to manage your avatar, profile, and account. This is much simpler than performing these tasks on the console itself, especially if you are doing it on a computer with a keyboard and mouse.

Xbox SmartGlass

While the Xbox Games app is a central location to buy and manage games and to manage your account, the Xbox SmartGlass app is a tool for remotely controlling your Xbox console.

With this downloadable app, you can control every aspect of your console from your PC. This includes the ability to remotely control your games without having to use the dedicated Xbox controller (see Figure 7-2).

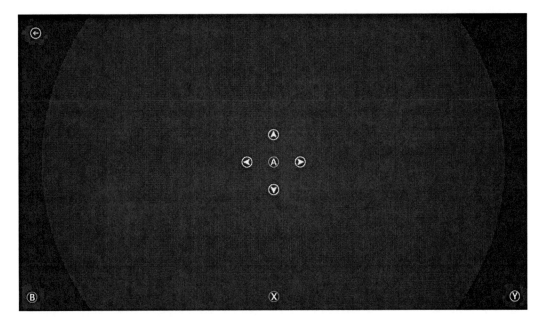

Figure 7-2. *Using your Windows 8 PC as a remote Xbox console controller*

In truth, this app is of limited use and the remote control facility is only useful if you own a Windows 8 tablet, on games where the repositioning of controls works in an ergonomic way, or where drag operations are useful. It will be interesting to see if future Xbox console games come with specific features that take advantage of this app.

In order to use the Xbox SmartGlass app, you need to be logged into the app, Windows 8, and your Xbox console on the same Live ID. So if, for example, you are playing a game that is logged into the Live ID of another user, the Xbox SmartGlass app won't connect to the console.

Managing Game Ratings for Children

One of the biggest concerns for parents is the suitability of the games their children play in Windows. With the Windows Vista introduction of the Games Center, you could set age ratings for games so that children could play only games that were appropriate.

In practice, however, this only worked with games that had bought into the Games for Windows branding, which few did. With the removal of the Games Center, this facility is gone, but not completely. Windows 8 Family Safety provides all the facilities you need to block unsuitable games (see Figure 7-3).

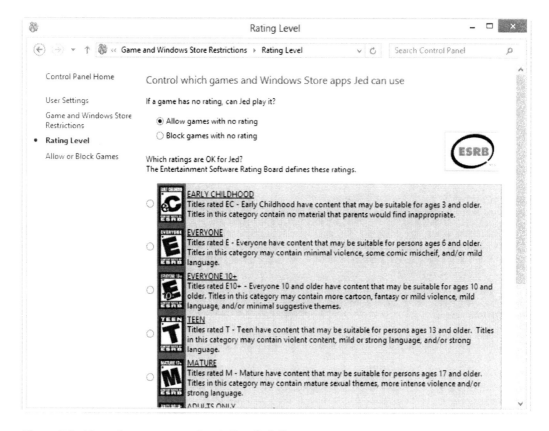

Figure 7-3. *Managing game age ratings in Family Safety*

I showed you how to set up Family Safety in Chapter 3. It is a fully-featured way to manage your children's game playing. I recommend it. With these controls, you can choose which games your children are allowed to play, the types of web sites they can visit, *and* the times they can use the computer.

To use this facility, each user must have an account on the computer. If you use local accounts rather than signing in with a Windows Live ID, you will need to create specific accounts for your children. This is most likely if you have very young children who do not need access to services such as e-mail.

Where Are the Traditional Desktop Games?

With Windows 7 Professional, you might know that the games—including Solitaire, Minesweeper, and chess—were hidden by default. They could be turned on in the Programs and Features page under Turn Windows Features On and Off.

With Windows 8, desktop games are no longer a part of Windows 8, though you might find the company you bought your computer from has preloaded some games for you.

Systems Administrators uses a Windows feature called AppLocker to specify which programs and apps are permitted to be installed on a Windows 8 computer. They use this facility to block games, and there's honestly no way around it on a managed system.

On an unmanaged Windows 8 system, you will still have access to the new games; but as I said, the old desktop favorites are gone forever.

Configuring Windows 8 for the Latest Games

Casual gamers will have little trouble playing the latest games from the Windows Store or Xbox Games on Windows 8 computers and tablets. Indeed, for some years now games have been far more popular on tablets than on desktop computers because of the new and fun ways in which we can interact with them and because the lower hardware specification of tablets means game companies have had to create simpler games overall.

But what if you're an enthusiast, which is fairly likely if you're reading this. How would you configure your computer to run the latest first-person shooters?

I'm not going to recommend specific graphics cards and other hardware, as these change so often that anything I write would quickly be out of date. There are some things you can look for when purchasing a new computer or computer parts, however, which I discuss in the next section. There are also things that you can do with Windows 8 itself.

So how can you configure Windows 8 to run the best and newest games? One of the first considerations is your antivirus software. Windows Defender, which is installed by default in Windows 8, is an excellent choice for games, primarily because it is lightweight but also because it doesn't do any major scanning when you are using the PC for other things.

Some third-party antivirus solutions also detect when games are running—usually by detecting something running fullscreen—and hibernates their scanning engines.

As a power user, I find Windows Defender perfectly adequate, so I don't use third-party antivirus software. If you are a gamer, however, this is something you should think about if you are considering purchasing a third-party package.

The amount of software you have running in the background can also make a difference. For example, you might have Microsoft's SkyDrive software running in the background, keeping a cloud backup of your files, or perhaps you have an alternative such as Google Drive, Dropbox, Mozy, and so on. These can slow down your Internet connection. If you are gaming, you may want to switch these off.

■ **Tip**   The upload speed on your Internet connection is as important for gaming as your download speed. If you have an older ADSL connection with a healthy download speed of 5Mbps but only a 0.6Mbps upload speed, for example, it can result in being kicked from servers. One player's slow connection adversely impacts the other players' experience (see Figure 7-4). The reason for this is that when you are gaming online, you are sending almost as much data as you are receiving.

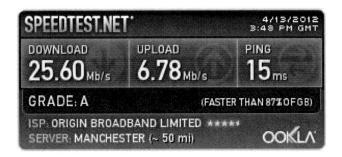

Figure 7-4. You can test your Internet connection speed using services like www.speedtest.net

Do the following to close an app:

1.   From the Start screen, move your mouse to the top left of the screen.

2.   When the thumbnail for the most recent running app appears, move the mouse downward to reveal all the running app thumbnails.

3.   Right-click the app you wish to close. Select Close from the options that appear.

Do the following to close a desktop task:

1.   From the desktop, click the Show Hidden Icons arrow in the far right of the Taskbar. This is the small Up arrow next to the system tray. If you do not see this arrow, there are no minimized programs running in the system tray.

2.   Right-click the program you wish to terminate (hovering over an icon will tell you what the program is).

3.   Select Exit or Close from the options that appear.

You may also have software and driver updaters running in the background that are slowing down your computer. You may be able to shut these down from the desktop in the same way, but perhaps you don't need them running to begin with.

Some of these updates can be very useful and are very important indeed. This includes the updaters from Adobe, which are used to fix security flaws that are very commonly exploited by malware. There may be other programs that you don't need, however. These include quick launchers for your scanner, printer, or Blu-ray software. It also includes utilities that came preinstalled on your computer, such as a quick launcher for media files.

To shut down these programs so that they don't autostart with Windows, do the following:

1.   Press Ctrl+Alt+Del on your keyboard.

2.   From the options that appear select Task Manager (this can also be launched by right-clicking the Taskbar).

3.   Click the Startup tab in the Task Manager (see Figure 7-5).

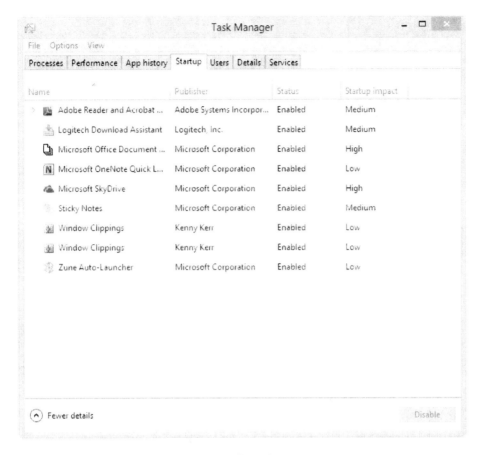

Figure 7-5. Managing Startup programs in the Task Manager

4.   Click the program you do not want to run at startup.

5.   Press the Disable button.

You should repeat steps 4 and 5 for all other software you want to disable at startup.

■ **Note**   Once you have configured your Startup programs, you should not need to switch off programs when you are gaming.

Choosing and Upgrading Your Gaming Hardware

Building a good gaming PC is a challenge, not least because the hardware can be extremely expensive for the best kit. But it is possible to choose or build a PC specifically for gaming on a budget. I want to talk you through what to look for and what to purchase.

Motherboard

When choosing a motherboard, it is best to select one that can run the highest overall speeds (in GHz), even if this makes the board capable of running much faster than the hardware you plug into it. This is to ensure that the motherboard is upgradable in the long-term. This will save you money and give you greater flexibility when it comes to upgrading.

Try to choose a board that offers the new SATA 600 ports so that you can attach the new generation of high-speed solid-state drives (SSD)—more on these shortly. Also, try to choose a board offering support for either Crossfire (AMD) or SLI (nVidia). I will talk more about this shortly.

Processor

The processor is probably the least important consideration when it comes to choosing or building a gaming PC because most of the gaming processing is done by your graphics card. The important consideration here is the clock speed (again in GHz).

A computer can only run as fast as its slowest component, so if you have chosen memory that runs faster than your processor, its overall speed will throttle to match that of the processor. The same applies to the motherboard. If this has a slow clock speed, then nothing will be able to run faster than it.

Memory

With your computer's memory, it's long been established that if you don't have enough memory installed on your computer for Windows and your installed programs, the computer will not run as quickly as it otherwise could. This is certainly true of a netbook upgraded from 1GB of RAM to 2GB, or a PC upgraded from 2GB to 4GB.

Above the 4GB level, the speed benefits decrease significantly. You can still get noticeable speed increases on some machines by installing 6GB or even 8GB of RAM, but there is no need to install more than this unless you are also using your computer for very memory-intensive applications such as mega-multipixel digital photo editing, video creation, or computer-aided design.

■ **Note**   If you are using the 32-bit version of Windows 8 on your PC, your computer will only be able to "see" a maximum of 4GB RAM. This includes any memory on your graphics card. If you have 2x 2GB memory cards and 1GB graphics card memory, Windows 8 will ignore one of the 2GB memory cards completely because it only sees complete cards.

Hard Disk

If you can afford it, put your money into a fast solid-state drive (SSD), preferably (if your motherboard supports the standard) one running on the new SATA 600 sockets. However, purchasing SSDs is more complicated than traditional hard drives. This is because manufacturers' memory chip speeds vary wildly. It is wise to seek up-to-date reviews of SSDs online before you buy. You can normally find these on computer magazines web sites.

Having an SSD as your main hard disk can significantly improve the speed of Windows 8 and your games. You need to make sure, however, that the main hard disk is of a suitable size. This is where the cost can rise sharply. In Appendix D, I will show you how to best determine the size of the hard disk that you need.

Graphics Card

Earlier in this chapter I spoke about SLI and Crossfire. These are technologies—by nVidia and AMD, respectively— that allow you to connect two or three graphics cards so that they can be used in parallel. This doesn't *actually* double or triple the graphics processing power—each extra card adds about an extra 50 percent of the overall computing power of the first card. You need to choose your motherboard carefully, however, because you are locked into using cards from a specific company if you use the multicard feature.

If you want to use only a single graphics card on your computer, then whether the motherboard supports SLI or Crossfire doesn't matter—you can use an nVidia or AMD card as you desire.

Some people have strong preferences regarding AMD and nVidia graphics cards. There is tremendous brand loyalty to one or the other. The overall quality and speed of the cards, especially in the price/performance mid-range, does vary quite substantially—with different companies pulling ahead periodically with new, faster, and more powerful hardware, only to lose ground to a competitor's innovation.

Before you choose a graphics card, or even a motherboard in this respect, it can be well worth checking out the online test reviews of graphics cards by PC magazines and other gaming web sites.

Working with Gaming Peripherals

Sometimes you will have USB gaming hardware attached to your PC, which could include a joystick or paddle controller. To access the controls for managing these in Windows, search for **game** at the Start screen and select **Set up USB game controllers** from the Settings results to run the Game Controllers dialog box (see Figure 7-6).

Figure 7-6. *Managing Game Controllers in Windows 8*

In this dialog box you can manage and change the properties of gaming controllers, such as inverting the horizontal and vertical axis of a joystick (see Figure 7-7).

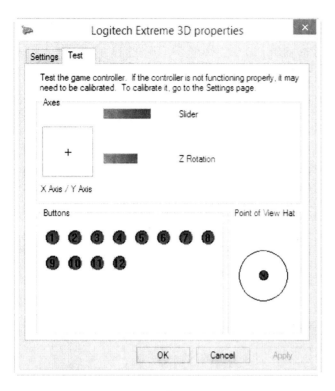

Figure 7-7. *Managing gaming hardware such as joysticks*

The Why of WEI

The Windows Experience Index (WEI) was introduced in Windows Vista to provide a simple way for people to benchmark their computers. You can access the WEI score by running System from the Control Panel, where you will see your WEI score listed (if it has been calculated yet) along with a link to access the full WEI information. To get to this, click Windows Experience Index and you will be presented with the full score figures (see Figure 7-8).

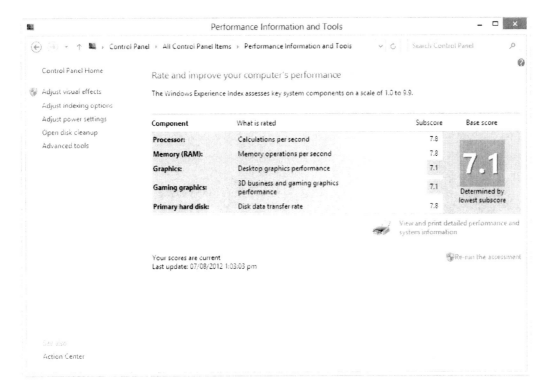

Figure 7-8. *The Windows Experience Index*

Gamers are fond of comparing their WEI scores. Web sites such as `www.weishare.net` allow you to do just that.

As an overall benchmark, however, the Windows Experience Index doesn't give you a great deal of information about how your computer will perform in actual use. Each component in your PC (the graphics card, memory, hard disk, etc.) contributes different things when running different types of programs. This is why computer magazines use other benchmarking tools when rating computers and their hardware.

3D Gaming on Windows 8

Three-dimensional gaming is relatively new to PCs. Windows 8 requires third-party drivers for it to work, although some graphics cards are increasingly coming with their own 3D drivers and controls.

In order to take advantage of 3D gaming on your computer, you will need a screen capable of displaying double the number of normal frame rates, upping the standard frequency from 60Hz to 120Hz.

To use 3D gaming on your computer, you will commonly launch your existing games through a 3D game management program or app into which you will probably have to download individual profiles for your games.

There are downsides to 3D gaming on PCs, however. First and most importantly, stable 3D profiles may not be released until well after the launch of the game. Also, 3D has a darkening effect on the image, especially in first person shooters, which can make distances more difficult to see. Finally, the 3D effect can cause headaches when used for more than 30 minutes.

That said, I've used a 3D-equipped gaming laptop myself and have played several 3D games on it. The effect can be extremely immersive and this can add, if you'll excuse the pun, a whole new depth to your existing games titles.

Viewing and Editing Photos in Windows 8

The new Photos app is your default software for viewing photographs. The old Windows Photo Viewer is gone forever. This doesn't mean that there aren't many other options for viewing and editing your digital photographs, and there are many apps of this type in the Windows Store, including those by big-name companies.

Adobe, for example, first showed us how powerful touch photo-editing apps can be on Android tablets. For everyone who doesn't want to use an app or who wants finer control over their photos, there are other options, including the excellent Windows Live Photo Gallery from Microsoft.

The Photo App

The Windows 8 Photos app is a relatively basic way to view your photos and pictures. By default, it has a view that shows a large, almost fullscreen images. It separates the different folders on your computer where you store your pictures. It also offers default photo access from cloud services such as Facebook, Microsoft's SkyDrive service, and the Flickr photo-sharing web site (see Figure 7-9).

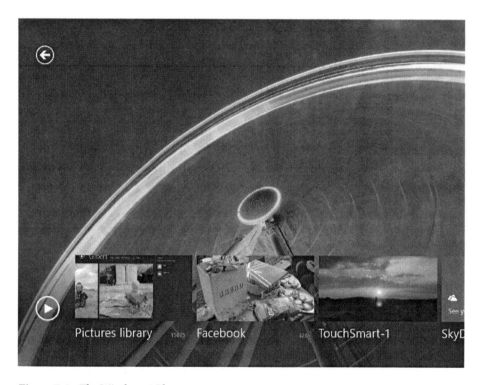

Figure 7-9. *The Windows 8 Photos app*

You can share photos and pictures by clicking the Share charm. Windows 8 will tell you which installed apps you can share the picture with (see Figure 7-10).

Figure 7-10. *Managing photos in Windows 8*

The editing facility in the Photos app extends only to deleting photographs, but as I mentioned earlier, there are plenty of third-party photo editing apps available for Windows 8. You can find these in the Photo category of the Windows Store.

When you are viewing a single photo in the Photos app, there are options you can display in the App bar (see Figure 7-11). These options include making a photo your Windows 8 lock screen image, or setting it as the default picture for the Photos app live tile, which cycles through all your pictures by default. From here, you can also display a photo slideshow.

Figure 7-11. *The App bar contains options for working with photos and pictures*

Windows Photo Gallery

Microsoft's free Windows Photo Gallery software is part of the company's Windows Essentials suite. You can download it from download.live.com or through the Windows Store. It is based around the company's Ribbon interface, so it will be instantly familiar to users of Microsoft Office 2007 and above (see Figure 7-12).

Figure 7-12. *Windows Photo Gallery*

The package allows you to perform many actions on your photos and pictures, such as

- Managing your photo library with drag-and-drop actions between folders
- Uploading photos and videos to cloud services, including Flickr and YouTube
- Basic editing (including automatic editing) of photographs

In Chapter 5, I discussed adding tags and ratings to your photo library to make individual images easier to find. I'll talk about this more shortly when I show you how to import photos and video from a digital camera, but Windows Photo Gallery offers excellent, easy-to-use methods for adding tags and ratings to photos.

Windows Photo Gallery also includes excellent face recognition software that can help tag friends and family. This makes it much easier to find photos of Gilbert, for example, who you see in Figure 7-16.

Other Third-Party Photo Editing Packages

There are many other photo management and editing apps, programs, and cloud services available. You may already have your favorite. I want to highlight three that I think are especially noteworthy.

Adobe Photoshop Elements

Adobe's Photoshop software has long been the king of photo editing, but the full package is extremely expensive and very complex. It's really only for creative professionals. At the lower end of the price range, however, is Photoshop Elements, which you can download from www.adobe.com. It is an excellent desktop program that provides a significant amount of power and flexibility while still being very easy to use.

Adobe Photoshop Express

Adobe also offers a free online photo editor, which you can find at www.photoshop.com. It is a reduced version of Photoshop Elements, but that doesn't mean that it isn't flexible or powerful.

Pixlr

If you want something closer to the full version of Photoshop—but without its high price—I have never found a cloud service better than www.pixlr.com. It is an extremely powerful, flexible, and—best of all—free, cloud-based photo-editing service that offers many of the features you find in the full desktop version of Adobe Photoshop (see Figure 7-13).

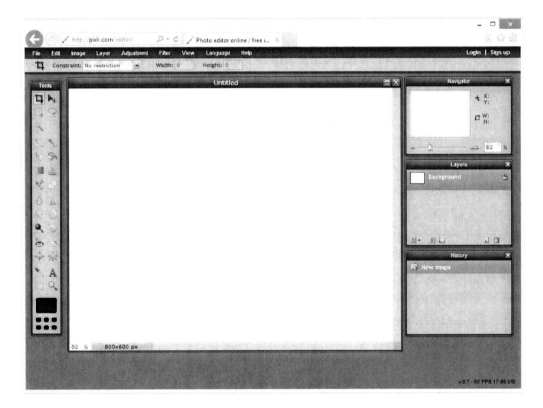

Figure 7-13. *Pixlr.com*

Importing Digital Photographs and Videos from a Camera

When you insert a memory card from your digital camera or camcorder into your computer, you are asked if you want to import photos and video from the device.

There are several advantages to allowing Windows 8 to import photos and video, rather than manually copying the files using Windows Explorer. The first advantage is that the import wizard allows you to add tags to the files. The second advantage is that Windows 8 is fantastic at determining the correct "up" position for photos and automatically rotates them for you.

To import photos or video, follow these instructions:

1. Insert your memory card, card reader, or camera into your Windows computer.

2. Windows prompts you that storage media has been inserted. Click the prompt (see Figure 7-14).

Figure 7-14. *Windows alerts you when you insert a storage device*

3. You can now choose what to do with the files on the device. By default, Windows displays the options for your default photo-viewing app or program. Click **Import photos and videos** [Photos] (see Figure 7-15). Based on the applications you have installed, the

Figure 7-15. *Windows asks what you want to do with the files*

options you see might vary from those shown.

4. The photo import wizard will appear (see Figure 7-16). Click Import to import all the photos to your computer. You can select or deselect images by clicking with your mouse or dragging down with your finger.

Figure 7-16. *The Windows 8 photo import wizard*

You can also specify a folder for the photos to be imported to. By default, this folder is named after the current date.

Sometimes you want more control over importing images. Let's say, for example, that you have been on vacation and visited several different places or countries. You might not want all your photos stored in the same folder.

You can use Windows Photo Gallery (click **Import pictures and videos [Windows Photo Gallery]** when asked what you want to do with your inserted memory card) if you have Windows Photo Gallery installed.

With the Import Photos and Videos wizard (see Figure 7-17), you can simply choose to import all the items on the memory card or to first review, organize, and group items to import. I'll show you how to do this in a moment, but if you want to import all items now, you can click **Add tags** to include descriptive tags with the images.

Figure 7-17. *The Windows 8 Import Photos and Videos wizard*

183

These descriptive tags, which you separate with a semicolon (;), help you find and organize photos on your computer and enable you to search for files. For example, you can search for "Dusseldorf" or "Gilbert" to bring up all the related files and images in the Files search results once tags have been set (see Figure 7-18). For more information on using tags to organize files and photos, see Chapter 5.

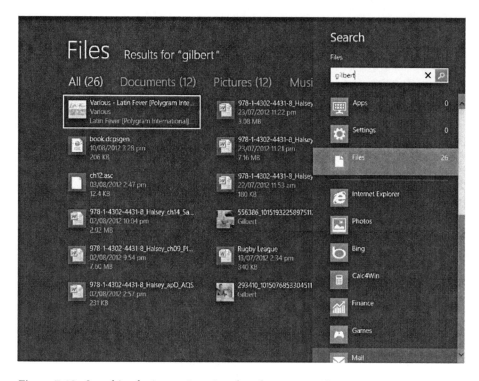

Figure 7-18. *Searching for images is easier when they are tagged*

The Import Photos and Videos wizard in Windows Photo Gallery also has an option to **Review, organize and group items to import**. This brings up a page where you can see photos and videos on the disk and select which ones you want to import (see Figure 7-19).

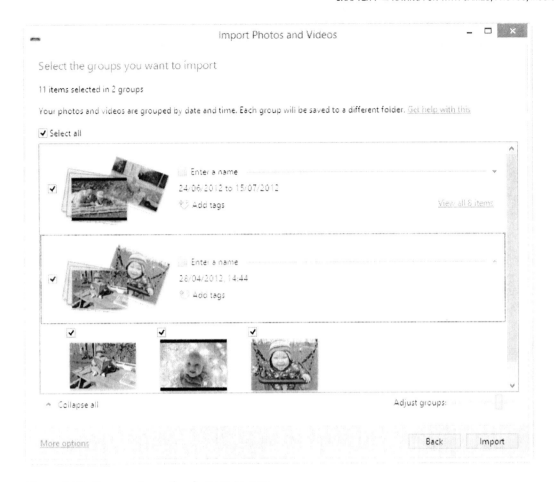

Figure 7-19. *You can choose the photos to import*

A slider near the bottom right of this window is particularly useful when it has been a while since you downloaded photos and videos from your camera. Let's say, for example, you have been on vacation for two weeks, during which time you visited several European cities (Amsterdam, Dusseldorf, and Cologne).

Using this slider, you can separate the photos by the date they were taken. You can then tag photos as "Amsterdam; Netherlands," "Dusseldorf; Germany," and so on.

Clicking More Options on either of the import pages offers storage locations for the imported items, the ability to batch-rename imported items, and automatic rotation of photographs. If you want, Windows 8 can delete items from the device or memory card after they have been imported (see Figure 7-20).

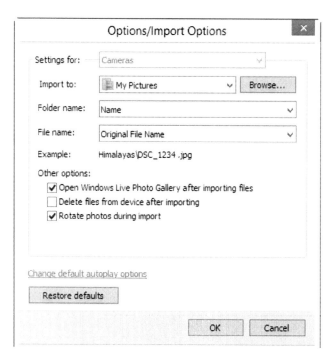

Figure 7-20. *There are additional import options available*

Playing and Enjoying Music and Video in Windows 8

Windows 8 also ships with Music and Video apps and Windows Media Player (note that Windows Media Player isn't available in the ARM version of the operating system). Unlike Windows Media Player where you play and manage your music and video libraries all in the same place, the Music and Video apps in Windows 8 are separate from one another, but both operate in the same way.

When you load the app, you are shown links to music or video that you can either view online or purchase with your Microsoft account. Your own music and video is hidden to the left of the screen (see Figure 7-21), so you need to scroll left to view it.

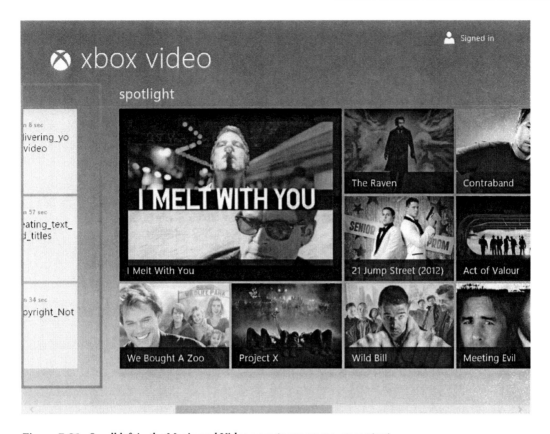

Figure 7-21. Scroll left in the Music and Video apps to see your own content

When you scroll to the left, you see your most recently played content, but in the top left of the screen is a link to My Music or My Videos (see Figure 7-22). Click this to view your Media Libraries in different ways—by artist, for example).

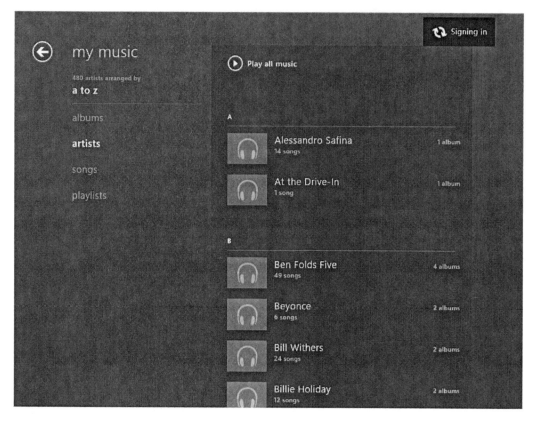

Figure 7-22. You can view your music and video collections in different ways

The music and video players in Windows 8 are rather good, having clearly evolved from Windows Media Center. They feature large onscreen controls that are simple to use with both touch and mouse, and as with all apps, can be docked to the left or right of the screen.

Creating and Managing Playlists in the Music and Video Apps

You can create music and video playlists in Music and Videos apps by selecting the artists, tracks, videos, or genres you want, and from the App bar, clicking the Add to Playlist button (see Figure 7-23). If you already have playlists created, they appear here as well, so that you can add items to any of them with a single click.

Figure 7-23. Adding music and video to playlists in the Music and Video apps

You manage playlists in the main My Music or My Videos view, where a link to your playlists is on the left of the screen. Clicking it displays your current playlists. Click to open one and you can select tracks to remove from the playlist. When you select tracks, a Remove from Playlist button appears in the App bar (see Figure 7-24).

Figure 7-24. Managing playlists in the Music and Video apps

Audio and Video Codecs in Windows 8

Windows 8 comes with excellent audio and video support. Out of the box it supports more music and video file types than any other version of Windows before it. There are three notable exceptions, however: the popular MKV video format (an open-source video codec) and support for both DVD video and Blu-ray video discs.

The MKV codec can be added using a codec pack such as the popular shark007.net, which is the only one I recommend. Adding the Blu-ray and DVD codecs requires an upgrade to Windows 8 Pro and purchasing Windows Media Center.

There are free third-party programs that can provide you with DVD and perhaps even Blu-ray playback codecs. Probably the best and most widely used is the VLC player, which you can download from www.videolan.org.

Windows Media Center

Windows Media Center doesn't come with Windows 8 as standard, unless included by the manufacturer of your computer. It can be added to Windows 8 Pro, however, through purchasing the Media Center add-on that you can get by clicking Add Features to Windows in the Control Panel. If you do not have Windows 8 Pro, you can upgrade the standard Windows 8 to this version here as well. Once you have purchased Windows Media Center, an icon for it will appear on the Start screen.

Visually and functionally, Windows Media Center has not changed from the Windows 7 version except that it now supports Blu-ray disc playback. The interface, which is a precursor to the one now used for the Start screen (yup, that's where it all began!), operates on a four-directional crosshairs system (up, down, left, and right) and supports viewing pictures, music, video, and live television if your computer has a compatible TV tuner (see Figure 7-25).

Figure 7-25. *Windows Media Center*

▨ **Note**   The DVD and Blu-ray codecs provided with Windows Media Center only allow playback within the Media Center software, not through any other app or program. You can add additional DVD and Blu-ray codecs to support playback through video players obtained from third-parties. Your computer may have been provided with software that plays DVD videos and Blu-ray discs.

You can also purchase a separate remote control and sensor (if your computer did not come with one) specifically for use with Media Center in what is commonly known as the ten-foot interface. It is great for viewing across a room and has made the all-in-one PC with TV tuner popular in student dorm rooms worldwide.

Organizing Your Media Libraries in Media Center

Your Windows Media Center Media Libraries automatically include all the pictures, music, and video that are in your File Explorer libraries. Crucially, Windows Media Center allows you to do something that's impossible with File Explorer: add network locations and external hard drives to these libraries.

Any network and external file locations that you add to the Media Libraries in Windows Media Center are automatically added to the main libraries in Windows 8. This is a great workaround for a missing feature in the operating system.

Manage the Media Libraries in Media Center by clicking Settings on the main menu. It is listed at the bottom of the main Settings screen (see Figures 7-26 and 7-27).

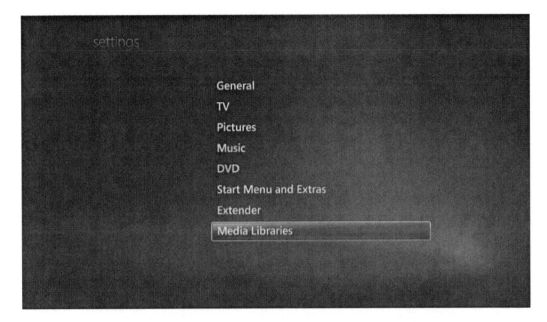

Figure 7-26. *Managing the Media Libraries in Windows Media Center*

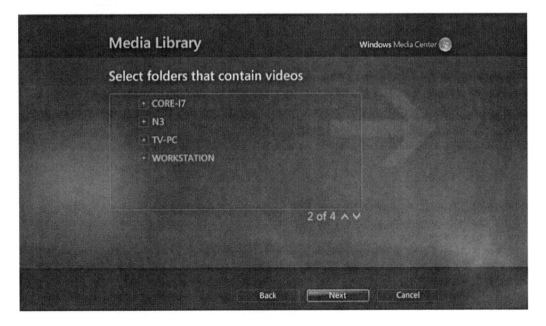

Figure 7-27. *Adding media to libraries in Windows Media Center*

Setting Up, Watching, and Recording Live TV

If you have a compatible television tuner card built into your computer or attached via USB, you can set up Live TV from the main menu. After it confirms the country and region that you live in, Windows Media Center scans for TV channels automatically (see Figure 7-28).

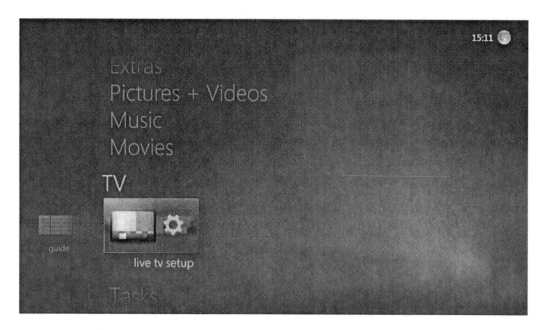

Figure 7-28. *Setting up Live TV in Media Center*

■ **Tip** Are you considering buying a cheaper Windows 8 ARM tablet instead of an Intel-based Windows 8 Pro tablet? One of the advantages that Windows 8 Pro tablets have is full support for USB devices *including television tuners*! This means that you can use it to watch Live TV if your tablet has a stand or a dock—giving you a mobile television set that can be used wherever you have a signal or with a mobile television aerial.

Windows Media Center supports a wide variety of television tuners, including cablecard, digital terrestrial, and digital satellite.

The automatically updating EPG (electronic program guide) is where you set programs to record. To record a television program, click the Record button on your remote control or right-click the program name. Press the Record button twice to record the entire series.

As with the very best digital TV recorders, Media Center is clever in that if you miss a program that was set to record (perhaps because you switched the computer off instead of putting it to sleep), it will look for a repeat of the program, and if one exists, records it.

In the TV section of the main menu, you can also search for television programs by name, genre, or other filters, such as actor or director.

Tip   MillieSoft provides a Windows Media Center plug-in called TunerFree MCE, which gives you access to on-demand Internet television services around the world (provided those services are available in your country). This includes the BBC iPlayer and the complete Hulu catalog. It also provides live streams from organizations, including NASA and TWiT (This Week in Tech) podcasts (see Figure 7-29). You can download TunerFree MCE from www.milliesoft.co.uk.

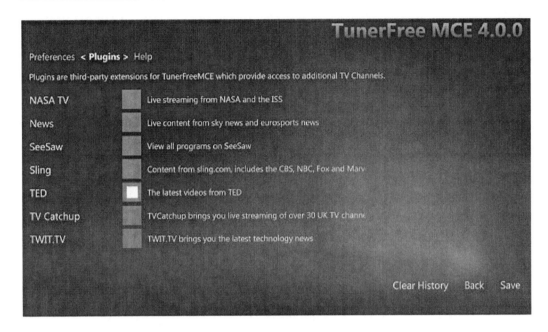

Figure 7-29. Using TunerFree MCE

Managing Windows Media Center

The main Settings screen in Media Center, shown in Figure 7-31, allows you to control all aspects of the software:

- You can determine the way Windows Media Center starts up and appears on screen; for example, whether it runs fullscreen, whether the Media Center window is always on top of other windows, and whether it runs automatically when you turn the computer on.

- You can add a pin code so that children cannot view programs with an inappropriate rating.

- You can edit the EPG to remove unwanted channels or that have a poor reception.

- You can control how and when subtitles appear in programs.

- You can control the default language and subtitle options for DVD and Blu-ray discs.

- You can set up an Xbox 360 console in another part of the house to work as a Media Center extender. This will include the broadcast of live television to that extender if you have a compatible TV tuner in your computer.

■ **Tip**   By default, subtitles will appear on screen when you mute the sound while watching live television in Windows Media Center.

Using Xbox 360 to Access TV, Music, Video, and Pictures from Windows 8

You can use your Xbox 360 console to stream music, video, and pictures from your PC if it has Windows 8 Pro with Media Center. You can do this through the Add Features to Windows 8 link in the Control Panel.

To do this from the Xbox 360 dashboard, select Media Center in the Video section to launch the connection wizard. The PC hosting the video and other content will need to be switched on and logged on to.

As a part of the setup process, you are given a Setup Key (see Figure 7-30). Enter your Setup Key by clicking Add Extender from the main Windows Media Center menu.

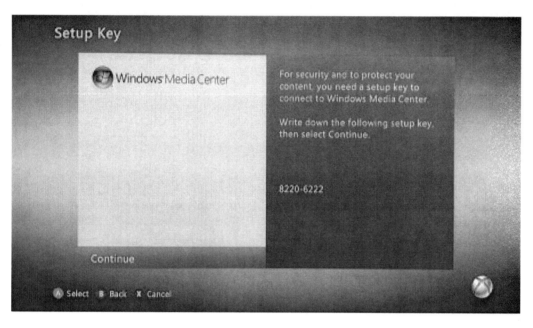

Figure 7-30. *Connecting an Xbox 360 to Windows Media Center*

Once you have successfully paired your Xbox 360 and PC, you are able to launch Windows Media Center on the Xbox 360 console to stream music, video, and pictures whenever the PC is switched on.

Converting Recorded TV to DVR-MS Format

When you record a television program using Windows Media Center, the video file is captured in a Windows TV (.wtv) format. Not every video editor will open WTV files, though the free Windows Live Movie Maker does, so if you want to edit the program, you can convert it in Windows 8 to the widely supported DVR-MS video format used with Windows Media Center in Windows XP.

In order to convert recorded TV WTV files to DVR-MS format files, Windows Media Center *must* be the default playback program for your recorded television. You may find that this isn't the case even with Windows Media Center installed, so you can change this by right-clicking a WTV file and clicking Choose Default Program from the options that appear (see Figure 7-31).

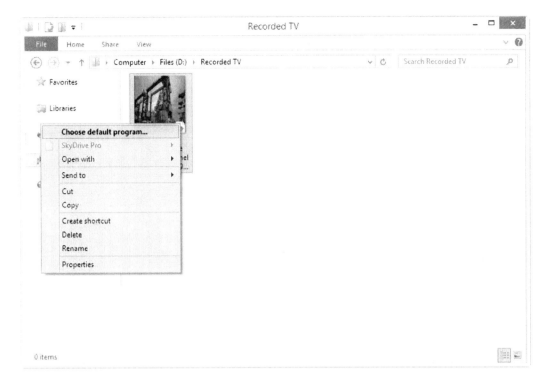

Figure 7-31. *Changing the default program to play back live TV*

When Windows 8 prompts you to choose the default playback program for this file, click Windows Media Center (see Figure 7-32).

Figure 7-32. *Select Windows Media Center from the options*

The file will start playing automatically, but you can close it. When you want to convert your recorded television programs to the DVR-MS format, you can right-click them and select Convert to .dvr-ms Format in the options that appear (see Figure 7-33).

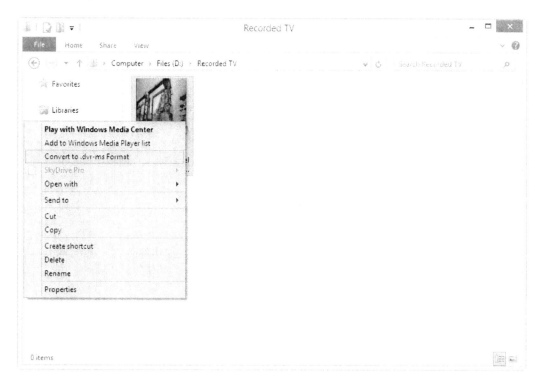

Figure 7-33. *Converting recorded TV to DVR-MS Format*

This doesn't delete the original WTV file—you will still be left with that—but it will create an additional video file that can be edited. My favorite free editing programs for recorded TV are DVREdit and DVR-2-WMV, which need to be used together for the best results. While the official download sites for these software packages are long gone, you can still easily find them available for download through a quick search online.

The good news though is that if you don't want to use or can't find these tools, you can also edit your WTV and DVR-MS files in Windows Live Movie Maker, which is available for free download as part of the Live Essentials Suite at download.live.com.

Summary

Windows 8 is a very consumer-oriented operating system and has some great apps for photos, music, video, and more. The finer control is still available in tools such as the Import Photos and Videos wizard.

If you're an enthusiast gamer, you might find Windows 8—with Xbox Live and Xbox console remote control built in for the first time—to be just the platform for you. With support for gaming technologies like 3D gaining ground, it will be interesting to see the innovative uses for this operating system.

The new Music and Video apps are also excellent and can be easily docked to the side of the screen while you work. Although you now have to pay extra for Windows Media Center and DVD/Blu-ray playback, it is a fantastic addition that allows you to customize the Windows 8 libraries in ways that are otherwise impossible.

CHAPTER 8

Maximizing Your Productivity

Windows was born into the business space. It was the original IBM PC, equipped with software such as Lotus 123 or WordPerfect, which was the powerhouse of the "modern" office in the 1980s. The introduction of the Windows user interface and the Microsoft Office suite solidified the PC's position as the productivity tool of choice. It was the flexibility of PCs that eventually brought them into homes, and now we take it for granted that we'll have access to our own PC at work; many people expect to be provided a laptop—and a smartphone as well.

Despite all this, the computer itself is probably the biggest barrier to productivity in the workplace. Enormous barriers can be encountered during a power outage or when the Internet connection goes down. There are ways to keep working in these circumstances, however; some of which are cleverer than buying laptops.

Some 90 percent of all e-mail is spam. There are alternatives to the spam mountain, though; some people argue that the days of e-mail are numbered and that instant messaging is the way forward.

As computers become more ubiquitous and we all get older, the ever-higher pixel densities on our screens can make text and other information difficult to read. Couple this with the barriers encountered by the disabled and people with fine motor control problems. Windows 8 includes some excellent tools to include everybody in a computing life. There is also excellent support to be found elsewhere.

These are just a few of the topics I'll cover in this chapter, the aim of which is to help you maximize your productivity with the operating system.

Managing and Arranging Running Apps

One of the features (some might say "limitations") of the new interface is that apps are designed to run fullscreen, with only the *in focus* app displaying on your screen at any given time. On a small tablet screen, this isn't a problem, but you still might want to have a second window open showing e-mail or messaging.

You can open two apps side by side by having the main app you want on screen and dragging the secondary app in from the left of the screen. To do this, you need to observe the rule that the app you want to drag in must be the app that you last accessed, just before the one you are viewing.

Think of this as a stack of playing cards from which the Start screen is excluded. The card on the top is the one you are currently looking at. The card directly under this one, the most recently used card, is the one you can bring alongside if you wish.

Note To display two apps side by side in Windows 8, you need a monitor resolution of 1366×768 pixels or higher.

There are several ways of displaying two applications side by side: by touch and with the keyboard. The easiest method is to drag the app downward from the top center of your screen, using either a mouse or touch. It will become a large thumbnail as you approach the center of the screen and can then be dropped on the left of right of the screen to dock it.

Another method is with the current app displaying on your screen, drag inward from the bezel on the left side of your screen, and the previously running app slides in from the side of the screen as a card.

Windows 8 then signifies that it is ready to dock that card to the first quarter of the screen. Separating the apps is a vertical bar with three dots on it. You can drag this bar left and right of the screen to change the primary focus from the main app to the side app. For example, if you have an app locked to the left quarter of the screen and you then drag the bar separating the two apps to the right side of the screen, the app that was on the left side now occupies the left three-quarters of the screen. The app that previously filled most of the screen now resides in the right quarter.

In Figure 8-1, the desktop counts as an app insofar as viewing two apps side by side is concerned. This means you can view the desktop in most of your screen while also seeing an app pinned to the left or right side.

Figure 8-1. *Two apps side by side in Windows 8*

There is one way to snap any running app to the left or right side of the screen, regardless of where it sits in your stack of running apps. If you move your mouse to the top left of your screen (note this cannot be done by touch), then thumbnails of all running apps appear. You can right-click any running app and select an option to snap it to the left or to the right side of your screen.

Switching Between Running Apps

You can switch between any of your running apps by using the Win+Tab keyboard shortcut. In Windows Vista and Windows 7, this displayed the Flip 3D view, where you could switch between running desktop apps in a three-dimensional stack. Flip 3D is not a part of Windows 8.

■ **Note** It is important to note that Win+Tab, which is used to switch between apps, won't allow you to select a running desktop program. To do this, you should use the Alt+Tab keyboard shortcut.

You can also use a mouse to switch between running apps from the Start screen or the Windows desktop. To do this, move your mouse cursor to the bottom left or top left of the screen; you will see, at the bottom of the screen, a thumbnail representation of your Start screen, and at the top, thumbnails of your running apps.

You can mouse up or down in this view to select the app to switch to, and then click it.

■ **Tip** You can shut down an app in this view by right-clicking it and selecting Close. You can also snap any app to the left or the right side of the screen in this right-click menu.

To switch between running apps with touch, you can drag apps in from the left of the screen. Start your swipe gesture on the left-hand screen bezel, and the apps will appear one at a time in reverse order from when they were last used. Swiping an app inward makes it run fullscreen. You can then continue swiping, one app at a time, until you reach the app that you want. This is one of the features in Windows 8 where the keyboard and mouse offer more control than touch.

You can snap the current window to the left and right of the screen using the keyboard combinations Win+, (comma) and Win+. (period) (note that the , and . symbols on your keyboard are the keys on which you will also see the symbols < and >). The reason to refer to these key combinations in this way is to remind you that there is no need to hold down the Shift key.

The next app you launch from the Start screen will then automatically fill the remaining space, leaving your snapped app where you put it.

Snapping Two Apps Side by Side

Working with side-by-side apps is straightforward; you can only have a maximum of two on screen at once. This view is called *split-screen* and it enables you to have one app in a side bar docked to either the far left or far right of the screen, while another app takes up the remaining space on your screen (see Figure 8-2).

Figure 8-2. *Side-by-side apps*

▪ **Tip** You can snap an app to one side of the screen using a mouse. Click the top of the app and drag it from the top of the screen toward the left or right of the screen, where the dock bar appears.

There are several ways to get apps to display side by side. It depends on whether you're using a touchscreen or a keyboard and mouse. To run side-by-side apps using touch, perform the following steps:

1. Open the app you want to pin to a side pane.

2. Return to the Start screen.

3. Open the app you want to pin in the main area of your screen.

4. Drag your finger inward from the left of the screen. The last running app appears.

5. Hold this app at the left side of the screen for a second. A vertical bar appears, indicating that split-screen mode is enabled.

6. Drop the app into the side pane.

You can drag the vertical bar separating apps from the left to the right of the screen to change the focus between the two running apps.

To arrange split-screen apps using a keyboard and mouse, perform the following steps:

1. Run the app you wish to pin in a sidebar.

2. Press Win+. (period key) on your keyboard to pin this app to the right of your screen.

3. Return to the Start screen and run the second app.

4. Move your mouse to the top left of your screen to display app thumbnails.

5. Click the app you want to run in the main part of the screen.

▪ **Note** In order to use the split-screen view in Windows 8, you need a horizontal screen resolution of 1366 pixels or higher.

Another way to snap apps to the left or the right of the screen is from the thumbnails of running apps.

1. Move your mouse to the top left of the screen to display the thumbnails of running apps.

2. Right-click the app you wish to snap to the left or right of the screen.

3. From the context menu, click Snap Left or Snap Right.

Working with Multiple Programs on the Desktop

Arguably, having only two apps displayed at a time can be limiting, but in fact, on the desktop, this is what I tend to do myself, with everything else minimized. So how can you maximize your desktop window productivity?

Minimizing and Restoring All Windows on the Desktop (a.k.a. Boss Mode)

If your desktop is getting *really* cluttered and you're struggling to concentrate, then there is a quick and easy way to minimize all the windows open on your desktop. On the far right of the taskbar, click the blank space to the right of the clock (see Figure 8-3). There is a hidden button here that automatically minimizes all the Windows on your desktop.

Figure 8-3. *The hide-all-windows button is on the far right of the taskbar*

■ **Tip**   The best way to find the Minimize Programs button is to move your mouse to the far right of your taskbar.

Clicking this button again restores all the windows to their previous positions on screen. This feature is sometimes referred to as *boss mode* because if you're having a moment of downtime at work and the boss walks past, he doesn't have to see that you're playing a game or shopping on Amazon.

■ **Note**   Some laptops come with a feature that allow you to run your fingers downward on the trackpad (usually four fingers) to automatically minimize all windows.

Minimizing and Restoring Windows Using Shake

Another way to minimize and restore all the windows on your screen is to shake your mouse. Doing this minimizes everything; another shake restores everything. It is useful for many people, but for those who have fine motor control problems, this feature can prove annoying. You can switch it off in the accessibility options (see Chapter 10).

Snapping Two Windows Side by Side

One of the most useful features in Windows, which I use all the time, is Snap. It allows you to view two windows on the desktop side by side, with each occupying exactly 50 percent of the screen. You can use it by dragging windows to the very left or very right of your screen. As you do this, a ghost outline of the program appears on screen to show you that when you release the window, it will snap to one half of the screen.

This feature is useful for many scenarios, including moving or copying files from one location to another, comparing two documents side by side, or working with two Internet Explorer windows side by side (see Figure 8-4).

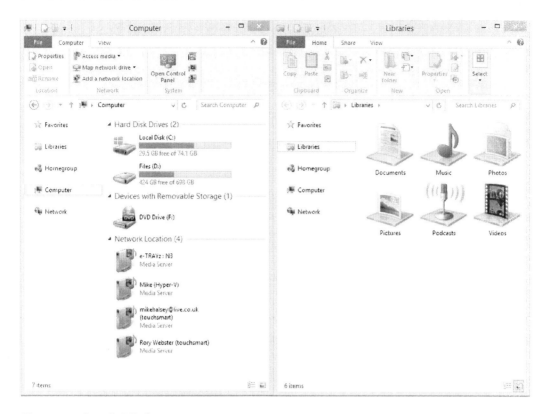

Figure 8-4. *Snap in Windows 8*

Peeking at and Closing Windows from Thumbnails

Another extremely useful way to arrange Windows on the desktop is through the use of taskbar thumbnails. When you move your mouse over the taskbar button of an open program, thumbnail images of that program appears. There are several actions you can perform here.

- Hovering your mouse over a thumbnail for about one second displays that window in the main screen, even if the program is minimized. It shows only that program and temporarily hides all others that are open.

- You can select this window to bring to the foreground by clicking the thumbnail.

- You can close a window by clicking the Close button in the top right of the thumbnail (see Figure 8-5).

Figure 8-5. You can close windows from their taskbar thumbnail

Pinning Programs to the Desktop Taskbar

You can pin a program to the desktop taskbar in Windows 8 by right-clicking its tile in either the Start screen or the All Apps view, and selecting Pin to Taskbar from the App bar (see Figure 8-6).

Figure 8-6. You can pin programs to the taskbar from the Start screen

Once you have your programs pinned to the taskbar, you can rearrange them by dragging and dropping them so that they are in the order that best suits you. My advice is to use the taskbar to pin all the programs that you use on a regular basis, and unpin software (such as utilities) that you don't regularly use from the Start screen.

You are still able to access these lesser-used utilities when you need them, but the aim is to keep the taskbar relatively uncluttered by showing only the program tiles that you *genuinely* use on a regular basis.

■ **Tip**   You should set a quick-to-open program as the first button on the taskbar because you may find yourself automatically clicking it as you try to open the nonexistent Start menu.

Maximizing Productivity with Jump Lists

Jump Lists, first introduced in Windows 7, are a great way to organize the files you work with on a regular basis, or for a current project. You can open a Jump List from the taskbar in one of two ways:

- Tap and push up with your mouse or finger

- Right-click with your mouse

Jump Lists show the files or places that have been opened most recently in a program. By default, it's the ten most recently opened documents.

You can pin documents, as many as you like, to Jump Lists by clicking the Pin button that appears next to the document name when you mouse over it. Pinning a document to a Jump List ensures that it always appears on the list (see Figure 8-7). This makes access to commonly used files extremely quick and simple.

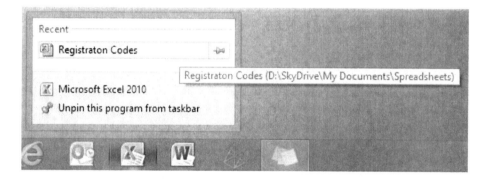

Figure 8-7. *Pin and unpin recently accessed files to Jump Lists*

Using Microsoft SkyDrive with Windows 8

Microsoft's SkyDrive cloud storage service is built into Windows 8 in the form of an app (see Figure 8-8). It allows you to view and open any files you have stored in Microsoft's cloud backup service. This can be very helpful on tablets and ultrabooks, where local storage space is at a premium, or if you want to access the same file on multiple computers.

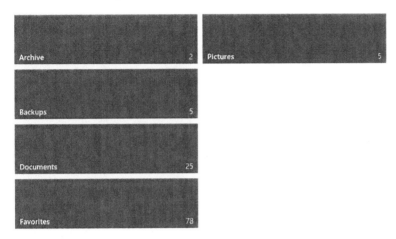

Figure 8-8. *Viewing your SkyDrive folders and files in Windows 8*

There are no files in the SkyDrive account shown in Figure 8-7, so how do you get them there? You can go to www.skydrive.com in your web browser and upload files manually, but this can be a chore. A better alternative is the free Microsoft SkyDrive program, which you can download from the Windows Store or directly from http://windows.microsoft.com/skydrive. You have automatically have it with a Hotmail or Microsoft account.

This program allows you to synchronize folders on your PC. All synchronized files and folders appear in File Explorer with a small button in the bottom-left corner that informs you of their sync status (see Figure 8-9).

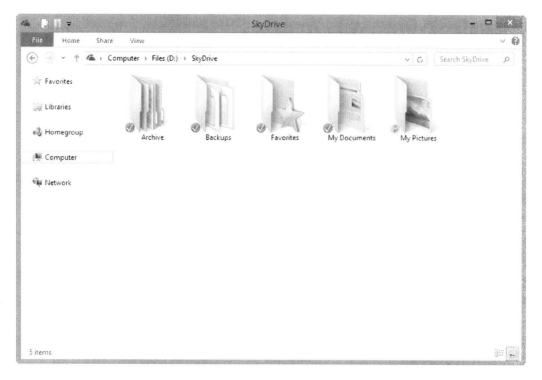

Figure 8-9. *Microsoft's SkyDrive software automatically backs up your files for free*

There are two main advantages to this. The first is that you always have an up-to-date cloud backup of your files. The other advantage is that these files are automatically synched and updated on every computer that you run the SkyDrive software.

By default, a SkyDrive account gives you 7GB of free storage, which is plenty for a lot of people. You can expand this amount, however, at the SkyDrive web site by purchasing additional space for reasonable rates.

SkyDrive is a good service to use with Windows 8, primarily because the amount of free storage you get is quite generous, but also because it is easily accessible by other Microsoft products, such as Windows Phone.

The Windows Mobility Center

The Windows Mobility Center (see Figure 8-10) is designed to help keep you productive on devices like laptops, ultrabooks, and tablets. The easiest way to find it is to type **mobile** or **mobility** at the Start screen; you'll find it in the Settings results. I want to discuss the areas of the Mobility Center by the type of tasks you wish to perform.

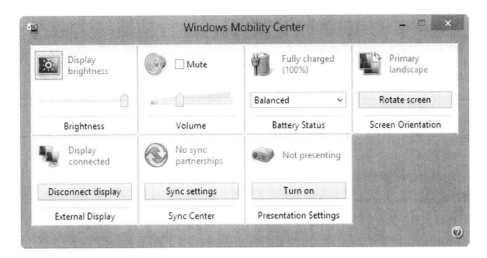

Figure 8-10. *The Windows Mobility Center*

■ **Tip** You can access the Windows Mobility Center by right-clicking the battery button on the taskbar, or through the Win+X administration menu.

Managing Battery Life on Laptops, Ultrabooks, and Tablets

Battery life is critical on laptops, ultrabooks, and tablets. Although many computer reviews and manufacturers now claim that some devices manage eight hours of life on "light use," the definition of light use means not really using the machine the way you want to in an average day. There are several tools you can use in the mobility center to optimize your battery life.

- **Brightness** is a simple slider to adjust the brightness of your screen. Lower levels of brightness prolong battery life.

- **Battery Status** provides a quick indication of the amount of power your battery has remaining. It also provides a drop-down menu that includes a power-saving mode to prolong battery life.

For more information on battery power management in Windows 8, see Chapter 9.

Maintaining Productivity Without Electricity/Internet Access

If you have ever been in a workplace during a power outage or when the Internet connection fails, you know that it commonly results in the stoppage of work and the appearance of playing cards.

The absence of electricity or an Internet connection doesn't need to mean that you can't get any work done. There are ways around these problems. Most obviously, if you have a laptop, then it can continue to run as long as its battery lasts, which is often long enough to see out a power outage.

You can also install Uninterruptable Power Supplies (UPS) in your workplace, which keeps computers, and even the Internet connection, running smoothly. Remember that your broadband line comes through a phone cable that is on its own external power circuit. Having a UPS plugged into your router (and perhaps a switch box if required) keeps your Wi-Fi and network online.

PCs plugged into UPS boxes can keep running for an hour or more in the event of a power outage. This means that you should have plenty of power to continue working while you wait for the electricity to come back.

Sharing a Mobile Broadband Connection

When your Internet connection goes down, you don't have to do without web access. If you have a laptop containing a mobile broadband (3G or 4G SIM card), then you can share this connection through the laptop (or even an Intel-based tablet) and with other computers in the office.

▪ **Tip** Many modern smartphones can be set up as mobile Wi-Fi hotspots so that their connection may be shared with other computers and devices. This feature may be called *Tethering* on your smartphone.

To share a mobile broadband connection, perform the following steps:

1. In the Control Panel, open the Network and Sharing Center.

2. In the left pane, click Change Adapter Settings.

3. Right-click the Mobile Broadband connection and select Properties from the context menu.

4. Click the Sharing tab in the dialog box (see Figure 8-11).

Figure 8-11. *Sharing a mobile broadband connection in Windows 8*

5. Select the check box to **Allow other network computers to connect through this computer's Internet connection**.

6. Set the Home Networking Connection type to Wi-Fi.

Other computers in the vicinity are now able to get online using the mobile broadband connection of the host laptop.

Note   Be aware that mobile data can be costly, and you should not use metered mobile broadband connections for Internet activities that are bandwidth intensive.

Mobile operators sell 3G and 4G Wi-Fi mini routers that act in the same way as a standard DSL router in the home or workplace. Also, some standard DSK and cable routers include SIM card slots as a backup connection. They can usually be set to automatically switch the data connection if the main Internet connection stops working.

Working with Secondary Displays

When you are a road warrior, you are often working with projectors or secondary displays. You can normally access these in the Charms menu on the Start screen under Devices. But if you are presenting, perhaps using PowerPoint, then you are using the desktop.

In the Mobility Center, you have options to connect to and manage an external display, as well as to rotate the orientation of your screen (perhaps if you are working on a tablet or a vertically aligned screen).

Note   What is Presentation mode? This option, found in the Presentation settings, disables all Windows, e-mail, and other notifications when you are using your computer for a presentation. It also disables Sleep mode during a presentation. This prevents the machine from switching itself off to save power (remember to have a main power adapter handy). It also prevents e-mail pop-ups from appearing so that your audience doesn't see that a friend just tagged you in a picture on Facebook.

Using ActiveSync to Synchronize Files with Other Computers and Devices

The Windows Mobility Center contains a quick link to the Windows Sync Center. It is here that you manage any ActiveSync devices your computer or Windows Server domain account is linked to. These include smartphones and tablets. If you have a device managed through ActiveSync, it is commonly set up by your systems administrator through Microsoft Exchange.

The Sync Center allows you to manage your synched devices (see Figure 8-12). You may have a hardware device that you want to sync with your computer, but you can also use the Sync Center to keep an offline version of server files so that you can work on the move.

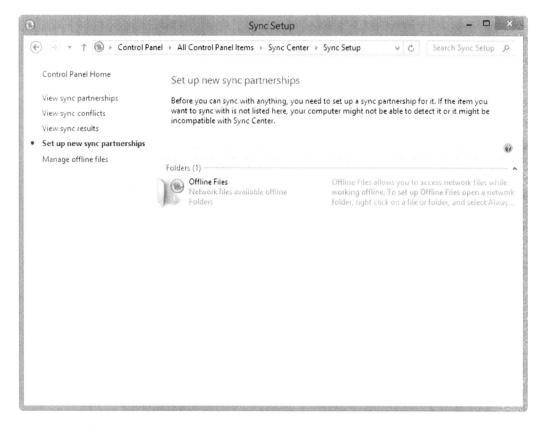

Figure 8-12. *The Sync Center*

On the Sync Setup page, you can view your current sync partnerships and any conflicts that you might have. To check that everything is up-to-date, you can also get the current status of synchronization with devices.

Click **Set up new sync partnerships** to synchronize files with another device on Windows 8. Note that the other device needs to be connected to your computer to set up the partnership.

If you are using the Sync Center to keep offline copies of files from a Windows Server, click **Manage offline files** to control your settings for the sync partnership.

In the Offline Files dialog box (see Figure 8-13), you can control the current state of the partnership, including the ability to specify the amount of hard disk space on your computer is available for syncing. You do this in the Disk Usage tab. The more space you make available, the more files you can synch with your computer and store locally.

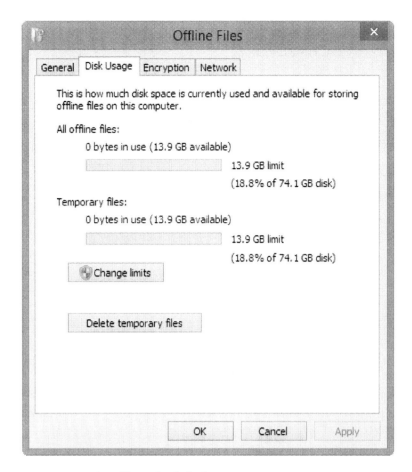

Figure 8-13. *The Offline Files dialog box*

This dialog box also allows you to make sure that offline files are automatically encrypted. This is very useful if you keep offline versions of files on a laptop that you travel with.

Working with Multiple Screens and Desktops in Windows 8

Many people like to use multiple monitors with their computers. Laptops especially might have a secondary monitor, or you might work in a financial or design environment where multiple displays are commonplace. In this section, I show you how to manage multiple displays in Windows 8, and how you can get the best from those displays through use of multidesktop wallpapers and new taskbar options.

Managing Multiple Displays in Windows 8

You can manage multiple displays in Windows 8 in one of two ways. From the charms, you can select Devices; management of secondary displays is located here. If you are using multiple monitors, however, you are most likely going to use the Windows desktop.

To manage multiple displays, see Figure 8-14, from the desktop, right-click anywhere in free desktop space. From the context menu, select Screen Resolution.

Figure 8-14. *Managing multiple displays from the desktop*

■ **Note** You cannot span the Windows 8 Start screen across more than one display; it always appears on the primary display. One exception to this is if you are using a computer with a built-in display such as a laptop or all-in-one where that built-in display always displays the Start screen, even if an external monitor is set as the primary display.

The Screen Resolution window displays shows each monitor connected to your computer. Here you can drag and drop the monitor displays to the left and right, and even up and down to organize them. You also have several other options, including whether to duplicate or extend the main display onto the secondary screen.

You can also select to make a screen your *main display* (I'll explain why you might want to do this shortly). Simply select the display icon that represents the one that you want to be your primary display, and then check the box **Make this my main display**.

Several very useful new multimonitor tools in Windows include the ability to display the Start screen and the desktop on separate monitors simultaneously, though you cannot stretch the Start screen across multiple displays.

■ **Tip** Many laptops now come with a new feature called Wi-Di (wireless display), which allows you to project your screen to a compatible projector or screen that also supports the Wi-Di technology. If you use this feature, the Wi-Di device may now appear on the Screen Resolution page. There are two ways to activate the Wi-Di device. The first is to press Win+P (project to a second screen) and the other is to find the device in the Devices charm.

There are also some new tools for managing the taskbar in Windows 8. In Figure 8-15, I have right-clicked the very far right of the Windows taskbar. What is noticeable is that there is no system tray shown. This is only shown on one screen. If you want to move the system tray to another screen, you can do this by right-clicking the taskbar on the target screen and from the context menu, click **Make this my main taskbar**.

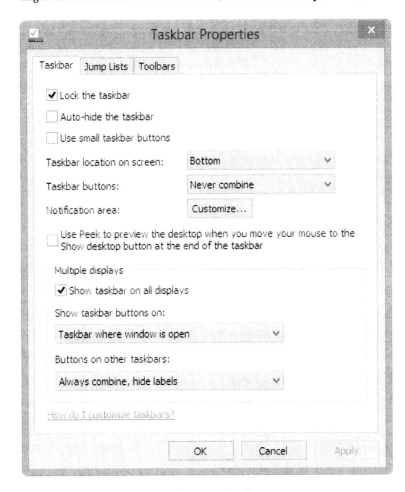

Figure 8-15. Managing the taskbar on multiple screens

You can also manage the taskbar in other ways when you have multiple monitors attached. By right-clicking the taskbar and selecting Properties, you are presented with a dialog box that shows additional multimonitor controls.

In taskbar Properties, you can uncheck the box to automatically display the taskbar on all displays. If you do this, then you only see the taskbar on your primary screen. There are other options that you might find useful.

- Show taskbar buttons on **all taskbars** shows all your pinned buttons for both open and inactive programs on every screen.

- Show taskbar buttons on **main taskbar and taskbar where window is open** shows all the pinned application buttons on your main display, but only the buttons for open programs residing on the secondary display(s).

- Show taskbar buttons on **taskbar where window is open** shows all your pinned buttons, but open programs are only indicated on the screen where they are actually open.

You may want to only show the taskbar on a single display, however, because this enables you to use the whole of each secondary screen for programs without a (likely empty) taskbar getting in the way.

Note You can take screenshots of multiple monitor displays in Windows 8 by pressing Win+PrntScrn (see Figure 8-16).

Figure 8-16. *Take multiple-monitor screenshots in Windows 8*

Using Multi-Monitor Wallpapers in Windows 8

Windows 8 now supports widescreen desktop wallpapers that can be spanned across multiple displays. Windows 8 also allows you to set different wallpapers on different screens. You select your multiscreen wallpaper in the usual way: by right-clicking a blank space on the desktop and selecting Personalize, or by right-clicking an image and then selecting **Set as desktop wallpaper**.

It is in the Personalization options that you choose the new Span option. It sits in the Picture Position drop-down box (see Figure 8-17). Windows 8 now automatically spans your display across several different screens.

Figure 8-17. *Desktop wallpapers can be set to span multiple screens*

■ **Note** Spanned wallpapers only really work when all the attached screens are running at the same resolution. If they are not, you may see areas of black.

Summary

Windows 8 contains volumes of productivity tools and ways to make the operating system, your programs, and documents easier to use. The mobility features also help squeeze more life out of your laptop's battery.

There are other productivity tools that I discuss later in this book, including the new Hyper-V virtualization software. As a guide to help you maximize your time with Windows 8, this chapter has covered what most people need to know.

CHAPTER 9

Personalizing Your Windows Experience

Windows has always been one of the most customizable operating systems available. It is one of the things that has made it so popular over the years. Indeed, a whole industry of third-party products is well established with companies providing evermore imaginative ways for you to personalize your copy of Windows.

Windows Vista introduced the Aero Glass interface. Here was something that had a much nicer appearance than the Teletubby blue of XP or the battleship gray of Windows of old, and so fewer people felt the need to customize their Windows installation.

When Aero Glass was further refined in Windows 7, changing the look of Windows to a metallic or movie-style theme, it became even less likely that people would personalize the desktop.

In Windows 8, we have the new Start screen and apparently fewer personalization options than the desktop. There are no wallpapers, fewer color options, and a sea of colored squares and rectangles.

So how can you personalize your copy of Windows 8? What options exist to allow you to change the desktop in imaginative ways? What hacks and third-party software exist to change the look of Windows 8 by perhaps customizing the taskbar or even bringing back the Start menu?

You'll be pleased to hear that Windows 8 is just as customizable as its predecessors. In this chapter, I'll show you how to give it a look and feel that best suits you.

Personalizing Windows 8

Again, Microsoft doesn't really allow a great deal of personalization with the new UI. When you first install Windows 8, you're asked to choose a color for the background—but there are other ways you can make the Start screen your own.

The main personalization options for the Start screen are in the PC Settings' Personalize section. Here you have three tabs across the top of the page: Lock Screen, Start Screen, and Account Picture. In the following sections, we'll look at these primary options and other ways that you can personalize Windows 8.

Personalizing the Lock Screen

There's not a great deal you can do with the Windows 8 lock screen except change the background picture. However, you can choose from a selection of stock photos or any picture file on your computer.

Figure 9-1 shows a selection of standard photographs you can choose from for your lock screen image. You can also click the Browse button to choose an image from your computer or network attached storage.

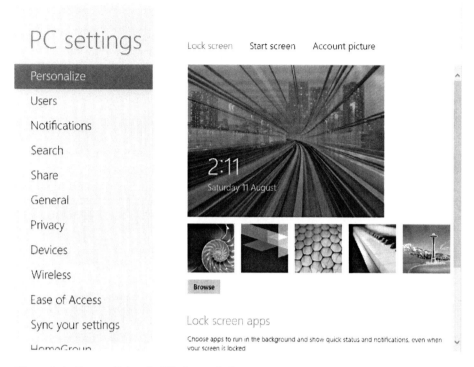

Figure 9-1. Personalizing the Windows 8 lock screen

More interesting are the lock screen apps. You can choose from installed apps that are capable of displaying live information on the lock screen. Not every app is capable of this, but those that are greatly increase the functionality of the lock screen.

To examine just how useful this can be, let's have a look at earlier Windows versions and the way we use our computers. In every earlier version of Windows, the lock screen didn't provide any information except which user was logged on.

With Windows 8, the lock screen always provides the time and date. It can also show additional information, such as the number of unread e-mails, the number of instant messages you have received, the current weather, and much more.

As I mentioned earlier, not every app is compatible with the lock screen, and some are only capable of displaying limited data. This includes the e-mail app, because you don't necessarily want people who are walking past your computer to be able to read the names of the senders and the subjects of the e-mails you have waiting.

You can add up to seven apps to the lock screen in Windows 8. They will always display in the bottom left of the screen, under the date and time.

Some apps provide much more information, including the calendar. It is very useful for providing details about your afternoon schedule, or perhaps what your friends are doing on social networks, or for informing others that you'll be at the dentist for the next hour—so that they can mess around with your computer.

You can only have one of the seven apps display additional information, and this is optional. If you wish to turn off this feature so that you only have the basic apps appearing, click the Detailed Status app and select **Don't display detailed status on the lock screen**.

■ **Tip**   You can remove any or all of the apps from the lock screen by clicking them in the Personalize page and selecting **Don't show quick status here** from the options.

Personalizing the Start Screen

There are a great many ways to personalize the Windows 8 Start screen. Changing the color and background picture are just two. Depending on how you use Windows, you may want to use the Start screen in one of several ways, so I'll show you how to configure it for different scenarios. Let's begin with the color and background.

The options for personalizing the Start screen are in PC Settings. The Start Screen tab is next to the Lock Screen tab.

The main options are to select a background image. You can only select one of the preinstalled images from Microsoft. You cannot use your own. These images are specially designed to pan sideways as you scroll around a crowded Start screen. They're very similar to the background images provided with Microsoft's Zune desktop media player.

Beneath the images are the color options. As you change the background image and color options, a live display shows you exactly how the new image/color combination will look (see Figure 9-2).

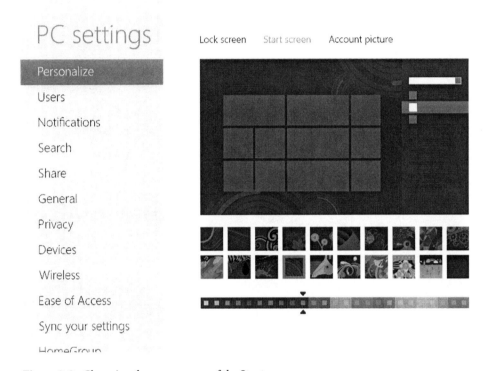

Figure 9-2. *Changing the appearance of the Start screen*

There is no need to press an OK or Apply button—just clicking a background object and moving the color slider is enough to apply your selections.

■ **Tip** By default, Windows 8 doesn't give you many options for changing the default wallpaper on the Start screen. Fortunately, software is available to help in the form a handy little utility called Windows 8 Start Tweaker. You can download this program from `ruanmei.deviantart.com/art/Windows-8-Start-Tweaker-1-01-259453275`, and it will allow you to add whatever background image you want to the Start Screen.

So what are these mythical Start screen scenarios of which I spoke, and how can you personalize the Start screen to make it suitable for both app and hard-core desktop users? To examine this in greater detail, let's split it into specific scenarios. For this, I'm going to assume that a person is happy to use both the apps and the Windows desktop, and switch between them.

The Switcher

The Start screen offers compelling new ways to use Windows. If you have a touchscreen laptop or a professional-grade tablet, you might want to use both the apps and the desktop programs. This would make you a *switcher*, someone who wants to use both Windows 8 interface types equally.

The Start screen allows you to arrange your tiles and icons into groups that you can name. Tiles and icons can be moved around the Start screen by simply dragging and dropping. If you want to create a new group, move slowly when you are between two groups (or at the very left or right of the Start screen) and a vertical colored bar will appear. If you drop an icon onto this bar, you will create another group.

To name a group, you need to zoom out of the Start screen, either with a pinch-out touch gesture or by clicking the bottom right of the Start screen. In this zoomed-out view you can right-click (or tap and drag downward) on a group, and from the App bar, an option to name the group will appear. Naming groups can prove handy, as seen in Figure 9-3.

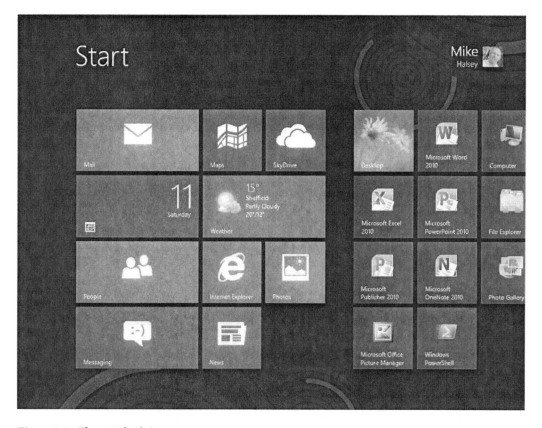

Figure 9-3. *The switcher's Start screen*

The Intensive Desktop User

Let's say you're not especially fussy about apps because you use your computer for work and you have enough desktop software anyway. You can hide any app or program from the Start screen by right-clicking it or dragging it downward slightly (you can select multiple apps this way too). On the App bar, you will see an option to unpin the app from the Start screen.

■ **Tip** Don't forget you can bring up the All Apps view by right-clicking or touching and dragging downward anywhere in a blank space on the Start screen. From All Apps, you can repin apps and programs to the Start screen or just run software you don't use very often.

By unpinning your apps, you can turn the Start screen into a very organized alternative to the former Windows Start menu, with all your programs and software organized into groups (see Figure 9-4). You may also want to name these groups to make programs easier to find using the method I described for switchers.

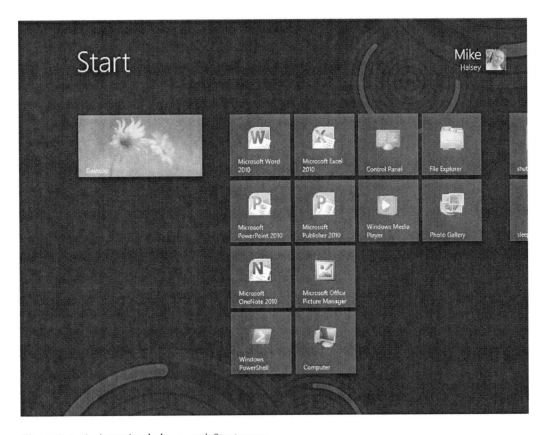

Figure 9-4. *An intensive desktop user's Start screen*

The Light Desktop User

Many people don't use very many desktop programs, so their Start screens might look quite barren and dark. If you are one of these people and you're not really interested in using apps, you can scale up everything on the Start screen to make things easier to see and click, and so that your desktop software icons take up more space.

To do this, you need to go into PC Settings and turn on one of the usability settings. Under the Ease of Access controls, turn on the option to **Make everything on your screen bigger** (see Figure 9-5).

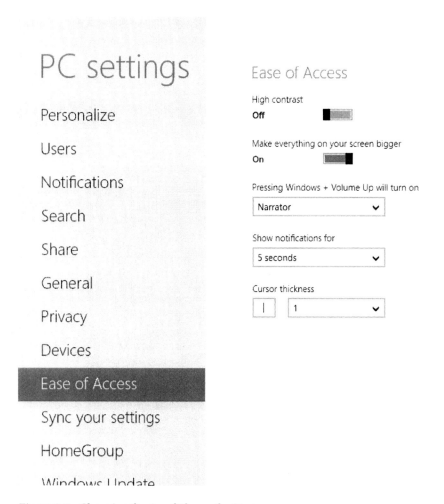

Figure 9-5. *Changing the size of tiles on the Start screen*

The advantage of this is that it only affects the Start screen and not your desktop, where you scale up everything separately. As you can see from Figure 9-6, it has quite a profound effect on the Start screen.

Figure 9-6. The Start screen of a desktop-only light user

The Work/Life Balance User

One of the most compelling things that the new Start screen offers people who use their computers for both home and work is a unique way to separate the two. By using the desktop for work and the Start screen for leisure time, you can completely ignore all of your desktop programs, such as Outlook and Microsoft Excel, and just use the app equivalents for play.

This makes sense in a lot of ways because apps are extremely different from their desktop equivalents—especially the Mail and Calendar apps, which can be set up for different e-mail accounts than your desktop e-mail software if you use an Exchange account for work.

You also have different photo viewers, video players, and music players. You might be surprised at how it feels as if you're using a completely different computer in the evening than what you're using during the day at work.

To set this up, you'll want to make the desktop tile the very last thing on your Start screen because you don't want to click it by accident when you're not at work (see Figure 9-7). It's fine at the far right of the Start screen anyway because it's extremely easy to remain working on the Windows 8 desktop all day without ever having to see the Start screen, something I will talk about later in this chapter.

Figure 9-7. *The work/life balance user*

The Widget Dashboard

There are those among you who really don't want to know about the new UI, who don't want to use the apps, and aren't interested in the Start screen, but who are interested in some of the new features in Windows 8, such as Windows To Go or Hyper-V.

It's possible to turn the Start screen into a widget dashboard—reminiscent of the widget dashboard in Apple's OS X desktop operating system (see Figure 9-8).

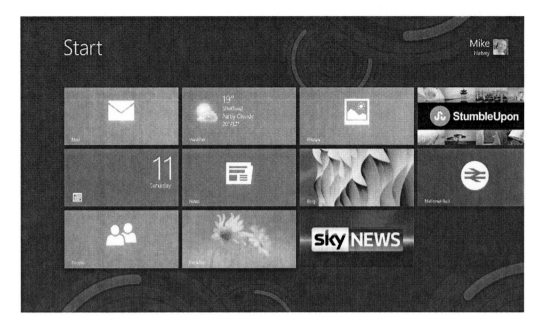

Figure 9-8. The widget dashboard

To do this, you first need to remove all the tiles and icons from the Start screen that you won't use or that can't give you live information. You can then scale up the Start screen using the Ease of Access feature that I described for light desktop users.

This will turn the Start screen into a dashboard with live widgets that can provide you with information on everything from e-mail and calendars, to foreign currency exchange rates, stock market figures, the local weather, and more.

■ **Tip**   Even though this type of user is unlikely to be much interested in apps, it's a good idea to look in the marketplace occasionally to see what new apps are available that have Live Tile displays.

Displaying Administrative Tools on the Start Screen

The Windows 8 Start screen doesn't show any of the administrative tools. Sure, you can access most of these by pressing Win+X to bring up a menu, but there is another way to display them on the Start screen.

To display the administrative tools on the Start screen, open the charm from the Start screen (it doesn't work from the desktop) and click the Settings icon. You will see Tiles at the top right of the screen. Click it.

You will see an option to show the administrative tools on the desktop (see Figure 9-9). Turning it on will automatically display a wide range of new icons on the Start screen (see Figure 9-10), and if you don't want them all, you can still right-click individual tiles (and groups of tiles) to hide them.

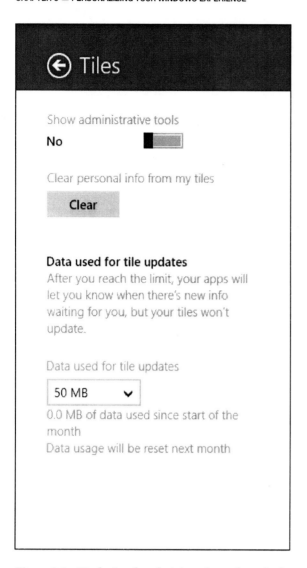

Figure 9-9. Displaying the administrative tools on the Start screen

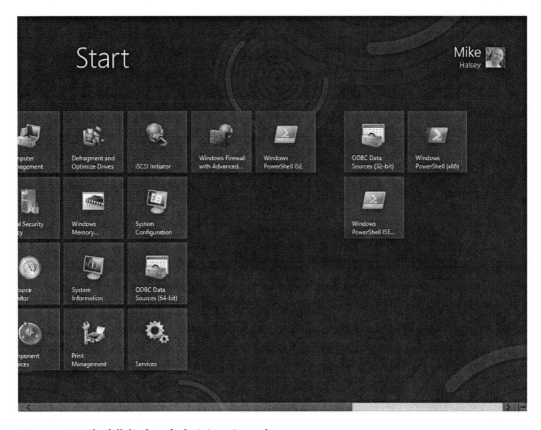

Figure 9-10. *The full display of administrative tools*

Personalizing the Windows 8 Desktop

If you've been using Windows 7, then you're already familiar with the Windows 8 desktop personalization options because little has changed. The Start button is gone, but I'll talk about alternatives later in this chapter. Everything else is accessed in the same way.

The main desktop personalization options are accessed by right-clicking (or touching and holding) any empty space on the desktop, and then selecting Personalize from the options that appear.

There have been a few changes, and one of these is the themes that change the color of your windows to complement your desktop wallpaper.

Personalizing the Desktop Wallpaper

As with Windows 7, you are able to choose themes with desktop backgrounds. You can also manually select several backgrounds and have Windows rotate them at a set frequency. Windows 8 can also change the color of the surrounding Windows furniture to match.

There are two ways to do this. The easiest way is to go to the Personalization page and click a theme that is overlaid by a color swatch (see Figure 9-11). A foldout card shows a range of colors overlaid onto the background image(s) of the theme.

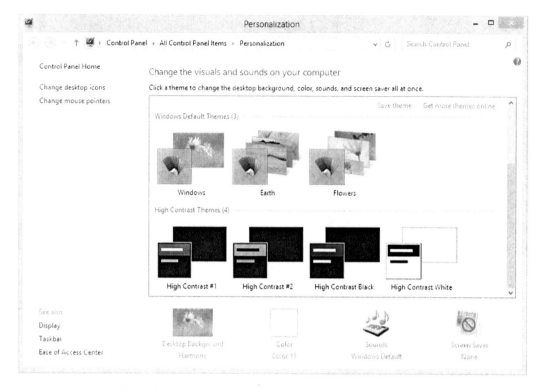

Figure 9-11. *The desktop Personalization options*

I'll come back to this automatic color-changer shortly, but first let's have a look at changing the background image.

You can change the desktop wallpaper by clicking Desktop Background at the bottom of the Personalization page. This brings up a new page that has several different elements to it.

In the main part of the window are currently available wallpapers. By default, you see all the wallpapers that ship as standard with Windows 8, including those that are for dual-screen setups.

In the Picture Location section, you can choose from several commonly or recently used picture locations. You can also click the Browse button to search for any picture (or pictures) on your computer to use as wallpapers.

At the bottom of the window is an option that changes how the wallpaper fills your screen (see Figure 9-12). The default option is to have the wallpaper fill the screen so that you don't have any areas of black. There are other options to consider, however, especially if you are using a 4:3 ratio screen.

Figure 9-12. *Changing the desktop wallpaper*

If you have multiple wallpapers selected, you can decide how often you want Windows 8 to change the desktop wallpaper. The options range from every ten seconds to once a day. You can check the Shuffle box to randomize the order in which they appear.

▪ **Tip**   Graphics can adversely affect your battery if you are using a laptop or other portable device. If you have your desktop wallpaper set to change regularly, there is an option at the bottom of the Desktop Background screen to pause the changing of the desktop when running on battery power.

Personalizing the Window Color

I mentioned that Windows 8 can automatically change the color of the windows on your desktop to complement the color of your desktop wallpaper. Clicking Window Color and Appearance on the Personalization page displays these options.

The Window Color and Appearance page features a color swatch and cards in various colors. This signifies that the window color will be changed and managed automatically by Windows 8.

Elsewhere in these options are 15 other window colors, each of which can be modified by sliding the color intensity slider. If you can't find the color you want (perhaps you are after a rich brown, for example), you can click **Show color mixer** to create your own custom color by setting hue, saturation, and brightness levels (see Figure 9-13).

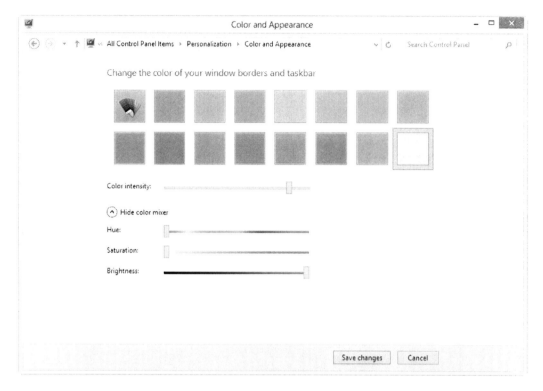

Figure 9-13. *Changing the window color*

Personalizing Sounds in Windows 8

It's much less common for people to personalize the sounds in Windows. There are modifications you might like to make, however, especially if you've never been a fan of the critical-error "*donk!*" sound, or if you want to turn the Windows startup sound on or off.

You can most easily access the sounds in Windows 8 by right-clicking the volume icon on the far right of the desktop taskbar and selecting Sounds from the options. You can also go to the Personalization page to display the Sound dialog box (see Figure 9-14).

Figure 9-14. *Changing the sound options*

You can easily and quickly turn off all Windows sounds by selecting No Sounds from the Sound Scheme drop-down list, or you can modify any individual Windows sound in the list.

You can even use your own sounds—any type of playable sound file can be used, including MP3s—in place of the standard sounds. Once you have chosen your sounds and created your own customized sound scheme, click the Save As button. You can share your personalized sound with friends and family, as well as keep a copy as a backup.

Choosing a Screen Saver

The screen saver options are last on the Personalization page. Unlike earlier versions of Windows, Windows 8 does not use a screen saver as the default setting, but instead turns off the display after ten minutes (see Figure 9-15). This is because screen savers are only necessary for older CRT monitors (a fuller explanation follows).

Figure 9-15. *Choosing a screen saver*

Some screen savers come with additional settings. You can preview the screen saver before turning it on by clicking the Preview button.

There is also an option to control the amount of time the computer is inactive (i.e., not using the keyboard, mouse, or touchscreen) before the screen saver switches on.

By default, Windows 8 returns you to the desktop when you return to the PC, but for extra security, you can check the option to instead return you to the logon screen.

■ **Note**   Do you need a screen saver? Screen savers are necessary for older cathode ray tube (CRT) monitors, where a beam of electrons is fired at a phosphor layer inside the screen to display a picture. If a single electron beam fires for too long at the same patch of phosphor, the image could end up physically burned into the phosphor layer—an effect called *phosphor burn in*. Modern flat-panel monitors do not suffer from this, however, and so Windows 8 is set by default to simply turn off the screen instead. This saves a considerable amount of power over the lifetime of your computer.

Changing the Desktop Icons

In the top left of the Personalization page is the option to **Change desktop icons**. To be honest, I love the argument about whether people have icons on their desktop or not. Many people like a desktop with icons and folders scattered over it, whereas other people, including myself, like a clean desktop. Frankly, this is why some of the arguments surrounding the new Start screen have been so intense.

So let me be fair here. The Desktop Icon Settings dialog box is where you can both turn on *and* off desktop icons in Windows 8. You can turn on and off the icons for the computer, your user folder, your network, the recycle bin, and the Control Panel (see Figure 9-16).

Figure 9-16. *Changing the desktop icons*

You can also restore default icons or prevent desktop themes from automatically changing the icons to custom icons.

Changing the Mouse Pointer

Also in the Personalization page is the option to **Change mouse pointers**, which opens the Mouse Properties dialog box. The mouse properties options, including those for mouse pointers (see Figure 9-17), are much more useful than you might think. I want to look at each tab in this window to explain what it does.

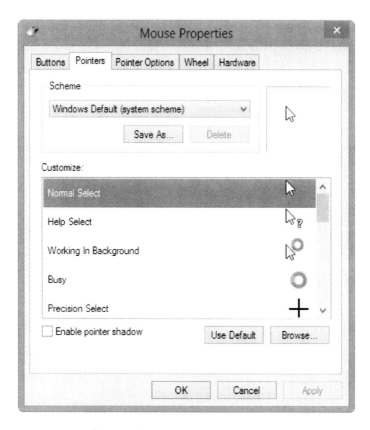

Figure 9-17. *Changing the mouse options*

- The **Buttons tab** is where left-handed people can switch the left and right mouse buttons. It also swaps the buttons on a laptop trackpad. You can also slow down or speed up the double-click speed, which is extremely useful for people who can't click as quickly. ClickLock allows you to avoid having to hold down the mouse button to drag items around the screen. These last two features are excellent for people with weaker motor skills.

- Under the **Pointers tab** are options to change the mouse pointer to a variety of high-visibility options, which is excellent for people who have difficulty seeing or reading the computer screen. There is more information about this in Chapter 10, where I show you how to change the mouse and keyboard options in detail.

- The **Pointer options** allow you to turn on useful features such as mouse trail so that you can see the mouse moving across the screen more easily. You can also display the position of the mouse by pressing the Ctrl key on your keyboard. You can slow down the mouse speed (or speed it up for gaming). You also can have the mouse automatically snap to the closest button. This is a great feature for those with weaker motor skills.

- The **Wheel tab** contains the vertical and, if your mouse supports it, horizontal scrolling options for Windows 8. If you do not have a wheel on your mouse, you may not see this tab.

- The **Hardware tab** allows you to view information on the hardware driver and driver settings for your mouse.

■ **Tip**   If you find Windows 8 difficult to use because of challenges with eyesight or motor skills, changing your mouse settings can help make Windows 8 more accessible and usable.

Personalizing the Taskbar

I would imagine your biggest question about the taskbar is how to get the Start menu back. Okay, I'll get to that, but I want to talk about other ways to personalize the taskbar first.

Access the taskbar personalization options (see Figure 9-18) by right-clicking the taskbar and selecting Properties from the options.

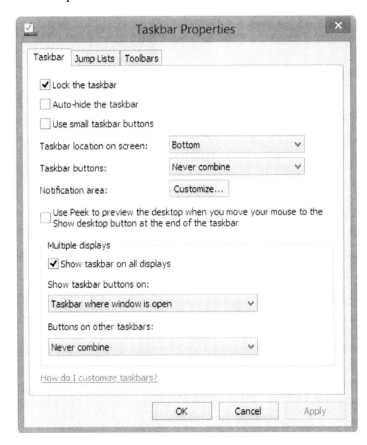

Figure 9-18. The Taskbar Properties dialog box

The options allow you to automatically hide the taskbar so that you can take full advantage of your screen when running programs. You can also lock the taskbar to prevent toolbars (if you use any) from being moved around, and you can change how icons appear on the taskbar.

Tweaking the Taskbar

The three views available of the taskbar are useful, but I've always felt there was something missing— the ability to have separate buttons for running instances of a program without the text labeling (see Figures 9-19 and 9-20). It's possible to add this feature, however, with a simple registry change.

Figure 9-19. Combining buttons into stacks(with labels hidden)

Figure 9-20. Never combining buttons

One thing to note is that whenever you make a change to the Windows registry, you should create a backup copy of the registry first. You can do this in the Registry (from the File menu) by clicking the Export option. Should a problem occur, you can later restore this backup by clicking Import from the File menu in the Registry Editor.

1. Right-click the taskbar and select Properties.

2. In the pane that appears, change the Taskbar buttons option to **Never combine**, and then click OK.

3. Open the Registry Editor by searching for **regedit** at the Start screen.

4. Navigate to Computer ➤ HKEY_CURRENT_USER ➤ Control Panel ➤ Desktop ➤ WindowMetrics (see Figure 9-21).

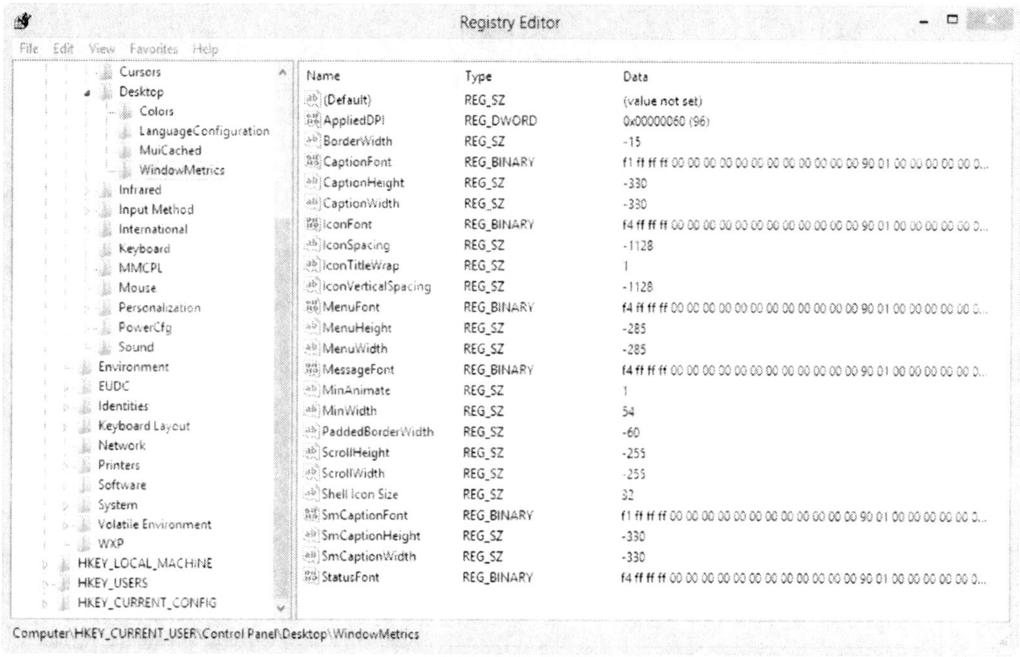

Figure 9-21. Personalizing the taskbar using the Registry Editor

5. Right-click in the right pane. From the options that appear, click New.

6. Click String Value.

7. Name the string value **MinWidth** and press Enter.

8. Right-click MinWidth. From the options, select Modify.

9. Change the value data to **54** and press OK.

10. Close the Registry Editor.

You should restart the computer. Your taskbar buttons are now separated for different instances of a program and the text labels are gone.

Personalizing Jump Lists

If you click the Jump Lists tab in the Taskbar Properties dialog box, you can change the number of recent items that appear in Jump Lists for Taskbar buttons. This is useful if you share your computer (and the same user account) with others and you want your file activity to remain private.

Personalizing the System Tray

By default, Windows 8 hides all your system tray icons and their notifications. Some people want to be able to see the tray icons, however, and you can turn them on or further hide icons. Click the small white Up arrow to open the system tray. Click Customize (you can also click Notification Area Icons in the Control Panel). You can also right-click near the system tray or on the clock and select **Customize notification icons** from the options.

In the Notification Area Icons window (see Figure 9-22), you can change the options for all the installed software for which a system tray icon already appears. The options are

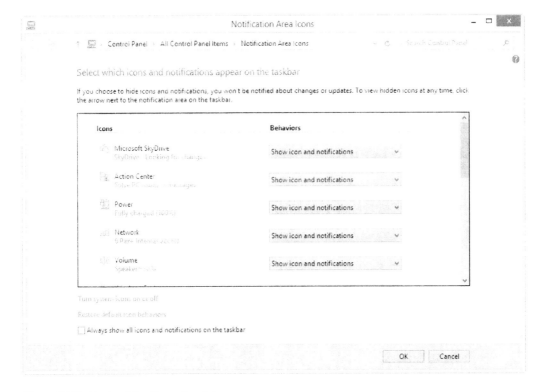

Figure 9-22. *Customizing the system tray*

- Show icon and notification

- Hide icon and notifications

- Only show notifications

Completely hiding icons and notifications is useful if you find a particular piece of software annoying, but showing icons and notifications makes the system tray more like the one in Windows XP (if you like that sort of thing).

Perhaps you really want to minimize things on the desktop and don't want to even see the standard notification icons or the clock. You can turn these icons off completely by right-clicking in the notifications area or on the clock and selecting Properties from the options. The System Icons screen in Figure 9-23 will appear.

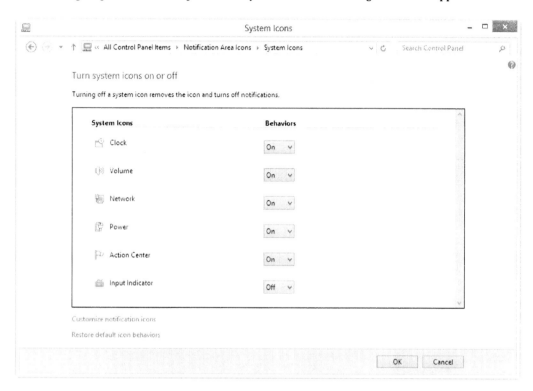

Figure 9-23. *Turning the system icons on or off*

Bear in mind, however, that if you turn off the icon for the Action Center, you won't be alerted when security issues arise. Also, turning off the laptop battery indicator could leave you running low and needing a recharge without realizing it.

Setting the Date and Time

In the Date and Time dialog box, you can quickly change the time and date on your computer, use time-synching services on the Internet to automatically keep your time and date correct, change your time zone, and control automatic adjustment for daylight saving time (see Figure 9-24). (You can also get to the Date and Time dialog box by right-clicking the clock on the taskbar.)

Figure 9-24. *Changing the date and time*

You also have the ability to add extra clocks to Windows! They appear when you click the date and time on the Windows taskbar. You can add up to two for different time-zones, each with a custom name (see Figure 9-25).

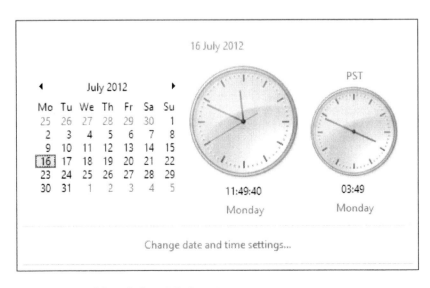

Figure 9-25. *Adding clocks to Windows 8*

Changing the Default File Explorer View

When you launch File Explorer in Windows 8, you are automatically taken to your Libraries view. But what if you don't want this and instead want File Explorer to default to the Computer view or perhaps even to a specific folder on your hard disk?

You can do this by modifying the shortcut for the Explorer icon on the Windows 8 taskbar.

1. Right-click the File Explorer icon to open its Jump List.

2. In the Jump List, right-click File Explorer, and then from the options that appear, click Properties (see Figure 9-26).

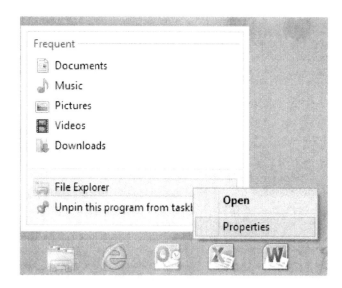

Figure 9-26. *Selecting File Explorer Properties from the taskbar*

3. Change the contents of the Target box to **%SystemRoot%\explorer.exe /e,::{20D04FE0-3AEA-1069-A2D8-08002B30309D}** and click OK to finish. This changes the default File Explorer view to Computer.

You can change this target to anything you like; for example, you can put a folder location in there instead. If you click the icon on the far left of the Address bar, the text in the Address bar will change to display the current folder location. It can be copied and pasted into the Target box (see Figure 9-27).

Figure 9-27. *Copying the current folder location from the Address bar*

To change this back to the default view, change the Target box text to **%SystemRoot%\explorer.exe /e,::{450D8FBA-AD25-11D0-98A8-0800361B1103}**.

Changing and Customizing Your Region Settings

The Region settings in the Control Panel allow you to do much more than tell Windows the country that you are located in. You can customize the time, date, and numerical systems in Windows so that, for example, you can change the digit grouping symbol from a Western comma (,) to an Arabic point (.) or change the negative number format from a minus sign (–) to having the digit appearing in parenthesis (). You can control these options by clicking the Additional Settings button.

Perhaps of more use is the ability to change the default date and time display options. These are two options I always change. I set the time to h:mm tt (single-digit hour:minutes seconds) and make the AM and PM labels lowercase text.

Additionally, you can display the full day of the week by adding dddd to the date options or the first three letters of the day of the week (see Figure 9-28).

Figure 9-28. *Customizing Region options*

Working with Multiple Languages in Windows 8

If people who speak different languages use your computer, or perhaps if you are an interpreter or language student, you can add additional languages to Windows 8 by clicking Language from the Control Panel (see Figure 9-29). You can click Add a Language on the main Language page to add languages to Windows, as well as change other regional settings, such as number and date formats, which may be applicable to a certain language. These options are accessible from the left side of the page.

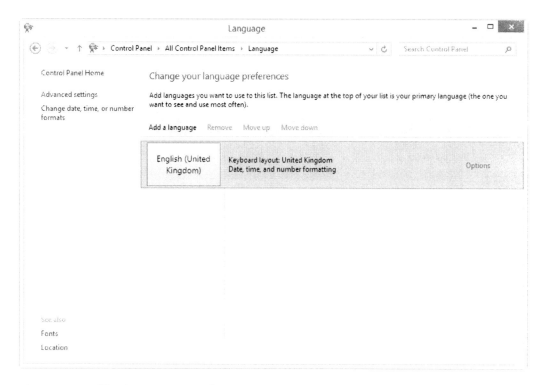

Figure 9-29. *Adding languages to Windows 8*

If you click Advanced Settings in the left pane of the main Language page, you find additional options, including the option to turn on or off the *language bar*. This helpful tool, which can be docked to the taskbar, enables you to quickly and easily swap between installed languages on your computer.

░ **Tip** Clicking the Options for a language allows you to change the handwriting recognition options from freehand to single characters. This is useful for pictographic languages like Chinese.

Personalizing the Power Management Options

It doesn't matter if you're using a laptop, ultrabook, tablet, or even a powerful desktop computer, you will still probably want to customize the power options for your Windows 8 computer. So why would desktop users want or need to change the default power settings? After all, the default settings of turning off the display after 10 minutes and putting the computer to sleep after 30 minutes must be pretty perfect, right?

Well, by default, when Windows 8 turns off the display, touching the keyboard or mouse returns you to the workspace you were at when you left the computer. Instead, you might want Windows 8 to return to the logon screen. This is especially useful if you are using your computer for work or perhaps don't want other people easily seeing your e-mail correspondence or your social networking (especially if they're mischievous like *my* friends are).

When you put your computer to sleep, it also keeps drawing power. Many people say that the average power draw for a Windows 8 PC in sleep is tiny. Multiply that by millions of machines, however, and you quickly see how this can balloon into a very considerable sum. When Windows 8 is capable of booting to the logon screen from a cold start in just ten seconds, do we still need sleep at all?

In this section, I want to look at the power options thoroughly and holistically, so that you can select the best options for you.

Changing the Power Plan

You can access the main power settings by clicking Power Options in the Control Panel. You get quick and easy access to the power plans, which are preconfigured options for your screen, shut down, sleep, and more, as well as the default plans added by PC manufacturers.

Figure 9-30 shows a Dell laptop—on which this book was written—that has three default power plans, which is standard for Windows. Your laptop or tablet may come with more, however, because hardware manufacturers may add their own power plans.

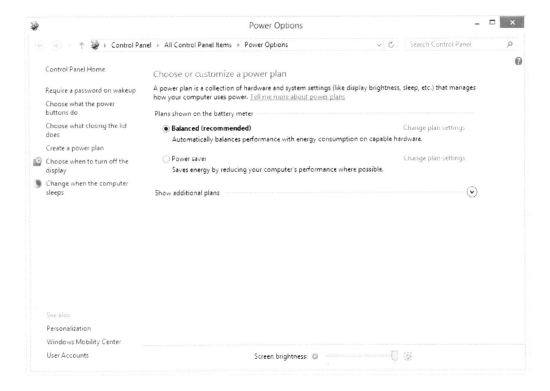

Figure 9-30. The Power Options page

The following are the default power plans:

- **Balanced**: The computer balances performance with energy consumption.

- **Power Saver**: Energy consumption is given top priority to extend battery life.

- **High Performance**: Battery life isn't an issue and you want the maximum performance from your PC.

You may have additional power plans, such as Quiet or Cool. In the pane on the left of the page is the option to create your own power plan. It displays a wizard from which you can base your plan on one of the three default plans, but you can also choose from four more options: dimming or turning off the display, putting the computer to sleep, and the overall screen brightness.

You can choose a plan by clicking it. Each one can be modified by clicking **Change plan settings**.

Controlling the Power Button, Power Options, and Password Wakeup

You might want more control over the power options. Click **Require a password on wakeup** to take you to the System Settings screen (see Figure 9-31).

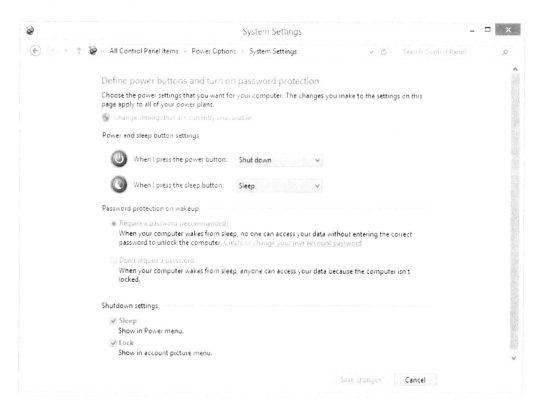

Figure 9-31. *Changing the Power button options*

You can determine what the physical power and sleep (if you have one) buttons on your PC's case and keyboard do, as well as any actions that happen when you close the laptop lid. For example, if you set the close-the-lid action to Sleep, but the battery dies because you thought the computer was actually turned off, you will lose unsaved work.

On the main Power Options page, you can also click **Choose when to turn off the display** or **Choose when the computer sleeps** in the left pane and you are shown the Edit Plan Settings options, which control the amount of time the computer remains idle before turning off the screen or putting the computer to sleep (see Figure 9-32). Note that if you have a desktop computer that does not have a battery, you will see a slightly different screen.

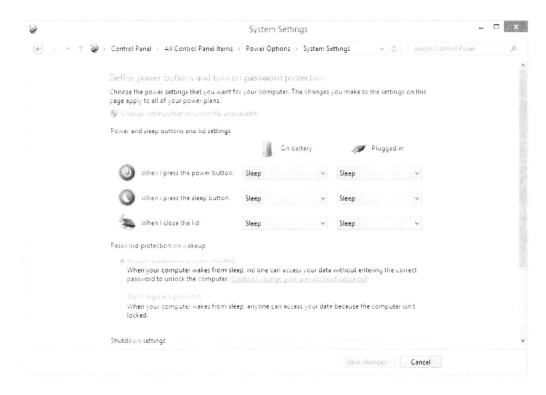

Figure 9-32. *Changing the display and sleep options*

If the computer is sleeping and Windows detects that the battery is very low, it will change to hibernate mode, where the contents of memory are saved to the disc. This can prevent unsaved work from being lost, but it is always wise to check that your work is saved before you step away from your computer.

Alternatively, if you use your laptop with an external keyboard, mouse, and monitor, you may not want it to sleep when you close the lid. You can change this setting. I do not personally recommend that you use a laptop with the lid closed, however, because this can cause some models to overheat.

Caution   Remember that if you set a PC to shut down instead of sleep, you will lose any work that hasn't been saved.

Many of the options on this screen are grayed out and you cannot change them. To change these options, click **Change settings that are currently unavailable** at the top of the screen. Some of the additional options can be extremely useful.

- **[Don't] Require a password** has Windows 8 return automatically to the logon screen after returning from sleep or hibernation, or if the screen saver is on or the screen is turned off. If you share your computer or keep it in a room shared by other people, you might want to leave this setting turned on. But if the computer is not physically accessible to others, you may find this setting unnecessary.

- **The shutdown settings** allow you to turn on and off the sleep and hibernate functions on your computer. It also permits you to turn off the new Fast Startup feature of Windows 8, which allows Windows 8 to boot to the lock screen from a cold start in just ten seconds. It does so by hibernating the kernel (the core OS) so that it doesn't have to load everything from scratch; it just opens the hibernation file and reads it back into memory.

  Some computers, especially older machines, have trouble with sleep and/or hibernation, and some don't support these features at all. If you are having trouble getting Windows to sleep, hibernate, or start quickly, you could turn these off these settings.

■ **Tip**   There was a proof-of-concept attack on Microsoft's BitLocker security system a few years ago, when it was proven that the encryption key could be retrieved from a hibernating (or sleeping) computer because Windows keeps the key in memory while you are working. This key is readable from a hacked computer in sleep or from an extracted hibernation file. It can be used to gain access to BitLocker-encrypted computers. At the time of writing, there is no word on whether this vulnerability has been fixed with Windows 8. So it is best to assume that it still exists.

You can also turn off the display of your logon picture on the lock screen. This is most useful if you have chosen a really embarrassing photo of yourself.

Controlling Sleep and Hibernation

You can choose the sleep and hibernation options for your computer by clicking either **Choose when to turn off the display** or **Change when the computer sleeps** on the Power Options page. You probably have seen these options available in other sections of Power Options; they remain the same.

What is the difference between sleep and hibernation? When you put your computer to *sleep*, it retains its memory by drawing a very small electric charge. This means that when you turn the computer back on, you are up and running extremely quickly at exactly the point at which you put the computer to sleep because nothing needs to be read into memory. It's already there.

Hibernation writes the contents of memory to a file on the hard disk. This means the computer can be shut down without requiring any power to keep the memory live, but it won't restart quite as quickly.

Changing the Advanced Power Settings

When you are viewing the sleep options, you see the option to **Change the advanced power settings**. Here you have many more options (click **Change settings that are currently unavailable** to edit them all). Figure 9-33 shows the advanced power settings.

Figure 9-33. *Changing the advanced power settings*

I want to talk about some of these settings and look at how they can be useful.

- **Hard disk**: Why might you want to turn off the hard disk? Hard disks unnecessarily consume a lot of energy when not in use. Perhaps you have multiple hard disks on your computer, and most of the time they are used only for file storage (perhaps files you don't often access) or for backups. Setting Windows 8 to turn off the hard disks on drives you are not using reduces overall power consumption on your computer. On any hard disk in use, the power will remain. Remember that when you want to access a mechanical hard disk that is powered down, there will be a slight delay as the disc spins up.

■ **Tip**   If you want to set any timings in the advanced power settings to Never, change the default time to 0 (zero).

- **Wireless Adapter Settings**: Wi-Fi and mobile broadband are a huge power drain for a laptop, ultrabook, or tablet because they turn your computer into a radio transmitter and receiver. If you change the default setting for locations where you have a strong signal, you will still get a good signal, which means the computer uses less electricity to power the Wi-Fi system.

- **Sleep**: You can turn sleep and hibernate off completely if they cause problems on your computer.

- **USB Settings**: If your computer is connected to USB devices that draw power from the PC—perhaps an external hard disk or optical drive, you can enable a setting that will cut power to the devices when they are not in use. This can dramatically extend the life of a portable computer such as an ultrabook.

- **Display**: While the main power options allow you to choose when to dim your computer's display to save power, these options give you finer control over exactly how much the display dims and how bright it is when plugged in. If your computer comes with a built-in light-meter, you can turn on the Adaptive Brightness, which automatically changes the brightness to match the available lighting.

- **Battery**: The battery options allow you to control what Windows 8 sees as low and critical battery levels. If you know that your battery is generally excellent and you don't want to be nagged, you could lower the low battery alert by ten percent. If you often step away from your computer while it is running on batteries, however, you might want to set Windows 8 to automatically hibernate when the battery runs low.

Maximizing Battery Life on Mobile Devices

If you are using a laptop, ultrabook, or tablet on the go and want to maximize your battery life, there are certain things you can do that will help.

1. Dim your screen brightness as much as you can. The less power needed to display an image, the longer your battery will last. Your screen is a real power hog.

2. Turn off your backlit keyboard (if you have one) because this will save power as well.

3. Set the screen to turn off after two minutes of inactivity and perhaps set the computer to sleep after ten minutes.

On a laptop or tablet, you might want to set the screen to turn off after only a couple of minutes—until you touch the screen, keyboard, or mouse to wake it up. The screen on a mobile device is the most power-hungry component. Having the screen switch off when not in use will greatly extend battery life.

You might also want to turn off features such as 3G and GPS, both of which consume power through broadcasting and receiving radio signals.

Also, have Windows 8 cut power to any attached USB devices that can also drain the battery on your computer.

Adding Power Buttons to the Start Screen and Taskbar

While the main Shut down, Restart, and Sleep options for Windows 8 might be hidden away in the Settings charm, it's still possible to add them to the Start screen and the taskbar.

1. Right-click a blank space on the desktop, and from the options that appear, click New ➤ Shortcut (see Figure 9-34).

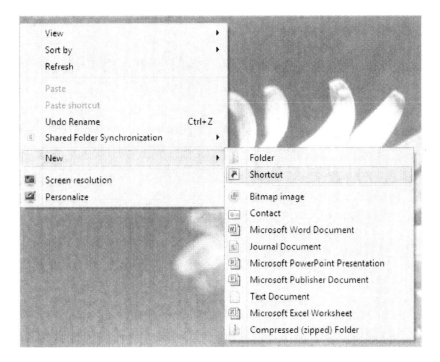

Figure 9-34. *Creating a new shortcut from the desktop*

2. In the window that appears, type **shutdown.exe –s –t 00** and then click Next (see Figure 9-35).

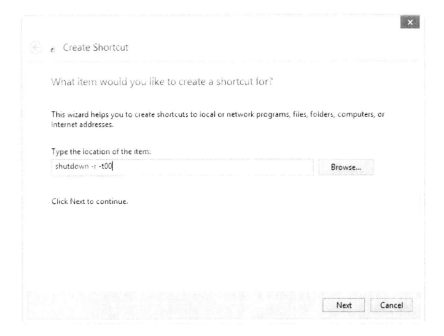

Figure 9-35. *Setting the shortcut code*

■ **Tip**   To create a Restart shortcut, type **shutdown –r –t 00**.

To create a Sleep shortcut, type **rundll32.exe powrProf.dll,SetSuspendState 0,1,0**.

To create a Hibernate shortcut, type **rundll32.exe powrProf.dll,SetSuspendState**.

To create a Lock Computer shortcut, type **rundll32.exe powrProf.dll,LockWorkStation**.

To enable sleep from a RUNDLL32 command, you also need to disable hibernation on the computer. To do this, open a Command Prompt (Admin) window and run (type) the **powercfg.exe /hibernate off** command. You can use the **powercfg.exe /hibernate on** command to switch it back on. Note that disabling hibernation on a laptop or tablet can result in the battery running to empty, and you will lose work on unsaved files and documents.

3.   Give the shortcut an appropriate name, and then click Finish (see Figure 9-36).

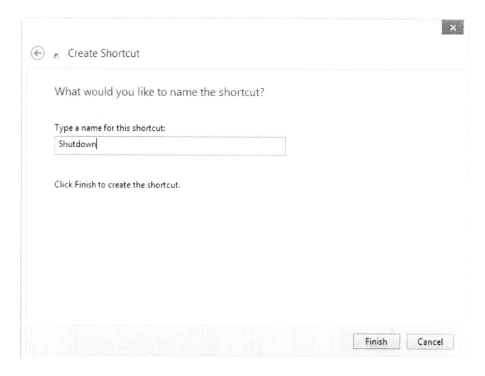

Figure 9-36.   *Giving the shortcut a name*

4.   Right-click the newly created shortcut, and then select Properties from the options.

5.   In the Shutdown Properties dialog box, under the Shortcut tab, click the Change Icon button (see Figure 9-37). You will be told that icons for this shortcut don't exist. This is fine—just click through it.

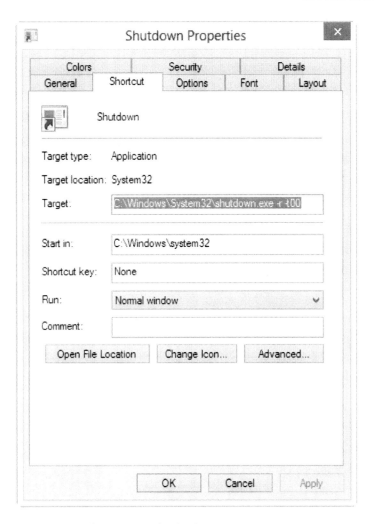

Figure 9-37. *The properties for the shortcut*

6. Choose an icon from the Change Icon dialog box, and then click OK (see Figure 9-38).

▓ **Note**   If you add an icon to a Sleep, Hibernate, or Lock icon, double-click the Shell32.dll file at the next view to display icons.

Figure 9-38. *Adding an icon to a shortcut*

7. Right-click your new power shortcut icon in File Explorer. Select Cut from the options.

8. In File Explorer, click the icon to the left of the Address bar. Navigate to C:\ProgramData\ Microsoft\Windows\Start Menu\Programs (see Figure 9-39).

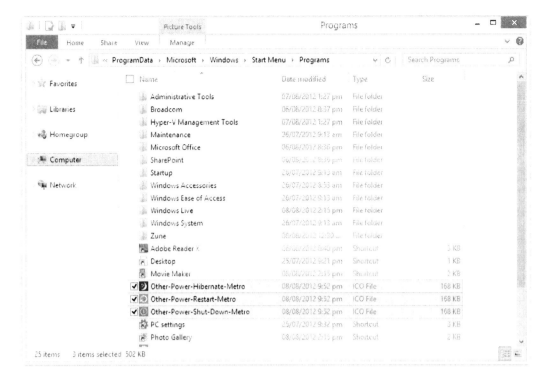

Figure 9-39. The C:\ProgramData\Microsoft\Windows\Start Menu\Programs folder

■ **Note** You can also use your own .ico icon files. Many custom icons can be created from web sites, including the excellent www.iconarchive.com.

9. Paste the shortcuts into this folder.

10. At the Start screen, open the App bar and click All Apps.

11. In the All Apps view, find the shortcut(s) you have created. Right-click it/them to open the app options for each shortcut. Here you can pin it/them to the Start screen (if they are not already pinned there) and to the taskbar (see Figure 9-40).

Figure 9-40. *Pinning your power icons to the Start screen and the taskbar*

■ **Note**   Sometimes these shortcut links won't work because of security that Windows 8 puts in place to prevent malware from shutting down your computer. If this happens, reopen the C:\ProgramData\Microsoft\Windows\Start Menu\ Programs folder and right-click each shortcut, selecting its Properties. With each shortcut, re-paste the command (e.g., **shutdown.exe –s –t 00**) into the Target field, and then click OK. The shortcut should now work.

Creating a Power Buttons Toolbar

If you pin the power buttons to your taskbar, you will probably not want them right next to your program buttons where they're far too easy to click by mistake. You can create a custom toolbar for the taskbar to keep the buttons on the far right of the screen, next to the system tray.

1.   Right-click in a blank space on the taskbar, and then uncheck **Lock the taskbar** in the options

2.   Right-click the taskbar again, and then select Toolbars ➤ New Toolbar (see Figure 9-41).

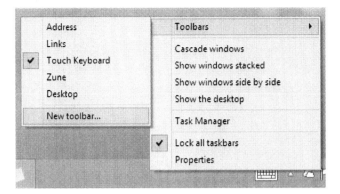

Figure 9-41. *Creating a new toolbar on the taskbar*

3. Create a new folder for the toolbar. Copy your power shortcut files into it. When you have created your folder, select it, and then click the Select Folder button (see Figure 9-42).

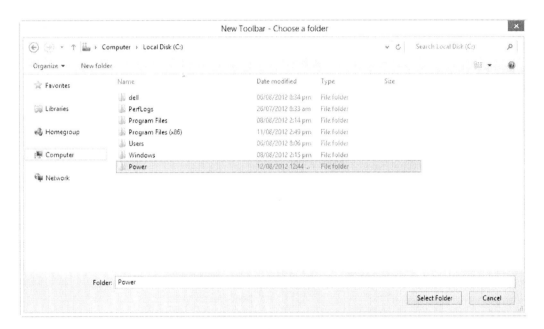

Figure 9-42. *Creating a folder for the toolbar*

4. Your toolbar will now appear on the taskbar. Drag the vertical bars to the left of it to resize it

5. You can also right-click within the new toolbar to select different options (see Figure 9-43). These include turning off the toolbar's text title and labels and changing the View options so that it displays large buttons.

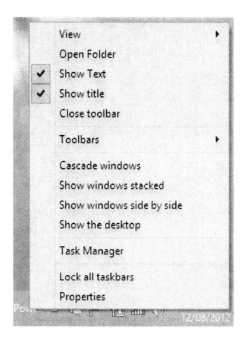

Figure 9-43. Changing toolbar options

Your finished toolbar will display on the right of the taskbar, keeping the power buttons safely away from your program buttons (see Figure 9-44).

Figure 9-44. A power toolbar on the taskbar

▪ **Tip**   You can turn off Sticky Keys, which is a keyboard accessibility feature that automatically starts when you press the Shift key five times. It might interfere with gaming or another activity. To do this, open the Ease of Access page from the Control Panel, and then click Make the Keyboard Easier to Use, followed by Set up Sticky Keys. You can completely turn off the Sticky keys feature.

Summary

Despite many of the initial reactions to Windows 8 when it was unveiled to the public and press, this operating system is extremely customizable. Even the new Start screen can be customized in a variety of ways to suit many types of users. This includes turning the Start screen into a very useful widget view. You can turn the Start screen off completely with third-party software, should you choose.

Being able to personalize your computer is important to many computer users and it is a mainstay of the Windows operating system. Personalization options go far beyond what is included in this chapter. Chapter 10 shows how these options can be configured further to assist people who have difficulty using computers.

This all helps make Windows 8 the customizable operating system you want, while at the same time still affording you all the cool new features it brings, such as Hyper-V and better multimonitor support.

Making Windows 8 More Accessible and Easier to Use

User accessibility is one of the biggest challenges facing companies that make computers, operating systems, and software. Accessibility is particularly important for touch-controlled systems, which improve computer use for people who have difficulty using a keyboard and mouse.

Who are Windows' accessibility features for? People of all ages, from all walks of life, and of all abilities can benefit from them. Perhaps you need text to be larger; perhaps you've never used a computer; perhaps you're left-handed; or perhaps you find it difficult to stare at a screen for a long period of time.

There are several ways to access the settings that can make Windows 8 considerably easier to use. The options available on each page vary, depending on what is likely to be required for the interface, Start screen, or desktop.

Making Windows 8 Easier to Use

You can access the Windows 8 Ease of Access settings through the charms by selecting Settings ➤ Change PC Settings ➤ Ease of Access (see Figure 10-1).

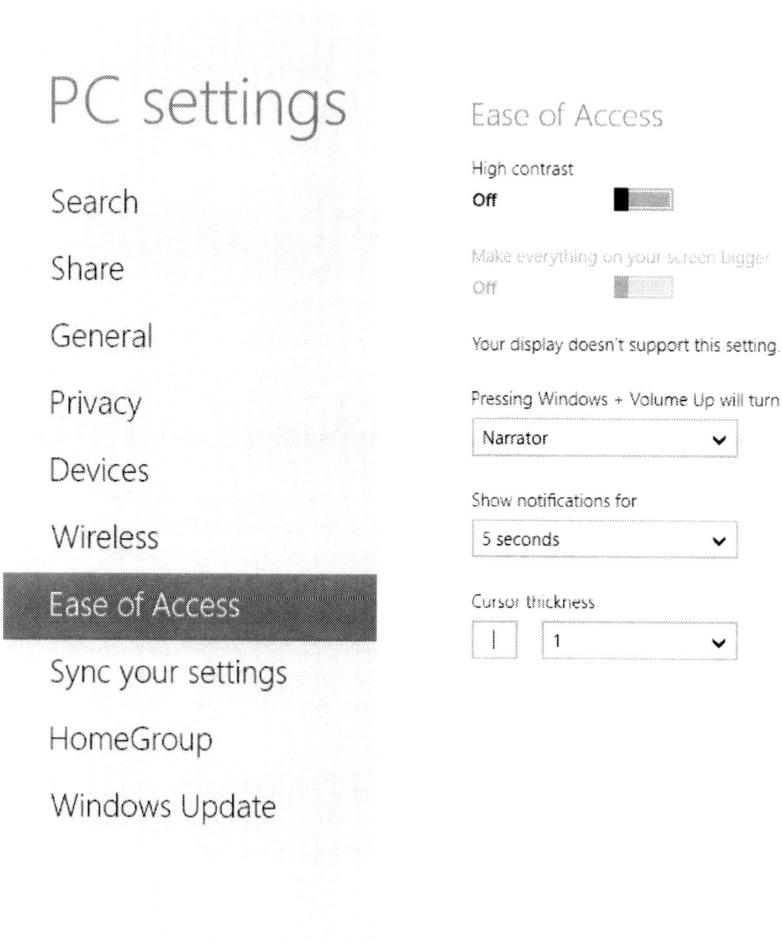

PC settings

Ease of Access

Search

High contrast

Off ▮▮▮▯▯

Share

Make everything on your screen bigger

Off ▯▯▯

General

Your display doesn't support this setting.

Privacy

Pressing Windows + Volume Up will turn on

Devices

| Narrator ⌄ |

Wireless

Show notifications for

| 5 seconds ⌄ |

Ease of Access

Cursor thickness

| ❘ | 1 ⌄ |

Sync your settings

HomeGroup

Windows Update

Figure 10-1. *The Ease of Access settings in Windows 8*

The following are the options listed in Ease of Access.

- **High Contrast** turns on a high-visibility color scheme that enables people to more easily see and read what's on the computer's screen.

- **Make everything on your screen bigger** scales up the Windows 8 interface without distorting buttons or text. This not only makes things easier to see and read, but it also makes buttons and tiles easier to click with a mouse or touch with a finger.

- **Tab through webpages and app using caret browsing** allows users to move around web pages and apps using the keyboard's cursor keys and other keys—including Home, End, PageUp, and PageDown—instead of having to use the mouse.

- **Pressing Windows + Volume Up will turn on** gives you a choice in the accessibility features (or nothing) that activate when you press the Windows key + Volume Up on your keyboard (assuming you have a Volume Up key on your keyboard). You can have this key combination turn on the Magnifier, the Narrator, or the onscreen keyboard.

- **Show notifications for** is a useful setting for people who feel that onscreen notifications disappear before they can be read. In this setting, you can set notifications to appear on screen for up to 5 minutes.

- **Cursor thickness** allows the width of the main cursor to be increased when editing text or entering text in a field (such as the Internet Explorer address bar). This option makes the cursor much easier to see.

■ **Note**   The Ease of Access features in PC Settings and on the desktop work independently of one another. This means that in order to use Ease of Access features in both the Start screen and on the desktop, you need to set the options for both.

The Ease of Access Center

So far, we've discussed how the Ease of Access options affect the way you interact with Windows 8. If you use the desktop, however, there are many more options available to you. This is because of the differences between the desktop and standard Windows 8 interfaces, and the added complexity of desktop software.

You can access the full Ease of Access Center through the Control Panel on the desktop. In the main part of the page are clear and large controls for turning on the Magnifier, Narrator, onscreen keyboard, and high-contrast color scheme (see Figure 10-2).

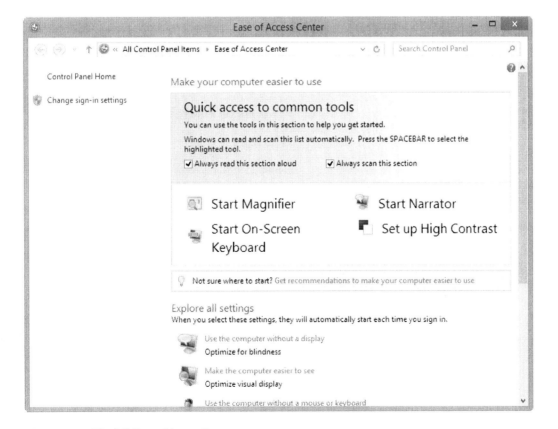

Figure 10-2. *The full Ease of Access Center*

Below this, you see **Not sure where to start? Get recommendations to make your computer easier to use**. This option activates a wizard that asks you simple questions. The wizard automatically sets the Ease of Access Center settings according to the answers that you provide.

The following are the full Ease of Access Center options.

- **Use the computer without a display** optimizes the PC for use by the blind or partially sighted. It reads instructions aloud to help guide you through the settings.

- **Make the computer easier to see** contains many options, including turning on a high-contrast color scheme, making the cursor thicker, and turning on the Magnifier.

- **Use the computer without a mouse or keyboard** includes settings for permanently turning on the onscreen keyboard and also for using speech recognition with your computer.

- **Make the mouse easier to use** switches the mouse buttons (if you are left-handed). It also offers other functions, including the ability to use the numeric pad on your keyboard as a mouse substitute.

▨ **Tip** As muscular problems such as repetitive stress syndrome (sometimes knows as repetitive strain injury) become more commonplace, it is becoming easier to find and purchase mice designed to help people continue to use their computer when a standard mouse and keyboard are uncomfortable to use. To find these devices, search online for **RSS** or **RSI mouse**.

- Make the keyboard easier to use turns on sticky keys so that you don't have to press two keys simultaneously when performing Ctrl+ actions, among other functions.

- Use text or visual alternatives for sounds activates visual clues, such as flashing the desktop, on occasions when Windows 8 would ordinarily play a warning sound.

- **Make it easier to focus on tasks** turns off background images and animations. This option is useful for people who find background images distracting.

- **Make touch and tablets easier to use** offers the Windows key + Volume Up button options.

In the left navigation pane of the Ease of Access Center is an option to Change Sign-in Settings. It is here that you find additional options to automatically turn on Ease of Access features at Windows logon. This includes the onscreen keyboard, the Magnifier (so that you can see where to enter your password), and the Narrator (see Figure 10-3).

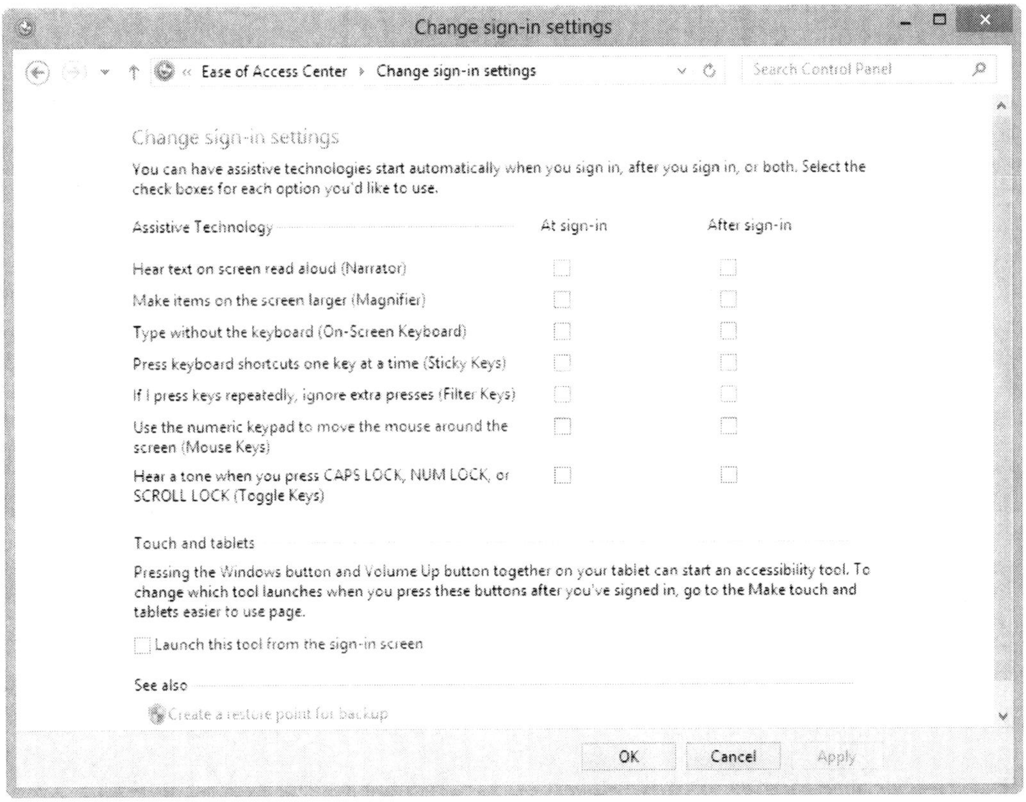

Figure 10-3. *Changing the Ease of Access sign-in settings*

Making Text and Windows Easier to Read

If you find the Windows desktop text and buttons difficult to see and read, there are several options you can select and features you can activate to help. These include the ability to scale up everything on the desktop to a maximum of 150 percent its normal size. Windows can do this without distorting anything on the screen.

To access this feature, right-click anywhere in a blank space on the desktop. From the context menu, select Screen Resolution. Next, click **Make text and other items larger or smaller** for scaling options (see Figure 10-4).

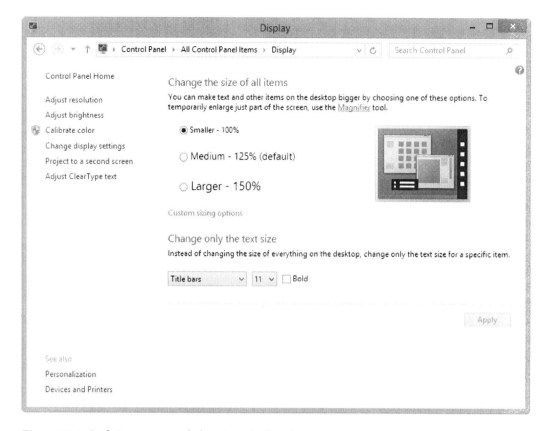

Figure 10-4. *Scale items on your desktop to make them larger*

This option makes everything on the screen proportionally larger without causing blurring, which is a common side effect of lowering the PC's screen resolution. You may only want to scale up certain types of text, however; perhaps even greater than the 150 percent offered.

Below the main scaling options is an additional option to individually specify the size of a variety of text items on the screen. You can change the Title bars on windows, menus, message boxes, palette titles, items, and tooltips. What this option won't allow you to do is further scale up the main text within windows and programs; but many software packages—including Internet Explorer and Microsoft Office—allow you to do this anyway, as I will detail shortly. Also with this option, you can specify that items always appear in bold to help them stand out.

In the left navigation pane, you see an option to Adjust ClearType Text. ClearType is a system that Windows uses to make text more legible on screen. There are many different types of screens, however, and people see in different ways, so the default settings may not be best suited for an individual user.

Clicking Adjust ClearType Text displays a wizard in which Windows shows you different blocks of text. At each stage, you click the one that is most legible, and Windows automatically adjusts the ClearType settings accordingly, so that the text on screen is at its most legible for you.

It is also possible to scale web pages and some document types. Not only does this make text easier to read, it also makes some web sites easier to navigate because buttons and links become larger.

In Internet Explorer 10, you can zoom in and out of web sites by pressing the Ctrl++ and Ctrl+- keys. These controls are also found in IE10 settings (see Figure 10-5).

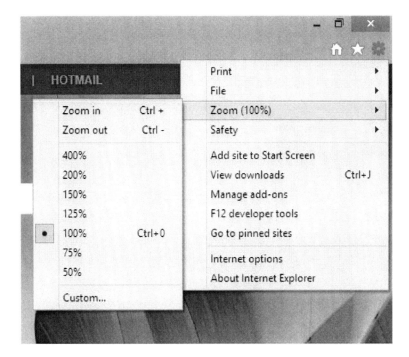

Figure 10-5. *Zooming web pages*

Some document types allow zooming. For many years, Microsoft Office has offered a tool that is located on the bottom-right of the Open window (see Figure 10-6). With this tool, you can zoom in and out of a document by using the slider or clicking the current percentage.

Figure 10-6. *Scaling Documents*

Many Windows 8 apps support pinch-touch gestures to zoom in and out. You can take advantage of these is you have a touchscreen on your computer.

■ **Tip**   You can zoom in and out of many apps and desktop programs in Windows 8 by pinch-zooming outward with a touch gesture. Some laptops come equipped with multitouch trackpads that support pinch-zoom gestures if you do not have a touchscreen.

Zooming in and out of documents and the desktop may not be sufficient enough. A high-contrast color scheme may be required if you are colorblind. To access this option, right-click anywhere in a blank space on the desktop and from the context menu, click Personalization (see Figure 10-7).

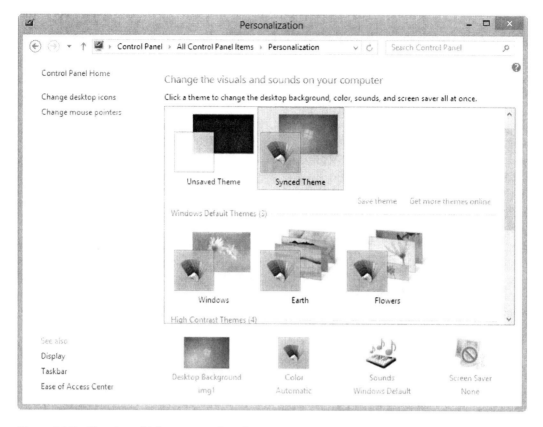

Figure 10-7. *Choosing a high-contrast color scheme*

In the Personalization window, there are several high-contrast color schemes for you to choose from. Alternatively, if you don't need a high-contrast scheme but have trouble with the look of Windows, you can switch to a different Windows color scheme, which makes some parts of the window furniture—such as the Minimize, Maximize, and Close buttons—much easier to see.

There are also high-contrast desktop themes available to help with issues varying from poor eyesight to color-blindness. These are also from the main Personalization page. Some public and charitable organizations provide additional themes for Windows. They can advise on the best combination of options for your specific circumstances.

If the scaling options and high-contrast themes don't make it easier for you to see in Windows 8, you can turn on the Magnifier from the Ease of Access Center. By default, this tool zooms everything on your screen. You can click the magnifying glass icon near the top left of the screen to access additional Magnifier controls (see Figure 10-8).

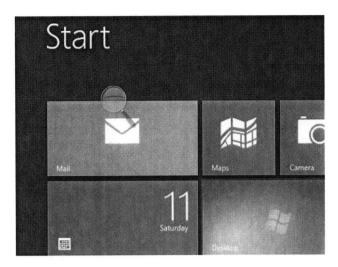

Figure 10-8. *The Magnifier displays a magnifying glass that you can click for more control*

The main controls for the Magnifier allow you to zoom in and out, as well as display the Magnifier in different ways.

- The Magnifier can be **Docked** to the top of the screen to display a larger version of the portion of the screen where your cursor is located.

- A **Lens** follows your cursor around the screen, zooming in on that small portion of the screen.

All options are selected by clicking the magnifying glass icon to reveal the full Magnifier options (see Figure 10-9).

Figure 10-9. *Clicking in the magnifying glass reveals the full Magnifier controls*

Clicking the Cog button displays a menu of options for the Magnifier, including inverting screen colors to improve contrast, and automatically jumping to text input boxes.

You can make the mouse cursor easier to see independently of the desktop theme as well. In the Ease of Access Center, click Make the Mouse Easier to Use. This displays some high-contrast options for the mouse, complete with images of what the cursor will look like with each option selected (see Figure 10-10).

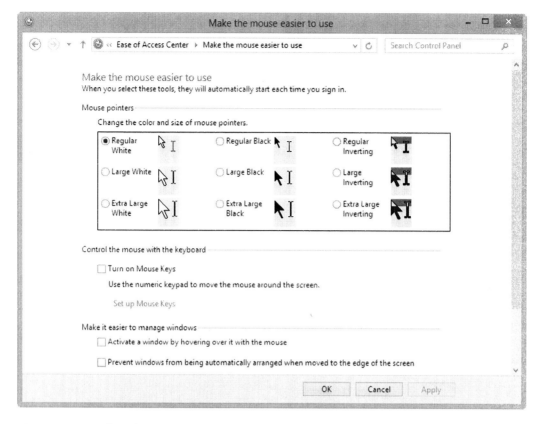

Figure 10-10. *Making the mouse easier to use*

By turning on Mouse Keys, you can also use the keyboard as a mouse, either as a replacement to or in conjunction with your regular mouse. This feature allows you to use the arrow keys on your computer's number pad (if your keyboard has one) to move the mouse cursor. This can also be useful if you have trouble using the mouse for long periods of time.

Other useful features include making a window active simply by hovering over it with your mouse. If you have difficulty with mouse buttons, you might find this option helpful.

Using the Narrator to Read Text Aloud

The Narrator tool assists those who are blind, partially-sighted, or simply have trouble reading the computer screen. This feature reads out text and other items on your screen as you mouse over, touch, or click it. It also read text in panels, such as web sites and Windows alert messages. As an item on screen is read, it is highlighted by a blue box. This helps people who are partially sighted track what is being read. The Narrator is most easily switched on by pressing the Windows key to return to the Start screen and then typing **narrator** followed by pressing the Enter key.

Controls are available both from **Control whether Narrator starts when I sign in** and from the sign-in screen (in the bottom-left corner) to make sure the Narrator is automatically turned on when you sign in to your computer.

There are also a significant number of keyboard shortcuts that you can use to control the Narrator. You can display a complete list of them at any time by pressing the Caps Lock+F1 key combination. Most of the Narrator commands use the Caps Lock key because it isn't used for any other purpose. While the Narrator is on, you need to use the Shift key for capital letters.

Windows 8 enhancements to the Narrator include the welcome ability to speed up and slow down the narrator's voice. In the Voice section of the Narrator Settings window, there are slider controls that adjust the speed of the voice, which by default is set at 50 percent; the volume of the voice, which is set at maximum by default; and the pitch of the voice, which is set at 50 percent. There are also a variety of voices that you can select. The commands available for reading web sites have also been expanded to ensure that more items on a web page can be read aloud.

The main Narrator Settings window is shown in Figure 10-11.

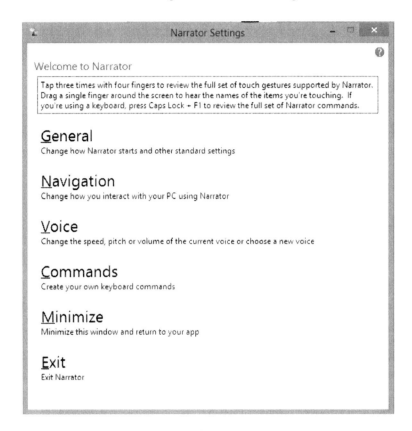

Figure 10-11. *The Narrator in Windows 8*

Windows 8 Narrator enhancements include ways to assist people with using touchscreen devices, including sounds to accompany actions that are performed with touch. These actions audibly confirm that your touch gesture was successful. The Narrator can also read text under your finger as you move it across the computer's screen.

It is important to note that if you want to use the Narrator with a touchscreen, the screen will need to support four or more touch points. This is because some of the Narrator touch gestures use three or four fingers. If you are buying a new touchscreen computer on which you want to use the Narrator, it is important to be aware of this.

Making Your Keyboard and Mouse Easier to Use

It is common for people to have trouble using devices like the mouse. Windows features such as Shake, although perhaps very useful for some people, might prove to be hugely irritating for others. Shake is a desktop feature that minimizes all the windows on the screen when you shake the mouse; it is not very useful if you have difficulty in using a mouse.

To turn off Shake and Snap (they can only be switched off together), follow these instructions:

1.   Open the Ease of Access Center from the Control Panel.

2.   Click **Make the mouse easier to use**.

3.   Check the box **Prevent windows from being automatically arranged when moved to the edge of the screen**.

Additional settings for the mouse are located in the Control Panel or by searching for **mouse** at the Start screen. Some of these functions are extremely useful (see Figure 10-12).

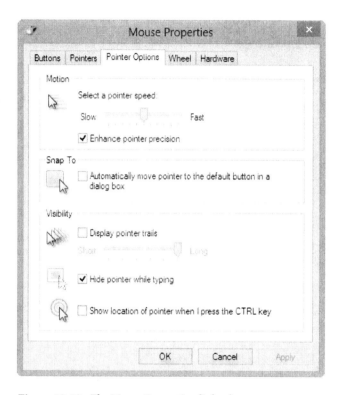

Figure 10-12. *The Mouse Properties dialog box*

- The **Double-Click Speed** of the mouse can be modified to suit you. If you find that you can't double-click the mouse at the speed Windows wants, you can slow it down.

- **ClickLock** is a feature that makes it easier to drag items on the screen. With this feature activated, you don't need to hold down the mouse button to drag. Click the mouse button once to select an item, and then click it again to drop it. This works with both the mouse and the trackpad.

- Windows 8 includes several different schemes to modify the mouse **Pointers,** including the option for large and high-visibility pointers.

- The **Pointer Speed** can be modified in Windows so that the mouse moves more slowly.

- **Snap To** is a useful feature that moves the mouse pointer automatically onto a button when you get close to it.

- **Pointer Trails** can be displayed so that you can more easily see where the mouse is on the screen.

- The ability to **highlight the location** of your mouse pointer on the screen is particularly useful. It is made available when you press the Ctrl key on your keyboard.

Tip   Left-handed computer users can switch the mouse buttons in the Mouse Properties settings.

At the Ease of Access Center, you can turn on various additional features for the computer's keyboard by clicking **Make the keyboard easier to use**. A feature called Sticky Keys is particularly useful.

Sticky Keys allows you to use the keyboard one key at a time. If you need to press a keyboard combination involving the Shift, Ctrl, Alt, or even the Windows key (it is supported even though the Sticky Keys options don't specify it), just press one of these keys, wait to hear a tone while pressing the key, and then press the letter associated with that keystroke (for example Ctrl+C).

Filter Keys is a useful feature that prevents repeated instances of a letter, number, or other character when a particular key is pressed.

Using Text or Visual Alternatives for Sounds

There may be times when you can't hear an alert or other sound on your computer; or to hear, you need the volume turned up to a level where other people complain about it. To help with these issues, Windows 8 offers visual cues to alert you when it would normally use a sound.

From the Ease of Access Center, click Use Text or Visual Alternatives for Sounds. The options include a flashing caption on the screen or flashing the whole desktop to alert you that something needs your attention. Alternatively, Windows can speak the caption (this is useful if you hear voices fine but have difficulty with other sounds).

Making It Easier to Focus on Tasks

To help navigate through the many and varied options in the Ease of Access Center, there is a clickable option to Make It Easier to Focus on Tasks. This page includes many of the common accessibility controls, such as Sticky Keys, the Narrator, and Filter Keys. You can also turn off the desktop background image in this option.

Finding Accessible Apps in Windows 8

With the new Windows Store, Microsoft is making it easier for customers to find accessible apps and for developers to write apps that are accessible. The tools for creating apps that support Windows accessibility are now much simpler for app developers to use.

To find accessible apps, open the Windows Store. Then, open the charms to click the Settings charm. In the top right of the screen, a Preferences option, when clicked, displays a switch to make it easier to find accessible apps. With this selected, the Windows Store will only display apps that support accessibility features.

Where to Find Accessibility Help and Support

Many of the option pages in the Ease of Access Center offer you the option to **Learn about additional assistive technologies online**. Clicking this link directs you to Microsoft's web site at www.microsoft.com/enable. Here you can read more about the accessibility features in Windows 8, as well as view video and other tutorials on their use.

This web site also contains links to third-party help, support, and commercial web sites where you can find advice and products designed to help make your computer more accessible and easier to use.

Summary

The accessibility features in Windows 8 are extensive. They make Windows 8 the most accessible operating system available today. I recommend starting at the desktop Ease of Access Center wizard. Run it by clicking **Get recommendations to make your computer easier to use**. The wizard asks you a series of questions about how you use your computer and where you find it difficult to use. It then makes recommendations for settings that you can select to make Windows 8 easier to use.

CHAPTER 11

Keeping Yourself, Your Files, and Your Computer Safe

Despite Windows' history of being very insecure and a hotbed for malware and viruses, this really isn't true any more. It's also not true that the security systems in Windows 8 are annoying, or lacking in flexibility, or difficult to use.

By default, Windows 8 is actually very good at taking care of itself. It needs to be. Most users don't want to worry about updates to Windows and antivirus software. They certainly don't want to have to change firewall settings to allow a game through a port.

If anything, the default settings for security in Windows 8 really are perfectly all right for general computer usage. If anything is going to be exploited, it's the soft, squidgy thing sitting at the keyboard, vulnerable to criminals who get them to click something that allows malware through the already excellent security in Windows 8.

Windows 8 includes more than just anti-virus software and security features though as there are also government-level file and disk encryption technologies that can be as simple to set up and use as a fresh user account.

In this chapter, I'll talk you through all the security features in the operating system, explain what they do, and show you how you can customize them to meet your own individual needs.

How Secure Is Windows 8 Really?

Windows 8 is arguably the most secure version of Windows in the history of the operating system due to the inclusion of anti-virus security software. It builds on previous security features, including User Account Control (UAC), which was first introduced in Windows Vista.

Some security researchers claimed that Windows 7 is even more secure than some UNIX-based operating systems; they will no doubt applaud Windows 8 as well. This is primarily due to the proactive approach that Microsoft takes to patching security flaws as they are discovered.

However, you cannot rely on an operating system to be secure on its own. Every time you install a program or app, you open the possibility of compromising your security. When you go online or check your e-mail, you open the possibility that someone, somewhere might attempt to trick you into installing malware.

It is important to look at Windows 8 security in a holistic way and not in isolation. In this chapter, I'll show you how to make sure that Windows 8 is completely secure. This chapter also refers back, in parts, to Chapter 3, where I showed you how to stay safe when you are connected to the Internet.

Maintaining Security When Using Windows 8 with Other Windows Versions

Windows 8 is secure, and Windows 7 and Windows Vista are also secure, at least when all precautions and safeguards are put in place and when features such as UAC remain turned on at their default setting.

Commonly, computers are used in a networked environment with other Windows PCs, not all of which will be running the same version of Windows. It is possible that some of these PCs are running Windows XP. All security and update support ends (or ended, depending on when you are reading this) for Windows XP in April 2014. This means that after this date, there will no longer be updates or patches to fix security or other vulnerabilities. If you are using your Windows 8 computer in an environment where there is an XP machine, you should not share files and folders with it.

The reason for this is that Windows XP is still widely used in the developing world and some countries in Asia. The arrival of Windows 8 is unlikely to change this situation much in the near future and, as such, after April 2014, the Windows XP operating system will be a huge target for malware writers and hackers.

After twelve years of patches and updates, there really shouldn't be any security flaws left, but you can be certain that some will still exist and be the targets of criminals.

You should also be wary of sharing files and folders with Windows 7 and Windows Vista, which are the main way malware would spread on a home or work network. This is because you may not know how the other computers on that network are managed or what their security is like. You may be using your Windows 8 computer in a workplace where all computers are managed the same way. Here you can be confident that the environment is enclosed with an SEP field[1] and is the responsibility of the IT department.

Maintaining Security When Using Windows 8 with Non-Windows Operating Systems

If you are using Windows 8 in an environment where there are other operating systems, then people's views might differ. If the other computers were Apple iMacs, for example, then some would argue they're more secure than Windows. In fact, I would argue that the opposite is true because Apple doesn't adopt the same stringent policy for maintaining security that Microsoft does and, as a result, Apple can be slow to respond to threats such as the malware attack in early 2012, which infected some 600,000 Apple Mac computers.

Computers running Linux are unlikely to pose a threat to your own computer security because the overall market share for this operating system isn't large enough to get the attention of malware writers.

This brings us to tablets, where Apple's iOS operating system and Windows 8 are perfectly secure—but Google's Android is anything but. This is because Google does not vet programs submitted to their app store in the same way that Apple and Microsoft do. As a result, any tablets or computers running Android should always be treated with caution.

---

[1] In the comedy science-fiction book *Life, the Universe and Everything* by Douglas Adams (Pan Macmillan, 1982), an SEP field is described as ". . . something we can't see, or don't see, or our brain doesn't let us see, because we think that it's somebody else's problem. . . . The brain just edits it out, it's like a blind spot. If you look at it directly you won't see it unless you know precisely what it is. Your only hope is to catch it by surprise out of the corner of your eye."

The technology involved in making something properly invisible is so mind-bogglingly complex that 999,999,999 times out of a billion it's simpler just to take the thing away and do without it. The "Somebody Else's Problem field" is much simpler, more effective, and "can be run for over a hundred years on a single torch battery."

This is because it relies on people's natural predisposition not to see anything they don't want to, weren't expecting, or can't explain. This description comes about when somebody parks a spaceship, actually a small Italian bistro, on the field at Lords cricket ground in London.

⬛ **Note   The Myth of Mac Security:** While it's true that, historically, Apple's Mac computers have been *almost* invulnerable to virus attacks due to the way the security of the operating system's UNIX-base was designed, this is sadly no longer the case. In recent years, malware writers, primarily in response to improved security in Windows, have focused more on tricking the Mac user into installing and permitting malware. This—along with Apple's slow response to some malware threats, as well as the rapid market growth for Apple computers—has greatly increased the threat to the platform.

Windows Defender

I started this chapter by saying that Windows 8 is the first version of Windows to come with built-in security software. Some of you may balk at the suggestion that Windows Defender, a rebadged version of Microsoft's free antivirus solution, Security Essentials, is actually effective at defending against malware at all.

In truth though, so long as you're aware of the online threats, Windows Defender is a perfectly good antivirus package and is all the malware protection you need on your computer.

It is based on Microsoft's award-winning Forefront antivirus package for Windows Server and it is very effective. When you look at the quarterly reports for the effectiveness of all the major antivirus packages, there is always some fluctuation in the brand rankings, depending on the threats that have been found in the previous six months and how effectively the manufacturers dealt with them.

There is no reason not to use Windows Defender, however. I never recommend installing any software that duplicates functionality that's already in Windows because this adds layers of complexity that can lead to problems. Shortly, I will detail some of my recommended alternatives, should you wish to use something else.

Configuring and Updating Windows Defender

One of the problems for Windows 8 users is that Windows Defender (see Figure 11-1) is very difficult for casual users to find. It doesn't appear in the PC Settings window; it is hidden on the desktop. You can most easily find it by searching for **defender** at the Start screen.

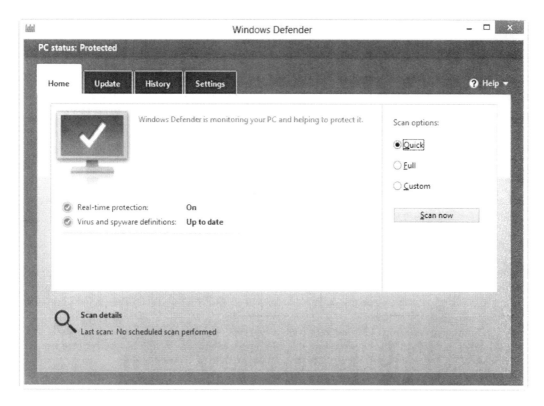

Figure 11-1. *Windows Defender*

Windows Defender has quite a simple interface with just four tabs: Home, Update, History, and Settings.

- The **Home tab** provides details on the current update and scanning status of the software. It allows access to perform quick, full, and custom scans. A custom scan would include scanning an external hard disk, for example.

- The **Update tab** provides information on when the software was last updated. The large Update button updates the software. It really is that simple.

- The **History tab** allows you to view reports of any suspicious or dangerous files.

- The **Settings tab** contains advanced settings for the program. It is here that you can exclude certain files (perhaps a program is being reported as malware when you know it isn't) and you can also join the Microsoft Active Protection Service and report details of suspicious files back to Microsoft.

■ **Note**   Real Time Protection should remain switched on. If you deactivate it, Windows Defender is not able to scan new files or web sites as you open them.

This does mean that Windows Defender isn't as configurable as some other packages, but why do we need antivirus software to be configurable anyway? I would argue that the whole point of antivirus software is to always provide complete protection, while staying out of the way.

Staying out of the way is something that Windows Defender does extremely well because it only runs scans and downloads updates when you're not using the computer. This means that if you're working, gaming, or doing some other intensive job on your PC, Windows Defender won't hog processor cycles or memory trying to update itself or run a full scan.

■ **Note** Windows Defender is updated through Windows Update, so it is extremely important not to switch this service off.

You can configure Windows Defender, however, in the options under the Settings tab. Here you can exclude certain file locations. For example, perhaps you work in computer security or for a computer magazine and have a drive containing viruses so that you can test antivirus products (in which case you've made a good choice using Windows Defender, I might add). You can also exclude certain file types.

■ **Note** You can set Windows Defender to automatically create a Restore Point when it scans. This can slow your computer slightly but if you have a fast PC, you won't notice. It can improve resiliency if virus removal causes Windows to become unstable. Using System Restore might also risk restoring the virus!

To be honest, I wouldn't recommend using either of these two settings unless it is absolutely necessary. The next setting, which excludes certain processes, is of much more use. You can use this feature to exclude some programs from scans if they cause conflicts or report as malware (see Figure 11-2).

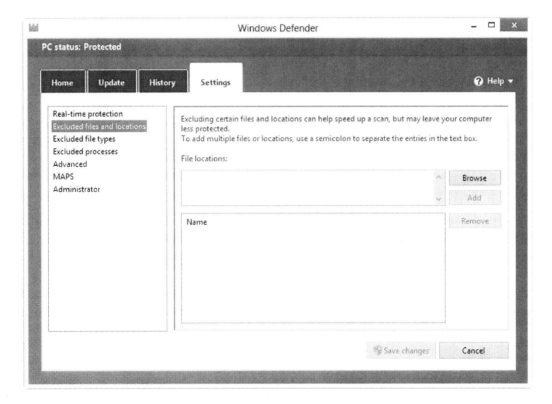

Figure 11-2. *Configuring Windows Defender*

It is actually more common than you might believe for programs to register as malware when they're not. These are called *false-positives*. It might be because the software has to perform the same type of actions on your computer that malware would, perhaps as a diagnostic tool. If you have software installed that registers as malware when it is not, you can exclude it here.

The Advanced settings (shown in Figure 11-3) offer some excellent features that you may want to turn on. These include the full scanning of USB-attached drives when a scan is in operation (remember that malware loves to infect USB flash drives because it's a great way to propagate). You can also set Windows Defender to automatically create a Restore Point when removing a virus. I thoroughly recommend this in case something does indeed go wrong.

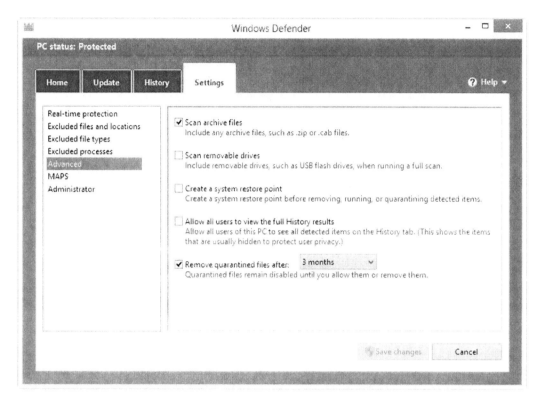

Figure 11-3. *Windows Defender advanced settings*

⬛ **Tip**   It is well worth turning on the Scan Removable Drives and Create a System Restore Point options in Windows Defender. They provide extra security and reliability.

Finding and Installing Third-Party Antivirus Software

So what other antivirus packages are available? Which should you choose? I recommend four that I believe are worthy of consideration because they have consistently scored highly in antivirus scanning tests over the last few years.

- **AVG Anti-Virus Free** (http://free.avg.com) has long been considered one of the best packages available. There is a free version, though in recent years it's become rather obtrusive with annoying ads encouraging you to upgrade to the full paid suite.

- **Norton AntiVirus** and **Norton 360** (`www.symantec.com`) provide some of the finest malware scanning available. It isn't free but is well worth considering. It has a friendly, simple interface and is extremely effective at protecting your computer.

- **Trend Micro Titanium** (`www.trendmicro.com`) is another highly effective antivirus package. It isn't free.

- **Kaspersky Anti-Virus** (`http://usa.kaspersky.com`) isn't quite as effective as the others, but it is extremely configurable. For the power user who wants a fine level of control, it is a very suitable option. This is not a free product.

It is not as easy to recommend McAfee's antivirus products because they have been know to cause problems in recent years. Also, McAfee's scanning and protection abilities are not anywhere near as good as they used to be.

Disabling Windows Defender

If you choose not to use Windows Defender because you are using third-party anti-virus software instead, you can switch it off. This is done under the Settings tab, in the Administrator section (see Figure 11-4).

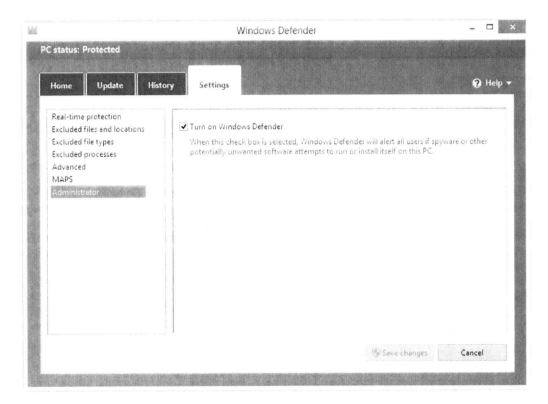

Figure 11-4. *Disabling Windows Defender*

If you are using a third-party antivirus product, you should turn Windows Defender off. I never recommend having two antivirus packages running concurrently because one can interfere with the operation of the other.

Offline Antivirus Scanners

There are some very effective offline virus scanners that start your computer from a USB flash drive to scan for and remove malware.

Regardless of what I said earlier about McAfee, it is difficult to criticize the quality of their offline offerings (`www.mcafee.com/us/downloads/free-tools`), which include the malware removal tools GetSusp and Stinger.

Microsoft also has an offline version of Windows Defender called Windows Defender Offline (`http://windows.microsoft.com/en-US/windows/what-is-windows-defender-offline`), which uses a USB flash drive to scan your computer for malware and remove it.

You should only download these tools as required. Do not use older versions. This ensures that the software version you use includes the most up-to-date malware data.

Using the Windows Firewall

Unlike Windows Defender, the Windows Firewall could be described as having a split personality. On initial examination, it's no more complicated to use than its antivirus brother is; but under the surface, the number of configuration options are huge.

Configuring and Maintaining the Windows Firewall

The basic Windows 8 Firewall window, which you can open by searching for **firewall** at the Start screen, doesn't offer many features and certainly doesn't offer a large Turn the Firewall Off button. It gives you information about the network you are currently connected to and shows you the current state of the firewall as it pertains to that network (see Figure 11-5).

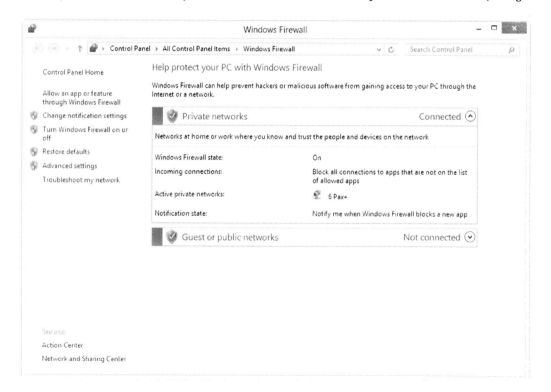

Figure 11-5. *The basic Windows 8 firewall*

There are many additional options, however, even for the basic firewall. You access these options through the left navigation. I want to talk you through each of them individually.

Allow an app or feature through Windows Firewall allows a program that has been blocked by Windows 8 because of suspicious activity (which is known to happen with older programs especially) or because you accidentally denied it permission.

It's not just simply allowing a program or app to install, however. You first have to click the Change Settings button to confirm to Windows that this is something you really want to do. This prevents malware from automatically coming through if you have inadvertently allowed it to install through UAC.

If a program or app doesn't appear in the list, you can click the Allow Another App button to manually browse for and permit a program or app (see Figure 11-6).

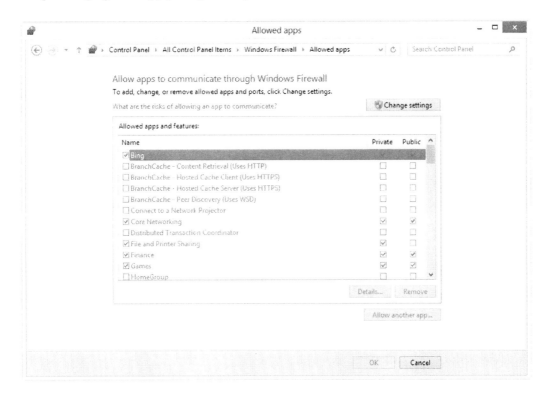

Figure 11-6. *Allowing a program or app through the firewall*

▓ **Tip**   If you are having trouble with your firewall, you can click Restore Defaults in the main firewall window to reset it to its default configuration.

Change notification settings and **Turn Windows Firewall on or off** allow you to turn off the firewall if you *really* want to. Both links take you to the same place (see Figure 11-7). I only recommend using these options if you are using a third-party firewall that you're happy with.

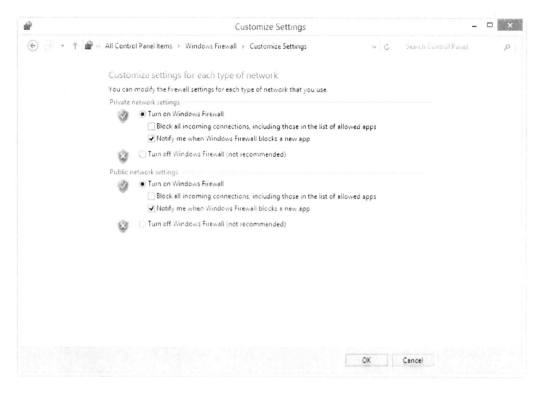

Figure 11-7. *You can turn off the Windows Firewall*

What's more, you can choose to have the firewall switched off in private networks, but remain on in public networks.

So why would you want to do this? Well, you might be a gamer and the firewall interferes with your online gaming at home, or you might be an office worker whose IT department asks you to switch off Windows Firewall because it conflicts with something on their system.

On a laptop, however, you still want to have the protection of the firewall when you're out and about. This is where you can leave the firewall turned on for public networks.

There is also a check box for blocking all incoming connections. This provides better security, especially on public networks, but you might find that some programs or apps won't work because they require this feature to be switched off.

Restore defaults resets Windows Firewall to its default setting. This is very useful if you've made advanced changes and can't remember what they were to undo them.

Using the Advanced Firewall

From the main firewall window, clicking Advanced Settings takes you to a different management console (see Figure 11-8), where you can set specific rules for both inbound and outbound traffic, and perform other operations, such as opening and blocking specific connection ports.

Figure 11-8. *The advanced firewall settings in Windows 8*

The main pane in the center displays the current firewall status, but there are two other panes here that you need to be familiar with. On the left side is a tree showing different options within the firewall. These are inbound and outbound rules, connection security rules, and firewall monitoring. (I will discuss each of these shortly.) On the right side are controls, including options to create and manage rules for the firewall.

To create a new firewall, first click Inbound Rules, Outbound Rules, or Connection Security Rules in the left pane, and then click New Rule in the right-hand pane to open the New Rule wizard (seeFigure 11-9).

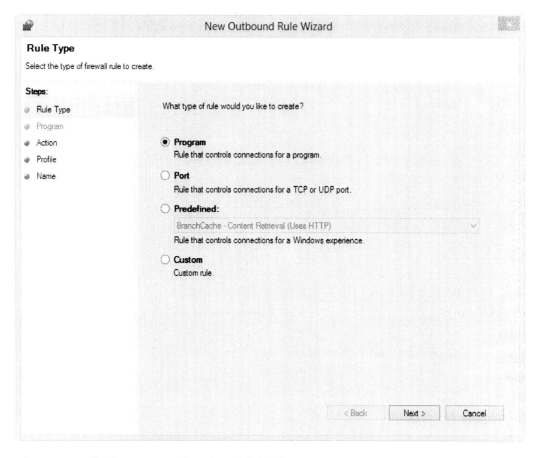

Figure 11-9. *All rules settings are done through helpful wizards*

Inbound Rules and **Outbound Rules** allow you to monitor and set rules for individual programs. You can click New Rule in the right-hand pane to create a new rule for a program or to allow or block a port on your computer.

Port opening and blocking is common with applications such as gaming and file sharing, where communications ports that are not normally used are blocked by firewalls by default.

Here you can set, for example, certain programs or ports to only operate if the data connection is secure. If you use your computer for work and perhaps work in an industry such as security, government, research, or pharmaceuticals, you might want your work applications to only transmit and receive data when you are connected to a secured and properly encrypted network. It is here that you can set specific programs or apps to only operate under these circumstances (see Figure 11-10).

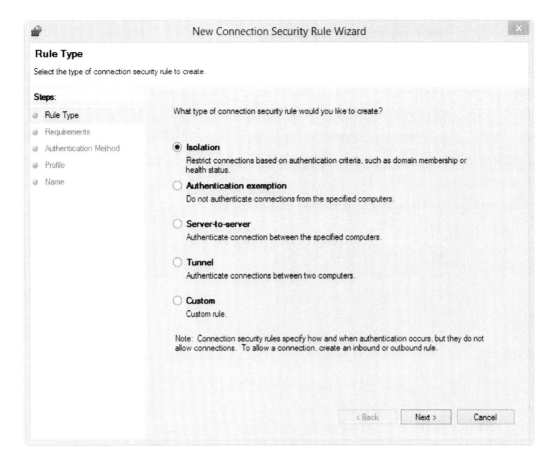

Figure 11-10. *Setting connection rules*

On the issue of secure connections, even if you only connect to your company through a virtual private network (VPN), you might be asked to set specific connection security rules so that your computer can be authenticated. You do this in the Connection Security Rules section, which specifies the type of connection you want (there are descriptions to assist you) and the type of authentication required by both computers before the connection is allowed.

When setting this up, you will likely have specific settings to input from your company or organization, and these will be specific to them alone.

One very useful feature is to create a custom connection rule whereby you can set—either with or without encryption or authentication—connections between two or several specific computers on specific IP addresses (see Figure 11-11).

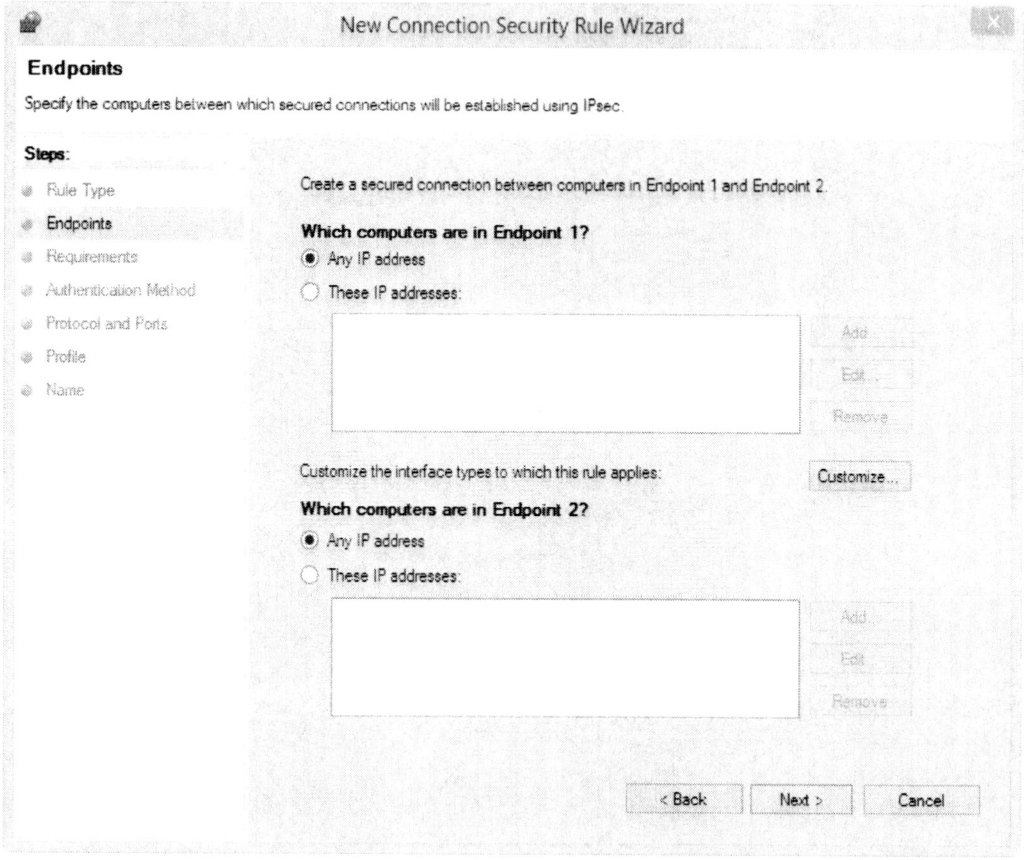

Figure 11-11. *Creating custom connections*

If you have a closed connection in an office and only want computers in the payroll department (for example) to be able to see and connect to other payroll computers, you can set their IP addresses here. However, you would need to set both inbound and outbound rules, as well as rules to clock all other IP address connections to the computer.

■ **Note** If you are only allowing connections from your computer, you need to make sure that the permitted computers have static IP addresses set in your router.

User Account Control

First introduced with Windows Vista, UAC is your main line of defense against unwanted software being installed on your computer, or unwanted changes being made to your copy of Windows or your computer's settings.

When a change is made to your computer that can affect other users, or potentially allow the installation of malware, or cause the computer to become unstable, UAC changes the desktop to a secure mode (the same one used when you log on to your computer) and only displays the UAC prompt on the screen. Unlike Windows 7, you won't see anything else.

In this mode, no software is permitted to act, and as such, malware cannot automatically click itself through. You have to choose a yes or no option, though Windows 8 can give you additional information about what is happening—and sometimes it is useful and written in plain language.

■ **Tip**   The best rule to follow is that if a UAC prompt appears at a time when you personally are not installing software or changing a Windows setting, you should *always* click **No**.

You can change the setting for UAC by searching for **uac** at the Start screen, where you will find it in the settings results (see Figure 11-12). I always recommend that you leave UAC with its defaults setting because it offers the best security without the feature becoming annoying.

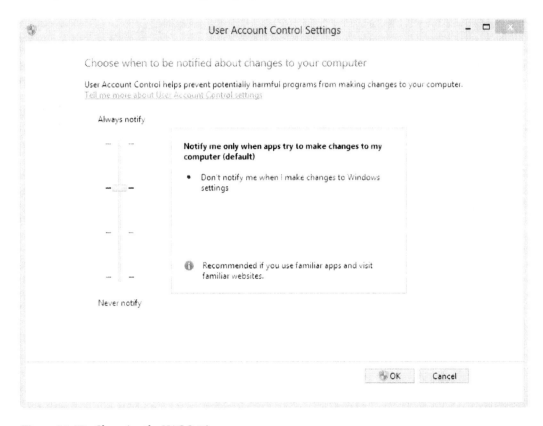

Figure 11-12. *Changing the UAC Settings*

There are four settings for UAC that vary from off to annoying.

- **Never notify me** turns UAC off completely. I recommend never using this setting.

- **Notify me only when apps try to make changes to my computer (do not dim my desktop)** is another setting I don't recommend. While this setting allows you to make whatever settings changes you want to Windows 8 without being bothered by UAC, it doesn't switch to the secure desktop mode when software is installed. This may permit malware to autoclick the UAC prompt for you.

- **Notify me only when apps try to make changes to my computer** is the default setting. I strongly recommend you leave it as is.

- **Always notify me** is otherwise known as "annoying mode."

So what is the difference between the default and the annoying modes? Some Windows 8 controls have a UAC shield icon next to them. This is to alert you that whatever you're doing here can affect other users or how the computer behaves.

In the default mode, Windows allows you to make changes that only affect your own user account, without popping up a UAC prompt. It is only when you're installing software or making changes that can affect other users (if you only have a single-user account it assumes more could be added later) that a UAC prompt appears.

Conversely, when in annoying mode, UAC gives you a security prompt for everything that can affect your own user account as well. This is much more secure but . . . well, it is plain annoying.

Encrypting Files, Folders, and Drives

On your Windows 8 computer—be it a desktop, laptop, or tablet—you can encrypt your data and the entire hard disk. But should you? I want to carefully look at and consider the usefulness of each of the three encryption technologies in Windows 8.

Encrypting Files and Folders Using the Encrypting File System

The question of whether to use a Windows encryption technology applies especially to the Encrypting File System (EFS). This system can be used to encrypt individual files or folders in Windows. It has been with us since Windows 2000. It uses 256-bit keys and a mix of several encryption systems based around AES to provide overall security.

You can encrypt an individual file or folder (or a selected group) by following these instructions:

1. Right-click the item(s) to be encrypted. Select Properties from the options that appear.

2. Click the Advanced button in the Attributes section.

3. Check the **Encrypt contents to secure data** box (see Figure 11-13).

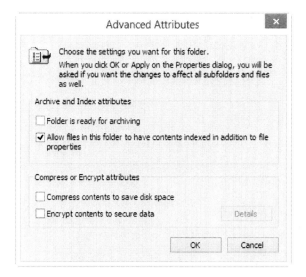

Figure 11-13. *Encrypting files and folders using EFS*

4. Click OK to begin the encryption.

The encryption process could take some time, depending on the number of files and folders that you are encrypting. You should not cancel the dialog box that appears on screen because this will cancel the encryption process.

You can *decrypt* files in the same way by following the same instructions and unchecking the **Encrypt contents** box.

How EFS Works

EFS is tied to your Windows user account. Whenever you log on to Windows using this account, you are automatically able to read, write, and modify EFS-protected files. If you log on to your computer using another account, however, or even if you have to reinstall Windows 8 and then log on using the same username and password you used before, you will be unable to access these files until you import your EFS key. Once you have imported the appropriate EFS key, you will be able to read the files again.

Backing Up and Restoring Your EFS Key

When you have encrypted files or folders using EFS Windows, a desktop Taskbar alert will prompt you to back up your EFS key. It is extremely important that you back up this key and keep it in a safe location *away* from the computer.

You will be asked to set a password for your key, which prevents anyone from importing it onto their computer or user account and opening your files.

You can manually back up and restore EFS keys in Windows 8 by searching for **encrypt** at the Start screen and then clicking **Manage file encryption certificates** in the Encrypting File System window that starts the wizard (see Figure 11-14).

Figure 11-14. Backing up and restoring an EFS key

This is a wizard-based tool and it's extremely simple and easy to use. You can also set the EFS system to only grant access to files if used in conjunction with a smartcard (assuming that your computer has a reader).

Should you change your EFS key—let's say you've moved to a different computer—you can update the cipher used to encrypt the files to the new key on the new computer as well.

Working with EFS-Encrypted Files

In practice, there are several reasons why I can't recommend using EFS. The first and probably the most important is that while it encrypts the contents of files, it still allows people to drill down into your files and folders and view all the file names, which can give away important information in themselves (e.g., `P. Grant Disciplinary 2012-08-21.docx`).

EFS also has what I personally consider a significant flaw. It lost my files on both occasions that I've used it. Because it encrypts individual files and folders, and not a whole disk, those files and folders are *still* encrypted when you copy them elsewhere.

If you have an automated backup solution that copies your files to an external hard disk or network attached storage (NAS) drive, the backed up files will also be encrypted. "Great!" you say. This is exactly what you want.

Unfortunately, EFS requires NTFS-formatted hard drives in order to work, but some external hard disks, especially NAS appliances, are often formatted using different methods. In such cases, you may find that your backups are completely scrambled and unreadable when you try to restore them.

Encrypting Drives with BitLocker

A much better encryption solution is BitLocker, which is a full-drive encryption system that was first introduced with Windows Vista. It uses a 128-bit AES cipher and can combine a Trusted Platform Module (TPM) chip on your motherboard with a pin and/or a USB flash drive to enhance security.

The main advantage of this method is that the encryption is tied to a chip on your motherboard, which contains the decryption cipher; not even the removal of the hard disk will allow people to read your encrypted files. The downside is that you need a TPM chip on your motherboard for BitLocker to work on your computer's hard drive(s), and it's uncommon for desktops to come with one fitted.

TPM chips are much more common on laptops, but they can push up the price and, as such, are most commonly found only on high-end business and workstation laptops.

This is disappointing because modern data protection regulations around the world demand that data is protected securely—and BitLocker is an absolutely brilliant way of achieving it.

░ **Note**   BitLocker is only available in Windows 8 Pro and Enterprise.

Because BitLocker provides full disk encryption, any files that you copy from your computer are decrypted automatically. While this might sound like a disaster, it does mean that backups are always readable (you do need to keep them safe, however) and that nobody can read any of the file names on your computer without unlocking the drive(s) with the appropriate key.

Preparing Your TPM Chip

Before you can use Bitlocker on your computer with a Trusted Platform Module (TPM) chip you need to activate the chip. You can do this by clicking the *TPM Administration* link in the bottom left of the main Bitlocker window, see Figure 11-15. The main TPMr administration page (see Figure 11-15) shows the status of your Trusted Platform Module chip. Before you can use BitLocker, however, you need to turn on the TPM chip on your motherboard.

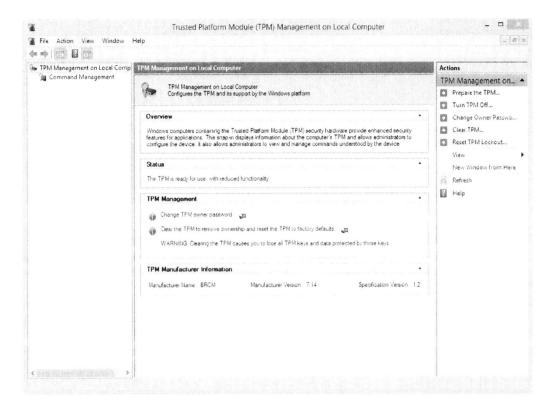

Figure 11-15. *Managing your TPM chip in Windows 8*

If you do not have a TPM-enabled computer, you won't be able to encrypt your hard disk. If your computer is TPM-enabled, however, you will see options to Prepare the TPM and more. For example, you can turn off TPM (be certain that you have no encrypted drives when you do this— see "When to Decrypt Your Hard Disks" later in the chapter) or clear the TPM of all its stored ciphers completely. If the TPM chip has locked you out of your computer (more on this later), you can reset a lockout once you have gained access.

To use BitLocker, you need to Prepare the TPM, which requires rebooting your computer because settings are changed in the BIOS or UEFI firmware (you can also turn it on there). Should you need to manage the TPM later on, this page provides all the controls to do so.

Activating BitLocker

Once your TPM chip is enabled, use the main BitLocker page to turn the feature on (see Figure 11-16), which you access from the Control Panel. You can encrypt all the hard drives on your computer, but you must complete the encryption of the drive on which you have Windows 8 installed. In order to encrypt any extra drives with BitLocker, your Windows 8 drive *must also* be encrypted.

■ **Note** BitLocker does *not* work with dual-boot systems! If you have or are planning to have a dual-boot system on your computer, BitLocker will lock you out of your computer each time you try to start it.

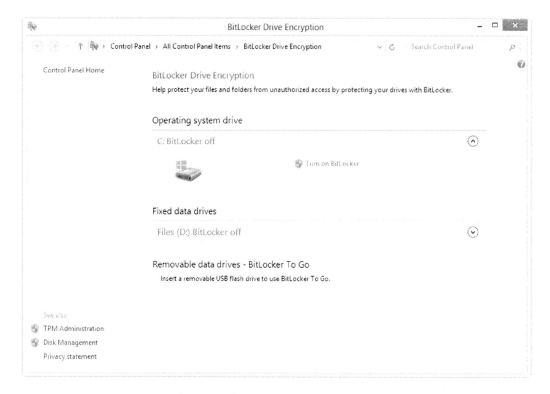

Figure 11-16. *Managing BitLocker in Windows 8*

Unlike EFS, BitLocker encrypts your hard drive in the background and it is perfectly fine for you to shut down your computer during the process because BitLocker will simply continue when you next log on. This is useful because it can take many hours to encrypt a large hard disk that is already full of files and folders.

You can also turn off BitLocker on protected drives. This is where decrypting drives is slightly easier than encrypting them. If, for example, you have two or more physical hard disks or partitions on your computer and you want to encrypt several of them, you must first complete the encryption of your Windows 8 drive before you can manually start encryption of the others. When decrypting drives, however, you can start all the jobs at the same time—and Windows 8 happily continues if you shut down the computer occasionally.

Backing Up and Restoring Your BitLocker Keys

When BitLocker has encrypted your hard drive, you are automatically prompted to back up your BitLocker key. There are three locations where you can do this:

- **A file on your computer**. Do *not* save the key to a drive that has been encrypted with BitLocker, or else you may not be able to read it again.

- **A USB flash drive**. I strongly recommend you save your key. I shall explain the reasons in the next section.

- **Microsoft SkyDrive**. This cloud service is a secure location. I recommend that you store a copy of your key on a cloud service like this, but it's no good for your main backup.

Starting a BitLocker-Encrypted Computer

The reason I recommend you keep a copy of your BitLocker encryption key on a USB flash drive is because if something happens to make BitLocker unhappy, such as boot change, you will be completely locked out of your computer until you can input the key.

You can type the encryption key, but it is a very long and complex string of characters. You can insert a USB flash drive containing the key, however, and the Windows boot loader will recognize it and grant you access again.

Surely, you say, this defeats the purpose of having an encrypted computer. I would argue that you should never keep your computer *and* the USB drive containing the unlock key in the same place (there is a separate key for each encrypted hard disk or partition). If you are traveling, however, you don't need BitLocker locking you out. It might be some time before you can get to another Internet-connected computer to download the backup.

Therefore, I always recommend that you keep a copy of the backup key(s) on a USB flash drive in a safe location—because you never know when you might need it.

Using BitLocker After a Reinstall of Windows 8

If you are using BitLocker on a computer where it has been used before—perhaps because you have reinstalled Windows 8 or performed a clean install to upgrade from Windows 7 (you should never upgrade an operating system encrypted with BitLocker), you will probably be asked to enter the owner password for your TPM chip (see Figure 11-17). This is set when you activate BitLocker. It is stored in the chip.

Figure 11-17. Clearing the TPM

You will only need to do this if you still have BitLocker-protected drives on the computer, which I don't recommend because you never know what might go wrong, such as electricity surges or laptop drops that cause hard disk corruption. What you can do, however, is clear the TPM chip completely and start afresh, which is the best option if you have no BitLocker encrypted drives in the computer.

You may be prompted to enter the owner password when restoring from a backup— if that backup was made before you encrypted your hard drives with BitLocker. Which brings me to the next section.

When to Decrypt Your Hard Disks

There are times when you should turn off BitLocker—purely to prevent disasters from occurring, as always happens with security technologies. These times include:

- When upgrading your copy of Windows or when installing a new operating system, such as migrating from Windows 7 to Windows 8.

- When moving a hard disk from one computer to another.

- When sending a computer out for repair (I always recommend wiping the data drive in this case).

When you restore your computer from a backup, your drives won't be encrypted. You will have to re-encrypt them.

Using BitLocker To Go

The BitLocker To Go feature doesn't require a TPM chip. This is a full-disk encryption system for USB and other attached flash drives and external hard disks. Unlike BitLocker, it is compatible with a variety of drive formats, including FAT32, exFAT, and NTFS—making it perfect for USB drives.

You encrypt an attached USB or other device with BitLocker To Go through the main BitLocker Window. Again, there is the same on/off control as there is for your internal hard disks (see Figure 11-18). BitLocker To Go only requires that you set a password, which is entered when you want to read or access the disk on another computer.

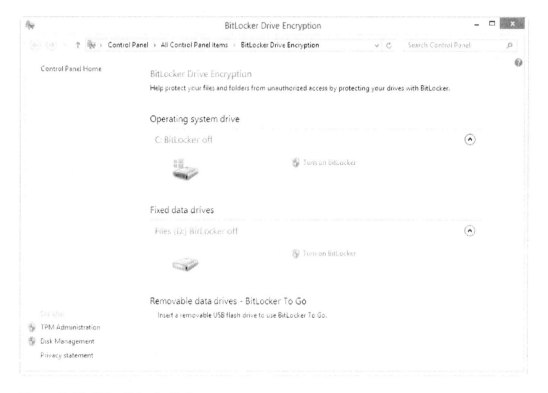

Figure 11-18. *Using BitLocker To Go*

When using a BitLocker To Go encrypted drive on another computer, there are limits to what you can do. For example, in versions of Windows that support the same version of BitLocker, namely Windows 7, you can get full access to the drive.

On Windows Vista and Windows XP, however, you have the BitLocker To Go Reader, which is software that, on entering your password, allows you to read the contents of the protected drive, but doesn't allow you to write files back to it.

This is an important consideration when using BitLocker To Go. You should ask yourself, "Am I going to want to edit these files on another computer?" If the answer is yes, as long as the computer is running Windows 7 or Windows 8, you will be fine. If not, then you will have more difficulty.

Because you can open and read files, however, there is nothing to stop you from saving a copy of that file locally and e-mailing the modified file to yourself once you have edited it. This is really the only way to edit files on a protected drive in Windows Vista or Windows XP.

Encryption Best Practice

BitLocker is an incredibly useful technology and there are many situations where you will want to use it. Having a password on your computer is not normally enough protection because a hard disk can be removed from a computer and read on another device.

If you are using a tablet or an ultrabook, you *do* have an advantage because the hard disk is a slim sliver of circuit board that requires specialized equipment to read it if it is removed. Even so, unless you store all of your documents and files on a cloud service such as SkyDrive or Dropbox and only access them over a live Internet connection, you probably have files on your computer that contain personally identifiable information (PII) about yourself or others.

Even the contacts database in your e-mail account is valuable because it can contain not only names, addresses, and e-mail addresses, but also dates of birth and other information that can be used to clone a person's identity.

If you are using an office laptop for work, you have tougher data protection rules governing how you use and how you protect the data of individuals. If you lose your laptop or it is stolen, you can face considerable fines or jail time if the laptop contains unencrypted data on individuals. This is on top of the damage done to your reputation or business, should it be discovered that you have lost sensitive and important information. If you travel abroad on business, you can also face penalties from data protection authorities in the country that you are in.

For these reasons, I recommend that you buy a laptop that comes equipped with a TPM chip, if you can afford it, so that you can take advantage of BitLocker. It is true that it is commonly just the high-end laptops that come with TPM chips, but if you shop around, you can normally find other laptops, ultrabooks, and tablets containing the chip. For businesses, a TPM chip is an essential business expense. For consumers, it can be a very worthwhile addition.

If you are on the road, it is a good idea to carry—separate from your laptop—a USB flash drive containing the BitLocker keys for your computer. The system has been known to lock out users at the most inopportune moments.

Using Biometric Devices with Windows 8

Encryption isn't the only way to secure your computer. There are a variety of biometric devices available for computers. They require third-party tools because they are not normally controlled by Windows, but Windows 8 does contain controls, which you access through the Control Panel, for working with biometric devices installed on your computer (see Figure 11-19). This is a central location from which you can manage devices such as smartcard readers and fingerprint scanners.

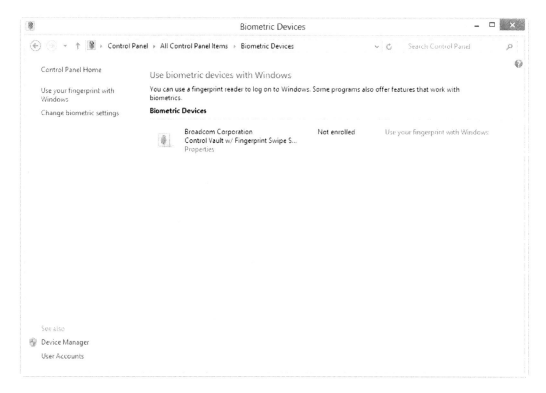

Figure 11-19. *Managing biometric devices in Windows 8*

You will probably find that when you open the management options for a particular biometric device in Windows, it starts a third-party security utility rather than a Windows 8 wizard.

This is very common for biometric devices, but it is useful for Windows 8 to have a central location to manage them.

■ **Note** Biometric devices use features unique to human physiology to identify a user. This commonly includes fingerprints but can also include retinal scanners, voice and facial recognition, handwriting, and anything else that's non-invasive for the user.

Some companies offer software with webcams (or the Kinect controller) that use technologies such as facial recognition to lock and unlock your computer. One example is a webcam that automatically locks the computer when it can no longer see your face.

Unless these security devices appear in the Biometrics page in the Control Panel, or are listed as security devices in the Device manager, you should treat the actual security they offer with caution. For example, software that comes with a webcam is unlikely to prevent anyone who wants to hack into your computer from doing so (your photograph might be enough to fool a webcam, which can only see in two dimensions anyway).

Don't assume that because your computer comes with a facility like this that it is secure. It doesn't necessarily work that way.

Summary

When it comes to security, Windows 8 is very good at taking care of itself. With the default settings left unchanged for Windows Defender, User Account Control, and Windows Update, the operating system installs all the updates it requires as they become available.

Sometimes you may want to customize settings, perhaps to hide updates or to custom-configure the firewall. Some third-party antivirus vendors will tell you that in order to get full and flexible control of antivirus software and a firewall, you need their software. This simply isn't the case. Windows Defender is really quite flexible for a small, lightweight package, and Windows Firewall is very powerful and flexible indeed.

I never recommend changing the default settings in Windows. Making them tougher only makes life difficult for you, and turning them down takes away the protection that you need. These are parts of Windows 8 that you are wise to leave well alone.

When it comes to encryption, you have several options, and if you carry personal or sensitive files on your laptop or tablet, I strongly recommend that you purchase a device with a built-in TPM chip, allowing you to use BitLocker. If you are using a Windows RT device, device encryption technology is built into the operating system. It works in the same way as BitLocker and is just as secure, but it doesn't require the TPM.

CHAPTER 12

Maintaining and Backing Up Your Computer and Files

Once you are using your new Windows 8 computer, the most important consideration is keeping it running smoothly to avoid downtime. Sometimes, despite all your best efforts, problems arise. If they do, visit my web site (www.theLongClimb.com), which has articles and videos to help you through problems.

So how can you set up Windows to maintain trouble-free use? And how can you set up backups to help you return to work quickly and easily if something goes wrong?

Maintaining a Healthy Computer

Why is it important to maintain a healthy operating system and have backups in place? Surely, Windows 8 is the most reliable and robust version of the operating system Microsoft has ever released. It comes with more tools for diagnosing and mitigating problems than any version of Windows before it.

I have long found it ironic that as Windows becomes increasingly stable and reliable, the number of diagnostic and repair tools provided as part of the operating system also increases.

The simple fact remains, however, that your computer is not a domestic appliance and with the exception of Windows ARM-powered tablets, which have the operating system embedded on a chip, every single file that makes up Windows can potentially be changed, deleted, or become corrupt.

What Causes Computers to Become Unstable

I want to talk about why computers become unstable, crash, and fail to boot. There are actually many causes for these problems.

- **Spikes and surges in the electricity supply** can cause Windows files to become corrupt. You should always have your computer plugged into a surge protector (as well as an uninterruptable power supply if you live in an area with an unreliable electrical supply). The power lead coming loose in the computer and the dog leaning against the power button are also causes (I've suffered this many times, though it is very amusing when he switches on the Xbox and can't figure out why the floor makes a noise when he lies down).

  Any interruption in the electrical supply can come at a time when a Windows file is being amended; it happens quite a bit. This problem can also cause the partition table—the database listing the physical location of each file on your hard disk—to become scrambled if the power is cut when it's being written to.

- **Poorly written software and drivers** are a very common cause of Windows failures. Don't assume for a moment that drivers delivered through Windows Update will always give you trouble-free operation; I've seen many a Blue Screen of Death happen this way. The problem here is that there is no way to predict or accommodate for the truly limitless variations in hardware and software on a specific machine.

  This is one of the reasons why Apple computers are reliable. As the manufacturer of both their operating system and all their hardware, they have complete and very tight control over the quality of drivers for the platform. It is the same with the App Store. Don't think that these app stores are just money-making schemes for Apple or Microsoft—they are, in fact, ways to ensure that the correct development tools are used, which encourages apps to be written in the right way.

  With the withdrawal of the x86 versions of Windows in Windows 9 (expected in 2015), Microsoft is expected to move to a strict signed-driver model where all hardware drivers must be officially tested and signed off by Microsoft. At the moment, it is recommended but isn't mandatory, and because it can be expensive, many hardware manufacturers choose not to pay for it.

- **Malware and viruses** sneak onto the computer by taking advantage of the user. These malicious programs can cause all manner of havoc on a machine before you even know what's happened.

- **Installing too many programs and temporary files** causes a computer to fail over time. The more you try to do with your computer, the greater the risk that something will go wrong; and the more unnecessary files you have, the slower the computer will become over time.

How is Windows RT Different?

Windows tablets with ARM processors have an embedded version of the Windows 8 operating system— called Windows RT—programmed onto a silicon chip instead of written file-by-file onto a hard disk. This offers greater security and resiliency because it's much harder for malware to modify, write, or delete files and it's far less likely that a sudden power surge will corrupt any files (and the fact that tablets are much less likely to be in use when plugged into mains electricity). This is the core difference between files installed on a hard disk, where changes and file corruption are simple and common, and silicon chips, where such things are more difficult.

You also cannot install desktop software on ARM tablets; you can only download apps from the Windows Store. This reduces the chance of poorly written software causing problems.

Finally, you cannot use USB and other hardware on these tablets in the way that you can with desktop PCs, laptops, and professional-grade tablets. While this might limit their functionality a bit, it also means that you aren't susceptible to poorly written drivers, the largest single cause of computer problems.

Using the Windows 8 Action Center

The Action Center (see Figure 12-1) is the central location in Windows for all important system messages and help tools. You access it by clicking the white flag icon on the far right of the Windows taskbar.

The Action Center is split into categories for Security and Maintenance, and warnings and alerts are automatically highlighted in amber or red.

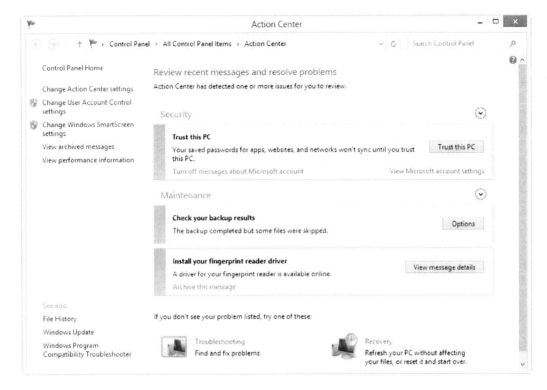

Figure 12-1. *The Action Center*

Although the collapsible Security and Maintenance lists provide you with a great deal of useful and helpful information about Windows 8, you may want to customize the messages that you receive. The reason for this is that the Action Center will still alert you about backing up your files, for example, even if you have a third-party backup solution installed on your PC.

Managing Action Center Messages

To customize the messages you receive in the Action Center, click Change Action Center Settings in the top of the left pane. This opens a settings window with check boxes that allow you to turn on or off messages for all the alerts in the Action Center (see Figure 12-2).

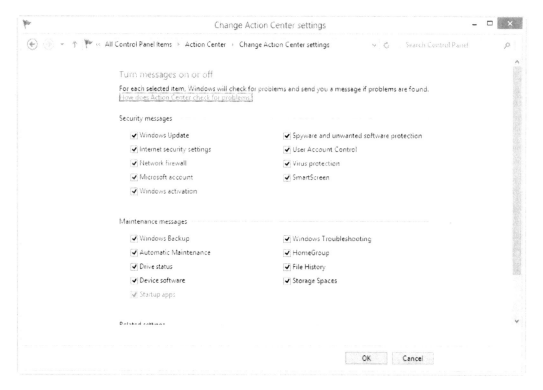

Figure 12-2. *Changing the Action Center settings*

■ **Tip** I would not advise turning off any of the alerts for Security Messages in the Action Center.

Using the Automatic Maintenance System in Windows 8

Windows 8 includes an automatic maintenance system that helps keep your computer running happily and healthily. These settings are in the Maintenance section of the Action Center. Click **Change maintenance settings** or search for **maintenance** at the Start screen.

The automatic maintenance includes deleting temporary and other unwanted files (such as those used by Windows Update), defragmenting of your hard disks, and checking for and installing updates for the operating system.

You can configure how and when you want this tool to run (see Figure 12-3) by choosing the time of day you want it to run or if you want it to run at all. The time of day selection is important because if you are using a laptop or a tablet, Windows 8 will wake from sleep to perform the maintenance. It won't wake the computer if it is switched off, however.

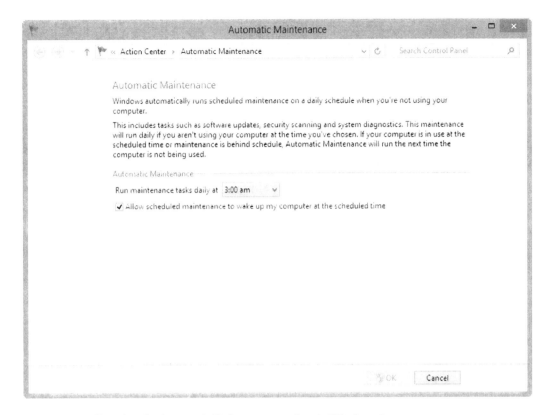

Figure 12-3. Changing the Automatic Maintenance settings in Windows 8

This means that if you think your computer will be switched off at the time maintenance is due to be performed, you can choose the time maintenance is performed.

You can run these tools independently as Disk Cleanup and Defragmenter, both of which are available by searches from the Start screen. I will show you how to use these tools and the additional options they provide in Chapter 13, should you want finer control over the automatic and manual maintenance options in Windows 8.

Using the Automated Troubleshooters

In the Action Center, you can run Windows 8's automated troubleshooters by clicking Troubleshooting (see Figure 12-4). There are many troubleshooters for almost every aspect of Windows, including networking and drivers.

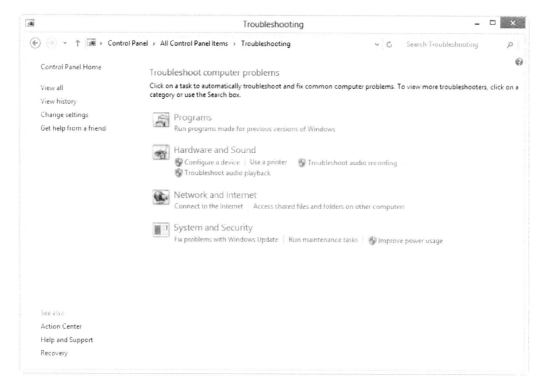

Figure 12-4. *The automated troubleshooters*

■ **Note** The automated troubleshooters resets Windows components and drivers to their default state. This is often enough to fix many problems, but if the issue is caused by a conflict with another driver or software package, the trouble-shooters are unlikely to fix the problem. You can visit my web site (`www.theLongClimb.com`) for more troubleshooting help.

The troubleshooters are wizard-based and give clear information. They can be run easily by users of any technical ability. They are split into handy categories covering Programs, Hardware and Sound, Network and Internet, and System and Security. Each troubleshooter is explained in plain language.

■ **Tip** You can also access the automated troubleshooters by clicking Troubleshooting in the Control Panel.

You can change settings for the Troubleshooters by clicking Change Settings in the left pane (see Figure 12-5). I do not recommend changing any of these settings, however.

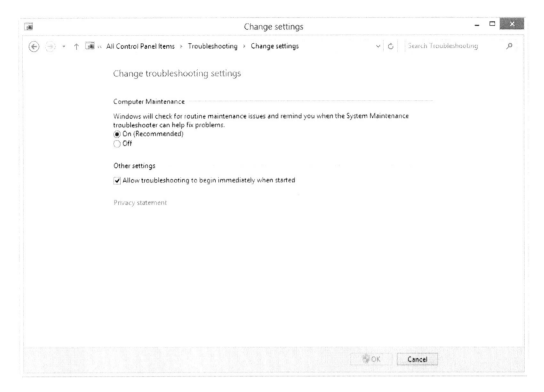

Figure 12-5. *Changing the Troubleshooting settings*

The Windows 8 Task Manager

The Windows Task Manager has been given its first significant overhaul in twenty years and the new look provides more helpful information about Windows than we've seen before. By default, you just see a list of running programs, but clicking the More Details button expands the window.

The Processes tab provides a heat-mapped display of the current processor, memory, disk, and network usage for all of your running apps and desktop programs. This means that if something is hogging huge amounts of memory, for example, you can see it straightaway (see Figure 12-6).

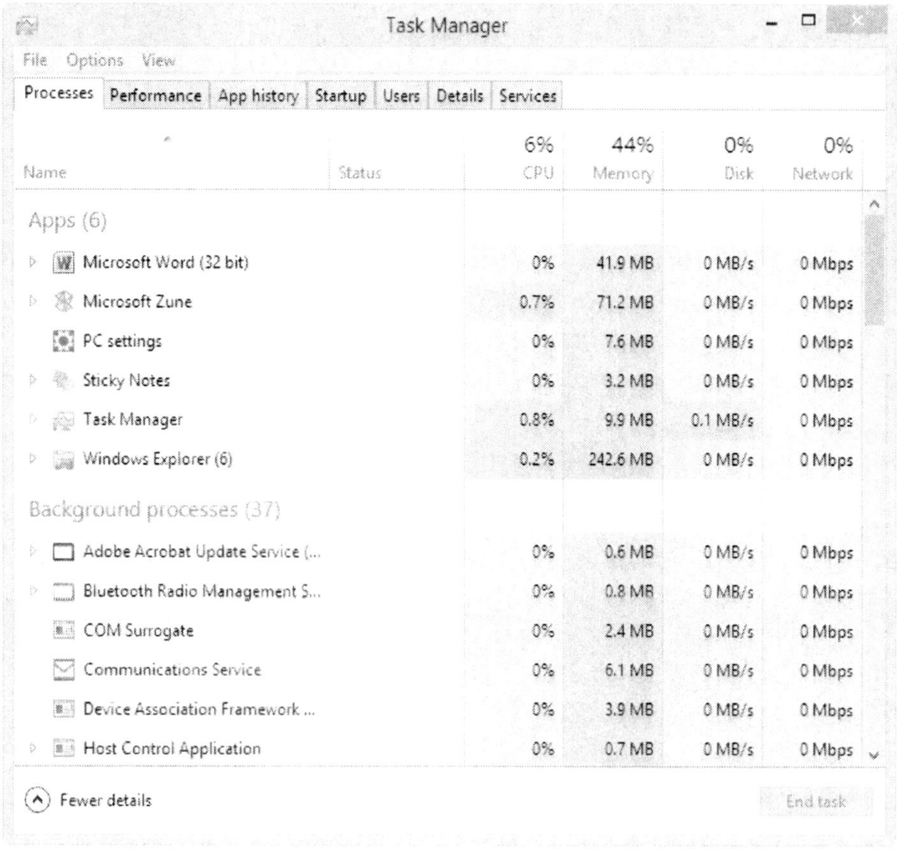

Figure 12-6. *Monitoring software in the Task Manager*

To close a program in the Task Manager, highlight the program and click the End Task button in the bottom right of the window.

■ **Tip** If you are unsure about which programs and processes you can shut down, the Task Manager offers several ways to find out. If you right-click a process, you can select options to view its Properties or open its File Location. Both reveal information about the process. You can also search online for this process from the context menu, which provides even more detailed information about the process.

There is a great deal you can now do with the Task Manager in Windows 8. The Performance tab now provides live graphs similar to the Performance Monitor, but with general overviews of performance information rather than the extremely detailed metrics offered by its big brother.

The App History tab is a great way to determine if the apps you are using in Windows 8 are well written and fit for purpose. Let's say, for example, that you are finding that something is chewing through your mobile broadband allowance. On the App History tab, you can see the total amount of data that your apps have used, even when those apps are not running (see Figure 12-7).

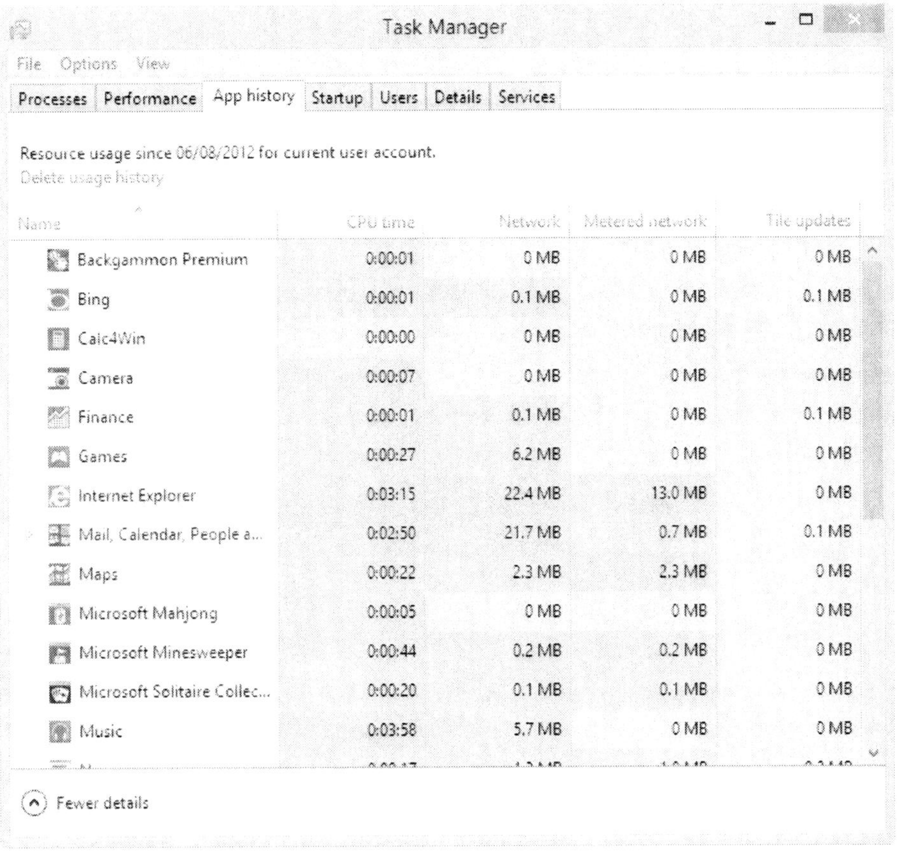

Figure 12-7. *The App History tab*

It includes the ability to see the amount of data consumed by the Live Tile for an app, if appropriate. Probably less useful is the processor time taken by an app. This chart doesn't take into account how much you use one app compared to another. Metrics that are more relevant are gained through the Processes tab when an app is running, or through the Performance Information and Tools page.

■ **Tip** You can open the Task Manager by pressing Ctrl+Alt+Del on your keyboard and selecting Task Manager from the options, or by right-clicking the taskbar, or from the Win+X administration menu.

The Details tab is more like the traditional Task Manager, if you prefer that look and usage. Here you see a complete list of every program, app, and process running in Windows 8. It works the same way as the old Task Manager in that you can right-click a program to shut it down.

It is interesting that only through the Details tab can you shut all the dependencies for a program. This means that when you shut down the program, all the processes and other programs that rely on it are also shut down automatically.

To shut down all the dependencies for a program, right-click in the program or process and select End Process Tree from the options.

Managing Startup Programs

The Task Manager is where you manage the programs that run at Windows startup. Not only does it make this feature simpler for nontechnical users, it also adds a very helpful Startup Impact column, which tells you—in simple *low,* *medium,* and *high* terms—how long the program slows down your computer when you turn it on (see Figure 12-8).

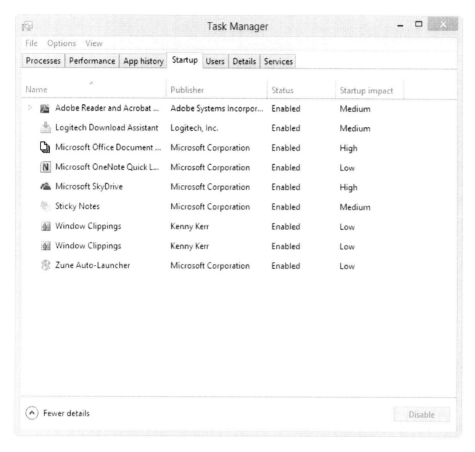

Figure 12-8. *Managing startup programs*

You can disable programs by highlighting them and then clicking the Disable button in the bottom right of the window. You can also re-enable programs the same way.

You will not see Windows 8 apps here because they cannot be set to run at startup, and any Live Tiles are automatically enabled unless you disable them by right-clicking the tile and selecting Disable Live Tile from the App bar.

Using Windows Update

Like Windows Firewall, Windows Update in Windows 8 has a split personality that is controllable through PC Settings and from the full Control Panel.

Managing Windows Update Settings in Windows 8

The basic Windows Update settings are located in PC Settings. They are a very simple affair. Windows Update automatically installs all critical, important, and recommended updates for a computer. There's very little the user has to do. In many ways, especially with regard to safeguarding people's personal privacy and security, it's exactly what the average nontechnical computer user needs (see Figure 12-9). The more technically savvy users, however, may prefer the added control that comes with the full Windows Update desktop settings, which are covered in the following section.

Figure 12-9. *Windows Update basic settings*

Managing Windows Update on the Desktop

Access to Windows Update is on the desktop through the Control Panel. The features here are instantly recognizable to anyone who has used Windows Vista or Windows 7.

The main control (see Figure 12-10) is color-coded to show at a glance your computer's current update status. There is a large green, amber, or red icon to alert you.

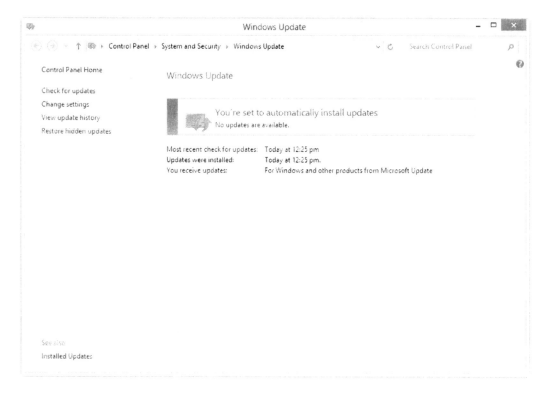

Figure 12-10. *Windows Update on the desktop*

Beneath this are details on when you or Windows 8 last checked online for updates, the updates received, and when they were installed.

■ **Tip** Windows Update on the desktop is able to check for updates to other Microsoft software, including Office and the Live Essentials suite. You can turn this feature on from the main Windows Update screen.

In the left pane are the options you may want to change. In Change Settings, you can decide when and how Windows 8 installs updates. First, it's important to note that Windows 8 has much fewer restarts than earlier versions of the operating system, waiting a good two days before forcing a restart in the hopes that during that time you'll shut your computer down anyway. This means that there is less of a requirement to change the autoinstall settings in Windows 8 by clicking Change Settings in the left navigation pane to open the full Windows Update controls (see Figure 12-11); though I personally recommend that they be left in the default state.

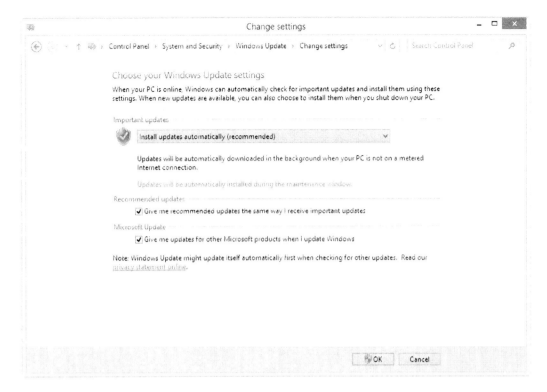

Figure 12-11. *Changing the settings for Windows Update*

The following are the four Change Settings options for Windows Update:

- **Install updates automatically** (recommended by both Microsoft and me).

- **Download updates**, but let me choose whether to install them.

- **Check for updates**, but let me choose whether to download and install them.

- **Never check for updates.**

Additionally, you have controls to allow Windows 8 to install recommended updates in the same way it receives important updates. Recommended updates can include new features to the operating system.

You can also choose if you want to receive more updates through Windows update, including:

- **Recommended updates**, which includes stability and feature updates that aren't deemed critical.

- **Microsoft Product Updates**, which include software such as Windows Live Essentials suite and the Bing Bar for Internet Explorer.

Hiding and Restoring Updates

On occasion, you may want to hide certain updates so that they don't appear and don't install. You might want to do this, for example, when Microsoft offers additional language packs that you don't want or need, or if a hardware driver issued through Windows Update is causing your computer to crash or the hardware to misbehave.

You can hide any update by right-clicking it in the main updates screen and then selecting Hide Update from the options. This prevents the update from appearing again (see Figure 12-12).

Note If you restore Windows 8 from an image backup or by using the Refresh option, all the hidden updates in Windows Update are visible once again. You will have to re-hide them.

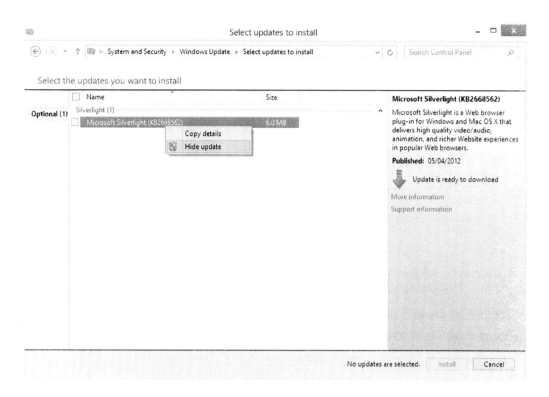

Figure 12-12. *Hiding Windows Updates*

You can also select a group of updates to hide. To select multiple consecutive updates, click the first one and then hold the Shift key while clicking the last update in the series. To select nonconsecutive updates, hold the Ctrl key while clicking the updates you want to select.

To unhide all the updates you have hidden (you can't do just a few), click Restore Hidden Updates in the left pane of the main Windows Update screen.

Managing Hardware Drivers and Rolling Back Windows Update

I mentioned that some updates, especially drivers, occasionally cause Windows to become unstable. Should this happen to you, be aware that Windows 8 creates a System Restore Point whenever it runs Windows Update, so you can roll back to the last restore point to undo the driver change.

To do this from the Start screen, search for **system restore** and (though this might seem odd) select Create a Restore Point from the settings results. In the dialog box, click the System Restore button.

You are now able to restore Windows to the way it was before the update was installed, and when you run Windows Update again, you can hide the offending update so that it doesn't bother you (see Figure 12-13).

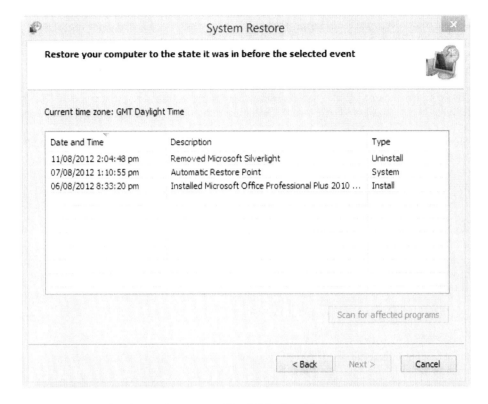

Figure 12-13. *Using System Restore to roll back Windows Update*

Getting Updates from the Windows Store

Updates for your purchased and downloaded apps don't come through Windows Update, even if you have Microsoft Update turned on and the apps are written by Microsoft. All updates for anything downloaded from the Windows Store comes *through* the Windows Store.

It's useful to keep an eye on the Windows Store tile on your Start screen, and if a number appears on it, this signifies the number of apps that have updates waiting to be downloaded and installed.

When you open Windows Store, there is a link in the top right of the screen that indicates that updates are available. Clicking this link shows you which apps have updates available. You can update them quickly and simply.

Installing Windows 8 Service Packs

About once a year, Microsoft releases a Windows service pack. Back in the days of Windows XP, some service packs, including the now famous XP SP2, included many new features for the OS. For example, XP SP2 brought with it the new security center and many new security features. Indeed, there was so much in it that some commentators said that Microsoft could have sold it as a completely new version of Windows.

This makes some power users quite excited about a new service pack, with some even wanting to download and install the beta of the service pack. In truth, however, Windows service packs these days are merely update rollups with perhaps a new piece of code in the background that allows Windows to perform better with a particular feature in Windows Server.

Over the years, Microsoft has been steadily uncoupling Windows software and features from service packs and updates. This means that when you install a Windows 8 Service Pack, you are unlikely to get anything that isn't already installed on your computer. Again, the service packs are simply rollups of the currently available updates that, if you have Windows Update turned on, you already have.

The biggest change here is the new app store. Many of the now traditional Windows programs, such as Mail, Calendar, Messenger, and the media players, are now apps. They are all updated via the Windows Store. Even other software has long since been moved into the Live Essentials suite and aren't included in the service packs. I should note that after installing service packs, some people have had problems that can cause their computer to crash—or worse! The people that usually experience problems are those who manually download the full service pack from the Microsoft web site and install it as a standalone package.

My best advice—and this applies to all versions of Windows, not just Windows 8—is to allow Windows Update to find and install the service pack for you. This has always been the least problematic way of doing it.

There shouldn't be any issues with waiting for Windows Update to install service packs forWindows 8 because it is unlikely there is anything in it that you don't already have installed on your computer.

Protecting and Repairing Windows

While it is simple and straightforward to keep your copy of Windows 8 running smoothly and in a healthy state, it can also be simple and straightforward to rescue the OS in the event something goes wrong. In this section, I'll show you what the various options are and how they work.

Creating a Recovery Drive

A *recovery drive* is a USB flash drive containing the tools required to repair Windows and get to options such as Startup Repair, Refresh, Reset, and System Image Restore if your copy of Windows 8 is unable to start.

You create a recovery drive from the Control Panel by clicking Recovery. You initially see options to refresh and reset the PC, but if you click Advanced Tools, an option to **Create a recovery drive** will appear (see Figure 12-14).

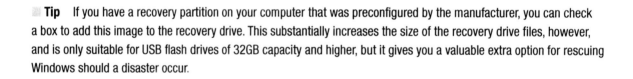

■ **Tip** If you have a recovery partition on your computer that was preconfigured by the manufacturer, you can check a box to add this image to the recovery drive. This substantially increases the size of the recovery drive files, however, and is only suitable for USB flash drives of 32GB capacity and higher, but it gives you a valuable extra option for rescuing Windows should a disaster occur.

Figure 12-14. *Creating a recovery drive*

Once the recovery drive is created, you can start your computer from it to access the recovery options. Note, however, that booting from USB will need to be turned on in the BIOS or UEFI firmware on your motherboard.

Creating a System Repair Disc

If you would rather create a CD or DVD recovery disc, you can do this in the Control Panel by clicking Windows 7 File Recovery. In the left pane, you have the option to Create a System Repair Disc. It is similar to a recovery drive in that it allows you access to the startup and repair options for Windows 8 if you boot your computer from the disc.

You cannot add a recovery partition to a system repair disc and it doesn't have the convenience of being on a USB flash drive. In many ways, a recovery drive is a better option, but for some people, the system repair disc is still a useful tool.

___

■ **Note**   You can only create a recovery drive or system repair disc for the type of Windows 8 installation you have (either x86 or x64). One created on an x64-bit version of Windows will not repair an x86 version of Windows 8.

___

Windows 8 Recovery

Back in the days of Windows XP, it was common to have to completely reinstall the operating system and all of your software every time something went wrong. Now there are several ways to secure your installed copy of Windows and restore it in the event of a crisis. In this section, I will show you how to do just that.

Creating an Image Backup of Windows 8

Windows Vista was the first version of Microsoft's operating system to include image backup functionality. Windows 7 brought this excellent and very useful feature to all editions of the operating system. It remains in Windows 8 largely unchanged, though there is a new interface for restoring an image backup.

I always recommend that the backup image be from a relatively clean installation in which you have only made essential changes and all temporary files have been deleted. It's a good idea to run Windows utilities such as the Disk Cleanup Wizard, which you can find by searching **clean** at the Start screen, and clicking **Free up disk space by deleting unnecessary files** in the Settings search results.

Access the Windows Image Backup creation utility by clicking Windows 7 File Recovery in the Control Panel, where you have the option to Create a System Image in the left pane (see Figure 12-15).

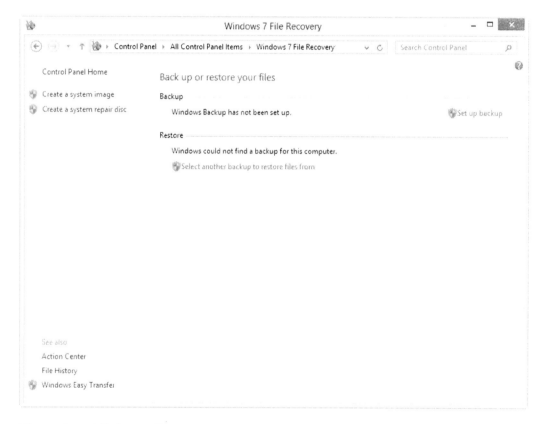

Figure 12-15. *Windows 7 File Recovery page*

Click Create a System Image to start the wizard, which guides you through creating a backup image of Windows 8. The backup image will be a complete snapshot of your PC at that time, including all of your installed software, their configuration settings and customized Windows settings, and all of your user accounts.

You will be asked where you want to store the image backup (see Figure 12-16). You can choose another hard disk or partition in your computer, one or more DVDs (though bear in mind these can degrade over time), or a network location.

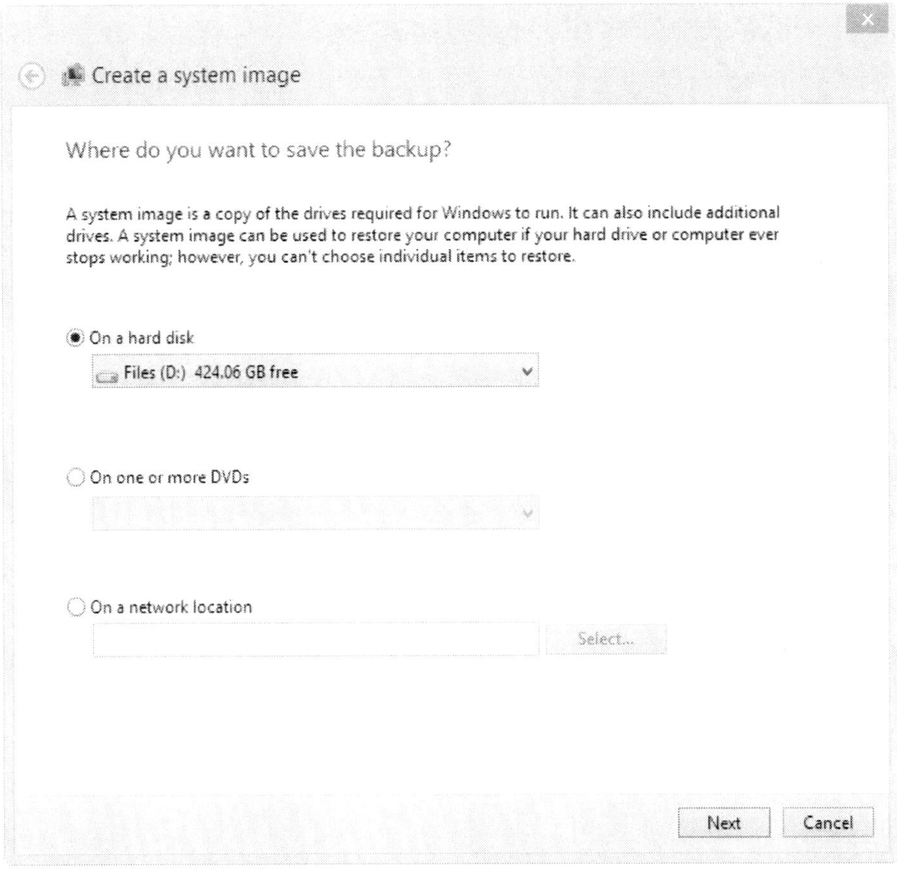

Figure 12-16. *You can save your backup in different locations*

If your computer always connects to your network via Wi-Fi, you should not choose a network location. This is because the image is restored from the Windows boot menu where no Wi-Fi drivers are loaded. When restoring from a network location, the computer needs to be connected to the network via a physical cable.

■ **Note**   If you have several hard disks or partitions in your computer, you will be asked if you want to add any of them to the image backup.

Before creating the backup, Windows 8 shows you what you're backing up and where the backup will be stored (see Figure 12-17). Click the Start Backup button when you are ready to begin.

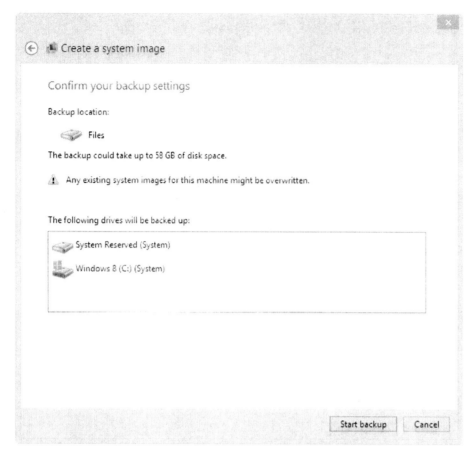

Figure 12-17. *Windows shows you the drives it will back up*

Restoring an Image Backup

There are several ways you can restore a backup image, all of which will lead you to the same menu system.

- Pressing F8 on your keyboard at startup to load the boot menu (see Figure 12-18).

- Starting your computer from a Windows 7 Recovery Drive. I will show you how to create one of these later in this chapter.

- Starting your computer using a System Repair Disc. I will show you how to create one of these later in this chapter.

- Booting your computer from your Windows 8 installation DVD and clicking Repair Your Computer at the install screen.

Some of these options will take you straight to the Windows 8 Startup Troubleshooting options seen in Figure 12-19. If not, you should choose Troubleshoot from the options on the boot menu shown in Figure 12-18.

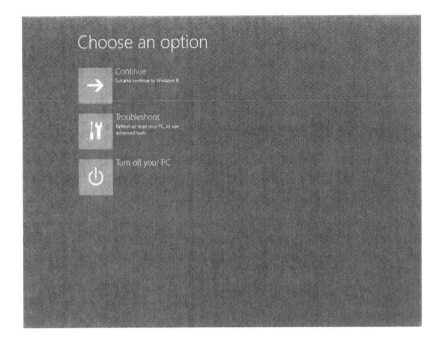

Figure 12-18. *The Windows boot options*

The next screen (see Figure 12-19) gives you options to perform a refresh or a reset. I will talk about these options shortly because they are different from restoring an image. At this screen, click Advanced Options.

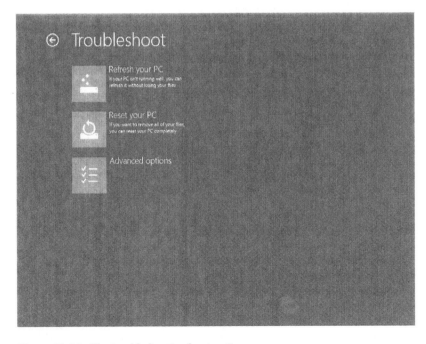

Figure 12-19. *The troubleshooting boot options*

You now see an option to use System Image Recovery to restore your computer (see Figure 12-20). Windows automatically finds the backup if it is kept locally on your computer. You will be prompted if Windows can't find it, perhaps because it is on a network location. If this happens, you will need to manually select the backup on the correct network location.

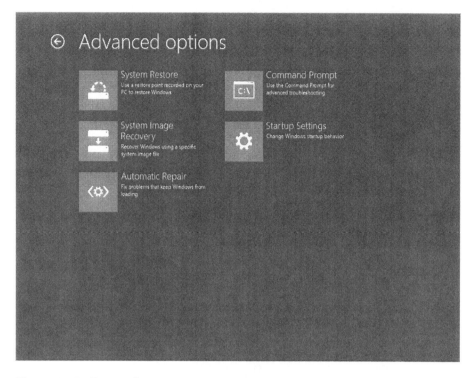

Figure 12-20. *You now have an option to restore using System Image Recovery*

Windows 8 will now restore your image backup. When this process has completed, your computer will be exactly as it was when you created the image, complete with all of your files and settings intact (though you may have to redownload Outlook e-mail and sync some other programs).

Repairing Windows 8 Quickly Using Refresh

Windows Image Backup isn't for everyone. Novice users might quickly become confused by the options presented to them. For this, Microsoft has introduced a new Refresh option that creates a system image backup that is easily and quickly restored from PC Settings.

There is one critical difference between a System Image Backup and Refresh that will affect power users, IT pros, and system administrators. While you can create a custom Refresh image that will restore all of your installed desktop software, it doesn't back up any of your settings for those programs. This means that software such as Microsoft Outlook will be returned to its *installation* settings and you will need to reconfigure e-mail accounts in it, and the settings and preferences in all of your other desktop software.

Many users won't be bothered by this, however. Let's look at average home users who won't customize any of their desktop software and probably won't mind having to set up their e-mail account in Windows Live Mail again, if they even use it.

Gamers will have their game settings automatically synced with cloud services like Xbox Live, Origin, and Steam, and so they won't notice a difference.

This can make the Refresh option excellent for anyone who supports friends or family and gets calls in the middle of the afternoon about a problem "that will only take a minute."

You can access the Refresh option from the Windows boot menu (as I detailed earlier and shown in Figure 12-19), but you also can access it from PC Settings by selecting General in the left navigation pane (see Figure 12-21).

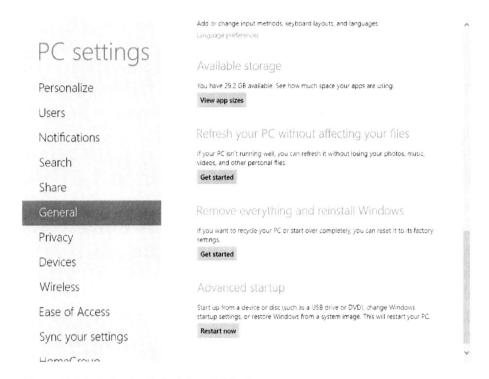

Figure 12-21. *Activating Refresh from PC Settings*

Refresh is explained, and when you are ready to refresh your computer, click the Next button. The process is completely automated from that point. You will need to restart your computer several times.

When you want to Refresh your copy of Windows, which will restore a working copy of Windows with all of your apps installed, click the Get Started button. Windows 8 explains the Refresh process and asks you to confirm that you want to refresh the computer. Click OK when you are ready to begin the process, which can take between 15 and 60 minutes depending on whether you have created a custom Refresh image or not (see the next section).

Creating a Custom Refresh Image

You can create a custom Refresh image. You may want to do this because, by default, this feature refreshes your copy of Windows 8 while keeping your files and apps intact, but it will wipe out all of your desktop software.

Creating a custom Refresh image turns this into a snapshot of your PC as it is *then*, complete with all of your desktop software installed.

■ **Note**   Remember that restoring from a custom Refresh image will reset all of your desktop software, so you will need to set up programs again.

Perform the following steps to create a custom Refresh image:

1. Press Win+X to open the Administration menu.

2. Select Command Prompt (Admin) to run the Command Prompt as an administrator.

3. Type **recimg -CreateImage D:\Folder.** D:\Folder is the location where you want the backup to be stored.

Windows 8 will create your custom Refresh image, which is restored using the Refresh feature.

Safe Mode and Diagnostic Startup Mode

With Safe Mode removed from the new boot menu, how do you get to it? By pressing Shift+F8 when starting Windows, you can see the older boot menu. Here you have the same familiar options, including Safe Mode and Safe Mode with Networking (see Figure 12-22).

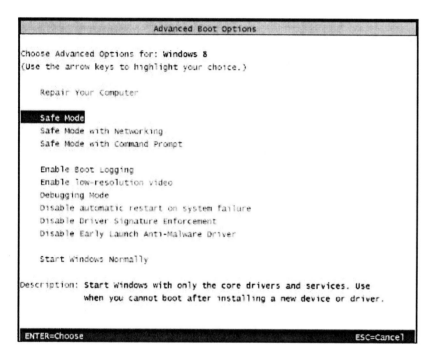

Figure 12-22. *Starting Windows 8 in Safe Mode*

Not all computers will allow you to press F8 or Shift+F8, however, especially ones that startup really quickly. If you need to get into Safe Mode in this case, you can do so from the Windows System Configuration page where Safe Mode comes with a whole variety of additional and useful options.

You access the System Configuration dialog box by searching for **msconfig** at the Start screen. Under the Boot tab, there is an option to turn the computer on in Safe Mode the next time it starts.

The most interesting option is under the General tab. While Safe Mode is very useful, it is also extremely limiting and doesn't allow you to perform many actions.

Under the General tab, there is the option to turn on a Diagnostic Startup (see Figure 12-23). It is equivalent to Safe Mode+ in that in addition to loading the bare operating system, it also loads some system drivers, such as for your graphics, and allows you to perform the full range of Windows 8 configuration operations.

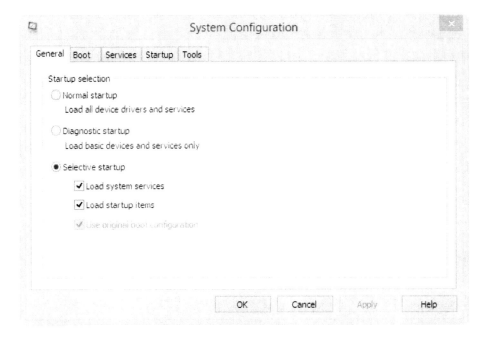

Figure 12-23. Turning on diagnostic startup mode

Note When you switch these options on in the System Configuration dialog box, they will remain on until you run msconfig again and switch them off.

Using Startup Repair

If Windows 8 fails to start three times and the System Reserved partition isn't damaged, Windows will launch Startup Repair (see Figures 12-18 and 12-19). This is an automated system that resets Windows components to their default settings in an attempt to get things working again.

If Startup Repair can't repair Windows, it will offer you advanced repair options, which are the menus shown in Figures 12-24 through 12-27. A Refresh might be the best option to get Windows 8 working again.

Figure 12-24. Windows 8 can self-repair when it can't start

Understanding the Windows 8 Startup Menus

The startup menus in Windows 8 have changed considerably to accommodate the mouse and graphical systems that were not supported on older computer systems.

This isn't to say that you can't access the previous DOS-type startup menu (it is still available with the Shift+F8 key press at startup), but the standard F8 key will now take you to the new graphical system if your hardware supports it.

At the first screen, you have three options: continue to start Windows 8, turn off your computer, or troubleshoot the machine (see Figure 12-25).

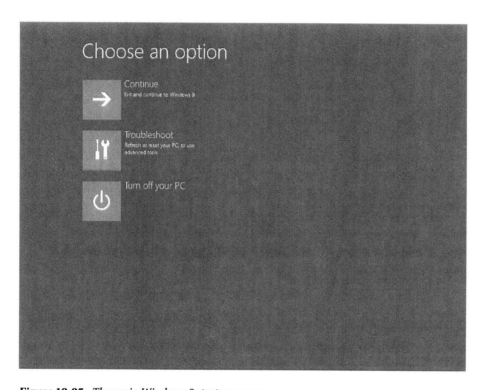

Figure 12-25. *The main Windows 8 startup menu*

The Troubleshooting options are quite basic, offering only the new options to refresh and reset your computer. You might expect to find the Startup Repair option here, for example, but it has been moved into the Advanced Options (see Figure 12-26).

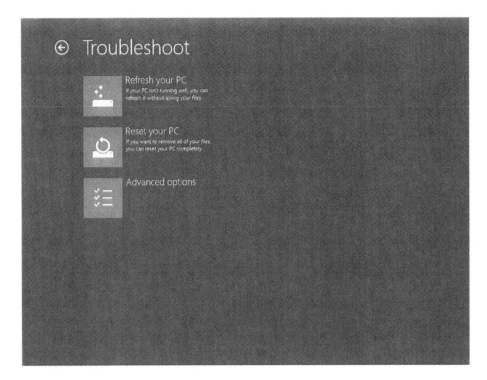

Figure 12-26. *The startup troubleshooting menu*

All the remaining options are found in the Advanced Options. Here you have access to the command prompt, in which you can perform such actions as manually repairing the boot options, performing a CHKDSK (check disk), and more. You can also change the Windows Startup Settings, which allows you to turn off the new graphical menu and have Windows 8 use the traditional DOS menu instead (see Figure 12-27).

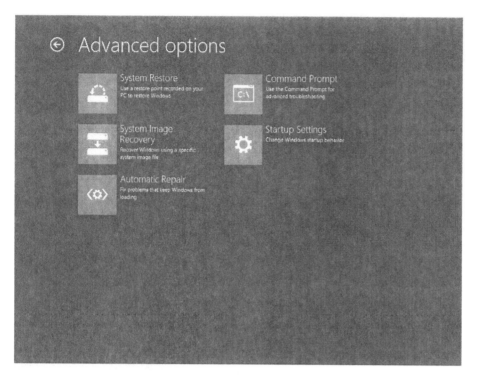

Figure 12-27. *The advanced troubleshooting menu*

■ **Note** The new graphical startup menu in Windows 8 excludes a few useful features that remain in the DOS menu. This includes the option to perform a memory test and the ability to start the computer in Safe Mode.

Restoring Windows 8 to Factory Settings

If you are selling your computer or giving it away, then you can use the Reset option to restore Windows 8 to its factory settings. This will wipe out all of your user accounts, files, settings, apps, and programs.

Remove Everything and Reinstall Windows is in the General options under PC Settings (see Figure 12-24). Make sure that you have backed up all of your files before performing a reset.

■ **Tip** Reset does not securely erase your files, so they could be recovered later on using a file recovery program. If you want to securely erase deleted files and data on your hard disk, there are many third-party utilities that can do this, but the excellent— and free—CCleaner (www.piriform.com/ccleaner) does this job along with providing other useful cleanup and maintenance tools for Windows.

Backing Up Files and Folders

Nothing is more important on your computer than your files and documents. Once you lose those precious family photographs of baby Gilbert's birth or last year's vacation in the Maldives, they're gone forever—and you have nothing but your memories from then on.

It is critical that you safeguard your files on your computer. I'll show you how to do this later in this chapter. It is very important that you make backups and keep them in safe and sensible places.

Where to Store Backups

Choosing where to store backups of your files is critical, because choosing to store your backups in the wrong location can often be as bad as having no backups at all. So where can you store your backups and what are the pros and cons?

- **A second hard disk on your PC** is the fastest and least difficult way to store backups because an automated system can update the backup every time you change a file. However, an electrical spike through the PC could fry the original data and the backup. A theft or a fire will destroy both copies.

- **Network attached storage** is a great way to store backups in your home or workplace. NAS drives are hidden in inaccessible places. They are still vulnerable to fire, however.

- **CD/DVD/Blu-ray discs** aren't advisable for backups any more. Partly because, with the exception of Blu-ray, the discs don't have large enough capacities for our ever-growing collections of digital photographs and home videos. Also, these discs degrade—and there's little way to tell if it will be three months or thirty years before they become unreadable.

- **USB hard disks** are probably the best option because they can be stored offsite in the home of a friend or family member, or at the home of the person responsible for backing up your vital business data.

- **USB flash drives** are of a size and price that you can consider storing backups on them. Bear in mind, however, that they are relatively easily broken (i.e., sat on, put in the washing machine, or chewed by the dog). If you store one on your key chain, you might never find it again.

- **Cloud storage** is becoming ever more popular and there are a lot of services to choose from, including Microsoft's SkyDrive, Google Drive, Carbonite, Mozy, Amazon S3, and many more. The problem here is the initial upload can be tens if not hundreds of gigabytes and unless you are on a super-fast broadband connection, this can take weeks or even months to upload.

░ **Tip** I always recommend using two backup solutions. I store backups locally on a NAS drive for quick restoration, but I also use Microsoft's SkyDrive service for cloud backup.

Remember to Encrypt Business Backups

You can normally consider your workplace relatively secure. You control who has keys and access to the building and the room(s) containing your computers. If you store business backups offsite, however, which is highly recommended, you should make sure those backups are either encrypted or kept in a very safe location.

Sending unencrypted backups home with a senior staff member is one thing, but given that you have no control over this person's home security presents a data protection risk. The only safe strategy with business data—and the one the data protection regulators are most likely to endorse—is a VPN or cloud-based encrypted solution designed specifically for business.

Using Windows 8 Backup

With Windows 8 having a built-in file and document backup solution, it makes sense that it is a good way to back up the contents of your computer. Windows Backup saves your files as a virtual hard disk (VHD) file. This means the entire backup appears as a single folder, which hides its contents from casually prying eyes. You can open this file and drill down into it to get to files, should you need them.

Windows Backup is run from the Control Panel by clicking Windows 7 File Recovery. In the main page, you turn on Windows Backup by clicking **Set up backup** (see Figure 12-28).

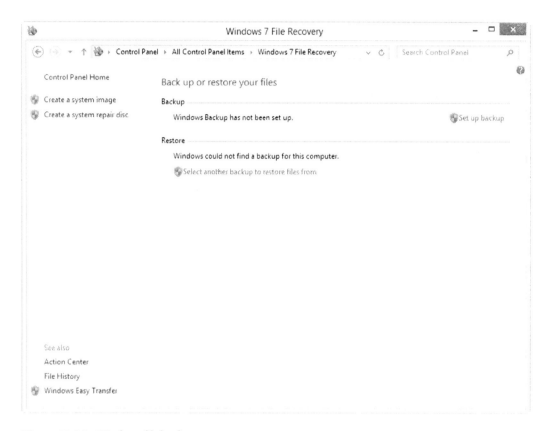

Figure 12-28. *Windows file backup*

You will be asked where you want to store your backup (see Figure 12-29). Local hard disks and USB attached hard disks appear in the options, but you can also choose a network location such as a NAS drive.

▨ **Tip**   Many Internet routers allow you to plug a USB hard disk into them to share on the network as storage. This can be an excellent local backup location.

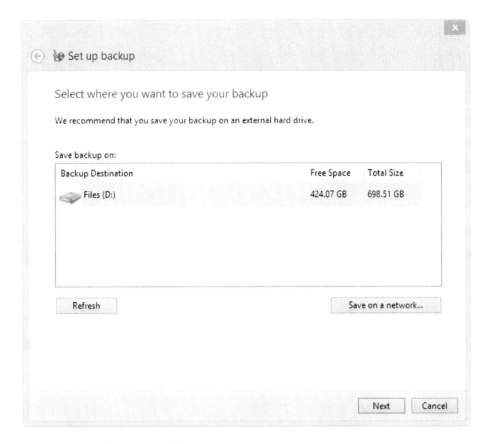

Figure 12-29. *Select a backup location*

On the next page, Windows asks if you want to choose what you want backed up or whether you should let Windows decide (see Figure 12-30). You should always choose to select items to back up yourself if you are a power user because, by default, Windows Backup keeps an up-to-date image backup of your copy of Windows.

Figure 12-30. *It is best to select Let me choose*

So why is this a bad thing? When Windows Backup maintains an image backup, it also copies any changes you made to the operating system into this image. This includes any problems and imperfections that can cause Windows to fail. When you create a backup image of Windows 8—and I'll show you how to do this shortly, you want to guarantee that you have a perfect working copy of Windows when you reinstall it.

On the next page, you can specifically select what to back up. You should uncheck the **Include a system image of drives** option because it creates and maintains a backup image of Windows 8.

You can also choose the folders and drives to include or exclude in your backup. You may have a second hard disk containing work files or documents for an ongoing project, for example. There are white arrows next to folder and document collections that you can use to expand folder trees outward. You can use this to select and deselect specific folders (see Figure 12-31).

Figure 12-31. *Choosing what to back up*

Finally, you will need to set a schedule for backups (see Figure 12-32). Click Change Schedule to choose from daily, weekly, or monthly backups on the day that you specify and at the time you're going to most likely have the computer turned on.

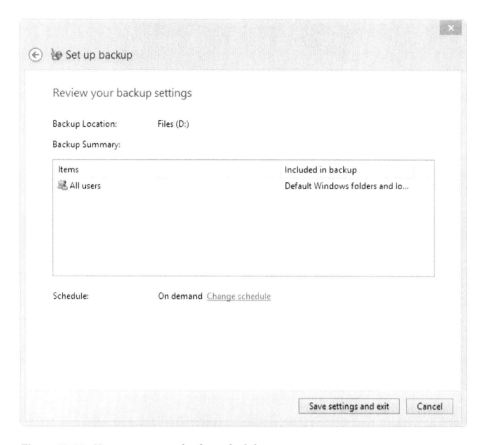

Figure 12-32. *You can now set a backup schedule*

This backup works automatically if the destination location for the backup is available. You can open Windows 7 File Recovery from the Control Panel at any time to see at a glance the current status of your backups, including the last date and time a backup was made. If you want, you can manually start a backup here as well.

Restoring Files in Windows 8

To restore files made in a Windows Backup, return to Windows 7 File Recovery in the Control Panel. If you have made a backup of files, you are presented with the option to restore these files.

Here you will be able to choose whether to restore all of your files or just a few of them. This is done through a helpful wizard interface similar to the one you used to select which files to back up.

■ **Caution**   Beware of synched network and cloud backups! If you use a service such as SkyDrive that syncs the files on your computer with those in the cloud, or a backup solution that keeps files in sync by *deleting the file on the backup destination when that file is removed from the computer*, you could find that your backup is wiped completely if you accidentally delete the files from your computer. To get around this problem, stop your backup software from running until you can restore the files.

Saving and Restoring Previous Versions of Files

Windows 8 comes with a new file versioning tool called File History, which keeps backup copies of files as you make changes to them so that if you accidentally make a change to a file that you didn't intend to make, the file can be restored.

File History can be incredibly useful if you use your computer for work and change files (such as Office documents) frequently. It can roll back accidental or unapproved changes.

File History is accessed from the Control Panel. You can use local internal hard disks, USB attached drives, and network attached drives (though the latter two don't work if they're not plugged in or are inaccessible). Figure 12-33 shows File History.

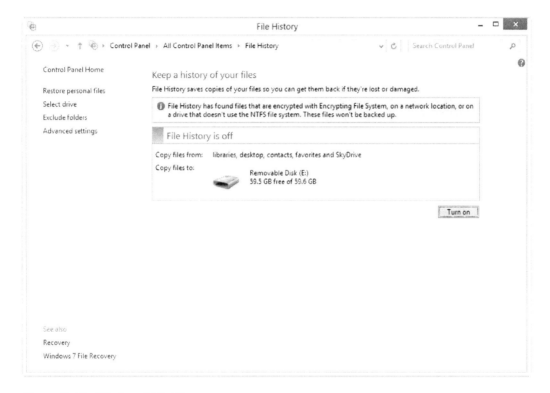

Figure 12-33. Windows 8 File History

▪ **Tip**   If you use a USB hard disk plugged into your Internet router for backups, why not use it for File History as well.

I would never use File History as a primary backup solution, however. You can never guarantee that the specific file(s) you need to restore will be there because File History keeps *every* file that has changed recently. Every time you open a file such as a picture or an MP3, the file is changed to update the Last Accessed timestamp. You could find that your File History is full of MP3s and nothing else.

You can rectify this from the File History pane by clicking Exclude Folders on the left of the page. Here you can exclude the drives containing file types that are only likely to change when the Last Accessed marker is set. These file types include music, pictures, and video.

Should you wish to change the location of the File History drive, you can do that in the left pane by clicking Change Drive. Bear in mind, however, that Windows will begin creating its versioning on files from scratch.

Clicking Advanced Settings in the left pane gives you more control over how File History operates (see Figure 12-34):

- You can choose how of ten it saves copies of files. Remember, it doesn't do it automatically when a file is saved. You can also choose from periods as low as 10 minutes. If you are using your Windows 8 computer for work, a shorter period may offer you more reassurance if you work on files that change regularly, like Word documents.

- You can also select how much of the available hard disk space is reserved for documents, from 2 percent to 20 percent. On a 1TB hard disk, 2 percent is 20GB and 20 percent is 200GB, so this is quite a lot of space for previous versions of files.

- You can also choose the amount of time a version is kept. The Forever option is a little misleading because it is the same as the Until Space Is Needed option. Keeping files until space is needed is probably the best option, however.

▓ **Tip**   If you are running short of hard disk space on the drive where you keep your File History, or if you just have too many old versions of files stored, you can click Clean Up Versions to delete older versions of files from the disk.

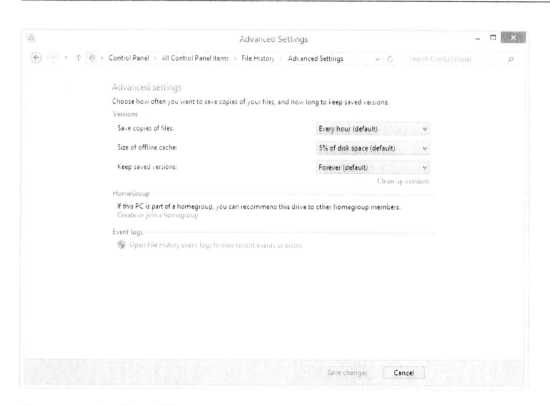

Figure 12-34. *The advanced file versioning options*

Note   If you are using a laptop or tablet that only has a single hard disk, you may not be able to keep File History versions locally on the computer because Windows 8 doesn't support keeping versions in the same location as the original files. Many Internet routers have USB ports so that you can plug in a hard disk to use as network storage. This is an excellent location for backups and File History versioning.

You can restore earlier versions of files using Restore Personal Files in the left pane of the File History page. It brings up a window showing you all the previous versions of documents that have been saved, along with their time and date. You can restore individual files or groups of files.

Safeguarding Your Personal Files and Folders

One of the problems with Libraries is the uncertainty of where files are stored. If your files and data are stored on the same partition as your Windows installation, and you are forced to reformat the hard disk and reinstall the operating system from scratch, you could lose everything.

While changing the default save location for Libraries is one way to do this, I prefer to move the user folders wholesale over to a new partition or hard disk in the computer.

A hard disk is a physical storage area where everything is put in the same place. This includes your copy of Windows and all of your files (see the left image in Figure 12-35). This means that if something goes wrong with Windows, you can face the possibility of losing all of your files as well.

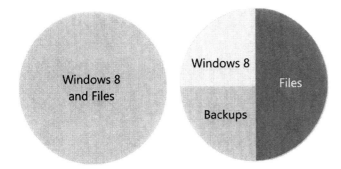

Figure 12-35. *An unpartitioned disk and a partitioned disk*

If you split your hard disk into several partitions, you are splitting that *physical* hard disk into several *logical* ones. File Explorer sees each partition as a different disk drive.

The image on the right in Figure 12-35 is my recommended setup. It has three partitions: one for Windows 8, a big one for files, and a third one for a backup copy of the operating system.

If you have a second hard disk in your computer, you may want to use it for files and backups. If something goes wrong with the hard disk on which Windows is installed, and this hard disk will see the most mechanical activity, your files and your backup copy of Windows will still be intact.

To create new partitions on your hard disk for files, perform the following steps:

1.   Press Win+X to display the Administration menu.

2.   Click Disk Management.

3. To create a new partition, you need to make space by shrinking an existing one. In the Disk Management window, right-click the hard disk partition you want to shrink (usually the C:\ drive containing your Windows 8 installation).

4. From the options, select Shrink Volume (see Figure 12-36). Note that "Volume" is the terminology used here to describe both disks and partitions.

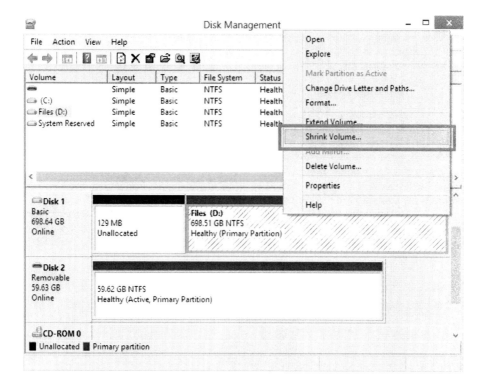

Figure 12-36. *Shrinking a partition*

▬ **Note** How big should you leave your Windows partition? For general light usage, 50GB is a good size (enter **51200** in the size box). A power user might want 100GB to 200GB (**102400** or **204800**), but a gamer might want up to 300GB (**307200**).

---

5. Choose the amount by which you want to shrink the disk. You'll need to leave enough space for all of your files and an image backup. On a larger hard disk (1TB or more), I suggest shrinking the drive down to 25 percent of its current size (e.g., 250GB).

6. In the *unallocated space* remaining after shrinking the partition, right-click with your mouse.

7. From the options, select New Simple Volume.

8. Create a partition of the appropriate size for files. I recommend 50 percent of the original volume size. Give it a name and drive letter (see Figure 12-37).

Figure 12-37. *Creating new partitions*

9. Repeat steps 6 to 8 for an Image Backup drive. Note that if you are using a professional-grade tablet or an ultrabook that does not have a large hard disk, you may not have enough space for an image drive.

■ **Note**   Many computers come with a backup partition containing a factory system image of Windows 8. If your computer didn't come with a Windows 8 installation disc, I recommend leaving this and creating your own secondary backup partition as well, because you never know when the factory image might come in useful.

Now we need to move the user folders and files to the new files partition.

1. Open File Explorer.

2. Click the small arrow in the File Explorer Address bar at the far left of the current address location.

3. From the drop-down location options, click your username (see Figure 12-38).

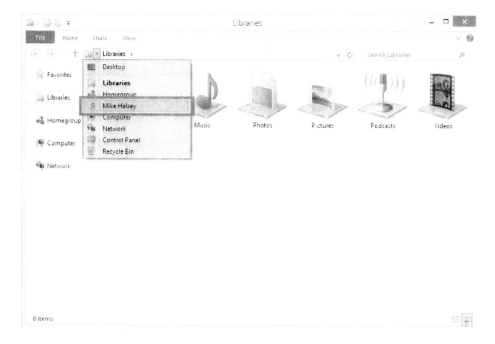

Figure 12-38. Selecting your user folders

4. Select the following folders: Downloads, Favorites, My Documents, My Music, My Pictures, and My Videos (see Figure 12-39).

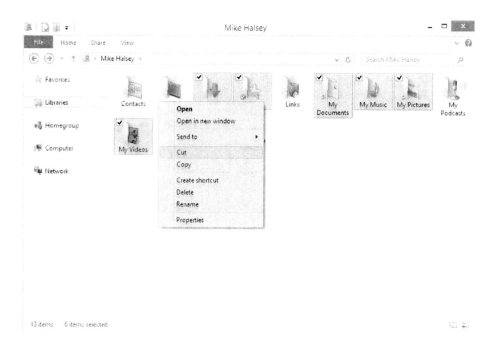

Figure 12-39. Selecting your user folders to move

5. Right-click the selected folders.

6. From the menu, click Cut (it is *very* important that you *do not* click Copy!).

7. In File Explorer, navigate to the new partition where you want your files to reside.

8. In a blank space, right-click.

9. Select Paste from the options that appear.

Taking Ownership of Files and Folders

With any selected file(s) or folder(s), you can change their security options. Go to the Share tab on the Ribbon to launch Advanced Security Settings (see Figure 12-40). By default, when a new user account is created in Windows 8, that user is given full permission to read, write, and modify the files in her user folders (Documents, Music, and so forth).

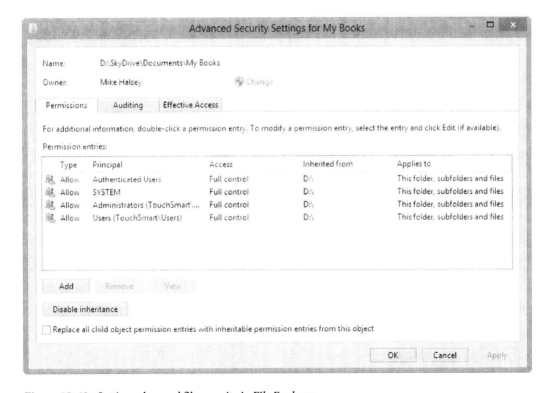

Figure 12-40. *Setting advanced file security in File Explorer*

At times, you may find that you have permissions set on files and folders from another user or another version of Windows. This is especially true if you have upgraded your system from an earlier version of Windows or if you store your files and folders on a separate partition or hard disk for added security and peace of mind.

When you try to access a folder for which you do not have permission, Windows 8 normally asks you if you want to take ownership of the folder; and if you say yes, it automatically changes the permissions on its contents.

Sometimes, however, you need to do it manually by following these steps:

1. In the Owner section of the Advanced Security Settings dialog box, click Change.

2. In the Enter the Object Name to Select section, type the username of the user you wish to make the owner.

3. Click the Check Names button.

4. If the names are correct, they will appear. Click the OK button to complete the ownership changes on the files/folders.

Summary

Because Windows has always been a very flexible and adaptable operating system, the options and features available to help you ensure that it keeps running properly and in a healthy way are very refined and advanced. It's ironic that the number of options to safeguard, troubleshoot, and repair increases at the same rate the number of problems and issues associated with the operating system decreases.

That said, using the tools available to you—and you should never need a third-party tool—you can create a very robust and resilient system.

■ ■ ■

CHAPTER 13

Advanced Configuration and Customization

Windows has always been renowned for being a very configurable operating system. Despite the new look, Windows 8 offers an immense number of ways to customize the OS, tweaked from within the OS itself and with third-party software.

The ability to configure Windows extends to the computer's internal and external hardware as well. In this chapter, I will show you even more Windows 8 configuration and customizations options. These options enable you to customize your Windows 8 installation in myriad ways, from simple changes to more complex customization that can help you build your computer skills.

The Control Panel

The Control Panel is where the full range of Windows controls and configuration options are found. Although throughout this book I've shown you how you can use various Control Panel options to configure specific features within Windows 8, there is much more to the Control Panel, including advanced and administrative tools.

The Control Panel is most easily accessed in Windows 8 by searching for **control** at the Start screen. There have been a few changes since Windows 7 and some Control Panel options aren't where you might expect to find them.

Customizing the Control Panel

By default, the Control Panel appears in the Category view, where all the Control Panel items are organized into groups, such as network and Internet controls (see Figure 13-1).

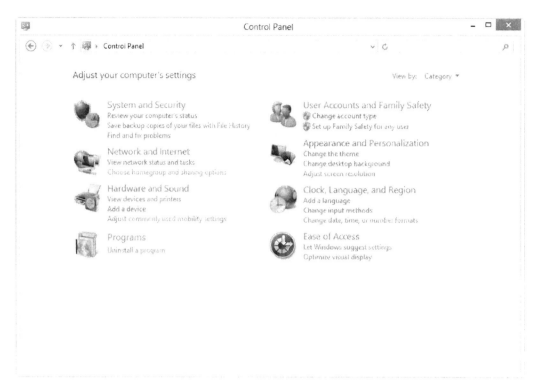

Figure 13-1. *The Control Panel Category view*

In the top right of the Control Panel window is a View By drop-down list where you can choose to display the Control Panel items as either large or small icons. The icon views simply list all the options available to you in the Control Panel (see Figure 13-2).

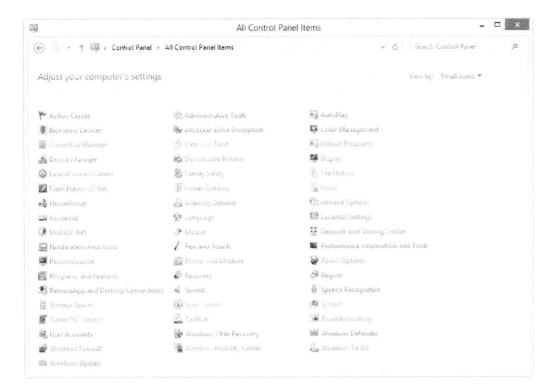

Figure 13-2. *The full Control Panel items list*

Your list of Control Panel items might differ from those seen in Figure 13-2 in that they might show fewer or slightly different controls. If you don't have biometric devices on your computer, for example, you won't see the Biometric controls, and if you don't have a touchscreen, you will likely not see the Tablet PC or the Pen and Touch settings.

The Control Panel only shows the controls that relate to your specific computer, and no more. This ensures that you're not distracted by controls that won't do anything.

I'm not going to detail every Control Panel item, but I do want to talk about the most important ones and show you how you can use them to configure your copy of Windows 8.

Choosing AutoPlay Options

Sometimes the AutoPlay options in Windows can be annoying. Do you really want Windows Media Player popping up every time you insert a CD or for File Explorer to appear whenever you insert a USB flash drive?

The AutoPlay options to select which program or app opens for a particular media or device are incredibly well-laid-out (see Figure 13-3). It's also very easy to stop Windows from asking you what you want to do with a device every time you insert it.

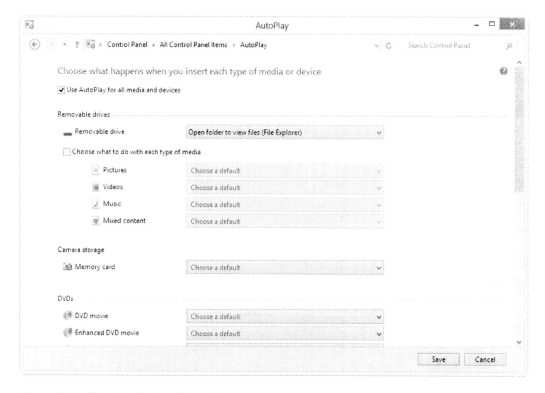

Figure 13-3. *Choosing the AutoPlay options*

This includes all removable drives for all types of media—including pictures, music, and video; storage cards for a camera (you might want to choose between the custom software that came with your camera or Windows importing the images); and DVDs, CDs, Blu-ray disks, and software.

At the bottom of this page is a Reset button to return all the settings to default, in case you make changes that you later decide you want to reverse.

■ **Note** When you insert some USB flash drives, you are asked if you want to use it to speed up your system using a Windows feature called ReadyBoost, a useful feature primarily for older computers with slower hard disks and small amounts of physical memory. It uses the flash drive as cache memory to speed up access to commonly opened Windows files. The speed improvements come with flash memory being much faster than a mechanical hard disk drive.

Setting Default Programs

There are four options in Default Programs:

- Set your default programs

- Associate a file type or protocol with a program

- Change AutoPlay settings (discussed in the "Choosing AutoPlay Options" section)

- Set program access and computer defaults

Set Default Programs lists all the software installed on your computer. Clicking a program in the left pane displays how many of its file defaults are set (see Figure 13-4). This means that the program will open a certain number of file types. The Windows Disc Image Burner, for example, will just open ISO files, but Microsoft Word will open many more files, including RTF, DOC, and DOCX. Windows Media Player will open even more file types.

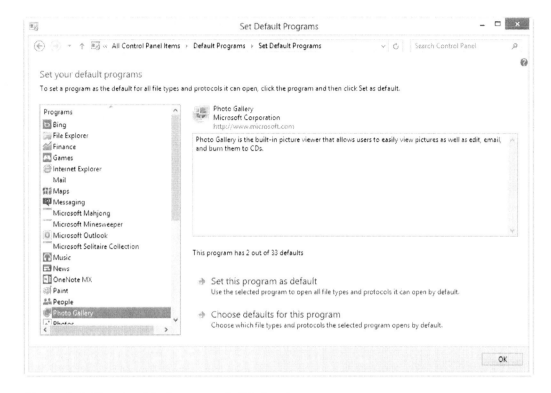

Figure 13-4. *Choosing default programs in Windows 8*

Here you have two options. You can **Set this program as default**, which sets the program as the default for *all* of the file types it can open. Otherwise, you can **Choose defaults for this program**, which takes you to the **Associate a file type or protocol with a program** options.

Associat[ing] a file type or protocol with a program offers finer control over the program or app that opens with a particular file type by displaying a long list of every file type Windows can open. You have the option to associate a single or multiple file types with a certain program or app (see Figure 13-5).

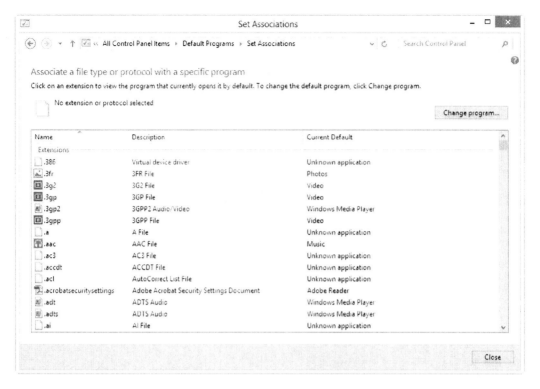

Figure 13-5. *Associating individual file types with programs or apps*

■ **Tip** File types can only be set one at a time. However, if you enter this page from Set Default Programs, you have check boxes that make it simpler to associate file types with programs.

Another way to control the default programs in Windows is through Set Program Access And Computer Defaults, which allows you to easily change the default programs for browsing the Internet, e-mail, media playback, and instant messaging (see Figure 13-6).

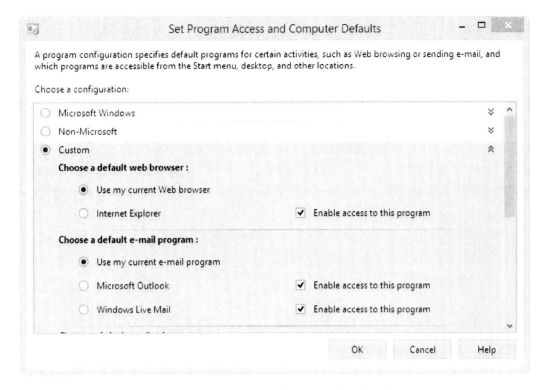

Figure 13-6. *Choosing the default web browser, e-mail client, and media player*

Managing Fonts in Windows 8

Windows 8 doesn't have a dedicated font manager, but the Fonts page is generally an excellent alternative. It shows thumbnail previews of letters and characters in the installed fonts (see Figure 13-7).

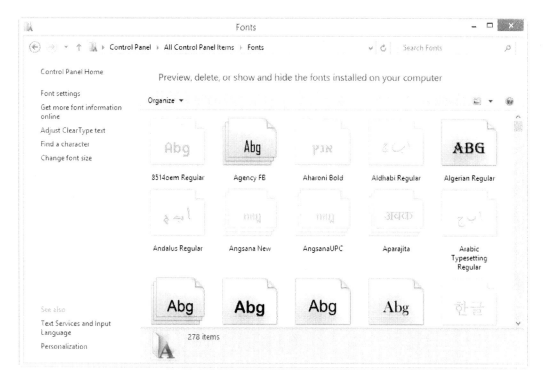

Figure 13-7. *Managing Fonts in Windows 8*

■ **Tip**   You do not need to be in the Fonts page to install a font. You can install a font from any location by right-clicking it and selecting Install.

If you want to view more of a font's characters, you can double-click it to open it. Some fonts will first open into a font group, but each font will show you more characters, though not the complete character set (see Figure 13-8).

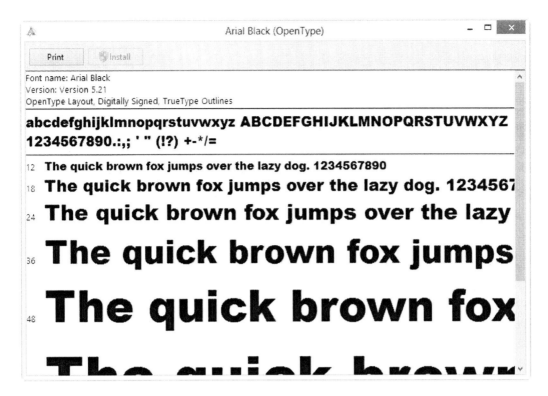

Figure 13-8. *Viewing fonts in Windows 8*

Using Location Settings and Other Sensors

In Location Settings, you can turn on (or off) settings that allow apps and other programs to use GPS and other location-aware sensors on your computer. You may not want apps to know your physical location, for example.

Managing Pen, Touch, and Tablet Settings

If your computer supports touch, the Pen and Touch and Tablet PC Settings will be visible in the Control Panel. They are separate options but they are linked in many ways. The Pen and Touch options only apply to using touch on the Windows desktop; you can't change the default controls for the Start screen and apps.

Of particular note, however, are the Flicks controls. These allow you to customize flick gestures on the screen to perform navigational and a variety of other actions, including editing controls such as copy and paste.

The Customize button edits flicks as well. There are plenty of options to choose from, including cutting and pasting. This can be extremely useful on professional-grade Windows tablets (see Figure 13-9).

Figure 13-9. *Using Flicks*

Tablet PC Settings allows you to tell Windows if you are left- or right-handed. And, should the calibration on your touch panel be out of alignment, you can recalibrate the touch layer on the display (see Figure 13-10).

Figure 13-10. *Changing the Tablet PC settings*

Configuring the Windows 8 Advanced System Settings

When you click System in the Control Panel, you are shown information about your computer. The System Properties page is where you find the type of processor and the amount of memory you have, as well as which edition of Windows 8 you are using. This information is useful when you need to describe your PC to a support professional.

Clicking Advanced System Settings in the left navigation pane brings up the System Properties dialog box, which has settings that you may want to change (see Figure 13-11).

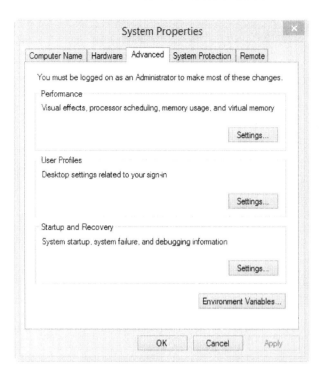

Figure 13-11. *Changing the advanced system settings*

In the Advanced tab of this dialog box, there is a page with three sections: Performance, User Profiles, and Startup and Recovery.

To open Performance, click the Settings button. In the Performance Options dialog box, the first tab is Visual Effects, which allows you to control some of the ways the Windows 8 desktop is displayed (see Figure 13-12). Some of the changes you can make here are purely cosmetic. For example, some people believe that removing **shadows under windows** makes the desktop look cleaner.

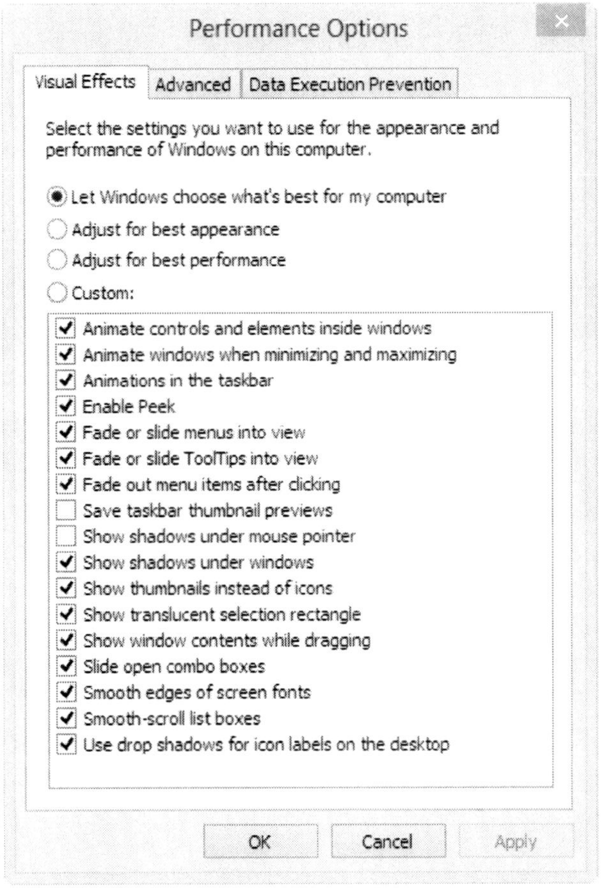

Figure 13-12. *Adjusting the Visual Effects*

If you have an older computer, you can adjust the look of the Windows desktop to get the best possible performance. Stripping the visual look of the desktop back to basics can improve the overall responsiveness of the computer.

Managing Virtual Memory Settings

The Virtual Memory settings are under the Performance Options' Advanced tab. Virtual memory is a file on the hard disk that your computer uses when it runs out of physical computer memory. This is much less of an issue than it used to be because computers ship with increasingly more memory, but you still may want to manage your Virtual Memory settings manually. The reason for this is that the Virtual Memory (sometimes known as the swap file or paging file) default settings have this file automatically increase and decrease in size. This can lead to disk defragmentation, which ultimately may cause the mechanical hard disk to slow down in accessing your files. If you use a solid-state disk where hard disk space is at a premium, you may want to reduce the overall size of the paging file. To do this, click the Change button on the Advanced tab. The Virtual Memory dialog box will appear, as seen in Figure 13-13.

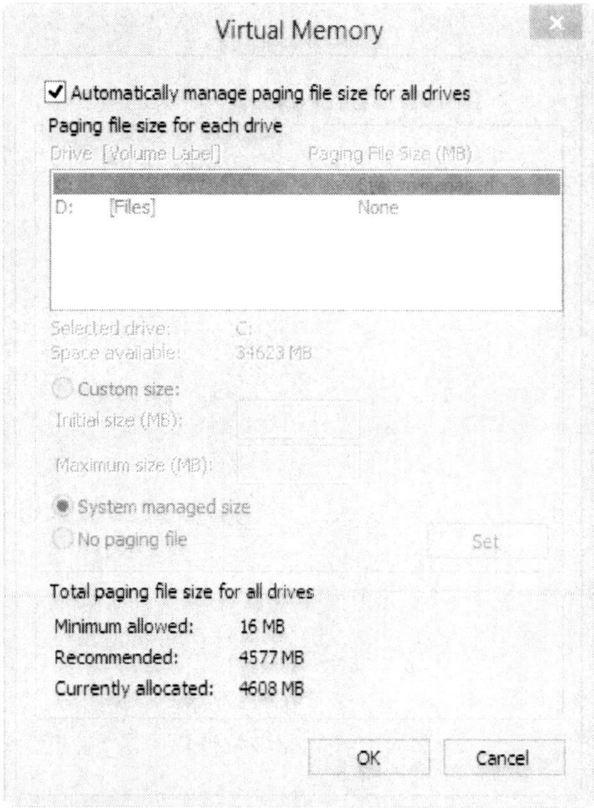

Figure 13-13. *Changing virtual memory*

To manage virtual memory manually, uncheck the box at the top of the Virtual Memory dialog box and instead select the Custom Size option. At the bottom of the dialog box, Windows 8 suggests minimum and recommended sizes for virtual memory. If you have large amounts of physical memory, however, such as 8GB or more and run Windows from an SSD, you may want to set virtual memory to the minimum settings. Otherwise, Windows 8 suggests a recommended amount for the Virtual Memory. Setting both values in the Custom Size fields to the same amount prevents the virtual memory file from shrinking, expanding, and ultimately fragmenting your hard disk.

In the drives view on the dialog box, you can also move the paging file to a different physical hard disk or partition, should you desire.

Managing Data Execution Prevention

Data Execution Prevention (DEP), accessed from the Performance Options dialog box, is a feature that prevents certain viruses and malware from damaging your Windows installation. On occasion, it can also prevent particular games or other software from running.

If you find that a program isn't running properly, you try allowing it through DEP. To do this, first select **Turn on DEP for all programs and services except those I select** and click the Add button (see Figure 13-14).

Figure 13-14. Managing DEP settings

Now you can navigate to the folder on your hard disk where the program is located and select it to allow it through DEP. It is possible that this will rectify the problem. You cannot turn off DEP completely.

Configuring and Managing System Protection

System Restore allows you to roll back changes to Windows settings if something goes wrong on your computer.

In System Properties, you can turn on System Protection for other drives and add them to the System Restore feature. You can also specify how much space on the disk is allocated to System Restore so that you can increase space if you have plenty available, or reduce it if you are using a small SSD (see Figure 13-15).

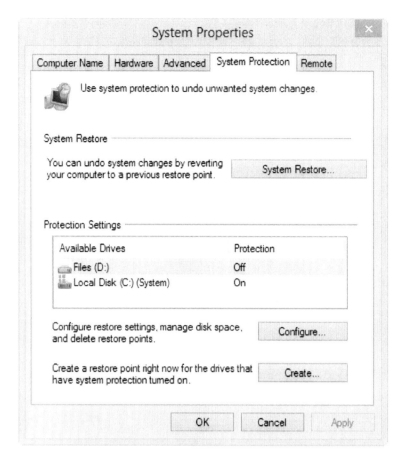

Figure 13-15. *Managing System Protection*

Let's have a look at these two options to see what they do.

- **System Restore** keeps copies of critical operating system files when a major change, such as software installation or an update, takes place. This information is kept in the System Volume Information folders on your hard disk, if you ever wondered what they were for. You can run System Restore to restore system files to an earlier point in time if a recent change has made your computer unstable.

- **System Protection** keeps version-controlled copies of the operating system and other files so that they can be reinstated if an unwanted change is made to a file. This system works closely with System Restore.

Using and Configuring Storage Spaces

Storage Spaces is a feature new to Windows that allows you to aggregate, or pool, several hard disks onto a single large storage drive. This pooled storage then appears on your computer as a single drive that you can expand by adding extra hard disks, as you require.

The advantages that Storage Spaces bring include ensuring that Windows automatically keeps a backup (mirrored) copy of your files, in case a hard disk fails. This should not be considered an alternative, however, to a good backup policy.

Hard disks that are connected to your computer by SATA, SAS, and USB links can be joined to the Storage Spaces (note that if you remove a USB drive at any time, you lose temporary access to the files stored on it). This means that you can use external hard disks to expand the storage of an all-in-one PC.

■ **Note** Hard disks that are added to Storage Spaces need to be formatted by Windows. They will be wiped of all data. You will then need to copy files back to them.

When you first set up Storage Spaces on your computer, you are shown a list of compatible hard disks. Windows tells you which hard disks are suitable for use with Storage Spaces, and you can choose which drives to add (see Figure 13-16).

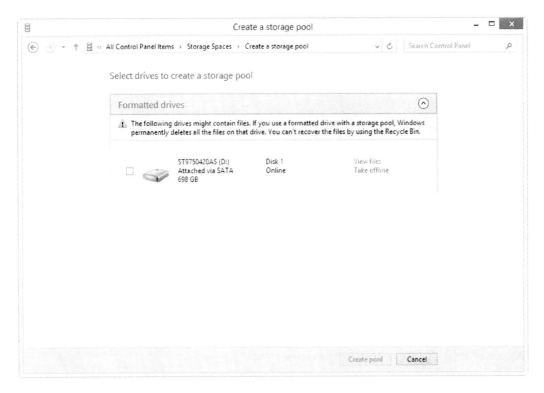

***Figure 13-16.** Using Storage Spaces*

There are three different types of storage layout from which you can choose for storage space (see Figure 13-17):

- **Basic Space:** The assembled hard disks are aggregated into a single hard disk.

- **Mirror Space:** At least two copies are kept of your files and data on separate physical disks.

- **Parity Spaces:** Saves parity information about the data stored. This information can be used to reconstruct data in the event of a disk failure.

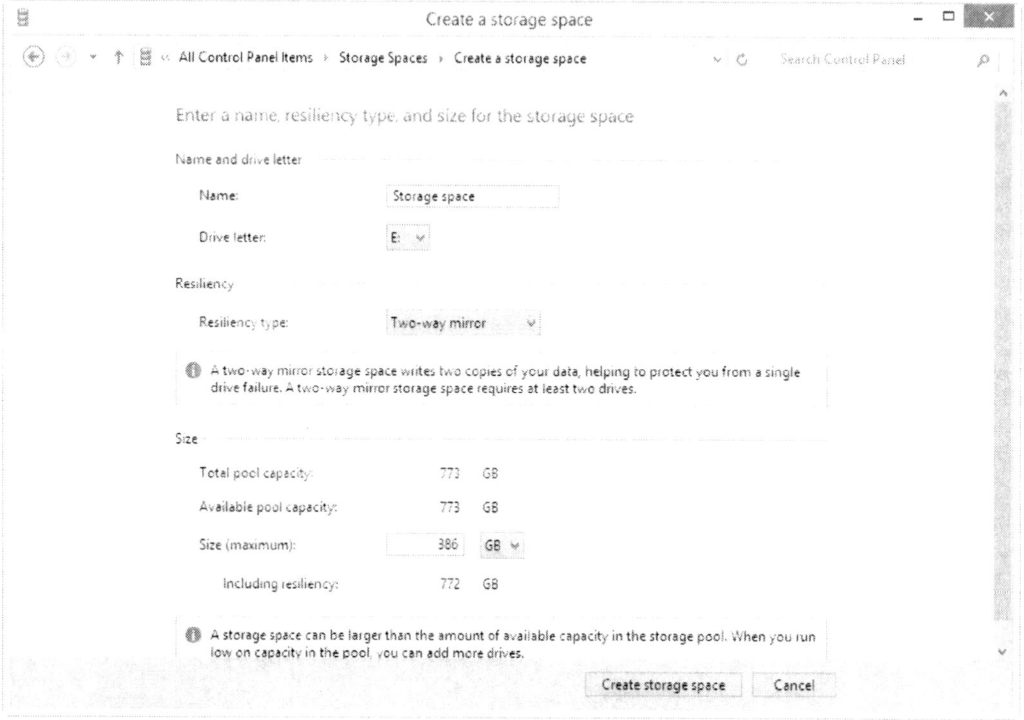

Figure 13-17. *Configuring Storage Spaces*

Storage spaces are configured via a helpful wizard that allows you to choose the storage layout that best suits you. Windows 8 explains what a particular layout does and how it can help protect your data. You can also choose a name for the new pooled drive and assign a drive letter to it.

Consider Storage Spaces to be a software equivalent of RAID (redundant array of independent disks), which is a collection of physical hard disks in a computer that are configured so the user sees them as a single, large drive. Storage Spaces is very useful in computers that have no RAID system or where storage can only be added via USB-attached hard disks.

■ **Tip** Unlike many RAID systems, you can add hard disks of any size to Storage Spaces.

Working with Hardware Devices

Whatever you do with your copy of Windows 8, there is no escaping hardware drivers. These pieces of code interpret the signals between your computer and both internal and external hardware, and allow everything to communicate.

Earlier in this chapter I spoke about how some hardware can be added through PC Settings. Indeed, Windows 8 is excellent at recognizing and installing hardware with network-attached hardware, such as Wi-Fi printers.

Drivers can cause problems, however, so I want to talk you through the process of installing, managing, and repairing troublesome drivers.

Device Manager

The Windows 8 Device Manager (see Figure 13-18) hasn't changed since earlier versions of the operating system. It contains some extremely useful tools that are commonly hidden.

Figure 13-18. *The Device Manager*

By default, it shows the hierarchical view of all of your computer's attached and installed hardware devices, grouped into collapsible sections. If there are any devices that are not properly installed, that have not been correctly configured, or that have been disabled, they will be highlighted in the list with a small yellow warning triangle. If a device is not working properly, it may have a warning icon superimposed on it.

There are other useful views in the Device Manager that can give you all sorts of additional information about your computer. From the View menu, you have several options. Looking at the resources on your computer provides information such as IO ports and Interrupt Requests (IRQs). These are the cycles on which information is exchanged with the processor. If you are experiencing problems, it is useful for determining if too many devices are set to communicate with the processor at any one time (see Figure 13-19).

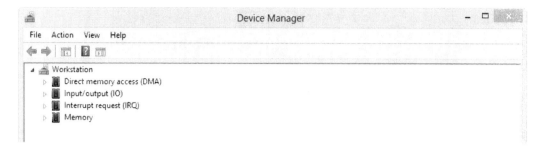

Figure 13-19. *Viewing resources in the Device Manager*

What types of problems might you have with your hardware that you can use the Device Manager to help resolve? The most common is a faulty or an incompatible driver. These can come from any source directly downloaded from the Internet or provided through Windows Update. I will show you how to resolve problems with faulty drivers in a short while. You can use the custom views to see if conflicting drivers are trying to use the same Windows Resources simultaneously. This problem is very uncommon and always caused by sloppily written drivers. Another rare problem is a driver inadvertently loaded twice by Windows. By looking at the way drivers are interactive with Windows, such as viewing IRQ requests, you can see if multiple instances of a driver have been loaded. A restart normally rectifies this problem.

You can also view hidden devices on your computer. These are commonly Windows system drivers that don't relate specifically to a piece of hardware. However, some hardware can also install hidden devices and you will want to check if this hardware is causing a problem (see Figure 13-20).

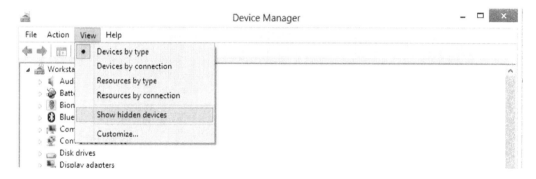

Figure 13-20. *Viewing hidden devices*

When you want to install a driver for a piece of hardware that isn't visible, select Scan for Hardware Changes from the Action menu in the Device Manager.

You will need to perform actions on hardware drivers when using Windows 8, including installing, removing, and updating them. The following sections describe how you to perform these actions.

Installing Device Drivers

Windows 8 commonly detects hardware and tries to install a driver for it. If the hardware came out after the release of the operating system, it may be unable to find a driver using Windows Update. If this happens, right-click the driver and click Update Driver Software (see Figure 13-21).

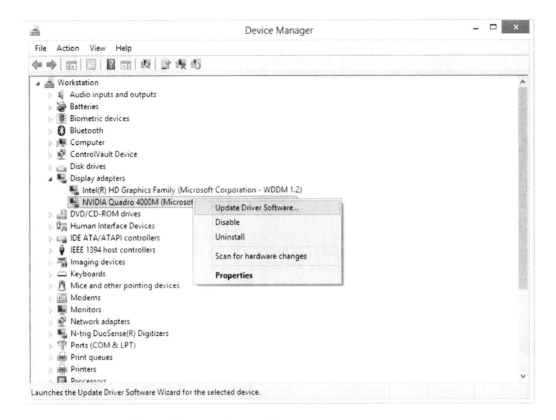

Figure 13-21. Manually installing or updating a driver

You will be asked if you want Windows to search for drivers or if you want to install the driver manually. If it is hardware that Windows 8 has already failed to correctly install, you should choose the **Browser my computer for driver software** option (see Figure 13-22).

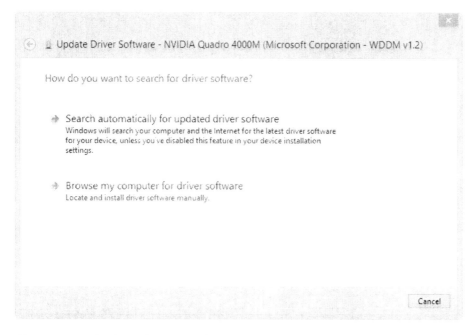

Figure 13-22. *The device driver wizard*

Here you have two options.

- **Search automatically for updated driver software** searches the preconfigured driver folders that come with Windows 8. If you have an active Internet connection, it also searches Windows Update. It also looks for drivers on any optical disc or USB-attached drive on your computer.

- **Browse my computer for driver software** gives you additional control. It allows you to manually specify the location(s) on your hard disk(s) or optical drives where the driver might be found. You can browse to a location on your computer, on an attached hard disk or flash drive, or on a network location. You can also choose from a very long list of drivers that Windows 8 comes equipped with (see Figure 13-23).

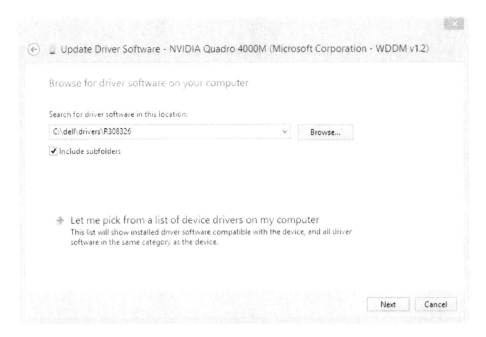

Figure 13-23. *Manually choosing a driver*

When might you want to choose which hardware driver to install? It might be useful if you are using older "legacy" hardware for which you know drivers exist because it's been out for years, but that perhaps Windows 8 doesn't recognize.

Should you choose the **Browser my computer for driver software** option, Windows will try to identify the hardware for you. It may not get it right, but if it does, select the correct option from the list and then click the Have Disk button to point Windows 8 at the correct driver (see Figure 13-24).

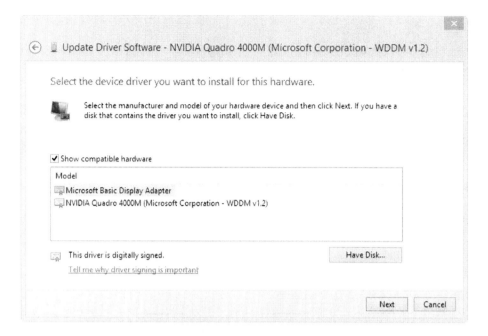

Figure 13-24. *Finding compatible hardware*

If you don't see your hardware in the list, uncheck the **Show compatible hardware** box. You are presented with a long list of hardware by various manufacturers. These are drivers that Windows 8 ships with, and if you find your hardware in the list, choose the manufacturer and product name that correctly matches the hardware you are trying to install (see Figure 13-25).

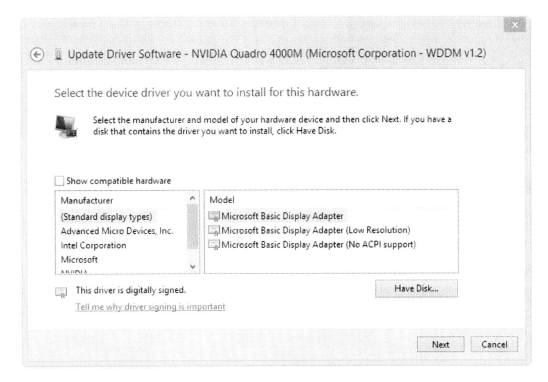

Figure 13-25. Selecting hardware from Windows 8 default drivers

Uninstalling and Repairing Device Drivers

Sometimes Device Drivers causes problems and needs to be uninstalled or reinstalled. When you uninstall most (but not all) of the hardware on your computer, you are given the option to also completely **Delete the driver software for this device** (see Figure 13-26).

Figure 13-26. Uninstalling device drivers

Checking this option will completely remove the driver software from your PC. This can prevent a faulty driver from being automatically reinstalled by Windows. If you need to repair a driver, you can now reinstall it from Windows Update or another source, such as the original driver disc that came with your hardware.

Also, if an updated device driver and is misbehaving, you can roll it back to the previous version of the driver software. You do this in the device driver properties window, as described next.

■ **Tip** You can disable hardware you don't need to use or that causes problems by right-clicking it and selecting Disable.

Working with Device Drivers

In addition to uninstalling drivers, you can roll a driver back to a previously installed driver (if it has been updated through a service such as Windows Update) by right-clicking the driver and selecting its Properties.

As shown in Figure 13-27, if an earlier version of the driver is available, the Roll Back Driver button is highlighted.

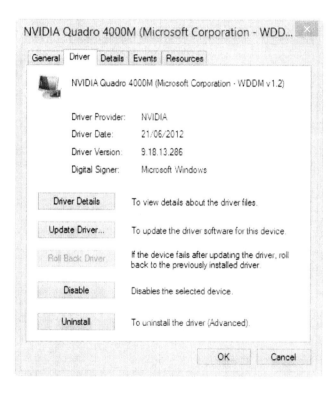

Figure 13-27. *Rolling back device drivers*

A driver's Properties dialog box provides a lot of information about it, but there's nothing here you can change or modify. The General tab is where Windows tells you whether the driver is working correctly or not.

Manually Connecting to Networks

Clicking Set up a new connection or network in the main pane of the Network and Sharing Center allows you to manually connect to a network. You might want to do this if you need to connect to a hidden Wi-Fi network, a virtual private network (VPN), or a dial-up Internet connection (see Figure 13-28).

Whichever option you choose, Windows opens a wizard to guide you through the process, including manually entering the SSID of a hidden Wi-Fi network and setting the type of encryption it uses.

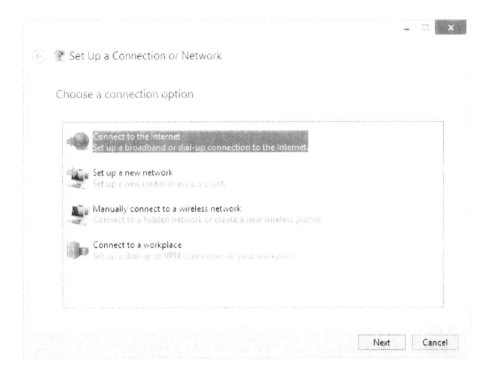

Figure 13-28. *Connecting to networks manually*

Choosing the Connect to the Internet option might be required for some broadband ISPs that require you to log on from your computer to gain access. If you must enter a username and password before getting online, click through **Set up a new connection anyway** and at the next screen select Broadband (PPPoE) (see Figure 13-29).

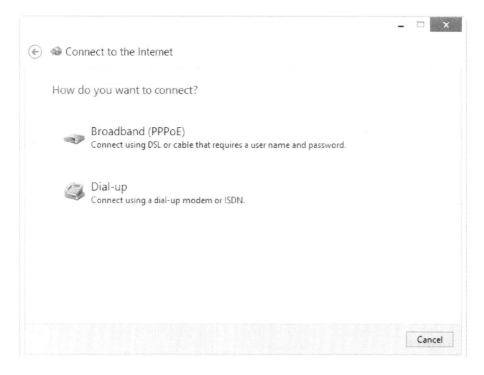

Figure 13-29. Manually connecting to dial-up or cable Internet

You will be prompted to enter the username and password that your broadband provider has assigned to you. This is only required if you must log on from your computer, not from your router, to get a connection. This will probably only apply if you have an ISDN connection.

Windows 8 Administrative Tools

So what are the Windows Administrative Tools (see Figure 13-30) and how do you get the best out of them? In this section, I'm going to focus on the tools that allow you to get the maximum benefit and performance out of your Windows 8 PC.

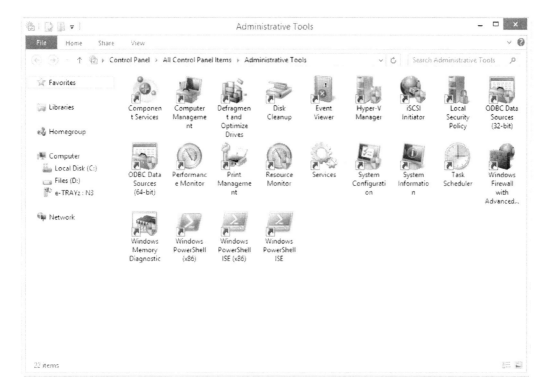

Figure 13-30. *The Windows 8 Administrative Tools*

Computer Management Console

The Computer Management Console provides access to other Administrative Tools but it is probably most commonly used to access the Disk Management tools. Here you can partition drives, grow and shrink partitions, and change, assign, and remove drive letters.

■ **Tip**   You can also open a dedicated Computer Management window from the Win+X Administration menu.

The main Computer Management window is split into a text details pane at the top and a graphical representation of your hard disks and partitions at the bottom (see Figure 13-31).

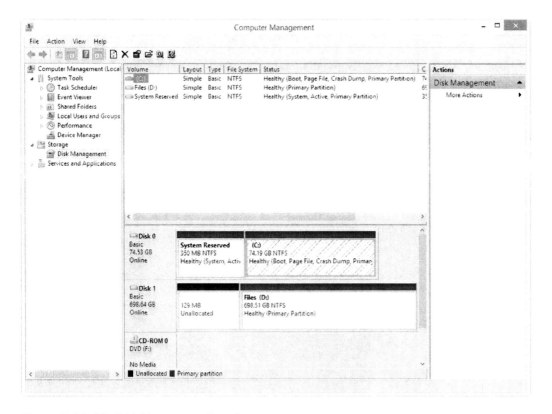

Figure 13-31. *The Disk Management Console*

You can right-click any hard drive or partition to perform a series of actions on it. These actions include the following:

- **Change Drive Letter and Paths**. If you have two disks that have the same drive letter assignment (perhaps one is an external drive), or if a disk does not appear to have a drive letter, you can change or assign it here. Another task you can perform is to turn the disk or partition into a folder within another disk.

■ **Tip** Some third-party software is available to help fix a USB-attached hard disk to a specific drive letter. This can be especially useful if you use a USB hard disk for backups and your backup software can only be set to work with a specific drive letter. One of the best is USB Drive Letter Manager, which can be downloaded from www.uwe-sieber.de.

- **Extend Volume** and **Shrink Volume**: These are used to resize the partition. Windows 8 has a fairly basic partitioning tool that may not be prepared to shrink a partition as much as you want. If this happens, try using the Defragmenter and then running the partitioning tool again. There is a simple wizard for partitioning and I've never known any reports of Windows corrupting partitions. That said, it is always a good idea to keep an up-to-date backup of all your files.

- Create a **New Volume** and **Delete Volume**: These are tasks that you can perform in blank space on disks or on existing partitions. You can use this to create RAID arrays as well as simple partitions, with Windows 8 supporting spanned, striped, mirrored, and RAID-5 arrays (see Figure 13-32). I will show you how to work with partitions in Chapter 14.

Figure 13-32. *Creating RAID arrays in Windows 8*

Defragment and Optimize Drives

The disk defragmenter helps keep file access on your computer quick by making sure that all parts of files are stored together on your hard disk. This also helps maintain file integrity and prevents files from becoming corrupt.

By default, it's set to automatically defragment all of your hard disks once a week and it automatically adds new hard disks to the defragmentation schedule as well (see Figure 13-33).

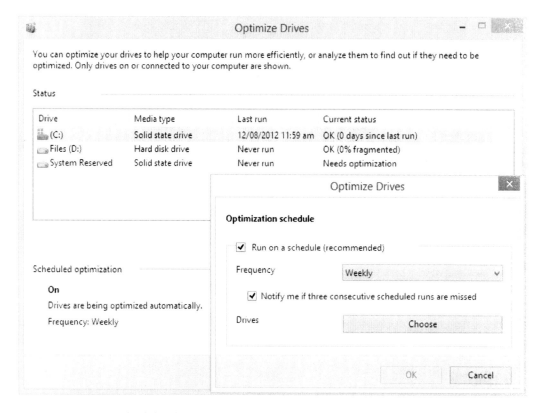

Figure 13-33. *Using the disk defragmenter*

There are some hard disks that you might want to exclude from the automatic defragmentation process, however. These include SSDs, in which there is no speed advantage to be gained from keeping files together because the drives are random access anyway.

Defragmentation also puts significant strain on mechanical hard disks, so if you have a disk in which the contents do not tend to change, such as for installers or for an image backup, it is worth excluding it from the defragmentation cycle.

Disk Cleanup

The Disk Cleanup tool removes temporary files from your computer. These files fill up space on a small SSD or generally slow down programs, including Internet Explorer. It's a very simple tool to use and as a basic alternative to more advanced freeware like CCleaner (www.piriform.com/ccleaner), it is worth running once in a while.

Event Viewer

No major event happens on your computer without being logged. This includes warnings and critical errors, including Blue Screen of Death errors.

You can view errors by type in the Log Summary to get additional information for clues as to what caused the error—so that you can rectify it. This can include error codes, descriptions, and details of the driver, program, or service that failed (see Figure 13-34).

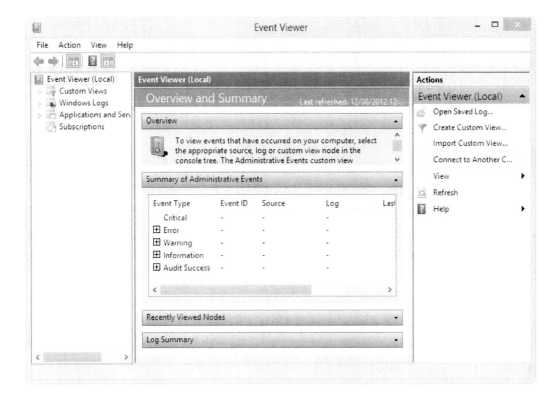

Figure 13-34. *The Event Viewer*

Errors are grouped by importance. For example, each event type can be opened with a double-click to display more information such as the error code, description, and any associated system file. You can look up these details online to get more detailed information about what this means, helping you to diagnose and repair the problem. You can find more information on Windows 8 troubleshooting on my web site (www.theLongClimb.com).

Local Security Policy

You probably won't need to worry about local security policies unless you are a systems administrator, in which case you will be administering group and security policies over a domain. There are a few settings here, however, that small business owners might be interested in.

You can set password expirations and rules governing the strength and length of passwords chosen by users. If needed for additional security, you can also lock out users after a specified number of failed logon attempts.

If you choose to turn on this feature, however, there must be several administrator accounts on the computer, otherwise, you could find that Windows 8 is completely locked out to you (see Figure 13-35).

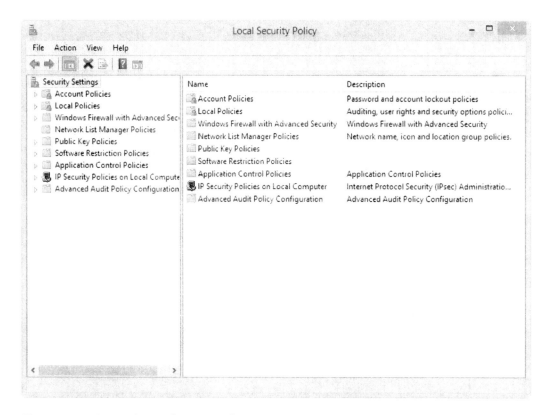

Figure 13-35. *Setting the Local Security Policy*

Performance Monitor

The Performance Monitor provides live graphs that show literally hundreds of metrics about Windows and your hardware. Are you concerned about your Wi-Fi traffic or your hard disk's write ability? To add data to the live graph, click the green + icon on the toolbar and choose the metrics to add from a Category view (see Figure 13-36).

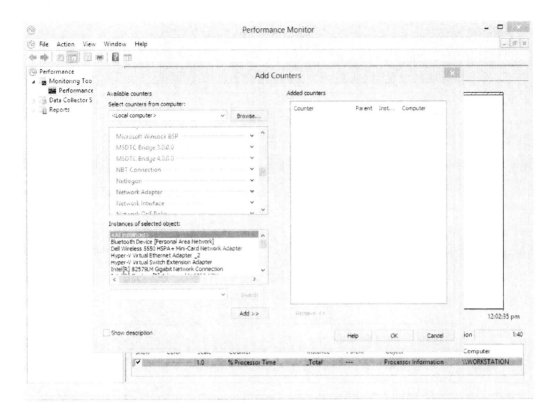

Figure 13-36. *The Performance Monitor*

These additional metrics provide valuable real-time information on the processes happening both inside and external to your computer. For example, you can see if all your processor cores are indeed working or if there are any bottlenecks with your networking.

Each counter is sensibly labeled and if you're not sure what counter to add, you can add a whole stack of related counters with a single click of the Add button.

When you are viewing the live data in the Performance Monitor, the graph could become confusing. You can turn a specific graph on and off in real-time by checking or unchecking the box next to its label at the bottom of the page.

Resource Monitor

The Windows 8 Resource Monitor provides even more detailed information about processes running on your computer, including the drivers, programs, apps, and Windows' services.

It works with tabs across the top of the page that give quick access to a general overview of your computer and more specific information about your CPU, memory, disk, and network.

Each of these sections contain collapsible panes with huge amounts of real-time information about your computer (see Figure 13-37).

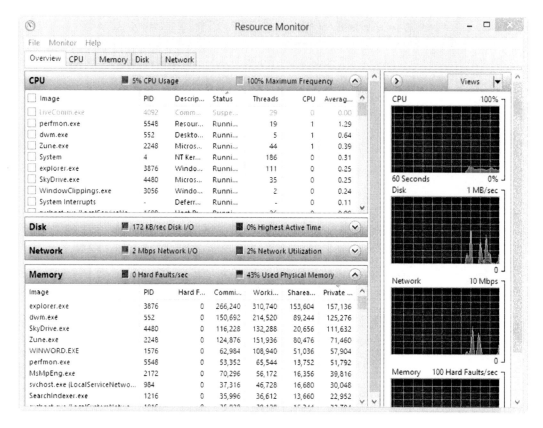

Figure 13-37. *The Resource Monitor*

In the top pane of each tab, each item has a check box next to it. Checking one or more of these will filter the graph information on the right of the pane to only show information about those particular processes. For example, you might be interested in the amount of data that your SkyDrive app is sending and receiving to diagnose if it is connecting correctly to the Internet.

Services

Services are programs that perform specific functions in Windows, such as running the print spooler or the firewall. Occasionally, you will want to disable a Windows or third-party service that you either don't need or that misbehaves.

You can do this in the Services page by right-clicking a service. From there you may start, stop, pause, resume or restart the service (see Figure 13-38).

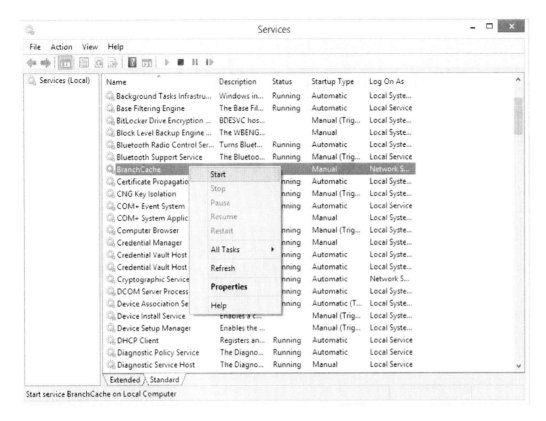

Figure 13-38. *The Services page*

It was common in the days of Windows XP and especially Windows Vista to completely disable services running in the background that you didn't need. With Windows 7, this was sorted so that only the services that you actually need are running at any one time.

You can disable a service though by selecting its Properties and setting its Startup Type to Disabled. Sometimes a service fails, however, especially if it is part of poorly written third-party software or a hardware driver. From this context menu, you can stop and restart services. Sometimes this can be useful if you find that a service is hung up and won't respond.

System Configuration

The System Configuration page is most commonly known to Windows users as MSConfig. It has been used in previous versions of Windows to disable unwanted startup programs. This is now managed through the Task Manager, but MSConfig is not without its uses.

The Boot tab allows you to manually set the computer to start in Safe Mode. This can be useful if you have a UEFI firmware system that won't allow you access to the F8 and Shift+F8 boot menu.

On the General tab are options that allow you to start the computer in a special Diagnostic Startup mode. This offers more functionality than Safe Mode in that it gives you more access to Windows features and controls, and it loads a few more hardware drivers. Diagnostic Startup is a great way to diagnose and repair problems with Windows 8 (see Figure 13-39). When you check this option, however, Windows will continue to boot into this new mode until you return to MSConfig and change the option back to Normal Startup.

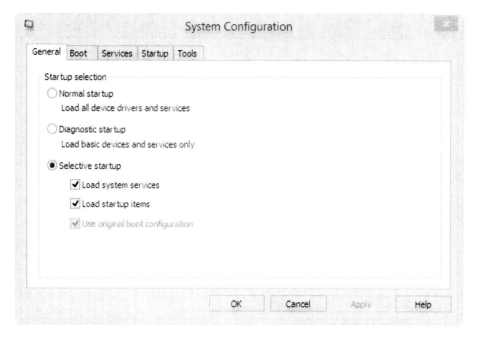

Figure 13-39. *MSConfig*

I do not recommend that you change the options under the Boot tab, especially not the advanced boot options. On the face of things, controlling the number of processor cores, which is an option here, might look like a tempting way to save electricity when using a high-power computer for lightweight tasks. In reality though, these features are strictly for IT pros because changing something here can render your copy of Windows 8 unbootable.

System Information

The System Information page provides extremely detailed information about your hardware, installed software and devices, running processes, and more. This information can be exported to a file through the File menu if you need to send comprehensive information about your computer to a support person.

Task Scheduler

The Task Scheduler can be used in several ways. First, you can use it to launch programs like the Disk Cleaner on a set schedule, such as once a month.

You can also set custom tasks that can be triggered in specific events, such as a driver failure. The Task Scheduler can then perform a series of tasks, including popping an alert window on screen to inform the user that a problem has occurred, to running a DOS or PowerShell script automatically.

The controls for setting up tasks are found in the right-hand pane, where you can either create tasks or import them from another computer (see Figure 13-40).

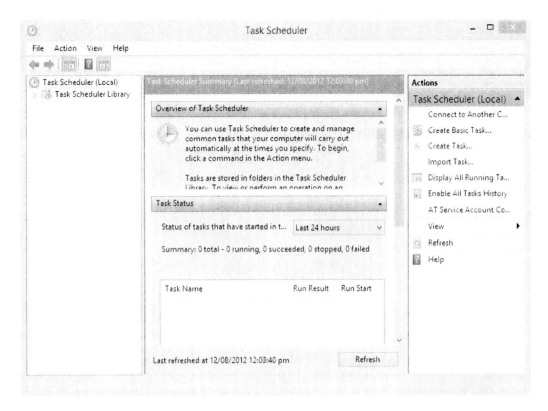

Figure 13-40. *The Task Scheduler*

Windows Memory Diagnostic

For many years, Windows has included a very useful and well-hidden Memory Diagnostic Tool (see Figure 13-41) that you can use if you suspect that your computer's physical memory has developed a fault.

Figure 13-41. *Windows comes with a memory diagnostic tool*

You can access the tool by searching for **memory** at the Start screen. It will scan your computer's memory, which can take considerable time so be prepared to walk the dog or have a coffee break. The tool will report any errors it finds.

Further Customizing Windows 8

Because of the way that Windows 8 is designed, it's possible to customize the operating system in an almost limitless number of ways. My mailbag regularly swells with questions about this. I'll discuss some of the more popular customizations. I should point out, however, that you should always be very careful making these kinds of changes to Windows. You should create a restore point, make sure that you have an up-to-date image backup of the operating system, and follow instructions very carefully because you could be making changes to the core OS. (See Chapter 12 for information on creating backup images and restore points.)

■ **Tip** Metro UI Tweaker is a great little utility for changing various aspects of the Start screen and Windows 8 interface. It also provides an easy way to add power buttons to the Start screen. You can download it at www.technobuzz.net/windows-8-metro-ui-tweaker.

Disabling the Windows 8 Lock Screen

The new Windows 8 lock screen provides valuable information over and above that available in previous versions of Windows, including the number of e-mails and messages received and appointment details.

Opening the lock screen is an another step you need to go through to log on to Windows 8. You may want to disable it completely and have Windows 8 start directly with the logon screen.

The lock screen can be disabled if you are using Windows 8 Pro or Enterprise, which includes the Group Policy Editor. To open it search for **gpedit.msc** at the Start screen.

Once in the Group Policy Editor, you need to navigate to Computer Configuration ➤ Administrative Templates ➤ Control Panel ➤ Personalization (see Figure 13-42).

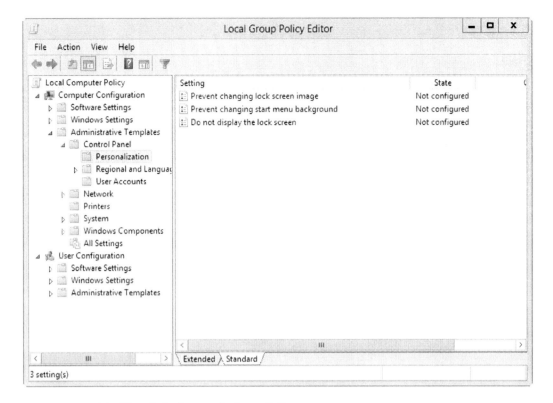

Figure 13-42. *Disabling the lock screen in Group Policy*

Here you will see an option labeled **Do not display the lock screen**. You should right-click this, select Edit from the options, and change the setting to Enabled in the next dialog box. The lock screen will no longer appear on the computer.

Automatically Logging into Windows 8

You may want to have Windows 8 automatically log on every time you start the computer. After all, if you are the only person using the computer and you log on with your Microsoft Account—bringing the benefits of automatically syncing your e-mail and calendar, and allowing you to buy apps, music, and video from the Windows Store—why would you need to type your password every time you start your computer?

It is very simple to do and requires unchecking a single box. Search for **netplwiz** at the Start screen. In the User Accounts dialog box that appears, click your main user account (it is the one labeled Administrator), and then uncheck **Users must enter a user name and password to use this computer** (see Figure 13-43).

Figure 13-43. *Automatically logging on users to Windows 8*

You will be asked to confirm your password to provide authorization. Afterward, Windows 8 will no longer ask you for your password at logon.

■ **Tip** If you want to restore the Start menu in Windows 8, you will need third-party software to do it. Solutions include ViStart (www.lee-soft.com/vistart), Start8 (www.stardock.com/products/start8), and Classic Shell (http://classicshell.sourceforge.net).

Booting Directly to the Windows 8 Desktop

While you can set Windows 8 to bypass the lock screen and also to automatically log on to your computer, you can also set it to start directly at the Windows 8 desktop.

Some third-party software, including Start8 and Classic Shell, can automatically boot Windows 8 to the desktop and perform tasks such as reinstating the Start menu.

You can manually set Windows 8 to boot to the desktop, however, using the following steps.

1. Open Notepad and type the following code:

```
[Shell]
 Command=2
 IconFile=Explorer.exe,3

[Taskbar]
 Command=ToggleDesktop
```

2. From the File menu select Save As and change the Save As Type to All Files.

3. Click the icon to the very left of the Address bar. When the address is highlighted, type **\%Appdata%\Microsoft\Windows\Start Menu\Programs\Startup** and press Enter.

4. Save the file as **desktop.scf** (see Figure 13-44).

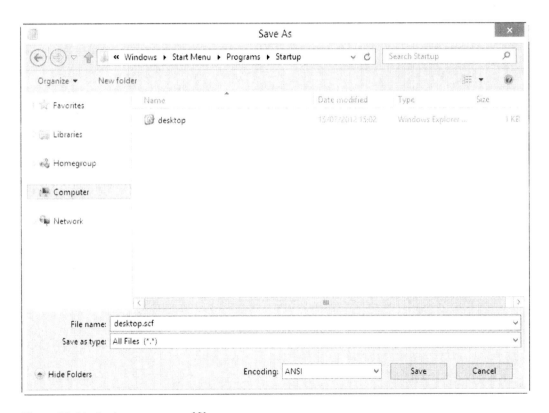

Figure 13-44. *Saving your new .scf file*

This creates a copy of the Windows Show Desktop button and sets it to autolaunch when Windows 8 starts. When you restart Windows 8, you will see the Start screen for a second or two before the file launches, but then you are taken directly to the desktop.

One important thing to note at this stage is that during the public beta of Windows 8, several methods for booting the operating system directly to the desktop appeared, and by the time the final release came around, none of them would work any more, perhaps because Microsoft found ways to block them. It's only sensible that I provide you with an alternate way to boot directly to the desktop in a way that can't be blocked.

This involves automatically launching File Explorer when you log on to Windows 8. It means that you have an open File Explorer window on your desktop whenever you start you computer, but you could easily change this to another program, such as Internet Explorer, and I'll show you how to do that too.

1. Search for **schedule** at the Start screen. From the Settings search results, click Schedule Tasks.

2. In the left pane of the Task Scheduler, click Task Scheduler Library (see Figure 13-45).

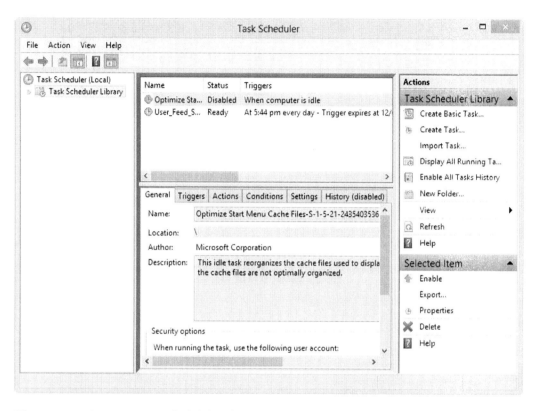

Figure 13-45. *Creating a new Scheduled Task*

3. In the right pane, click Create Basic Task.

4. Give the task a name, such as **Boot to Desktop**, and click Next.

5. At the next page, set the task to action When I Log On and click Next.

6. Make sure that Start a Program is selected at the next page and click Next.

7. In the Program/Script box type **explorer** (to automatically launch Internet Explorer, type **iexplore**) and click Next (see Figure 13-46).

Figure 13-46. *Setting File Explorer to launch at logon*

8. At the next screen, click Finish. You will now see your task listed in the top central pane of the Task Scheduler. You can right-click it to edit or delete it, if you wish.

Windows 8 will now switch to the desktop after a second or so of displaying the Start screen, and then autolaunch the program you have specified. If you want to launch any other program, type the full file name and address of the program, such as C:\Program Files\Google\Chrome\Chrome.exe.

Useful Windows Registry Hacks

One of the best things about the Windows Registry is how easy it is to edit, and how much control you can get over Windows by doing so. I'd like to share some of my favorite registry hacks. As with any work in the Windows Registry, be very careful adding, deleting, or changing settings, and always make sure you have both a backup copy of the registry and a backup image of your copy of Windows. Each registry change for a feature within Windows will require you to restart the computer; for registry changes involving programs, restarting the program is normally enough.

Backing Up the Windows Registry

The Registry is a database of all the settings and configuration options for Windows, your hardware, and all of your installed software. It's the main file (actually a series of files) that tells the operating system what's what and what's where. If you're making changes to the registry, you should make a backup copy of the files.

You can do this from within the Registry Editor. Search for **regedit** at the Start screen to find it. Then, from the File menu click Export and save your backup of the registry file in a safe place (see Figure 13-47).

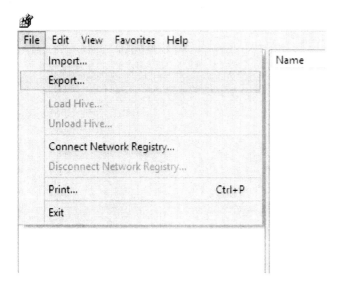

Figure 13-47. *Backing up the Windows Registry*

If you need to restore your backed up registry keys, open the Registry Editor and from its File menu, click Import. You will be asked which file you want to import and then asked to confirm that you *do* want to add this key to the Registry. Adding a backed up key will overwrite any changes made to that key.

Add Copy To/Move To Options to the File Explorer Context Menu

While it's useful for the File Explorer context menu to include Cut and Copy commands when you right-click a file or folder, it's also possible to add Copy To Folder and Move To Folder options to this context list (see Figure 13-48).

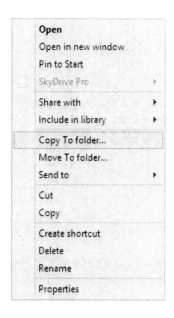

Figure 13-48. *Adding Copy To Folder and Move To Folder options to File Explorer*

Here's how to add the Copy To Folder command:

1. Open the Registry Editor by searching for **regedit** at the Start screen.

2. Navigate to the key HKEY_CLASSES_ROOT\AllFilesystemObjects\shellex\ ContextMenuHandlers.

3. Right-click the ContextMenuHandlers key and add a New Key with the name **Copy to folder**.

4. Double-click this new key's Default value and change its value to **{C2FBB630-2971-11D1-A18C-00C04FD75D13}**.

To also add a Move To Folder item to the context menu, repeat these steps but create a new **Move to folder** key with the default value **{C2FBB631-2971-11D1-A18C-00C04FD75D13}**.

Add Defragment to the File Explorer Context Menu

You can add a Defragment option to the context menu in File Explorer when you right-click a hard disk (see Figure 13-49). This starts a command-line version of the defragmentation tool.

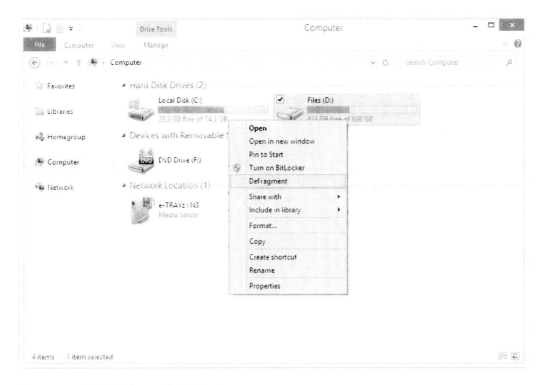

Figure 13-49. *Add Defrag to the File Explorer context menu*

Follow these steps to add Defragment:

1. Open the Registry Editor by searching for **regedit** at the Start screen.

2. Navigate to the key HKEY_CLASSES_ROOT\Drive\shell.

3. Create a new key under this called **runas**.

4. Double-click Default Value to open it and set its default value to **Defragment**.

5. Create a subkey under runas called **command**.

6. Double-click the Command subkey and change its default value to **defrag %1 -v**.

Change Taskbar Program Previews

With a simple registry tweak, you can change the size of the preview thumbnails for running programs in the Windows 8 taskbar.

1. Open the Registry Editor by searching for **regedit** at the Start screen.

2. Navigate to the key HKEY_CURRENT_USER\Software\Microsoft\Windows\ CurrentVersion\Explorer\Taskband.

3. Right-click and create a new Dword (32-bit) Value called **MinThumbSizePX**.

4. Double-click this new entry and change its value to the size (in pixels) you want your thumbnails to be. For example, you might want huge thumbnails that are 500 pixels across (so you change the number to 500) or you might want tiny thumbnails of 50 pixels (so change the value to 50).

There are other registry Dword 32-bit Value keys you can create to control thumbnail images:

- NumThumbnails (the number of thumbnail images)
- MinThumbSizePX (minimum thumbnail size)
- MaxThumbSizePX (maximum thumbnail size)
- TextHeightPX (thumbnail title text height in pixels)
- TopMarginPX (top margin in pixels)
- LeftMarginPX (left margin in pixels)
- RightMarginPX (right margin in pixels)
- BottomMarginPX (bottom margin in pixels)
- ThumbSpacingXPx (horizontal spacing between thumbnails in pixels)
- ThumbSpacingYPx (vertical spacing between thumbnails in pixels)

Show Drive Letter Before Volume Name in File Explorer

You might want to turn off the display of driver letters in File Explorer, which you can do by selecting Options and then opening the View tab. Select **Change folder and search options** and then uncheck **Show drive letters**.

You can also have File Explorer display the drive letter before the drive volume name.

1. Open the Registry Editor by searching for **regedit** at the Start screen.

2. Navigate to the following key HKEY_LOCAL_MACHINE\SOFTWARE\Microsoft\Windows\CurrentVersion\Explorer.

3. Right-click and create a new Dword (32-bit) Value called **ShowDriveLettersFirst**.

4. Double-click the new addition to open it and change its value from 0 to **4**.

Summary

Windows has traditionally been highly configurable and Windows 8 is no exception with its sheer volume of settings. This chapter could turn into an entire book on its own just talking about how to configure every setting.

I hope this chapter has given you a good overview of what the settings do, how you can change them, and why you might want to do so. There are some settings, such as changing the virtual memory, that I always recommend you change, but generally speaking, Windows 8 is fine out of the box. *Tweaking* Windows 8, on the other hand, is something entirely different.

CHAPTER 14

Getting Started with Virtualization

On average, a new version of Windows is released every three years. Each version brings new features and new ways of working, but also fresh challenges. One of those challenges is maintaining compatibility with the older software that we've used for years and that are as comfortable as an old shoe.

I am not excluded from this. I have used the same graphics package, Microsoft PhotoDraw, for over a decade. I love it—it does everything I want and it's extremely easy to use. Why should I change?

Sadly, with upgrades to Windows come software incompatibilities. The biggest change came with the move from Windows XP to Windows Vista. The whole core of the operating system was rewritten from scratch. It included some major restructuring, such as removing, replacing, or rewriting features. With PhotoDraw, I found that while most of the package still worked, some features treated me to only an annoying *"donk!"* noise when I tried to use them.

There are also times when you want to be able to use or try a different operating system on your computer, such as Linux or even the prerelease of the next version of Windows. Setting up a dual-boot system can be extremely complex, especially as Windows 8 commonly needs to be installed last (see Chapter 15 for notes on this). A good option is to install the second operating system in a virtual machine.

When Windows 7 was launched with the accompanying XP Mode virtualization client, I was delighted. At long last, I could use PhotoDraw again on the desktop without worry or problems.

The bad news now is that XP Mode is no longer supported and it isn't a feature of Windows 8. This is primarily because all support for XP ends (or ended, depending on when you're reading this) in April 2014, before the release of Windows 9.

It's not all bad news though. Windows 8 Pro and Enterprise editions contain a feature called Hyper-V. This is Microsoft's latest virtualization client ported from Windows Server. It's more than powerful enough to get your legacy software working again.

Virtualization isn't just about maintaining compatibility with older software, however, because it also has important roles to play in testing stability in software and updates for deployment, and also for providing customizable working environments for users. In this chapter, I'll show you how to set up and maintain Hyper-V for all these roles.

It is worth noting, though, that using virtualization is an advanced feature and something that less-technical Windows users will likely avoid. You can't do anything to harm or damage your current Windows installation, but if you want to use Hyper-V and you're not completely comfortable with computers, you should follow the instructions in this chapter very carefully to ensure the best results.

Note   Hyper-V is only available in the 64-bit versions of Windows 8 Pro and Enterprise, if running on compatible hardware.

What Is Virtualization?

Hyper-V allows any operating system to run inside another in a virtualized environment that simulates the hardware of a full PC. It effectively tricks the virtualized operating system into thinking its running on its own hardware. Older virtual machines that simulated the hardware were very slow because every hardware action had to be re-created in software.

Newer virtual machines, including Hyper-V, allow the virtualized operating system access to your computer's own hardware. They manage the sharing of that hardware between the host OS and the virtualized OS on the machine to make sure conflicts don't occur. This means that Hyper-V acts on your computer and your network as though they're just another computer attached to that network.

The main benefit of virtualization is that the hardware management allows virtual machines (VMs) to harness the full power of modern computers with multiple processor cores and large volumes of memory. For example, if you have a quad-core processor and 8GB of memory in your computer, a good virtual machine can assign each of three operating systems a single processor core and 2GB of memory each with the host OS using the remaining core and memory—maximizing the computer's potential and reducing overall costs.

When Would You Use a Virtual Machine?

There are several scenarios in which the use of a virtual machine is helpful, including keeping your older legacy software working. If you really must use software that worked fine in Windows XP but doesn't work in Windows 8, then installing a copy of XP into a VM is a way to continue using that software.

VMs are also commonly used for testing scenarios. Let's say you want to roll out a patch or software upgrade across your computers, but you're unsure of how it will interact with the existing software that you use. You can test it first in a VM so that you are certain that all works fine beforehand, and avoid the risk of any downtime.

You might also use virtualization to provide custom working environments. On one machine, you could set up VMs for design, accounting, or other purposes that provide workers with the tools and environment they need to be productive, while also making the environment easy to transport between computers in different locations.

I used Hyper-V while writing this book so that I could install a clean copy of Windows 8. There are all manner of scenarios where it is useful to have a VM running.

▓ **Note**   You need a valid license (product key) for each operating system you install in a virtual machine using Hyper-V.

Why You Should "Sandbox" Windows XP

For those who want to run XP on a virtual machine, I want you to examine if you should really continue using Windows XP to run your legacy software. While there is one scenario where it's perfectly safe to run XP (I'll come to it shortly), there are a couple of very good reasons why you should not.

Windows XP, while very well liked by many people, is an extremely insecure operating system. As shipped with Internet Explorer 6, it was responsible for many major security scares in the decade after it was released.

Those problems have never gone away. In countries such as China, XP usage was still very high when Windows 8 was released. Malware writers and criminals still want to target the OS and its vulnerabilities to steal personal data from users.

At the end of extended support for XP, all patches and updates for the operating system stop forever; any vulnerabilities that still exist, or any new vulnerabilities created through third-party software or malware, will be left unpatched. You can be certain that when XP support ends, malware for any remaining vulnerabilities—the ones that the criminals have identified but not yet exploited—will be released.

> ■ **Tip** Always make sure that Windows Updates is turned on and that antivirus software is installed on any operating system in a VM with Internet access.

I do not recommend that anyone continue using Windows XP, either on its own or within a virtual machine, in either Windows 7 or Windows 8. There is one scenario however, where it might be considered okay to use Windows XP in a virtual machine. This is when you're using software in XP that never requires Internet access. You can set up the VM with no networking and Internet support.

This "sandboxed" VM is completely isolated from your network and the Internet, with no traffic able to get in or out. You can still give it local file storage access so that you can work with files on your computer; but without direct ability to contact the Internet, the only way it can succumb to virus infection is if the host PC or the files on it are already infected.

> ■ **Note** While Windows XP Mode in Windows 7 allowed you to pin XP-installed software to the Windows 7 taskbar and use it on the Windows 7 desktop, Hyper-V does not support this. To use this functionality, you need to use Microsoft Enterprise Desktop Virtualization (MED-V), which is part of the Microsoft Desktop Optimization Pack (MDOP). It is only available to enterprises through Software Assurance volume licensing.
>
> There is a way to "sort of" get XP-mode running on the Windows 8 desktop using Oracle `VirtualBox.HowToGeek.com` has published a guide at `www.howtogeek.com/howto/12183/how-to-run-xp-mode-in-virtualbox-on-windows-7/`.

Installing an Operating System in Hyper-V

So how do you install an operating system into Hyper-V, and what types of operating system does it support? You can install any version of Windows or other Intel (x86 and x64)–based operating systems into Hyper-V, including GNU/Linux, by following these steps:

1. Find Hyper-V in Windows by searching for **Hyper** at the Start screen.

2. Click Hyper-V Manager. The Hyper-V Manager (see Figure 14-1) looks and operates much like the other administration windows in Windows 8. Your main controls are in the right pane.

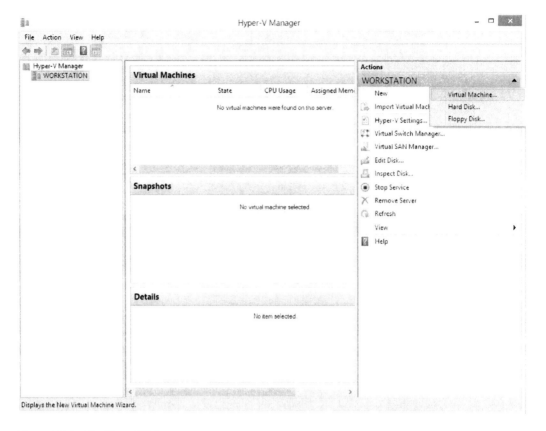

Figure 14-1. *The Hyper-V Manager*

3.   Click New ➤ Virtual Machine to create a new virtual machine.

░ **Note**   Is Hyper-V deactivated on your computer? If a search for Hyper-V displays no results, open the Control Panel ➤ Programs and Features ➤ Turn Windows Features On or Off. Turn on Hyper-V by checking the box and clicking OK.

---

4.   Click the Next button at the bottom of the New Virtual Machine Wizard (see Figure 14-2) to set up your own virtual machine.

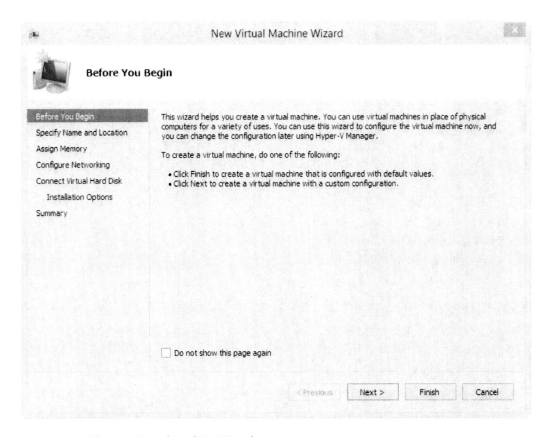

Figure 14-2. *The New Virtual Machine Wizard*

5. Give your virtual machine a name and a store location (see Figure 14-3). By default, Windows 8 suggests storing it on the same hard disk that Windows is installed. You may want to specify a different hard disk, however. Click Next.

Figure 14-3. *Specifying a name for the VM*

■ **Tip**   Storing your VM on a different disk or partition to Windows 8 excludes it from any system image backup you make, thus bringing down the overall size of that backup. If you always want to use the VM *with* your installed copy of Windows, however, then keeping it on the same hard disk as Windows (and therefore included in an image backup) might be the best choice.

---

6.   Assign the amount of memory you want to dedicate to the VM (see Figure 14-4). The amount depends on the type of operating system you are running in the VM and how much physical memory your PC has.

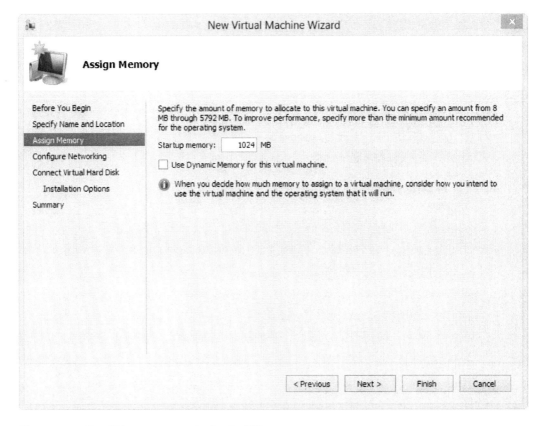

Figure 14-4. Specifying a memory size for the VM

For example, you might be installing XP into the VM, which means you would only need 512MB of RAM. If you plan to do graphics work in the VM, however, more memory would be required. If your PC only has 4GB of memory, you should probably not specify more than 1GB for the VM; but if you have 8GB, then you could dedicate a healthier 2GB of memory to the VM.

There is also the option to use Dynamic Memory. This feature allows the VM to automatically assign additional memory through Hyper-V if it is required and if there is available memory on your PC. You may find this option useful because it is only used when required. Click Next.

7. Configure the networking options for the VM (see Figure 14-5). Click Next.

Figure 14-5. *Configuring networking for the VM*

If you want a completely sandboxed operating system with no local computer, network, or Internet access, there is no need to configure a network adaptor to work with the VM. This isolates the VM completely from the outside world, but it also means that you are unable to access the files and documents on the host computer and that you won't have access to the VM using Remote Desktop.

■ **Note**   You may not be able to add networking options at this time because networking in Hyper-V must be configured independently of any individual VM. VMs can share individually configured networks to either give them Internet access, access to the local computer, or only access to other VMs. If this is the case, you need to install Integration Services into the VM when it is installed, and set up a virtual switch. I show you how to do these later in this chapter.

---

8. Connect the VHD. This wizard page lets you specify the size of the virtual machine's hard disk (see Figure 14-6). It will suggest a size, though you can change this if you require the VM to be larger or smaller. An alternate option is to reattach an existing VHD. Click Next.

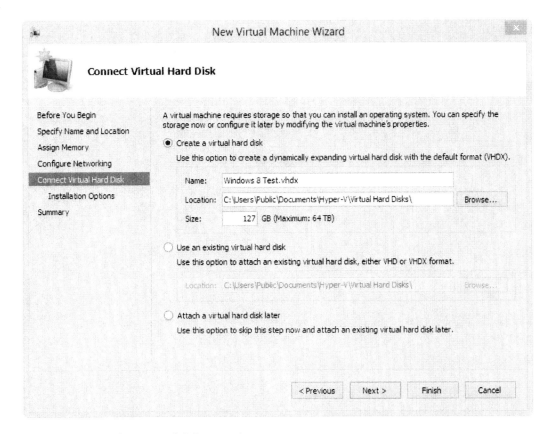

Figure 14-6. *Specifying virtual disk properties*

9. Install an operating system (see Figure 14-7). You can do this from a virtual floppy disk, CD, DVD, USB flash drive, or ISO file.

Figure 14-7. *Installing the OS into the VM*

10. Confirm all the details you have entered (see Figure 14-8). Click Finish when you are done.

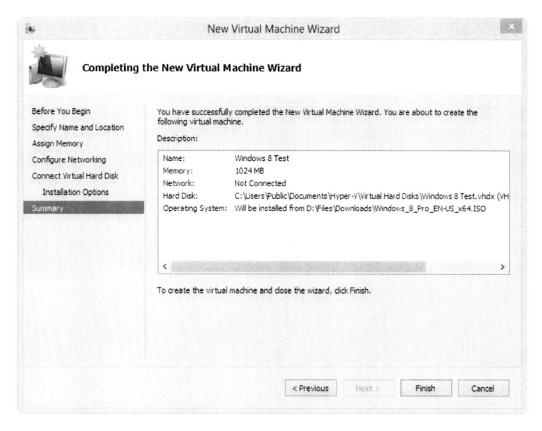

Figure 14-8. *Confirming the VM details*

11.   Start the VM. In the Hyper-V Manager, you now see your VM listed in the top center pane (see Figure 14-9). Click it. In the bottom half of the right pane, click Connect to connect to the VM.

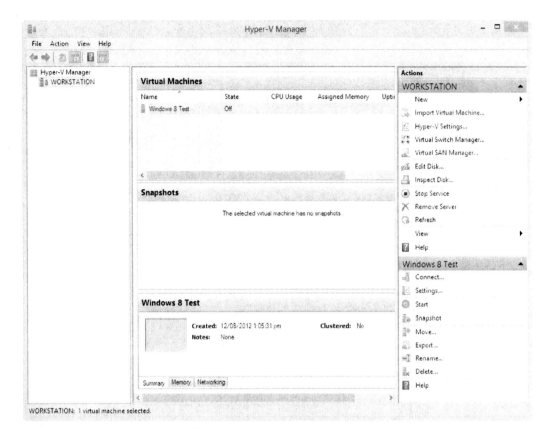

Figure 14-9. *Running a VM*

12.   Open the Action menu and select Start to launch the VM (see Figure 14-10).

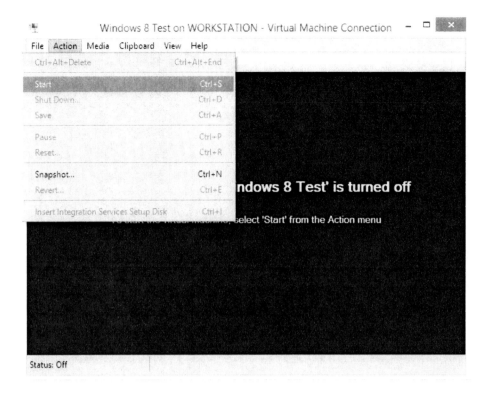

Figure 14-10. Launching a VM

Once you have started the VM, you see a window with the virtualized OS running inside it.

Setting Up Networking with Hyper-V

By default, all Hyper-V virtual machines are sandboxed and completely isolated from the computers and networks around them. When you want a virtual machine to interact with other VMs, your physical computers, the network, and the Internet, you need to create a virtual switch. This is done from the main Hyper-V Manager, where you click Virtual Switch Manager in the right pane.

You need to decide what type of virtual switch you want to create. The Virtual Switch Manager gives you a text description of each type of switch (see Figure 14-11).

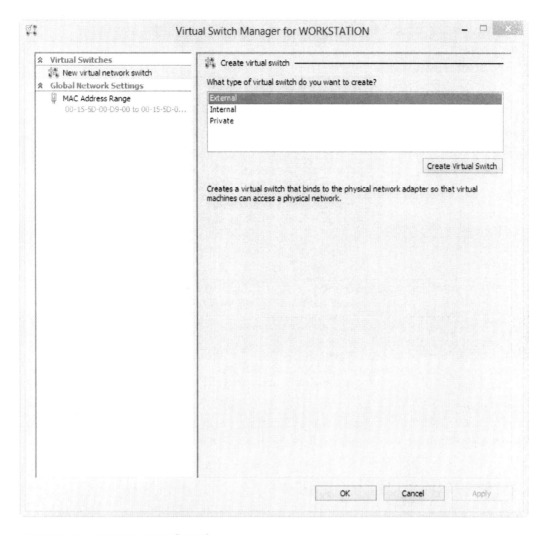

Figure 14-11. *Creating a virtual switch*

If you want your VM to see and access files on the host PC and on your network, you need to select External, which is also the option that gives the VM access to the Internet (so be careful with it if using XP). The Internal and Private options only allow Hyper-V VMs to communicate with each other.

When you have highlighted the option you want, click the Create Virtual Switch button.

You now need to configure the options for your virtual switch (see Figure 14-12). An important thing to determine is which network adapter in your computer you attach it to. You may have both wired and wireless network adapters in your computer; you need to choose the right one.

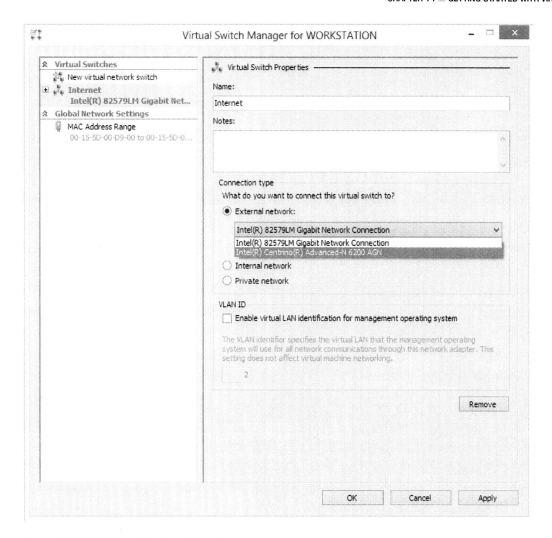

Figure 14-12. *Setting virtual switch options*

■ **Tip** Let's say you want a VM to access files on the host PC, but you do *not* want it to have access to the network or the Internet. If your PC has wired and wireless connections, connect the switch to the one that you *don't* use to get online. If you don't have a physical network cable plugged into the PC, choose the non-Wi-Fi connection. This gives the VM access to the host PC *only* and helps isolate it from malware and attack.

Once you have created your virtual switch, you need to attach it to your VM. Click the appropriate VM in the top-center pane in the Hyper-V Manager. Then in the bottom-right pane, click Settings. This brings up the settings for the VM (see Figure 14-13).

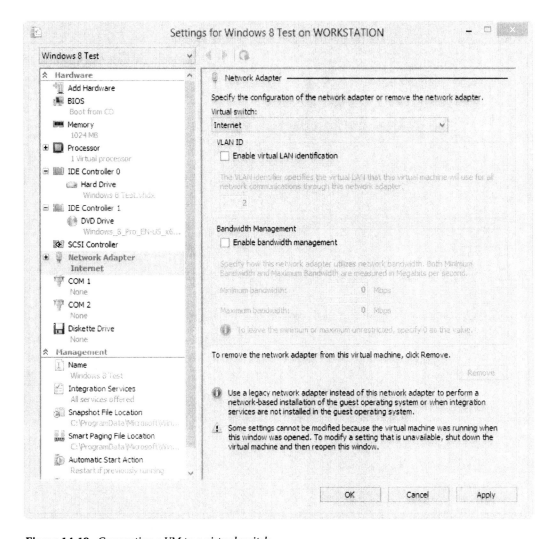

Figure 14-13. *Connecting a VM to a virtual switch*

Click Network Adapter option in the left pane. If you do not see this option, then click Add Hardware to add a network adapter.

Where you choose the virtual switch at the top of the Network Adapter settings, select the switch you created and press OK. No further configuration should be necessary. Your VM now has network access.

Other options may be changed in the VM Settings, however, some settings that are set when you first create the VM cannot be changed. To change these settings, the VM needs to be switched off.

Integrating Additional Services into a VM

Some operating systems, especially earlier versions of Windows, won't give you network access or other features at this point. This is where you need to plug extra features into the VM. You must do this with the VM running.

These additional features are required for some operating systems, and include the ability to move your mouse cursor freely between your main desktop and open VMs without having to first unlock it from the VM window. They also include networking and USB support for some operating systems.

From the Action menu, click Insert Integration Service Setup Disk. This loads an ISO file containing software that enhances the functionality of the VM.

Using Virtual Hard Disks

You can also use VHDs (virtual hard disks) within windows both as file containers and as boot drives for the operating system. You can create a VHD within Hyper-V but also from the Windows 8 Disk Management Console (available using the Win+X keyboard shortcut).

On their own, VHDs are of limited use because you need to manually reattach them to Windows 8 when the computer is restarted. It is in booting from a VHD that they become useful. Let's say you have a laptop that you repurpose for different roles within a company, such as sales, accounting, or management, for example. Rather than have a complicated multiboot system that is difficult to maintain, you can create a series of VHDs and copy the correct one to the laptop when you need to assign the laptop a different departmental role.

Creating a VHD in Windows 8

Create a VHD from the Disk Management Console (press Win+X to open options). From the Action menu, click Create VHD (see Figure 14-14).

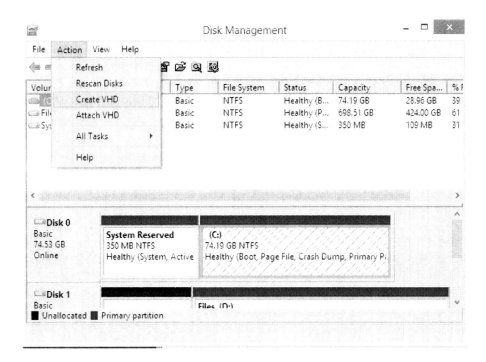

Figure 14-14. *Creating a VHD*

A dialog box allows you to specify the VHD size and the hard disk location for VHD storage (see Figure 14-15).

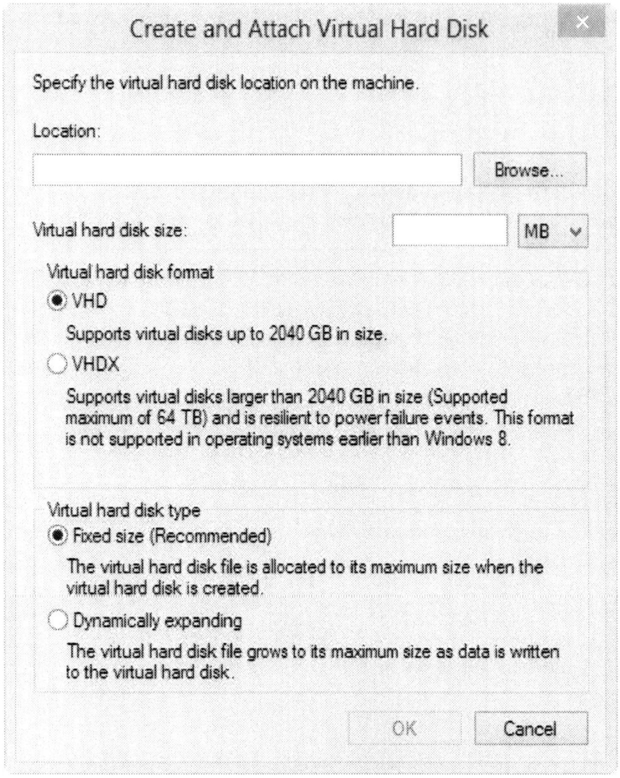

Create and Attach Virtual Hard Disk

Specify the virtual hard disk location on the machine.

Location:

[   ] Browse...

Virtual hard disk size: [   ] MB ▾

Virtual hard disk format

◉ VHD

   Supports virtual disks up to 2040 GB in size.

○ VHDX

   Supports virtual disks larger than 2040 GB in size (Supported maximum of 64 TB) and is resilient to power failure events. This format is not supported in operating systems earlier than Windows 8.

Virtual hard disk type

◉ Fixed size (Recommended)

   The virtual hard disk file is allocated to its maximum size when the virtual hard disk is created.

○ Dynamically expanding

   The virtual hard disk file grows to its maximum size as data is written to the virtual hard disk.

OK   Cancel

Figure 14-15. *Choosing VHD options*

When you choose the location for the VHD, you also specify its name. The size options are interesting, however, because you can specify a fixed size or you can have the VHD expand in size dynamically as and when you need more space within it.

When the VHD is created, you can attach it to Windows 8 in the Disk Management Console by selecting Attach VHD from the Actions menu.

Booting Windows from a VHD

Creating a VHD doesn't let you install an operating system in it or boot from it. To do this, you need to start your computer from your original Windows 8 installation media. Once you have selected your installation language, perform the following steps.

1. Press Shift+F10 at the installation screen to open a Command window.

2. Type **diskpart** and press Enter.

3. To use an existing VHD, type **Select vdisk file=C:\Path1\Path2\disk.vhd**, substituting the path and disk names for the location on the disk of the VHD and its name.

4. To create a new VHD, type **Create vdisk file=C:\Path1\Path2\disk.vhd maximum=20000 type=dynamic**, again substituting the path and disk names with where you want the VHD to be created and what you want it to be called (the path folders must already exist). Also, substitute the number of megabytes and create either a fixed or dynamic disk.

5. Type **Select vdisk file=C:zPath1\Path2\disk.vhd** and press Enter to attach the VHD if you have just created one.

6. Type **attach vdisk** and press Enter.

7. Type **exit** and press Enter.

8. Type **exit** again and press Enter.

9. Click Install ➤ Custom: Install Windows Only (Advanced).

10. Locate the newly attached VHD in the hard disk pane that you want to install Windows. This is Disk 1 if you only have one hard disk in your computer. You can identify it by its size. Click Next when you are ready to install Windows onto the VHD.

You can install Windows 7 Enterprise and Ultimate, Windows 8 Pro and Enterprise, and Windows Server 2008 and 2012 into a VHD.

▒ **Note**   Each operating system and software package you install into a virtual machine needs to have its own license and, if necessary for that product, its own product key. Some versions of Windows are not licensed for use inside a virtual machine. You can find out more about licensing for your particular copies of Windows and other Microsoft software at www.microsoft.com/About/Legal/EN/US/IntellectualProperty/UseTerms.

You now need to add the VHD to the Windows boot menu.

1. Press Win+X to open the Administration menu.

2. Click Command Prompt (Admin).

3. Type **bcdedit /v** in the Command window. Press Enter.

4. Locate the VHD you have installed and make a note of its global identifier (GUID) code. It is a long string of numbers and letters in the Identifier section for the OS (see Figure 14-16).

Figure 14-16. *Locating the GUID for an installed OS*

5. Type **bcdedit /set {GUID} description "OS Name"**, substituting the actual GUID for the OS for the letters GUID, and assigning the OS its proper name. Press Enter.

6. Optionally, you might want this VHD to be the OS that loads by default. Set this by typing **bcdedit / default {GUID}**. Press Enter.

You are now able to boot your computer from the VM in the same way that you boot into your normally installed copy of Windows. In fact, you won't even be able to notice the difference. Most people booting into a VM have no idea that they're not using an operating system that's installed onto the computer's hard disk.

■ **Note**   It is worth noting that the Secure Boot feature in Windows 8 on UEFI-equipped motherboards might prevent some VHDs from booting. You should check in the UEFI firmware settings to see if this feature can be turned off on your computer.

Summary

The virtualization options in Windows 8 are powerful; but remember that they are only available in the Pro and Enterprise editions.

I have shown you how it is also possible—so long as you have two network adapters in your PC—to isolate a VM from the Internet while still giving it access to your own PC. It can only really be done if you connect to the Internet via Wi-Fi and *do not* have a physical network cable plugged into your computer. Doing this can help isolate an older Windows XP installation from viruses and other malware infections.

CHAPTER 15

Installing Windows 8 on Your Computer

Whether you get your copy of Windows 8 with a shiny new PC, off the shelf from your local store, or on a software subscription package from Microsoft, you'll need to install it at some point; either to replace an earlier version of Windows on your computer or when something goes wrong.

Installing Windows 8 is something that can be done fairly simply and without fuss. In fact, it's the least fussy version of Windows ever. It allows you to upgrade from an earlier version of the operating system, or wipe out an existing one, while keeping all of your files intact.

Back Up Your Files and Documents First!

When you install Windows 8 onto an existing computer, you will want to make sure that you keep all of your files and documents intact. To guarantee this, you should *always* make an up-to-date backup of all of your files and documents beforehand.

While the Windows installation process is generally very robust, there's no knowing when and how something might go wrong. This could be due to a power outage, a driver failure, or simply forgetting that you had some important files in a different folder that Windows 8 doesn't save because it doesn't know it needs to.

The best place to keep a files backup is on an external USB hard disk; but if you have a second physical hard disk or a hard disk that's split into several different partitions on your computer, you can keep your files there. Bear in mind though that a *proper* backup should be one that's external to the computer, which covers you in case of fire, theft, or hard-disk failure. (See Chapter 12 for information on performing backups.)

Windows 8 Edition Differences

There the several editions (sometimes known as flavors or SKUs [stock-keeping units]) of Windows 8. Be aware that some are only available to certain customers and in certain ways.

- **Windows 8** is the general consumer version and comes preinstalled on most new PCs. It is also available through retail purchase.

- **Windows 8 Pro** is the version aimed at IT professionals and enthusiasts. It comes preinstalled on some PCs and is available for purchase.

- **Windows 8 Enterprise** is only available to business volume-licensing customers.

- **Windows 8 RT** (Runtime) is the ARM version of Windows 8. It is only available to Microsoft's hardware partners. It is not available through retail purchase and cannot be installed on a blank tablet by the end user.

- **Windows 8 Pro with Media Center** isn't actually an official version of Windows 8, but it is sold by some hardware partners or preinstalled on some media and entertainment-focused PCs. It is only available for purchase by upgrading Windows 8 or Windows Pro through the Add Features to Windows option in the Control Panel.

Deciding How to Install Windows 8 on an Existing Computer

One of the perennial questions asked in computing circles when migrating from one version of Windows to another is whether to perform an upgrade over your existing copy or whether to completely wipe the old installation and start from scratch. So what are the pros and cons of both?

Upgrade pros:

- Upgrading is much faster and easier overall, especially if you have a lot of software on your computer, because it saves reinstalling everything afterward.

- Performing an upgrade will leave your files intact if your files and documents are on the same hard-disk partition as your old copy of Windows and you don't have an external backup (more on this shortly because it's very important).

Upgrade cons:

- Any problems associated with your software or Windows installation might be carried forward into Windows 8.

- Upgrading does not guarantee that your software will work properly afterward, and some software programs might need to be uninstalled and reinstalled.

Clean install pros:

- Your new installation will be fresh and clean with no problems associated with it.

- There will be no bugs and incompatible software.

Clean install cons:

- Installation and configuration can be time-consuming, especially if you have a lot of software.

- You will need to have an up-to-date external backup of your files and documents.

In truth, you might not have a choice but to perform a clean installation, at least as far as the Windows 8 upgrade options go. This is because Windows 8 might not be able to migrate your software anyway.

Now let's look at the process of actually upgrading to Windows 8. Once you have physical media for installing Windows 8, be it a DVD or a USB flash drive, you can set about the process of installing the operating system on your computer. If you want to upgrade from a version of Windows other than Windows 7, you will have to reinstall your software, as I shall explain shortly.

When Is an Upgrade *Also* a Clean Install?

Each and every upgrade path to Windows 8 allows you to move *Just* [the] *personal files* for each user on the computer. Is this a clean install and is it a clean installation alternative? The answer to this question depends on the version that you're upgrading from and the setup that you have in place.

When Windows performs an upgrade, it copies your old Windows installation, complete with programs, into a `Windows.old` folder. This is so that you can recover any files from the installation that you need to—such as Internet Favorites from Windows XP, which weren't stored in a separate User folder and weren't considered part of the user's files.

This means that all new folders are created for the new operating system containing all new files. With this being the case, you essentially have a clean installation because there's nothing left over from your old Windows installation that can cause problems, malware infection, or incompatibilities.

When You Should Perform a Clean Install

So when shouldn't you choose Upgrade to perform a clean installation? There are a few scenarios where you should just choose to perform a completely clean installation, formatting your hard disk and starting from scratch.

- *If you already store your files and documents on a different physical hard disk or partition to your copy of Windows.* I always recommend storing your files on a separate partition of Windows for data security, and there is simply nothing to be gained from creating the `Windows.old` folder. In this circumstance, it's best to reformat the Windows drive, which removes any trace of doubt that the former installation might cause problems.

- *If your Windows disk isn't large enough to store both Windows 8 and your old Windows installation in a Windows.old folder.* If there isn't enough space on your hard disk to upgrade Windows, the installer will inform you before the upgrade process begins.

- *If you are upgrading from Windows XP,* you should always reformat your hard disk because Windows 8 (as with Windows 7) wants to create a System Reserved partition at the beginning of your primary hard disk (Disc 0), where it will place its startup and system repair files. This partition contains the boot information for Windows and, crucially, all the rescue tools and utilities for when the operating system won't start. If the Windows installer can't create this partition, you lose valuable Windows 8 features.

- *If you have UEFI firmware on your computer,* Windows 8 might create support and rescue partitions in addition to System Reserved. If you have a Windows 7 computer that you are upgrading to Windows 8, performing a format and clean installation is the only way to create these additional troubleshooting and rescue partitions.

Acquiring Windows 8

Windows 8 is the first version of the operating system that you can purchase online direct from Microsoft. You have the choice of downloading the operating system or ordering it on a DVD. You can purchase the operating system as a download on an existing computer that is running another version of Windows. There is no requirement, however, to install the downloaded copy of Windows 8 on the computer you download it to; you can install it on another computer if you wish.

If you choose to purchase a packaged DVD product, you can skip ahead to the "Preparing to Install Windows 8" section in this chapter.

Downloading Windows 8

The Windows 8 Upgrade Assistant is at `www.microsoftstore.com`. It helps you through the process of downloading and paying for your new copy of Windows 8. At the end of the process, it presents you with several options (see Figure 15-1).

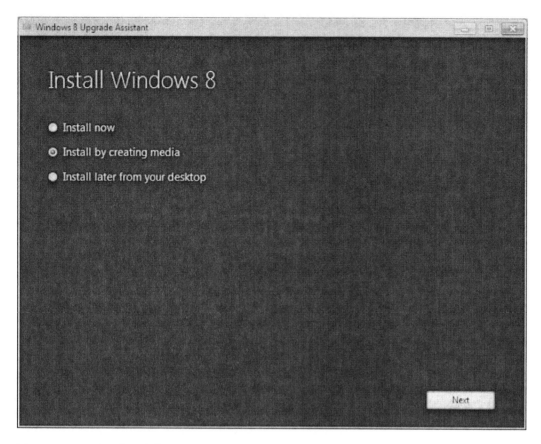

Figure 15-1. Using the Windows 8 Upgrade Assistant to purchase Windows 8

When you download Windows 8, you will want to keep a copy of the installer, as you never know when you might need to reinstall it. When you are prompted to **Install by creating media**, this is exactly the option you should choose because it gives you physical media that you can safely store in case you need it.

You can create this media on a USB flash drive or an ISO file that can be burned to DVD (see Figure 15-2).

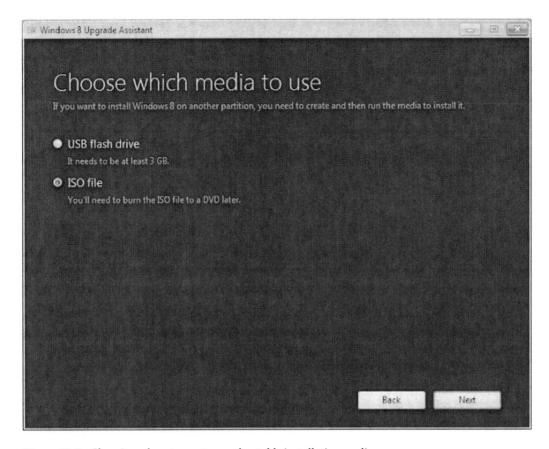

Figure 15-2. Choosing where to create your bootable installation media

I strongly recommend that you choose the ISO file option to create an installer file that can be used later. The reason for this is because the ISO file can later be burned to a DVD or copied to a USB flash drive (I will show you how to do this shortly). If you create a USB flash drive, you will never be able to use that flash drive for anything else unless you want to delete the copy of the Windows 8 installer that is on it. The ISO image file will be saved to your computer for later use.

The other important part of this purchasing process is to keep a safe record of your Windows 8 product key. It is displayed in the Windows 8 Upgrade Assistant. You should always keep a record of it in a safe place with your installation media.

Once the installation media is created, you can install Windows in place or from a restart. I will show you how to do these later in this chapter.

Creating Bootable Media from a Windows 8 ISO File

Once you have created your Windows 8 ISO file, you will want to create bootable media from it—using either a DVD or a USB flash drive. The easiest way to do this—the way that's supported in every edition of Windows—is by downloading the Windows 7 USB/DVD Download Tool. You can search for it online or get it directly from www.microsoftstore.com/store/msstore/html/pbPage.Help_Win7_usbdvd_dwnTool.

This tool allows you to burn a DVD of an ISO image file or copy it to a USB flash drive (see Figure 15-3). It first asks you to select the ISO image file you have downloaded, and then it prompts you to create an installer on a USB device or a DVD.

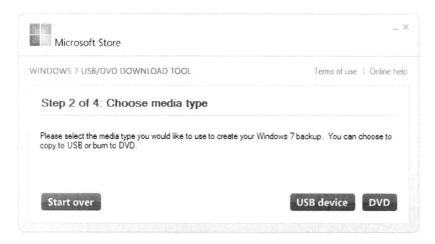

Figure 15-3. *The Windows 7 USB/DVD Download Tool*

If you are using Windows 7 and want to burn a DVD of your Windows 8 installer, you can double-click the ISO file in Windows Explorer to open a dedicated DVD burning tool. This might be a quicker and easier option for some people.

Preparing to Install Windows 8

After you have downloaded or bought a retail copy of Windows 8, or if you need to reinstall it, the process varies, depending on whether you are upgrading an existing Windows installation or if you are performing a clean installation; and if you are upgrading, the version of Windows that you are upgrading from.

The options that present themselves to you therefore can vary quite considerably, so in this section, I'll show you what those options are and how the installation will vary depending on how you choose to perform it. I'll also help you make sure that the installation you perform is stable and reliable.

Upgrading from Windows XP

Unlike Windows 7, Windows 8 *does* support a direct upgrade path for users of Windows XP, although you can't transfer your programs, user accounts, and settings. The upgrade process will only allow you to migrate your personal files and documents to the new operating system (see Figure 15-4).

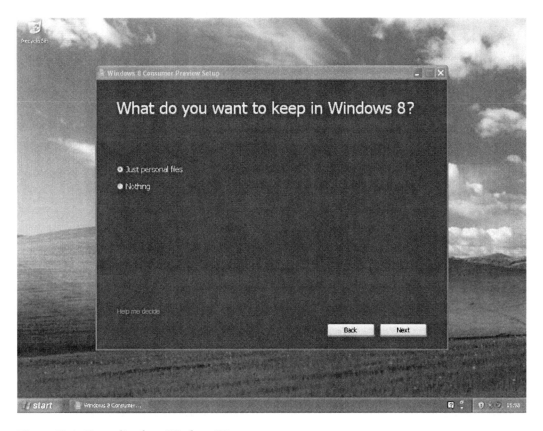

Figure 15-4. *Upgrading from Windows XP*

The reason you can't upgrade your full Windows XP installation to Windows 8 is because Windows XP and Windows 8 are based on completely different core code (the OS kernel) and are largely incompatible. When Microsoft migrated Windows to a new kernel with Vista, many Windows XP features became obsolete as they were replaced by newer, faster, and more efficient features. This is the primary reason for software incompatibilities with XP software. If you want to upgrade from Windows XP to Windows 8, you will need to reinstall all of your software afterward.

■ **Note** Some software packages will never run happily in Windows 8, not even in compatibility mode. To use older software in Windows 8, you may need to install it in a virtual machine. I show you how to do this in Chapter 14.

Upgrading from Windows Vista

If you are upgrading to Windows 8 from Windows Vista, you may be surprised to see that you still can't migrate your software to the new OS. Why?!, you might ask. After all, I did state in the last section that Microsoft moved to a new core kernel with Windows Vista, and that this is what makes XP software incompatible.

This limitation may seem all the more unusual because you could migrate software when upgrading from Vista to Windows 7. However, parts of the core kernel changed during Windows 7's life, and those changes have carried over into Windows 8. To avoid any risk of problems due to software trying to call Windows Vista functions, Microsoft has disallowed software migration from Vista to Windows 8.

In Figure 15-5, the upgrade path from Windows Vista allows you to migrate your personal files and your Windows Settings. This makes the process of configuring Windows 8 simpler and quicker.

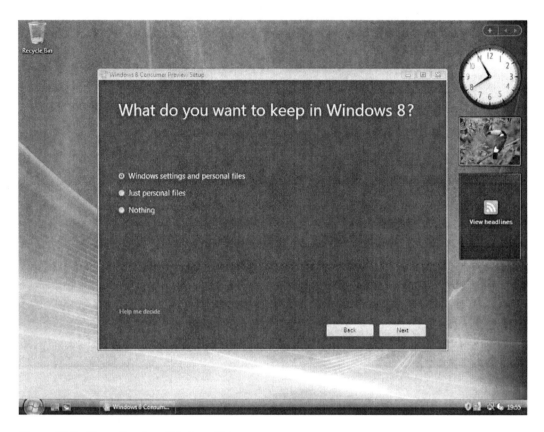

***Figure 15-5.** Upgrading from Windows Vista*

Upgrading from Windows 7

It is only when upgrading from Windows 7 that you can actually migrate all of your software to the new OS. Windows 7 and Windows 8 are similar in many ways, but this doesn't mean that software incompatibilities won't appear. I have encountered a couple of software packages that worked fine in Windows 7 but that were buggy or produced errors when ported to Windows 8.

As you can see in Figure 15-6, the Windows 8 installer gives you the options when upgrading from Windows 7 to migrate all of your *Windows settings, personal files, and apps* (for this, read desktop software) or just your *personal files*.

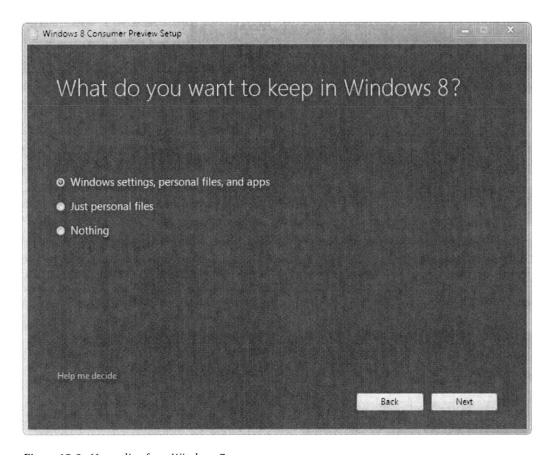

Figure 15-6. *Upgrading from Windows 7*

Moving from 32-bit (x86) to 64-bit (x64)

If you are currently running a 32-bit (x86) version of Windows, either because you're using Windows XP (where the 64-bit version was withdrawn some years ago), or you're using the 32-bit version of Vista or Windows 7 and you want to upgrade to the 64-bit version of Windows 8, there are some things you should know.

First and most important, you simply cannot upgrade any 32-bit version of Windows to the 64-bit version, not with XP, Vista, or even Windows 7; the installer simply doesn't support it (see Figure 15-7).

Figure 15-7. *You can't upgrade from a 32-bit version of Windows to a 64-bit version*

The reason for this is because the differences between the 32-bit and 64-bit versions of Windows are very pronounced, not the least of which is with the hardware driver support, where the x86 and x64 drivers are very different from one another.

This means that if you want to move to a 64-bit version of Windows 8, perhaps because you have already upgraded the memory in your computer to more than 4GB (including your graphics memory), you will have to reformat your hard disk and perform a clean installation of Windows 8.

This 4GB memory limit is important because it *does* include your graphics memory. Let's look at an example. Your computer has three 1GB memory cards installed, and your graphics card has a memory standing at just 512MB (0.5GB). In this situation, the 32-bit version of Windows will happily see *all* 3.5GB of your memory.

If you upgrade the graphics card, though, to one with 2GB of installed memory, you will have a total of 5GB. Windows will discard your memory in chunks of entire memory cards, and this means that the total amount of memory your PC sees will only be two of the three 1GB memory cards on your motherboard (in some configurations, it might only see one of them!)

In this circumstance, the only way to see above the 4GB memory ceiling is to install the 64-bit version of Windows 8, which is able to see *all* of your installed memory.

Windows 8 Minimum Hardware Requirements

If you have an older computer, you might wonder if Windows 8 will run on your computer. The good news is that the minimum hardware requirements for Windows 8 are very low, meaning it will run on most computers.

- **Processor**: 1GHz or faster

- **Memory**: Minimum 1GB (32-bit) or 2GB (64-bit)

- **Hard Disk**: 16GB free (32-bit) or 20GB free (64-bit)

- **Graphics**: DirectX 9 with WDDM 1.0 or higher driver

- **Resolution**: 1024×768 pixels for Start screen and apps, 1366×768 resolution for side-by-side apps

Bear in mind that these are the *minimum* requirements. You should not expect the full Windows 8 experience to run on older hardware as well as it will on a newer computer.

Installing Windows 8 on Netbooks

It is very important to carefully consider whether to install Windows 8 on your netbook. Windows 8 Start screen and apps will not work on screens with a vertical resolution of less than 768 pixels. Many netbooks, especially older ones that originally shipped with Windows XP, only have a vertical resolution of 600 pixels.

■ **Tip**   You can check the vertical screen resolution on your netbook in **Windows XP** by right-clicking in a empty space on the desktop, and then clicking Properties in the options. Then click the Settings tab and check whether the second number in the Screen Resolution section is 768 or higher. In **Windows Vista**, right-click in an empty space on the desktop and select Personalize from the options. Then click Display Settings. Check whether the second number in the current resolution is 768 or higher. With **Windows 7**, right-click in an empty space on the desktop and select Screen Resolution to show the current resolution of your monitor.

The other consideration for netbooks is that on horizontal screen resolutions lower than 1366 pixels, you cannot view two Windows 8 apps side-by-side. This is less of a concern than the vertical resolution issue, but is very relevant to some netbook users. To check your horizontal resolution, follow the steps in the preceding Tip but check the first number for your current resolution.

Upgrading to Windows 8

There are several ways to upgrade Windows 8—from a DVD or USB flash drive, or through a digital download—and all operate in the same way once started, except that if you choose to download your copy of Windows 8, this download (between 3.5GB and 4.5GB) will need to complete before the upgrade process can begin. When you have completed the download, you will be asked if you want to make a bootable DVD or USB flash drive from it, and you need to supply this item yourself. You can install Windows 8 directly, but I always recommend making a backup copy of the installer onto a DVD or a flash drive because you never know when you will have to reinstall Windows 8 or need to perform a clean installation. You can later capture this as an ISO file for backup using software such as WinISO (www.winiso.com).

1. When you first start the upgrade process from a DVD or USB flash drive, you will be asked if you want to get updates to the installer online. This is important and very worthwhile because it includes stability updates and new hardware drivers that can make the installation process more stable and robust (see Figure 15-8).

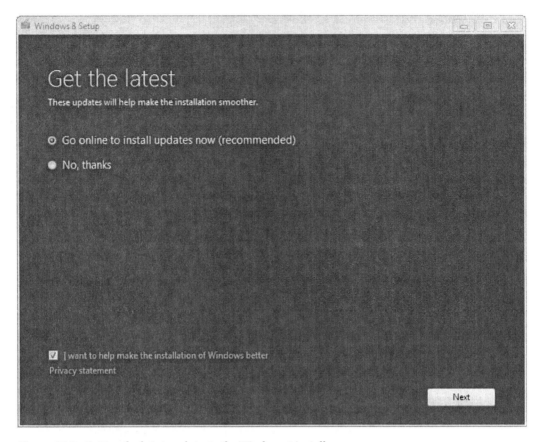

Figure 15-8. *Getting the latest updates to the Windows 8 installer*

2. After this process completes, you will be asked to enter your product key for Windows 8 and accept the license agreement.

3. Next, you are asked what you want to keep from your previous installation. As I showed you earlier, this will either be your files, settings, and apps (programs); only your files and settings; only your files; or if you want a clean installation, nothing at all (see Figure 15-9). This screen will vary depending on the version of Windows you are upgrading from.

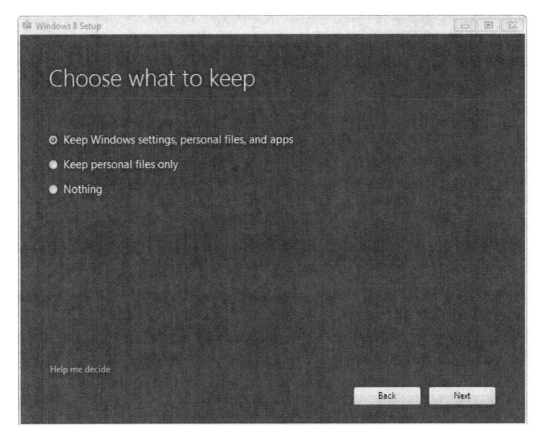

Figure 15-9. *Choosing what to keep from your previous installation of Windows*

4. It is at this point that the Windows 8 upgrade advisor will run automatically as part of the installer. It will inform you of any incompatible software and hardware (see Figure 15-10). As part of the upgrade process, it might recommend that you uninstall some hardware or software; that some hardware of software might need manual updating after the upgrade; or that some software or hardware might not function correctly or work at all.

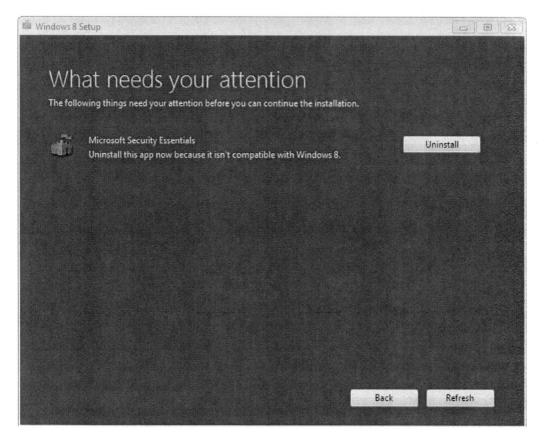

Figure 15-10. *The Windows 8 Upgrade Advisor*

■ **Note**   Don't be concerned if the upgrade advisor says you should uninstall your antivirus software. Windows 8 includes antivirus software by default.

An important thing to note here is that the Windows 8 installer might not let you proceed with the upgrade unless certain tasks that it deems important have been completed, such as uninstalling software identified as incompatible with Windows 8. The installer will help you uninstall this software.

Once these steps have been completed, Windows 8 will install. You will not be able to use your computer during this time, and the computer might restart several times during installation.

Performing a Clean Install

To perform a clean installation of Windows 8, you will need to start your computer from the boot media that you created (either a DVD or USB flash drive), or from your retail copy of Windows 8 (note that you won't get an installation disc with a new computer that has Windows 8 preloaded onto it). You may need to enter the boot menu of your computer (normally F12 when you start the PC, though this may differ on your computer) to tell the PC to start from the media that you have inserted.

1. When the Windows installer starts, you are asked to enter the country and language you want to install (see Figure 15-11). Click Next when you have selected the appropriate options.

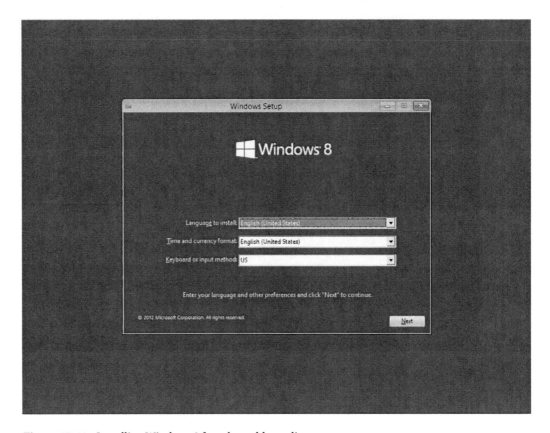

Figure 15-11. *Installing Windows 8 from bootable media*

---

2. The next screen is important. Because you are installing Windows 8, click the Install button in the center of the screen (see Figure 15-12). In the bottom right of the screen, notice Repair Your Computer. This is useful if you later need to rescue and repair a faulty Windows 8 installation.

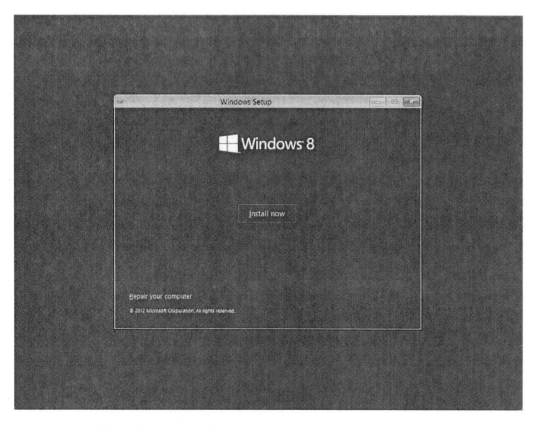

Figure 15-12. *Click Install Now to install Windows 8*

3. In the next screen (see Figure 15-10), you can upgrade your current copy of Windows to Windows 8 through the bootable installer. This feature is most useful when rescuing a faulty installed copy of Windows 8 because it will create a completely new and fresh (i.e., without your software and apps installed) installation of Windows 8 and place your old installation, complete with all your files, in a `Windows.old` folder so that you can save them.

4. To perform a clean installation of Windows 8, click Custom: Install Windows Only (Advanced) (see Figure 15-13).

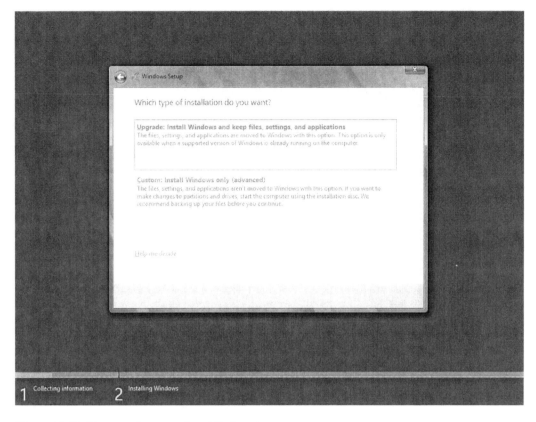

Figure 15-13. *You can also upgrade to Windows 8*

5. You are presented with a list of hard disks and partitions in your computer that you can install Windows 8 onto (see Figure 15-14). On most computers, you will most likely only see a single disk listed. This is where you will install Windows 8. You should choose to install Windows 8 on Disc 0 (zero) because this is where the System Reserved partition with the operating system boot files will be placed. If you have UEFI firmware in your computer, the Windows 8 installer will possibly create other startup and rescue partitions as well). The installer will *always* place these on Drive 0 (zero).

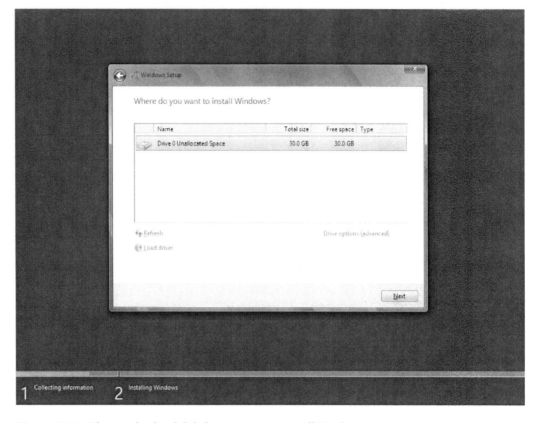

Figure 15-14. Choose what hard disk that you want to install Windows 8 on

6. The installation process is completely automated from here. You won't be required to do anything with your computer until Windows 8 is completely installed. When this happens, you will be asked to choose the color scheme for Windows and to either sign into the computer with a Microsoft Account or to create an account.

Best Practices for Installing Windows 8

Installing your copy of Windows on Drive 0 is important, because in computers with more than one physical hard disk, you might find that your *second* hard disk, which contains your files, might read as Drive 0 in the drives list (because of the motherboard socket you have plugged it into) and your Windows drive might read as Drive 1.

■ **Tip** In a tower PC with more than one physical hard disk, if you can unplug all but the Windows disk drive before installing Windows 8, it will mitigate any problems associated with the Windows and System Reserved partitions ending up on different disks. This will ensure the System Reserved partition is on the correct disk.

The problem arises here when you come to create a system backup of your computer. With the System Reserved partition *always* residing as the first partition on Drive 0, if that hard disk already has files on it, Windows will insist you back up the entire files disk as part of your Windows image backup.

■ **Note** Windows Vista and Windows 7 created a System Reserved partition of 100MB in size. Windows 8 contains more tools and creates a System Reserved partition of 350MB in size. If you have a System Reserved partition that is too small, Windows may not allow you to create an image backup.

The upshot of this is that your image backup file can be huge, and when you restore it, it is an older copy of your files, wiping out all of your new and updated files.

You should also make sure that you install your copy of Windows 8 onto Drive 0. With the System Reserved partition always on Drive 0, if your Windows installation is on another hard disk—let's say Drive 1—removal or failure of Drive 0 (where the boot menu resides) will result in a Windows installation that won't start and that will be very difficult to repair.

In the bottom half of the Where Do You Want to Install Windows? page is Drive Options (Advanced), which provides the basic partitioning and formatting tools you need to create a clean installation of Windows 8 successfully (see Figure 15-15).

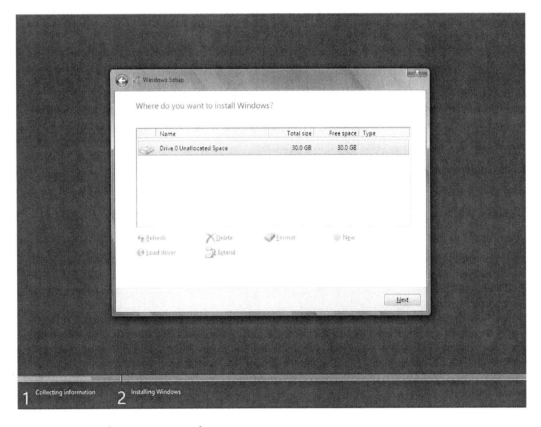

Figure 15-15. *Disk management tools*

Using these tools, you can perform the following actions:

- **Delete** an existing partition on a hard disk

- **Format** a partition or disk

- Create a **New** partition on a physical hard disk

- Join partitions to create an **Extended** partition

Sometimes, however, your hard disks won't appear in the drives list in the Windows installer. This happens if your computer contains RAID drives, but you can specifically load the driver required for the Windows 8 installer to be able to work with those disks if they don't appear in the drives list by clicking Load Driver. You will need a copy of the driver on CD, DVD, or a USB flash drive.

My best recommendation is to *always* delete your existing Windows partition and create a new one where one already exists (i.e., if you've used another version of Windows on the computer). The reason for this is because the boot and system partitions that Windows 8 creates are different from the ones used by Windows 7 and Windows Vista, and if you are upgrading from Windows XP, you won't have these partitions but you will need them.

On some computers, the Windows 8 installer might create four of these partitions, and you need to make sure there is space for them. The reason you want these partitions is because they contain all the tools you need to troubleshoot and repair Windows 8 when it won't start. If you don't allow the installer to create them, you could find that the troubleshooting and repair tools won't work when you need them.

If you have enough hard disk space, I also recommend that you create two (preferably three) partitions so that you can keep your Windows installation and your files (and optionally a backup copy of Windows) separate. Moving your files away from Windows 8 in this way helps make sure that if something goes wrong with Windows 8 and you need to reinstall it, there will be no question about the integrity of your files.

I recommend that you create partitions. The size of your main Windows partition will vary depending on how you use your PC. The following are some recommended Windows 8 partition sizes for different types of users:

- **General business user**: 50GB (enter 51200 in the partition size box)

- **General home user**: 50GB to 100GB (51200 to 102400)

- **Power user**: 100GB to 200GB (102400 to 204800)

- **Developer:** 100GB to 200GB (102400 to 204800)

- **Gamer**: 100GB to 300GB (102400 to 307200)

If you create a separate backup partition for a Windows image backup, it should be the same size as your Windows 8 partition, or double the size if you want to keep both a System Image Backup and a custom Refresh image. You should add to this any additional space you need for a backup copy of the hardware drivers and software installers for your computer, perhaps an extra 5GB.

Finally, the files drive should occupy all of the remaining space. Obviously, this is only really a suitable setup for computers with very large hard disks of at least 1TB and preferably 1.5TB or more. You might be installing Windows 8 on a tablet or ultrabook with precious little storage space, perhaps just a 64GB or 128GB SSD. If this is the case, you can install Windows 8 into a 30GB partition and save the rest for files, or you can simply create one big partition that occupies the entire hard disk. If you do this, however, you should make sure that you keep regular up-to-date backups of all your files and documents.

Transferring Files and Documents from an Old Computer

The Windows 8 install disc contains a tool called Windows Easy Transfer (see Figure 15-16), which is used to transfer files and settings from one physical computer to another. This is extremely useful if you have bought a new computer with Windows 8 preinstalled.

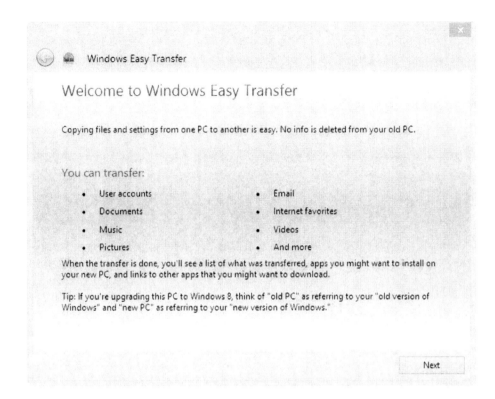

Figure 15-16. *Windows Easy Transfer*

Put your Windows 8 install DVD or USB flash drive into your *old* computer running Windows XP, Vista, or Windows 7 and from its Support/MigWiz folders, run the **migsetup** program.

This tool allows you to easily transfer files and settings from your old computer in a variety of ways (see Figure 15-17).

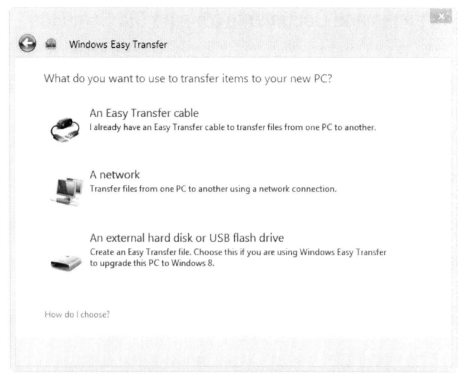

Figure 15-17. *Select how you want to transfer your files*

- **A dedicated Easy Transfer cable**. You can buy these at computer stores and online. It is a physical cable that connects the two computers, requiring them to be physically close together.

- **Transfer your files over a home or work network**. Bear in mind, this is significantly faster when both computers are connected to the network with a physical cable than it is over Wi-Fi.

- **Via an external hard disk or USB flash drive.** This has the added benefit of giving you a backup copy of your files.

On the next screen, after you selected your preferred transfer option, you need to specify whether it is the old PC or the new (destination) PC (see Figure 15-18).

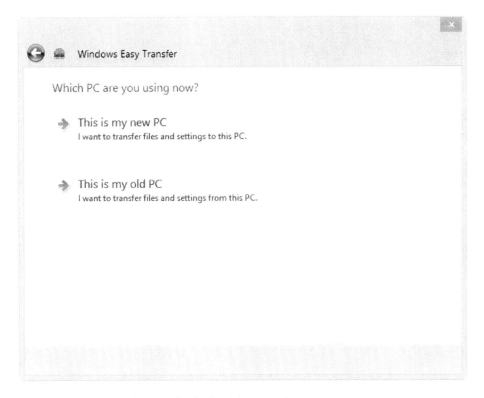

Figure 15-18. *You need to specify which PC you are using*

If you are transferring files and settings across your home or work network, you will be given a code and asked to run Windows Easy Transfer on your new Windows 8 computer (see Figure 15-19). You can find it by searching for **transfer** at the Start screen. You will need to specify on the Windows 8 computer that you are receiving files over your network and input the code provided on the old computer.

Figure 15-19. You can transfer your files over a network connection

Click Next, and then you are asked what you want to transfer and you are told how much space is required (see Figure 15-20). This could run to many gigabytes, so a USB hard disk is a good idea if you have one handy because it is a much faster way to transfer files than across a network.

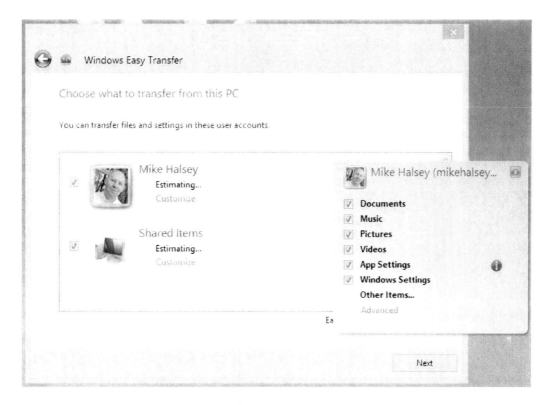

Figure 15-20. You can choose what to transfer

Windows Easy Transfer will now begin the process of copying your files. To accept imported files on your new Windows 8 computer, you will need to be running Windows Easy Transfer on that computer. Search for **transfer** at the Start screen to find it.

Summary

Migrating from an earlier version of Windows, even Windows XP, is simpler with Windows 8 than with any other version of the operating system, and moving your files and documents is relatively straightforward, even from a completely different computer.

Microsoft worked hard with Windows 8 to make the installation experience as straightforward as possible and they've succeeded with Windows 8 in ways that make moving to this operating system a joy.

When it comes to the choice between performing an upgrade or a clean install, it's only really relevant when migrating from Windows 7 or reinstalling Windows 8. This is because as you can't bring your software and hardware drivers from Windows XP or Windows Vista, you also can't bring any problems associated with them.

Some tools are relatively hidden—such as Windows Easy Transfer, which is an excellent tool that supports new features, including the transfer of files across a network.

Then there are the advanced administrator tools, such as Unattended Setup and SysPrep. These tools, especially when coupled with the Windows Automated Installation Kit, make very powerful ways to deploy Windows 8. If you are interested in learning about Windows deployment, this is a great next read for you. And you can find out about creating unattended Windows 8 installations at technet.microsoft.com/en-us/library/ff699026.aspx.

As for this book, I have covered all you need to be able to really get to grips with the power that lies under the surface of Windows 8, from ways to customize the look and feel of the OS to hidden tools and utilities that can make you more productive.

I hope you have found this book useful and informative.

—Mike Halsey

APPENDIX A

■ ■ ■

Windows 8 Touch Gestures

For many people, touch will be new to their Windows experience. In many ways, such as with tapping and double-tapping, touch operates in the same way you would expect a mouse click to work. Table A-1 contains a complete list of the touch gestures you can use with Windows 8. Those who already have been using touch will be pleased to hear that the gestures haven't changed. Some new gestures have been added, though, and those are included in the table.

Table A-1. *Windows 8 Touch Gestures*

Touch Gesture	Command	Action
Tap	Click	Tap the screen with your finger.
Double tap	Double-click	Tap the screen twice in the same place with your finger.
Drag vertically	Scroll	Touch the screen and vertically drag your finger upward or downward.
Drag horizontally	Drag selection	Touch the screen and horizontally drag your finger left or right.
Press and tap	Right-click	Touch and hold the screen with one finger while tapping it briefly with another finger.
Zoom	Zoom	Move two fingers apart (zoom in) or toward each other (zoom out).
Rotate	Rotate	Move two fingers in a circular motion.
Two-finger tap	Programmable in some apps	Tap the screen with two fingers.
Tap and pull down	Right-click (Start screen)	Tap the screen and drag your finger slightly downward.
Press and hold	Right-click (desktop)	Tap and hold the screen for one second, then release your finger.
Flick	Pan up, down, back, forward	Flick your finger up, down, left, or right on the screen.

Narrator Touch Gestures

The Accessibility features in Windows have long been a strength of the operating system, but with Windows 8, they have been extended to add support for touch gestures that work with the Narrator. To use Table A-2, the touch gesture listed in the left column will execute the corresponding command in the right column.

Table A-2. *Narrator Touch Gestures*

Touch Gesture	Command
Tap or drag	Read aloud the item under your finger.
Double tap or Hold with one finger and tap with a second finger	Activate an item (equivalent to a single mouse click).
Triple tap or Hold with one finger and double-tap with a second finger	Select an item.
Flick left or right	Move to the next or previous item.
Hold with one finger and two-finger-tap with additional fingers	Drag an item.
Two-finger tap	Stop the Narrator speaking.
Two-finger swipe	Scroll.
Three-finger tap	Show or hide the Narrator settings window.
Three-finger swipe up	Read the current window.
Three-finger swipe down	Read from the current text location.
Three-finger swipe left or right	Tab forward and backward.
Four-finger tap	Show all commands for current item.
Four-finger triple tap	Show the Narrator commands list.
Four-finger swipe up or down	Enable/disable semantic zoom(semantic zoom provides a view of large blocks of content; on a web site, for example).

▓ ▓ ▓

Windows 8 Shortcut Keys

Table B-1. *Keys with No Modifier*

Key	Function
Space	Select or clear active check box.
Tab	Move forward through options.
Esc	Cancel.
NumLock	Hold for 5 seconds: ToggleKeys.
Del	Delete file (File Explorer).
Left arrow	Open previous menu or close submenu.
Right arrow	Open next menu of open submenu.
F1	Display help (if available).
F2	Rename item.
F3	Search for next instance in a search.
F4	Display items in active list.
F5	Refresh.

Table B-2. *Windows Logo Key Combinations*

Windows Logo Key+	Function
No other key	Toggle Start screen/last app.
PrtScr	Capture screenshot (saved in Pictures as screenshot.png, screenshot(1).png, screenshot(2).png, etc.).
C	Open the charms.
D	Show desktop.
E	Open File Explorer.
F	Open files in Search charm (+Ctrl to find computers on a network).

(continued)

Table B-2. (*continued*)

Windows Logo Key+	Function
H	Open Share charm.
I	Open Settings charm.
J	Switch focus between snapped and larger apps.
K	Open Devices charm.
L	Switch users (lock computer if on a domain).
M	Minimize all windows (desktop).
O	Change lock-screen orientation.
P	Open the second screen and projection options.
Q	Open Search charm.
R	Open Run dialog box.
T	Set focus on taskbar and cycle through running desktop programs.
U	Open the Ease of Access Center.
V	Cycle through notifications (+Shift to go backward).
W	Go to Settings in the Search charm.
X	Quick-link power-users' commands (opens Windows Mobility Center, if present).
Z	Open the App bar.
1-9	Go to the app at the position on the taskbar.
+	Zoom in (Magnifier).
−	Zoom out (Magnifier).
, (comma)	Peek at the desktop.
. (period)	Snap an app to the right (+Shift snap to the left).
Enter	Narrator (+Alt to open Windows Media Center, if installed).
Spacebar	Switch input language and keyboard layout.
Tab	Cycle through app history (use Ctrl to use arrow keys).
Esc	Exit the Magnifier.
Home	Minimize nonactive desktop windows.
PgUp	Move Start screen to left monitor.
PgDn	Move Start screen to right monitor.
Left arrow	Snap desktop window to the left (+Shift to move to left monitor).

(*continued*)

Table B-2. (*continued*)

Windows Logo Key+	Function
Right arrow	Snap desktop windows to the right (+Shift to move to right monitor).
Up arrow	Maximize desktop window (+Shift to keep width).
Down arrow	Restore/Minimize desktop window (+Shift to keep width).
F1	Open Windows Help and Support.

Table B-3. *Ctrl Key Combinations*

Ctrl+	Function
Mouse wheel	Desktop: Change icon size, Start screen: Zoom in/out
A	Select All
C	Copy
E	Select search box (Explorer)
N	New window (Explorer)
R	Refresh
V	Paste
W	Close current window (Explorer)
X	Cut
Y	Redo
Z	Undo
Esc	Start screen
NumLock	Copy
Left arrow	Previous word
Right arrow	Next word
Up arrow	Previous paragraph
Down arrow	Next paragraph
F4	Close active document

Table B-4. *Alt Key Combinations*

Alt+	Function
D	Select Address bar (Explorer)
Enter	Open Properties dialog box
Spacebar	Open Shortcut menu
Tab	Switch between apps
Left arrow	Move to previous folder (Explorer)
Up arrow	Go up one level (Explorer)
F4	Close active item or app

Table B-5. *Shift Key Combinations*

Shift+	Function
No other key	Five times: Sticky keys
Tab	Move backward through options
Esc	Open Task Manager
NumLock	Paste
Left arrow	Select a block of text
Right arrow	Select a block of text
Up arrow	Select a block of text
Down arrow	Select a block of text

Table B-6. *Ctrl+Alt Key Combinations*

Ctrl+Alt+	Function
D	Toggle Docked mode (Magnifier)
I	Invert colors (Magnifier)
L	Toggle Lens mode (Magnifier)
Tab	Switch between apps using arrow keys

Table B-7. *Alt+Shift Key Combinations*

Alt+Shift+	Function
PrtScr	Left Alt+Left Shift+PrtScr: High contrast
NumLock	Left Alt+Left Shift+NumLock: Mouse keys

Advanced Query Syntax for Search

In addition to the search methods that I detailed in Chapter 5, there is a large volume of Advanced Query Syntax options that you can use when searching (especially for files) in Windows 8. These options are available both at the Start screen and in File Explorer.

Data Store Location

Table C-1. *Data Store Location*

Restrict Search by Data Store	Use	Example
Desktop	desktop	Gilbert store:desktop
Files	files	Mike store:files
Outlook	outlook	Jed store:outlook
A Specific Folder	foldername or in	foldername:MyDocuments or in:MyVideos

Common File Kinds

Table C-2. *Common File Kinds*

Restrict Search by File Kind	Use	Example
Calendar	calendar	kind:=calendar
Communication	communication	kind:=communication
Contact	contact	kind:=contact
Document	document	kind:=document
E-mail	email	kind:=email
RSS Feed	feed	kind:=feed
Folder	folder	kind:=folder
Game	game	kind:=game

(continued)

Table C-2. (*continued*)

Restrict Search by File Kind	Use	Example
Instant Messenger conversations	instant message	kind:=instant message
Journal	journal	kind:=journal
Link	link	kind:=link
Movie	movie	kind:=movie
Music	music	kind:=music
Notes	note	kind:=note
Picture	picture	kind:=picture
Playlist	playlist	kind:=playlist
Program	program	kind:=program
Recorded TV	tv	kind:=tv
Saved Search	saved search	kind:=saved search
Task	task	kind:=task
Video	video	kind:=video
Web History	web history	kind:=web history

Properties by File Kind

Table C-3. *Properties by File Kind*

Property	Use	Example
Title	title, subject or about	title:"Windows 8"
Status	status	status:pending
Date	date	date:last week
Date modified	datemodified or modified	modified:last week
Importance	importance or priority	importance:high
Deleted	deleted or isdeleted	isdeleted:yes (no)
Is attachment	isattachment	isattachment:yes (no)
To	to or toname	to:mike
Cc	cc or ccname	cc:chris
Company	company	company:Microsoft
Location	location	location:"office"
Category	category	category:pilot

(*continued*)

Table C-3. *(continued)*

Property	Use	Example
Keywords	keywords	keywords:"pending"
Album	album	album:"equinoxe"
File name	filename or file	filename:Report
Genre	genre	genre:metal
Author	author or by	author:"Mike Halsey"
People	people or with	with:(jed or gilbert)
Folder	folder, under or path	folder:downloads
File extension	ext or fileext	ext:.txt

Filter by Size

Table C-4. *Filter by Size (Note that the NOT and OR operators here must be in uppercase.)*

Size	Use	Example
0KB	empty	size:empty
0 > 10KB	tiny	size:tiny
10KB > 100KB	small	size:small
100KB > 1MB	medium	size:medium
1MB > 16MB	large	size:large
16MB > 128MB	huge	size:huge
> 128MB	gigantic	size:gigantic

Boolean Operators

Table C-5. *Boolean Operators (Note that the NOT and OR operators here must be in uppercase.)*

Keyword/Symbol	Use	Function
NOT	draft NOT edition	Finds items that contain *draft*, but not *edition*.
–	draft –edition	Finds items that contain *draft*, but not *edition*.
OR	draft OR edition	Finds items that contain *draft* or *edition*.
Quotation marks	"draft edition"	Finds items that contain the exact phrase *draft edition*.
Parentheses	(draft edition)	Finds items that contain *draft* and *edition* in any order.

(continued)

Table C-5. (*continued*)

Keyword/Symbol	Use	Function
>	date:>10/23/12	Finds items with a date after October 23, 2012.
	size:>500	Finds items with a size greater than 500 bytes.
<	date:<10/23/12	Finds items with a date before October 23, 2012.
	size:<500	Finds items with a size less than 500 bytes.
..	date:10/23/12..10/11/12	Finds items with a date beginning on 10/23/12 and ending on 10/11/12.

Boolean Properties

Table C-6. *Boolean Properties*

Property	Use	Function
is:attachment	draft is:attachment	Finds items that have attachments that contain *draft*. Same as isattachment:no (yes).
isonline:	draft isonline:yes (no)	Finds items that are online and that contain *draft*.
isrecurring:	draft isrecurring:yes (no)	Finds items that are recurring and that contain *draft*.
isflagged:	draft isflagged:yes (no)	Finds items that are flagged (Review or Follow up, for example) and that contain *draft*.
isdeleted:	draft isdeleted:yes (no)	Finds items that are flagged as deleted (Recycle Bin or Deleted Items, for example) and that contain *draft*.
iscompleted:	draft iscompleted:yes (no)	Finds items that are not flagged as complete and that contain *draft*.
hasattachment:	draft hasattachment:yes (no)	Finds items containing *draft* and having attachments.
hasflag:	draft hasflag:yes (no)	Finds items containing *draft* and having flags.

Dates

Table C-7. *Dates*

Relative to	Use	Function
Day	date:today	Finds items with today's date.
	date:tomorrow	Finds items with tomorrow's date.
	date:yesterday	Finds items with yesterday's date.

(*continued*)

Table C-7. (*continued*)

Relative to	Use	Function
Week/Month/Year	date:this week	Finds items with a date falling within the current week.
	date:last week	Finds items with a date falling within the previous week.
	date:next month	Finds items with a date falling within the upcoming week.
	date:last month	Finds items with a date falling within the previous month.
	date:this year	Finds items with a date falling within the current year.
	date:last year	Finds items with a date falling within the next year.

Attachments

Table C-8. *Attachments*

Property	Use	Example
People	people	people:gilbert

Contacts

Table C-9. *Contacts*

Property	Use	Example
Job title	jobtitle	jobtitle:author
Instant messaging address	imaddress	imaddress:mike@MVPs.org
Assistant's phone	assistantsphone	assistantsphone:555-1234
Assistant's name	assistantname	assistantname:Darren
Profession	profession	profession:designer
Nickname	nickname	nickname:Gilby
Spouse	spouse	spouse:Victoria
Business city	businesscity	businesscity:Seattle
Business postal code	businesspostalcode	businesspostalcode:96487
Business home page	businesshomepage	businesshomepage:www.thelongclimb.com
Callback phone number	callbackphonenumber	callbackphonenumber:555-555-2345
Mobile phone	mobilephone	mobilephone:555-555-2345
Children	children	children:Gilbert

(*continued*)

Table C-9. (*continued*)

Property	Use	Example
First name	firstname	firstname:Jed
Last name	lastname	lastname:Halsey
Home fax	homefax	homefax:555-555-1234
Manager's name	managersname	managersname:Tom
Business phone	businessphone	businessphone:555-555-1234
Home phone	homephone	homephone:555-555-1234
Mobile phone	mobilephone	mobilephone:555-555-1234
Office	office	office:sample
Anniversary	anniversary	anniversary:1/8/11
Birthday	birthday	birthday:1/8/11
Web page	webpage	webpage:`www.thelongclimb.com`

Communications

Table C-10. *Communications*

Property	Use	Example
From	from or organizer	from:Jed
Received	received or sent	sent:yesterday
Subject	subject or title	subject:"Editing Report"
Has attachment	hasattachments, hasattachment	hasattachment:true
Attachments	attachments or attachment	attachment:presentation.ppt
Bcc	bcc, bccname or bccaddress	bcc:Gilbert
Cc address	ccaddress or cc	ccaddress:mike@MVPs.org
Follow-up flag	followupflag	followupflag:2
Due date	duedate or due	due:last week
Read	read or isread	is:read
Is completed	iscompleted	is:completed
Incomplete	incomplete or isincomplete	is:incomplete
Has flag	hasflag or isflagged	has:flag
Duration	duration	duration:> 50

Calendar

Table C-11. *Calendar*

Property	Use	Example
Recurring	recurring	recurring:yes (no)
Organizer	organizer, by or from	organizer:Rory

Documents

Table C-12. *Documents*

Property	Use	Example
Comments	comments	comments:"needs final review"
Last saved by	lastsavedby	lastsavedby:mike
Document manager	documentmanager	documentmanager:mike
Revision number	revisionnumber	revisionnumber:1.0.3
Document format	documentformat	documentformat:MIMETYPE
Date last printed	datelastprinted	datelastprinted:last week

Presentations

Table C-13. *Presentations*

Property	Use	Example
Slide count	slidecount	slidecount:>20

Music

Table C-14. *Music*

Property	Use	Example
Bit rate	bitrate, rate	bitrate:192
Artist	artist, by or from	artist:Lacuna Coil
Duration	duration	duration:3
Album	album	album:"shallow life"
Genre	genre	genre:metal
Track	track	track:12
Year	year	year:> 2006 < 2013

Pictures

Table C-15. *Pictures*

Property	Use	Example
Camera make	cameramake	cameramake:sample
Camera model	cameramodel	cameramodel:sample
Dimensions	dimensions	dimensions:8×10
Orientation	orientation	orientation:landscape
Date taken	datetaken	datetaken:yesterday
Width	width	width:1600
Height	height	height:1200

Video

Table C-16. *Video*

Property	Use	Example
Name	name, subject	name:"Family holiday in Germany"
Ext	ext, fileext	ext:.avi

Upgrading Your Computer

A PC isn't just for Christmas, it's for life. You'll want to make sure that your computer lasts for as long as possible because, let's be honest, these things are expensive and you can't afford to be buying a new one before the current machine is out of its warranty period.

In this appendix, I'll talk you through not only the options for upgrading your copy of Windows 8 and its features, but also upgrading your entire PC—and even buying a new one. It's most likely you'll get Windows 8 with a new computer because it is the cheapest way to buy a copy of the operating system.

Choosing a New Windows 8 Computer

I went through the specific hardware requirements for Windows 8 in Chapter 15, but most computers you buy today can run Windows 8 with no problems whatsoever. This makes it more important to know what you need to buy, so that you don't get ripped off by unscrupulous salespeople when choosing and paying for a new computer.

I've split this section into three categories: desktop PCs (including all-in-ones), laptops, and ultrabooks and tablets.

Do You Need a New Computer?

So do you need a new computer anyway? Well, if you are using a computer that's running a copy of Windows Vista or Windows 7, then you probably do not need a new one because the hardware requirements for Windows 8 are the same and it'll run fine.

The only considerations you need to think about here are

1. Do you want to take advantage of the new multitouch technology in Windows 8?

2. Is your current computer more than four years old?

If the answer to either one of these is yes, then it could be the right time to buy a new computer. Any computer more than four years old is more prone to failure than you might like, and the new touch technology in Windows 8 enhances usability considerably. Also, if you have a laptop more than three years old, I recommend replacing it.

Remember that if you buy a new PC, your copy of Windows 8 is effectively free. That $500 budget-computer the salesman tried to steer you away from will probably be perfectly good for years to come.

Choosing the Right Desktop PC

When it comes to buying either a desktop PC, by which I mean a separate tower and monitor, purchasers have traditionally had the hardest time avoiding over-zealous salespeople. "You want to edit photographs? Then you'll benefit from having the fastest processor. . ." commonly goes the line.

The first decision to whether you want a desktop PC or an all-in-one. Both have their advantages and disadvantages.

Desktop PC pros

- More easily upgradable by the user

- If one part fails, the entire PC doesn't need to go for repair

- As you upgrade the PC, old parts can be sold secondhand

- More powerful than all-in-ones, making them more suitable for some tasks

Desktop PC cons

- Can look big and unsightly in the home

- Can be noisy

All-in-One pros

- Stylish and won't look unsightly in the home

- Commonly very quiet computers

- Only one power lead is required, reducing overall power consumption

All-in-One cons

- If one part fails, the entire PC needs to go out for repair

With computer parts changing so rapidly these days, you'll commonly find that all you can ever do with a tower is add more memory, add a second hard disk, and change the graphics card. You might be surprised how big a difference these changes can make, so if you want a tower case, even a small one, ask to see how easy it is to work with the components inside.

Does it have any spare memory sockets? Does it have a spare hard disk bay? If/when the internal power supply fails, how easy is it to replace? Is it a custom-made unit (common in small towers) or a standard, big-box PC PSU (power supply unit)? Does the PC have any expansion ports, and can these take a graphics card?

Never let the salesperson dictate to you what type of processor you *must* have to get the maximum benefit. These things change often, but Intel's Core series (which should be around for a few years yet) provide us with a good guide.

If you only want a PC for light e-mail, web browsing, and basic photo editing, then an inexpensive Core i3 is a great option. If you want to watch HD video but don't need a separate graphics card, you'll want a Core i5 with integrated graphics. That leaves the faster Core i7 processors for enthusiasts and those doing design, animation, HD video editing, and gaming.

You'd be hard-pressed to find a modern PC with less than 4GB of RAM, but do you need any more than this? For very light duties, such as e-mail and Internet browsing, this amount of memory is fine. Hard-core gamers and people using their computers for the other intensive tasks I mentioned need more RAM. You might need more if you want to edit your digital photos and videos. Go for the fastest speed memory you can get, such as 2 GHz instead of 1,333 MHz, because this is where the benefits are.

Next, do you need a solid-state (SSD) hard disk? These are expensive and do not yet come in big capacities at an affordable price. If you are a gamer, then you'll certainly benefit from the extra speed; but with modern games occupying 24GB or more or space, and Windows itself requiring up to 40GB with software and temporary files taking up room, you won't get more than two games on an average SSD before filling it up. This doesn't give you space for any of your files and documents.

If you use a mechanical hard disk, try to get a 7,200 rpm (revolutions per minute) drive, which operates faster than the 5,400 rpm hard disks.

You should only buy a dedicated graphics card if you have to do thoroughly intensive work such as HD video editing, gaming, or graphic design. For general use, including watching Blu-Ray discs, the onboard graphics of a modern PC are perfectly adequate.

When it comes to choosing between a tower and an all-in-one it's worth considering where the computer will live. If it's in a home office or a work office, then a tower is fine; but in your living room you may want something less intrusive and with a smaller overall profile.

Finally, does the monitor have a touchscreen or a built-in Kinect sensor? With Windows 8, these are two options well worth having.

Choosing the Right Laptop or Ultrabook

Many of the considerations for choosing a desktop or an all-in-one PC are the same for laptops and ultrabooks. One of the main differences is that whereas you can upgrade the memory and the hard disk in a laptop, you can never upgrade an ultrabook. What you get is what you're stuck with!

There is the consideration of how you will use a mobile computer. If you want to do serious work, storage is probably important and thus you should choose a laptop. Ultrabooks are perfect for light use if you enjoy working at the local coffee shop or if you want something that you can put in a bag and easily carry.

Get a touchscreen if you can, though it can make some smaller and lighter laptops topple over backward. A big factor is in the build quality. Poke the back of the screen to see if you can distort the picture).

Test the keyboard too. Is it genuinely comfortable to type on? Are all the keys a sensible size and in a sensible place? Is the touchpad usable? Does the touchpad have additional functions, such as multitouch? A keyboard with a backlight is a welcome addition.

More importantly with laptops and ultrabooks is the length of the battery life like and whether the battery be changed by the user.

Choosing the Right Tablet

With Windows 8 tablets there is a simple choice: Intel/AMD or ARM? On Intel and AMD chipsets, you'll have the advantages of the full version of Windows, with the full desktop, probably the same power as a modern laptop but with poor battery life and a high price.

With an ARM-based tablet, you'll get fantastic battery life but the machine won't have anywhere near the power, storage, or memory of an Intel/AMD machine, and you won't be able to install desktop software—ever!

There's also an argument on what size screen to get with a tablet. With a professional-grade tablet, a screen around 12 inches should be the maximum, otherwise it's far too big to hold and your arm will tire quickly. With an ARM tablet, I personally find 10-inch tablets (original iPad size) to be too bulky to carry around and even use casually on the sofa. Personally, I prefer smaller 7-inch screens.

Microsoft's Surface tablets provide a great deal of flexibility. They come with both lower power ARM processors that offer long battery life, and Intel processors that provide the full Windows 8 desktop experience. The integration of a keyboard in the cover is a bonus that may make a Surface tablet a suitable alternative to an ultrabook.

Windows 8 and OEM Installation Discs

I want to tackle one of the biggest problems facing people buying new computers. This is the omission of a Windows 8 installation DVD.

Original equipment manufacturers (OEMs) have worked with Microsoft for years now to reduce the number of pirated copies of Windows. Most OEMs no longer ship new computers with a copy of the Windows installation DVD; instead they provide recovery partitions with a copy of the installed factory image that can be restored if need be.

The downside is that if you need to restore the operating system and you haven't backed up your files and documents (which you have, right!?), then you will almost certainly lose them all because restoring the rescue image that came with your computer always destroys any files you have stored on the same partition as your Windows 8 installation. You will also take the machine back to its default state, reinstall all your software, and reconfigure the computer from scratch.

Sure, you can create your own custom disc image, even wiping out the factory one to save disc space, but haven't you paid for a copy of Windows, which includes the installation disc?

My best advice here is to always check the manufacturer's policy regarding installation discs before you buy. High-end and business computers commonly come with an option to get the disc, or they provide it automatically, but budget computers don't.

Many OEMs allow you to get a copy of the disc separately for a small shipping fee (usually $10) and many people think this is reasonable. If an OEM flatly refuses to provide a disc under any circumstances, however, I recommend that you spend your money elsewhere.

Note If you buy a Windows 8 ARM tablet, you can never get an installation disc. This version of the operating system is *only* available to OEMs and is not user-installable.

It is important to note that OEM discs are commonly tied to the computer's BIOS or UEFI firmware purchased with a new PC. This means that if you try to install them on another computer, they will not work.

SHOULD YOU BUY EXTRA SOFTWARE?

The subject of discs brings me to the age-old question of should you buy all the extra software that salespeople want you to buy because they make more money on that than on the PC itself. Most often, they try to sell you an antivirus suite and a full copy of Microsoft Office saying you need both because what comes with Windows 8 is just not good enough.

What comes with Windows 8, both in terms of antivirus and Office, is good enough for most people. The advice I've included throughout this book helps you get the most out of them. Perhaps you'd find a copy of Adobe Photoshop Elements very useful. Windows 8 doesn't come with DVD or Blu-Ray players, so you might like one of these. But antivirus and general Office—forget it!

Adding More Memory to a PC or Laptop

It is widely known and accepted that the quickest, cheapest, and fastest way to get a performance increase out of an older computer is to add more memory to it. You always need to make sure that you add the correct type of memory, however.

When you open the computer's case or the panel where the memory is located (see Figures D-1 and D-2), you see that the memory sticks have labels on them. The information you need from the labels are memory type (DDR, DDR2, DDR3, etc.) and speed in MHz.

Figure D-1. *Adding memory to a desktop PC*

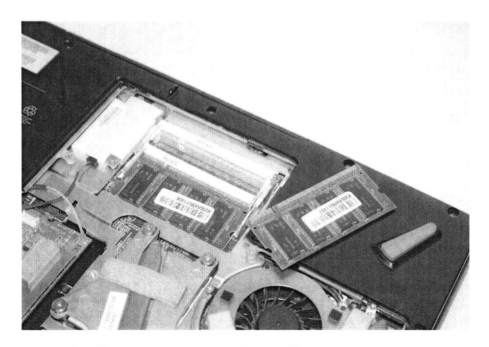

Figure D-2. *Adding memory to a laptop or all-in-one PC*

These are the two things you need to match when buying additional memory. You also need to check if there are any free memory slots. The documentation that came with your motherboard can tell you what types of memory are compatible.

There is a clip at each end of the memory slots on a desktop PC. When you insert the memory, you need to make certain that these are clipped into place firmly.

When adding memory to a laptop, you also find small clips that need to be firmly fixed in place on either side.

Note   If you are using the 32-bit (x86) version of Windows, adding more than 3GB of memory won't result in greater speed because Windows won't see it. A 32-bit operating system can only see a maximum of 4GB of memory, including what's on the graphics card. You can determine which version of Windows you are using in the System section of the Control Panel.

Changing or Adding a Hard Disk

In Figure D-3, you see two SATA hard disks and an SSD. The power and data plugs that attach to the back of these drives only go in one way. You shouldn't force them because the plastic on the connectors could snap.

Figure D-3. *Adding hard drives to a desktop PC. The drive on the far left is the SSD*

You should always make sure that hard disks are properly screwed into the computer's case.

When it comes to laptops and all-in-one PCs, hard disks commonly come in a slide-out caddy (see Figure D-4). They are less accessible than the memory in some laptops. You should check your computer's manual to determine whether the hard disk is a user-serviceable component.

Figure D-4. *Changing the hard disk in a laptop or all-in-one*

Changing or Adding a Graphics Card

At times, people want to change the graphics card on their computers. Doing it is usually a simple matter of pulling out the old card and slotting in the new one. Each type of card only fits in the correct slot (see Figure D-5). You should check the documentation that came with your motherboard to determine the type of slot it has before buying a graphics card.

Figure D-5. *Changing the graphics card in a PC*

You should always check if your graphics card requires additional power, usually provided by a six- or eight-pin plug, because not all power supplies come equipped with these.

If your power supply does not have the relevant plugs (apart from the question of whether you need a new power supply to supply the additional current the graphics card requires), you can buy a power lead adapter cable to give you the plug you need.

Changing the Power Supply in Your PC

The power supply is commonly the first thing in a PC to fail. The power supply is the big box in the back of the computer into which you connect the mains electricity cable. In the desktop PC, a power supply is simple to change. The leads coming from it need to be unplugged (make a note of what it's plugged into so you can easily reconnect everything again). There is a power lead for each drive, perhaps one for the graphics card and two for the motherboard.

There are four screws on the back of the case, at the top and bottom corners of the power supply (not the ones on the fan) that, when undone, allow the old power supply to pop out (see Figure D-6). Screw the new one in place and reconnect the wires, and all is done.

Figure D-6. *A power supply*

If you have an all-in-one or a small form-factor PC with an internal power supply, you will probably need to take the computer to an authorized service center to have it replaced.

Safely Working with Your PC, Laptop, or Tablet

To work safely with your computer when you are adding or changing hardware, you should always follow these instructions:

- Place the computer on a firm, flat surface.

- Make sure the computer is switched off and unplugged from the main electricity.

- Touch unpainted metal inside the computer's case to ground yourself and release any static electricity discharge from your body.

- Avoid working on nylon carpet or other locations where static electricity build-up is common.

Upgrading Windows 8

Throughout this book, I have made reference to features that are only available in the Pro edition of the operating system, such as Group Policy, or that need to be bought separately, such as Windows Media Center and DVD/Blu-Ray playback functionality.

You can add these features to Windows 8 by upgrading it. In the Control Panel, there is an Add Features to Windows 8 option (see Figure D-7). You can purchase upgrades and add-ons for the operating system that gives you new features.

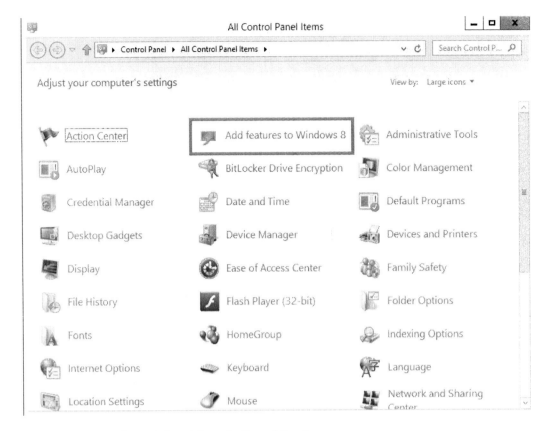

Figure D-7. *Upgrading Windows 8 from the Control Panel*

Summary

The instructions on how to upgrade and change the parts inside your computer are fairly short. This is because it is actually much simpler and easier to perform these actions than you might think.

On a computer, every cable only plugs into the right thing, so you never need to worry about incorrectly plugging in something somewhere it will cause harm or damage. Laptop and all-in-one PC sockets and plugs are all hard-wired and fixed in place, so you can only slot in components.

The short instructions prove just how easy it is to upgrade a PC and breathe new life into it.

Index

X, Y, Z

CPSIA information can be obtained at www.ICGtesting.com
Printed in the USA
LVOW111246170313

324645LV00004B/165/P